Indigeneity: Before and Beyond the Law

Examining contested notions of indigeneity, and the positioning of the Indigenous subject before and beyond the law, this book focuses upon the animation of indigeneities within textual imaginaries, both literary and juridical. Engaging the philosophy of Jacques Derrida and Walter Benjamin, as well as other continental philosophy and critical legal theory, the book uniquely addresses the troubled juxtaposition of law and justice in the context of Indigenous legal claims and literary expressions, discourses of rights and recognition, postcolonialism and resistance in settler nation states, and the mutually constitutive relation between law and literature. Ultimately, the book suggests no less than a literary revolution, and the reassertion of Indigenous Law.

To date, the oppressive specificity with which Indigenous peoples have been defined in international and domestic law has not been subject to the scrutiny undertaken in this book. As an interdisciplinary engagement with a variety of scholarly approaches, this book will appeal to a broad variety of legal and humanist scholars concerned with the intersections between Indigenous peoples and law, including those engaged in critical legal studies and legal philosophy, sociolegal studies, human rights and native title law.

Kathleen Birrell is based at Melbourne Law School, Australia.

Indigenous Peoples and the Law

Series editors

Dr Mark A. Harris, *La Trobe University, Australia*;
Prof. Denise Ferreira da Silva, *Queen Mary, University of London, UK*;
Dr Claire Charters, *University of Auckland, New Zealand*;
Dr Glen Coulthard, *University of British Columbia, Canada*

The colonial modalities that resulted in the pillaging of the 'New World' involved wholesale dispossession, genocidal violence and exploitation of their original inhabitants. It was not, however, until the latter part of the 20th century that Indigenous peoples attained some degree of legal recognition. This book series focuses upon the manner in which Indigenous peoples' experiences of law have been transformed from an oppressive system of denying rights to a site of contestation, and the articulation of various forms of self-governance. Encouraging a range of theoretical, political and ethical perspectives on Indigenous peoples and the law, this book series aims to provide a comprehensive survey of the experience of Indigenous peoples and their changing relationship with national and international juridical frameworks.

Titles in this series:

Aboriginal Peoples, Colonialism and International Law
Raw Law
Irene Watson

Forthcoming titles in this series:

Human Rights, the Rule of Law and Exploitation
Blood Minerals
Mark Harris

The Literary and Legal Genealogy of Native American Dispossession
The Marshall Cases Trilogy
George Pappas

Scales of Governance and Indigenous Peoples
New Rights or Same Old Wrongs?
Edited by Irène Bellier and Jennifer Hays

Indigenous Peoples as Subjects of International Law
Irene Watson

Indigeneity: Before and Beyond the Law

Kathleen Birrell

Routledge
Taylor & Francis Group
LONDON AND NEW YORK

First published 2016 by Routledge

2 Park Square, Milton Park, Abingdon, Oxfordshire OX14 4RN
711 Third Avenue, New York, NY 10017

a GlassHouse book

Routledge is an imprint of the Taylor & Francis Group, an informa business

First issued in paperback 2017

British Library Cataloguing in Publication Data
A catalogue record for this book is available from the British Library

Library of Congress Cataloging-in-Publication Data
Birrell, Kathleen Beth, author.
Indigeneity : before and beyond the law / Kathleen Beth Birrell.
pages cm. — (Indigenous peoples and the law)
Includes bibliographical references and index.
ISBN 978-1-138-79332-3 (hbk) — ISBN 978-1-315-76131-2 (ebk)
1. Indigenous peoples--Legal status, laws, etc.—Philosophy. 2. Indigenous peoples—Social conditions. 3. Indigenous peoples in literature. 4. Aboriginal Australians—Legal status, laws, etc. I. Title.
K3247.B57 2016
342.08'72—dc23
2015025501

ISBN: 978-1-138-79332-3 (hbk)
ISBN: 978-1-138-57037-5 (pbk)

Typeset in Baskerville and Gill Sans by
Florence Production Limited, Stoodleigh, Devon, UK

Contents

Acknowledgements

Writing, it has been surely suggested by many, is seldom the singular enterprise it may appear to be. On the completion of this book, I am indebted to many, as supervisors, colleagues, editors, institutional benefactors, friends and family. Derived as it is from my doctoral thesis, my greatest debt is to my doctoral supervisor, Professor Peter Fitzpatrick, whose remarkable scholarship and exemplary and generous supervision both illuminated and emboldened me. I am grateful for the intellectual rigour he brought to my own scholarship, and to regular meetings with other students, for his careful and unhurried guidance, and for his consistent attention to the detail of my work. But, more than this, I am grateful for his extraordinary kindness and friendship and, alongside Shelby Ferris Fitzpatrick, for welcoming us into their home and wondrous garden.

My gratitude extends to the Birkbeck Law School, University of London, and its stimulating and enriching community. I thank those who shared their intellectual endeavours and friendship with me in reading groups and beyond, particularly Maria Aristodemou, Richard Bowyer, Lucy Finchett-Maddock, Ben Golder, Richard Joyce, Chris Lloyd, Maria Carolina Olarte, Victoria Ridler, Matthew Stone, Illan Wall and Thanos Zartaloudis. I also thank the Birkbeck Department of English and Humanities for their facilitation of interdisciplinary work, particularly Sharon Holm. I am grateful for the provision of institutional financial support during my studies, through the Ronnie Warrington Studentship, the Birkbeck Overseas Research Studentship and the Birkbeck College Research Studentship. I also acknowledge the richly diverse community of Goodenough College, London, of which I was privileged to be a part, and the Menzies Centre for Australian Studies, Kings College London, which also supported my studies in London. I particularly thank Rebe Taylor, for her wonderful intellectual companionship, collaboration and enduring friendship.

In Melbourne, I am enormously grateful to Professor Lee Godden and Associate Professor Maureen Tehan, who provided wonderful collaborative opportunities at Melbourne Law School. I am also grateful to Professor Sundhya Pahuja, who made the initial introduction to Peter Fitzpatrick and encouraged my early ideas. Among many others, my debt also extends to Olivia Barr,

Julie Evans, Ann Genovese, Bec Goodburn, Kirsty Gover, James Parker, Marc Trabsky, Yoriko Otomo and Margaret Young.

I extend my thanks to the Routledge editorial team, most particularly to my reviewer for his very astute comments on my manuscript.

I am greatly indebted to the Indigenous communities of Australia and the Torres Strait Islands, whose stories inspired and animated my critique. I particularly acknowledge Alexis Wright, both for her extraordinary writing and for her invaluable insights in the context of my work, which extended to drawing my attention to the artwork of Ellen Roughsey, which appears on the cover of this book.

As ever, I extend my boundless gratitude to my parents, Ruth and John, for their extraordinary support. I also thank my parents-in-law, Dinny and Peter, for their encouragement. And finally, I dedicate this book to Will, whose faith, patience and love emboldened me to begin at all and sustained me throughout, and also to my children, Evelyn and Audrey, who daily remind me of the rich abundance of life, beyond intellectual endeavour.

Permissions

An earlier form of Part I ("Imagining Indigeneities") was previously published as "Indigeneity: Before and Beyond the Law" in (2010) 51 *Studies in Law, Politics and Society*, Special Issue: Interdisciplinary Legal Studies: The Next Generation 219.

Parts of "Narratives" and an earlier form of "The Legal Archive" were previously published as "An Essential Ghost: Indigeneity within the Legal Archive" in (2010) 33 Australian Feminist Law Journal, 81.

Parts of "Narratives" and an earlier form of "An Idea of Justice" were previously published as "An Idea of Justice" in (2013) 22(1) *Griffith Law Review*, 87.

Parts of "Beyond the Law" were previously published as a book review in (2012) 8(3) *Law, Culture and the Humanities*, 515.

Parts of "A Subversive Juridicity" were previously published as a book review in (2009) 5 *Law, Culture and the Humanities*, 156.

All are published with permission.

Part I

Narratives

Chapter 1

Imagining indigeneities

> The great life-story cycle has been the way for millennia. It is the birthright of all Aboriginal children to be born into the *right* story. Indeed, it is the birthright and greatest gift we can give all children. The *right* story connects us intimately to our country, giving us our place and our identity. The *right* story embeds us deeply in nature, connected to the living spirit.[1]

> If, 'in this land, stories have power' then we only have to choose what story we will tell, what story we will live, what story we will pass on to the children who will one day follow in our footsteps. As we make, so we are made . . . .[2]

This book is focused upon the animation of indigeneities within textual imaginaries, both literary and juridical, narratives that exist in "a strange play"[3] of mutuality. Law and literature – as texts, "signs on a page" – may be understood to be artificial abstractions, concerned with inscribing a story upon "bodies and . . . souls . . . fulfil[ling] as well as replac[ing] their unfulfillable desires".[4] In so doing, these abstractions inscribe 'indigeneity' upon the bodies and souls of their subjects, in a multiplicity of ways. Whether describing law *as* literature or law *in* literature, the (inter)disciplinary endeavour that is 'law and literature' is underpinned by the primacy of narrative. For Aristodemou, narratives "invent rather than reflect our lives, ourselves, and our worlds" and cannot be neutral; rather, they "investigate, but also suggest, create, and legislate meaning".[5]

1 Gladys Milroy and Jill Milroy, "Different Ways of Knowing: Trees are our Families Too" in Sally Morgan, Tjalaminu Mia and Blake Kwaymullina (eds), *Heartsick for Country: Stories of Love, Spirit and Creation* (2008) 22, 24.

2 Sally Morgan, "The Balance for the World" in Morgan, Mia and Kwaymullina, above n 1, 254, 278.

3 Patrick Hanafin, Adam Gearey and Joseph Brooker, "Introduction: On Writing: Law and Literature" in Patrick Hanafin, Adam Gearey and Joseph Brooker (eds) *Law and Literature* (2004) 31(1) Special Issue, *Journal of Law and Society* 1, 2.

4 Maria Aristodemou, *Law and Literature: From Her to Eternity* (2000) 1.

5 Ibid., 3.

The narratives of law and literature both create and legislate meaning. The focus of this book is their mutual creation and legislation of indigeneity.

As, arguably, postcolonial subjectivities, indigeneities are constructed within law and literature in terms of a process described as "deep" colonisation,[6] yet are also deconstructive of those terms. Indeed, law and literature have been described as disciplines that "interfere with one another",[7] as "sites of struggle where cultural meanings and dominant assumptions can be criticized and contested".[8] While legal narratives conceive of indigeneity in terms of a putative 'authenticity', I will suggest that the aesthetic of Indigenous literature disrupts and deconstructs the law. Furthermore, as an ambivalence or undecidability, articulated and represented within particular spaces of recognition, I will elaborate a conception of indigeneity as recognised and created within these discourses, ultimately revealing legal and literary narratives to be mutually constitutive.

In the course of a broader consideration of legal and literary renderings of indigeneity and, indeed, of indigeneities *before* and *beyond* the law, this book will examine constructions of indigeneity in the international arena, particularly in terms of rights discourses, and within the law of native title, particularly in Australia. In so doing, I will demonstrate that this law continues to embrace an antiquated anthropological notion of "the 'authentic' or whole Indigenous subject, framed and referenced by mythic time and complex kinship rather than by the impacts of colonialism", thereby "eras[ing] dispossession".[9] Accordingly, it would seem, this law (mis)recognises indigeneity as a static cultural 'authenticity', in a movement proceeding not "from combat to combat until it arrives at mutual reciprocity . . . [but] from domination to domination".[10] Indeed, for Foucault, as for Butler, "juridical systems of power *produce* the subjects they subsequently come to represent".[11] In the context of native title, the colonial schema in which the common law conception of indigeneity operates compels a particular performance from the Indigenous subject, in order to appear before the law at all. Such performance has been described as "the impossible object of an authentic self-identity . . . a domesticated nonconflictual 'traditional' form of sociality and (inter)subjectivity".[12]

6 Deborah Bird Rose, "Land Rights and Deep Colonising: The Erasure of Women" (1996) 28 *Aboriginal Law Bulletin* 6; see also Deborah Bird Rose, *Reports from a Wild Country: Ethics for Decolonisation* (2004).

7 Hanafin, Gearey and Brooker, above n 3, 1.

8 Aristodemou, above n 4, 10.

9 Patrick Wolfe, *Settler Colonialism and the Transformation of Anthropology* (1999), 197, discussed in Ann Curthoys, Ann Genovese and Alexander Reilly, *Rights and Redemption: History, Law and Indigenous People* (2008) 175.

10 Michel Foucault, "Nietzsche, Genealogy, History" in Michel Foucault (Paul Rabinow, ed.) *The Foucault Reader* (1984) 76, 85. Discussed in Majid Yar, "Recognition and the Politics of Human(e) Desire" (2001) 18(2–3) *Theory, Culture & Society* 57, 61–2.

11 Judith Butler, *Gender Trouble: Feminism and the Subversion of Identity* (1990) 2.

12 Elizabeth Povinelli, *The Cunning of Recognition: Indigenous Alterities and the Making of Australian Multiculturalism* (2002) 6.

In contrast, literature authored by Indigenous peoples provides an alternative mode of recognition for the Indigenous subject, as an "articulated"[13]or, alternatively, fluid subjectivity. While the "historical or positive"[14] narrative of the law persists in returning indigeneity to a fixed position of cultural authenticity, Indigenous literature dissolves – momentarily – this fixity, imagining fluid and manifold indigeneities. In this way, the law is opened to a multitude of Indigenous imperatives. Such fluidity or hybridity in Indigenous literatures allows for more expansive expressions of community and Indigenous Law,[15] whereby indigeneities are conceived not as as fixed identities, but as existing within a perpetual state of (re)creation.

This endeavour entails an interdisciplinary engagement with a variety of scholarly approaches and extant discourses, but the central arguments of the book

13 James Clifford, "Indigenous Articulations" (Fall, 2001) 13(2) *The Contemporary Pacific* 468, 478. Clifford describes Indigenous identity as "articulated", meaning something that's articulated or hooked together . . . [which] can also be unhooked and recombined"; "a social or cultural formation as an articulated ensemble . . . [which] does not allow you to prefigure it on an organic model . . . more like a political coalition in its ability to conjoin disparate elements, a cyborg. While the possible elements and positions of a sociocultural ensemble are historically imposed constraints that can be quite persistent over time, there is no eternal or natural shape to their configuration.

14 Jacques Derrida, "Force of Law: The Mystical Foundation of Authority" in Jacques Derrida (Gil Anidjar, ed.), *Acts of Religion* (2002) 228, 240, discussing Montaigne, *Essais* 2, Chapter 12, 601/*Essayes*, 482.

15 The "Law" of Indigenous Law is frequently capitalised by Indigenous authors. Indigenous Australian academic Irene Watson, for example, describes "Raw Law: a natural system of obligations and benefits, flowing from an Aboriginal ontology": Irene Watson, *Aboriginal Peoples, Colonialism and International Law: Raw Law* (2014) 5. From a non-Indigenous perspective, I may speculate that this is in recognition of the ultimate authority of this Law and, in a (post)colonial context, its authority over non-Indigenous law. For my purposes, this may also speak to its dwelling in the Derridean unconditional and as, perhaps, the "law of the law": Jacques Derrida, "Before the Law" in Jacques Derrida (Derek Attridge, ed.), *Acts of Literature* (1992), 191. It has also been capitalised as "Law" judicially, notably in *Sampi v Western Australia* [2005] FCA 777 (10 June 2005). At [1052], French J summarised the Bardi definition of Law, as submitted to the court in evidence (second emphasis added – hereafter, emphases are noted only where my own):

> Bardi law and custom as described in the evidence and as summarised by Mr Bagshaw, relies upon the belief that Bardi lands and waters and the cultural forms and practices which make up the body of their customary law were created and bequeathed upon their ancestors by supernatural beings, the *inamunonjin*. These beings occupied and/or moved across the Dampier Peninsula region before direct human experience of the world. They shaped the physical environment and informed it with their spirits. They set the boundaries of traditional territories, named sites and introduced songs, dances, designs and objects together with myths and rituals. They set up the basic rules regulating the social order. *The sum total of these rules, customs and resources is comprehended by the term "Law"*.

Furthermore, at [1053], his Honour applied this term to the specific subject matter of the native title claim: "The Law so understood, in my opinion, embodied the fundamental principle that the Bardi people as a community hold the traditional territory which is defined by the Law and is to be used and enjoyed in accordance with its rules."

are principally focused upon studies in law and philosophy, and law and literature. As an examination of indigeneity *before* and *beyond* the law, I am concerned with differing, yet mutually constitutive, narratives. Specifically, the hegemonic narratives of law *before* which the Indigene must perform, and the necessarily infinite responsivity of law to a *beyond* that constitutes and transforms it. These engagements encompass discourses of rights and dialectics of recognition, both in the international sphere and in the particular context of (post)colonial settler nation states, and discourses surrounding the very notion of 'indigeneity' itself.

To begin, I will elaborate upon this notion of indigeneity, as a thoroughly contested concept, a legal and political instrument for rights advocacy, and a global and indeed globalising discourse. This will include an overview of anthropological debates surrounding its cultural validity and legal and political instrumentalisation. International rights discourses, including human rights and their critique, will also be afforded attention, with particular reference to the normative classification and categorisation of Indigenous peoples in international fora. I will then provide a review of my theoretical orientations and philosophical underpinnings, and their application to questions of indigeneity in law and literature, critical approaches to rights and recognition, postcolonialism, and law and literature as an interdisciplinary paradigm.

This introductory examination will include a consideration of the constituently constraining quality of recognition, introduced in its strongest manifestation with Hegel,[16] and partially liberated by way of Fanon in a (post)colonial context.[17] The notion of a misrecognised indigeneity will then be developed in relation to a Derridean reading of subjectivity before the law, and the commensurable relation between law and literature.[18] This will include a discussion of attempts to define literature, as a "strategy"[19] or as a singular "event",[20] and will extend to an examination of the literary work as evocative of that which Derrida conceives as the unconditional, which animates the law in a perpetual motion between determinacy and indeterminacy, ultimately constituting it. Indeed, for Derrida, the unconditional is conceived as that which is "without condition", "without power", and "without defence",[21] arising in the moment of deconstruction, the event – *"what arrives, what comes about"* – resistant to all domestication and

16 Georg Wilhelm Friedrich Hegel, "Self-Consciousness: The Truth and Self-Certainty: Independence and Dependence of Self-Consciousness: Lordship and Bondage", in *Phenomenology of Spirit* (AV Miller trans., with analysis and forward by JN Findlay, 1977 edn) 111.

17 Frantz Fanon, *Black Skin White Masks* (Charles Lam Markmann trans., 1967 edn).

18 Derrida, above n 15, 181. See also Peter Fitzpatrick, "Juris-fiction: Literature and the Law of the Law" (2004) 35 (1–2) *ARIEL* 215; Peter Fitzpatrick, "Reading Slowly: The Law of Literature and the Literature of Law" in Ruth Buchanan, Stewart Motha and Sundhya Pahuja (eds), *Reading Modern Law: Critical Methodologies and Sovereign Formations* (2012) 193.

19 Terry Eagleton, *The Event of Literature* (2012), especially from 167.

20 Derek Attridge, *The Singularity of Literature* (2004).

21 Jacques Derrida, "The University Without Condition" in Jacques Derrida, *Without Alibi* (2002) 202, 206.

convention.[22] Accordingly, the apparent determinacy of a hegemonic law – including human rights, as " 'the perfect instrument of empire', of a globalized *imperium*" – may be (re)conceived as "its ultimate undoing, or even its transformation."[23] The relation between law and literature will be elaborated by way of a Benjaminian reading[24] of literary revolution and a recuperation and reassertion of Indigenous Law. I will then proceed to a discussion of ethical positions in "intercultural"[25] research – the capacity to speak of or for the other, and the means by which a non-Indigenous researcher, such as myself, might approach such articulations. I will close Part 1 with a synoptic account of the remaining chapters.

By necessity, the principal focus of this book is confined to Aboriginal and Torres Strait Islander peoples of Australia, but some limited comparison will be made to other Indigenous societies, particularly the First Nations peoples of Canada and the Native American peoples of the United States of America. To clarify, I use the term 'Indigenous' in order to be broadly inclusive, although specific individuals and communities have spoken from distinct and local perspectives. I have recorded these assertions as uttered or written, but in my own argument I use the broader term 'Indigenous'. This category, though highly contested, has now assumed national and international political and legal meaning, in international agreements and United Nations (UN) declarations, and carries particular social and cultural associations unique to the global processes of decolonisation. Its interrogation, in legal and literary discourses, is the very purpose of this book.

The question of indigeneity

The very question that is indigeneity,[26] and non-Indigenous interest in answering it, is the subject of vast scholarship and debate. As an inherently local *and* global discourse, the profusion of political, legal, literary, scholarly, and community

22 Derrida, above n 21, 234.

23 Peter Fitzpatrick, "The Revolutionary Past: Decolonizing Law and Human Rights" (2014) 2(1) *Metodo: International Studies in Phenomenology and Philosophy* 117, 127, citing Robert A Williams, *The American Indian in Western Legal Thought: The Discourses of Conquest* (1990) 59.

24 Walter Benjamin, "Critique of Violence" in Walter Benjamin, *Reflections: Essays, Aphorisms, Autobiographical Writings* (1978) 277.

25 See discussion of a decolonial "delinking" and associated "interculturality" in Ferdinando Menga, "Interculturality and the Limits of a Globalized Order. Some Paradigmatic Insights on the Unavoidable Intervention of Contingency Within Human Institutions" (2012) 3–2 *Rivista Internazionale di Filosofia e Psicologia* 254, 256–8. See also discussion in Fitzpatrick, above n 23, especially 128.

26 The terms "indigeneity" and "indigeneities", as used throughout this book, denote Indigenous subjectivities, Indigenous "life-ways" (Marcia Langton, "The 'Wild', the Market and the Native: Indigenous People face New Forms of Global Colonization" in William M Adams and Martin Mulligan (eds), *Decolonizing Nature: Strategies for Conservation in a Post-Colonial Era* (2003) 79, 80) and

engagements with expressions of indigeneity reflects its expanding international currency. The term "Indigenous", as a global expression of identity and concomitant struggle, is relatively recent. Once appearing only perhaps in "a scattering of botanical works on indigenous plants",[27] indigeneity now connotes not merely nativeness to land or region[28] but also a political, legal, and cultural identity with international valency – Indigenous peoples – most properly capitalised as a plural proper noun. The plurality of 'peoples' is a recognition of a 'collective, rather than purely individual, dimension to [Indigenous] livelihoods',[29] and an extension of self-determination to those who may not yet, or indeed ever, be defined as nations.[30] Furthermore, Tuhiwai Smith has described the plural of 'peoples' in 'Indigenous peoples' as the result of Indigenous activism – a recognition of 'real differences between different indigenous peoples'.[31] Articulation of Indigenous peoples as a 'global form of political identity' has also required recognition of entities that surpass extant political categories, who may be nations, yet do not pursue statehood.[32]

Irrespective of the implicit and explicit heterogeneity of Indigenous peoples throughout the world, which persists despite colonisation,[33] indigeneity itself has

Indigenous Law (see footnote 15, above). This denotation extends the elements of the definition of "indigeneity", defined in *The Oxford English Dictionary* (1991, Second edn) as "the quality of being Indigenous; indigenousness". For my purposes, "indigeneity" conflates the demarcations proposed elsewhere, such as Hamilton's use of the term in the context of the law, as "not the specific ontologies and epistemologies of [Indigenous] peoples . . . but rather the political, economic and legal articulations of indigenous difference (and the discursive and material effects of these articulations) in postcolonial settler nations" (Jennifer Anne Hamilton, *Indigeneity in the Courtroom: Law, Culture and the Production of Difference in the North American Courts* (2009) 1). I would also contrast my definition with Niezen's use of the term "indigenism", which he defines as "the international movement that aspires to promote and protect the rights of the world's 'first peoples'" (Ronald Niezen, *The Origins of Indigenism: Human Rights and the Politics of Identity* (2003) 4).

27 Niezen, above n 26, 2–3.

28 Lesley Brown (ed.), *The New Shorter Oxford English Dictionary on Historical Principles* (1993), defines "indigenous" as: Born or produced in a particular land or region; (especially of flora or fauna) native or belonging naturally *to* (a region, a soil, etc), not introduced; inborn, innate. Of, pertaining to, or concerned with the native inhabitants of a region.

29 Tom Calma, Aboriginal and Torres Strait Islander Social Justice Commissioner, Australian Human Rights Commission Native Title Report 2008, at www.hreoc.gov.au/social_justice/nt_report/index.html (accessed 6 October 2015).

30 Sharon Helen Venne, *Our Elders Understand Our Rights: Evolving International Law Regarding Indigenous Peoples* (1998) 70–2. For a critical consideration of the nation as the "universal form of collective political organization", see Peter Fitzpatrick, *Modernism and the Grounds of Law* (2001) 127; Sundhya Pahuja, "Decolonization and the Eventness of International Law" in Fleur Johns, Richard Joyce and Sundhya Pahuja (eds), *Events: The Force of International Law* (2011) 91, 96–7.

31 Linda Tuhiwai Smith, *Decolonizing Methodologies: Research and Indigenous Peoples* (1999) 7.

32 Niezen, above n 26, 51.

33 See Gayatri Chakravorty Spivak, "Can the Subaltern Speak?" in Cary Nelson and Lawrence Grossberg (eds), *Marxism and the Interpretation of Culture* (1988) 271, 284. Here, Spivak speaks of the subaltern subject in the Indian context: "Certain varieties of the Indian elite are at best native informants for first-world intellectuals interested in the voice of the Other. But one must nevertheless insist that the colonized subaltern *subject* is irretrievably heterogeneous."

become a multifarious yet globally cohesive marker of unity, defined in accordance with a cultural distinctiveness resistant to colonial imposition, spiritual and ancestral connections to land and waters, marginalisation and dispossession, and political agitation against neocolonial expansion. Soguk asserts: "Given the negations visited upon their histories, more than others, indigenous struggles compel a political calculus that registers indigenous identity practices".[34] In claims for rights to cultural integrity and expression, access to and management of land and resources, and to political and economic autonomy, Indigenous peoples of the world present a collective struggle. Such struggles have given rise to a "new kind of global political entity", termed "indigenism",[35] and an associated international discourse of indigeneity.

Much critique and debate surround the concept of indigeneity, particularly in anthropological circles,[36] despite gestures toward consensus. Barnard, citing Saugestad, argues that a "consensus in 'international discourse in politics, law, and anthropology'" suggests a "polythetic definition"[37] of indigeneity, in accordance with four criteria: "first-come, non-dominance, cultural difference, and self-ascription".[38] Nonetheless, contention remains, and a distinction has been drawn between notions of indigeneity as an anthropological concept, as a legal concept, and "as a useful tool for political persuasion".[39] With reference to the latter, it has been acknowledged that the essentialism required by the " 'indigenous people' category" may be "the only discourse the 'other' can use against the power of the coloniser".[40] Accordingly, the collective Indigenous political movement has been described as "a movement of movements",[41] comprised of those whose historical subordination "affords them a greater capacity to think imaginatively about possible alternative futures".[42] Marginalised groups described as "local,

34 Nevzat Soguk, "Indigenous Peoples and Radical Futures in Global Politics" (March 2007) 29(1) *New Political Science* 1, 5.
35 Niezen, above n 26, 3.
36 Anthropological debate concerning the concept of indigeneity was particularly concentrated in a series of responses to an article published in 2003: Adam Kuper, "The Return of the Native" (Current Anthropology Forum on Anthropology in Public, June 2003) 44(3) *Current Anthropology* 389. Responses appeared in Current Anthropology Forum on Anthropology in Public (June 2003) 44(3) *Current Anthropology* 389; (April 2004) 45(2) *Current Anthropology* 263; Alan Barnard, "Kalahari Revisionism, Vienna and the 'indigenous peoples' Debate" (2006) 14(1) *Social Anthropology* 1; Discussion: The Concept of Indigeneity (2006) 14(1) *Social Anthropology* 17–32. I will discuss this particular discourse in greater detail in Part II.
37 Barnard, above n 36, 7.
38 Sidsel Saugestad, *The Inconvenient Indigenous: Remote Area Development in Botswana, Donor Assistance and the First People of the Kalahari* (2001) 43, cited in Barnard, above n 36, 1.
39 Barnard, above n 36, 7.
40 Justin Kenrick, "Discussion: The Concept of Indigeneity" (2006) 14(1) *Social Anthropology* 19.
41 Tom Mertes, *A Movement of Movements: Is Another World Really Possible?* (2004), cited in Soguk, above n 34, 5.
42 Soguk, above n 34, 5.

native, autochthonous" and "traditional", "tribal", or "peasant"[43] are now also defined via an internationally recognised identity that has become a tool for empowerment, with which to harness previously inaccessible resources. At both a national and international level, claims may be made via the performance of such identity. Yet, its use as a tool – dependent as it may be upon fixity and stereotype – is highly fraught, encumbered with expectations that may bear little or no resemblance to lived realities. Notions of hybridity must contend with "the old misconception that 'the only real Aboriginals are tribal Aboriginals'",[44] or "the ones sitting on a desert rock with a spear".[45] Contested interpretations move between these polarities, offering arguably essentialist constructions, which reduce indigeneity to arguments over authenticity. Indeed, it has been suggested that the very notion of indigeneity, and claims to it, necessarily follow "a western social construction of 'indigenous' authenticity".[46]

First defined internationally in 1957 by the International Labour Organization, and now elaborated in various international instruments[47] – initially drafted largely by those who would not identify as Indigenous[48] – the term "Indigenous", while contested, is now imbued with enormous legal and political meaning. Particularly

43 Michael R Dove, "Indigenous People and Environmental Politics" (2006) 35 *Annual Review of Anthropology* 191, 192.

44 Eva Rask Knudsen, "Fringe Finds Focus: Developments and Strategies in Aboriginal Writing in English" (1991) 15(2) *Australian Literary Studies* 32, 33, citing Mudrooroo Narogin, *Writing from the Fringe: A Study of Modern Aboriginal Literature* (1990) 168.

45 Anita M Heiss, *Dhuuluu-Yala: To Talk Straight* (2003) 19, discussing Ruby Langford Ginibi, "My Mob, My Self" in Kerry Reed-Gilbert (ed.), *The Strength of Us as Women: Black Women Speak* (2000) 19.

46 Barnard, above n 36, 7, citing Richard Handler, "Authenticity" (1986) 2 *Anthropology Today* 2; Trond Thuen, "Anthropological Knowledge in the Courtroom: Conflicting Paradigms" (2004) 12 *Social Anthropology* 265, 279–82.

47 The term "indigenous" was included in the International Labour Organization (ILO) Convention (No. 107) *Concerning the Protection and Integration of Indigenous and Other Tribal and Semi-Tribal Populations in Independent Countries* (1957), and the accompanying International Labour Organisation Recommendation No 104 (1957). This Convention was revised by the International Labour Organisation Convention (No 169) (*Indigenous and Tribal Peoples Convention*) in 1989. It is also defined in the Martinéz Cobo Report to the United Nations Sub-Commission on the Prevention of Discrimination of Minorities in 1986; and the Chairperson of the United Nations Working Group on Indigenous Populations, formed in 1982: see www.iwgia.org/culture-and-identity/identification-of-indigenous-peoples (accessed 6 October 2015). See discussion of these definitions in Megan Davis, "Indigenous Struggles in Standard-Setting: The United Nations Declaration on the Rights of Indigenous Peoples" (2008) 9(2) *Melbourne Journal of International Law* 439, 442. It was further defined by the World Bank in 1991: The World Bank Operational Manual: Operational Directive 4.20 (September 1991): Indigenous Peoples. This definition has since been refined: World Bank Operational Directive 4.10 (July 2005, revised April 2013): see http://web.worldbank.org/WBSITE/EXTERNAL/PROJECTS/EXTPOLICIES/EXTOPMANUAL/0,,contentMDK:20553653~menuPK:4564185~pagePK:64709096~piPK:64709108~theSitePK:502184,00.html#F6 (accessed 6 October 2015).

48 Niezen, above n 26, 3; 53–93.

in the realms of natural resources and environmental and climate change politics, indigeneity is wielded as a weapon in large-scale debates over development and conservation. In the midst of such debates, Indigenous peoples may be both actors and pawns – at times active in the pursuit of rights to land, waters, and resources on the basis of cultural knowledge and connection, at others simply a part of the artillery used in efforts to protect areas of ecological significance or, more recently, in international schemes for climate change mitigation and adaptation.[49] Yet, it is the articulation of and identification with this internationally recognised notion of indigeneity that has catapulted peoples who may have been previously oriented toward the local into the international arena.

The global articulation of indigeneity has been attributed to the inauguration and development of human rights as inalienable and universal principles, the concomitant rise of identity politics,[50] and the delocalisation inherent within "totalizing systems of modernity",[51] which actually served to create indigeneity as a global concept: "[T]hrough the very process of being recognized as 'indigenous', these groups enter the realms of modernity".[52] Hirtz describes the current formulation of the 'Indigenous' as "[a] form of 'bureaucratic Orientalism' . . . constructing and reaffirming the Other through the minutiae of administrative procedures and contemporary representational processes", thereby "establishing the right to act as an indigenous group".[53] Indigeneity, he ultimately suggests, is an expression of modernity itself:

> Modernity needs the contrasting concept of indigeneity and tradition, whereas traditional societies in pre-modern or pre-colonial times did not need to establish their 'otherness' in opposition to modernity or their own history.[54]

The arrogations of modernity to an encompassing universalism are confounded by an origin that must necessarily be apart from it – that Other in relation to

49 See, for example, the United Nations Reducing Emissions from Deforestation and Degradation Programme (REDD+): www.un-redd.org/Home/tabid/565/language/en-US/Default.aspx (accessed 6 October 2015). For discussion, see Kathleen Birrell, Lee Godden and Maureen Tehan, "Climate Change and REDD+: Property as a Prism for Conceiving Indigenous Peoples' Engagement" (2012) 3(2) *Journal of Human Rights and the Environment* 196.

50 Niezen, above n 26, 3.

51 Dove, above n 43, 193, citing Arjun Appaduri, *Modernity at Large: Cultural Dimensions of Globalization* (1996); also citing Anthony Giddens, *The Constitution of Society: Outline of the Theory of Structuration* (1984); Alf Hornborg, "Ecology as Semiotics: Outlines of a Contextualist Paradigm for Human Ecology" in Philippe Descola and Gísli Pálsson, *Nature and Society: Anthropological Perspectives* (1996) 45.

52 Frank Hirtz, "It takes Modern Means to be Traditional: On Recognizing Indigenous Cultural Communities in the Philippines" (2003) 34(5) *Development and Change* 887, 889.

53 Hirtz, above n 52, 889.

54 Ibid. See also Peter Fitzpatrick, *The Mythology of Modern Law* (1992) ix: "No matter what its relevance to so-called primitive and ancient worlds, myth is vibrantly operative in modernity".

which modernity is defined.[55] These realms of modernity include human rights discourses, within which the concept of indigeneity has been encapsulated and defined as a unique and inviolable 'Otherness', to be protected as such. Indeed, the UN Declaration on the Rights of Indigenous Peoples[56] presents indigeneity in these terms, affirming Indigenous peoples as "equal to all other peoples", yet "recognizing the right of all peoples to be different, to consider themselves different, and to be respected as such".[57]

Recognition, it is suggested, is "a conceptual framework through which we understand the struggle to become . . . fully individuated beings" and, accordingly, is "a powerful and enduring philosophical discourse of being and becoming".[58] The modern subject of recognition, however, particularly in postcolonial contexts, is "thoroughly imbricated with relations of appropriation and ownership",[59]

55 Fitzpatrick, above n 30, especially 43–4. See also Said's seminal discussion of the construction of the Occident, in contrast to the Orient: Edward Said, *Orientalism* (1978); and Spivak's discussion thereof: Gayatri Chakravorty Spivak, *A Critique of Postcolonial Reason: Toward a History of the Vanishing Present* (1999) 203.

56 On 7 September 2007, the United Nations General Assembly adopted the *United Nations Declaration on the Rights of Indigenous Peoples*, taking note of the recommendation of the Human Rights Council contained in its Resolution 1/2 of 29 June 2006, by which the Council adopted the text of the Declaration. See http://social.un.org/index/IndigenousPeoples/DeclarationontheRights of IndigenousPeoples.aspx (accessed 6 October 2015; "*Declaration*"). Australia was one of the four countries that voted against the Declaration (alongside the United States of America, Canada and New Zealand). Following the change of Federal Government in November 2007, the new government informally indicated its support for the Declaration: see Statement on the United Nations Declaration on the Rights of Indigenous Peoples, The Hon Jenny Macklin, Minister for Families, Housing, Community Services and Indigenous Affairs, 3 April 2009, Parliament House Canberra: www.un.org/esa/socdev/unpfii/documents/Australia_official_statement_endorsement_UNDRIP.pdf (accessed 6 October 2015). It is of note that the Native Title Amendment (Reform) Bill 2011 (Cth), proposed by Greens Senator Rachel Siewert, at s 3A, provided: "It is an additional object of this Act that governments in Australia take all necessary steps to implement the . . . principles set out in the United Nations Declaration of the Rights of Indigenous Peoples" and, furthermore, that "the provisions of this Act are to be interpreted and applied in a manner that is consistent with the Declaration". This section has not been incorporated into the subsequent Native Title Amendment (Reform) Bill (No. 1) 2012 (Cth) (lapsed) or subsequent Native Title Amendment (Reform) Bill 2014 (Cth) (before Parliament at the time of writing). The Australian Law Reform Commission has also begun a formal review of the Native Title Act 1993 (Cth) and, in an Issues Paper (IP 45), suggests that "[r]eform should reflect Australia's international obligations in respect of Aboriginal and Torres Strait Islander people, and have regard to the United Nations Declaration on the Rights of Indigenous Peoples" (Principle 4). For further discussion on the impact of the Declaration on Australian law, see Davis, above n 47. More generally, see Claire Charters, Les Malezer and Victoria Tauli-Corpuz (eds), *Indigenous Voices: The UN Declaration on the Rights of Indigenous Peoples* (forthcoming).

57 Preamble to the *Declaration*, above n 56.

58 Brenna Bhandar, "Plasticity and Post-Colonial Recognition: 'Owning, Knowing and Being'" (2011) 22(3) *Law and Critique* 227, 228.

59 Bhandar, above n 58, 228.

whereby the self is recognised only in accordance with a preconceived subjectivity – that which Derrida describes as an "economy of the same".[60] This argument would extend to claims to "the universal as an ontological completeness"[61] in international rights discourses, such as the Declaration. This very document, however, presents paradoxical claims to universality and specificity – it purports to 'declare' the rights of individuals and communities that are both universally identifiable, yet are defined by cultural and geographic particularity. The language of difference contained within the Declaration might suggest the emergence of that which Tourme-Jouannet has described as "a legal status of difference . . . alongside the legal status of equality in international law".[62] In the context of settler nation states, however, recognition of such difference is violently constrained, the Indigenous legal subject "confined to a restricted economy of property ownership and subjectivity".[63]

The lineaments of an international Indigenous rights discourse may be traced from the inauguration of formal international human rights, which began with the Universal Declaration of Human Rights, adopted by the UN General Assembly in 1948.[64] Subsequent resolutions, covenants, and associated instruments and mechanisms reflect a commonly articulated succession of rights, usefully summarised by Messer as follows: the " 'first generation' of *political and civil rights* protect basic security of persons"; the " 'second generation' of *socioeconomic and cultural rights*" protect, among other things, rights to employment, standards of living and education, and rights of women and children; the " 'third generation' of *solidarity* or *development rights*" protect "rights to peace, a more equitable socio-economic order, and a sustainable environment"; and the " 'fourth generation' of *indigenous rights*", of which the Declaration on the Rights of Indigenous Peoples is the centrepiece, protect Indigenous peoples' "rights to political self-determination and control over socioeconomic development".[65] At the recent completion of the Second International Decade of the World's Indigenous People (2005–2014),[66] the extent to which the broad and ambitious objectives of the Decade were

60 Jacques Derrida, "From Restricted to General Economy: A Hegelianism without Reserve" in Jacques Derrida, *Writing and Difference* (2002) 317.

61 Fitzpatrick, above n 23, 118.

62 Emmanuelle Tourme-Jouannet, *What is a Fair International Society? International Law between Development and Recognition* (2013). See also Emmanuelle Tourme-Jouannet, "The International Law of Recognition" (2013) 24(2) *European Journal of International Law* 691, 667–90, 668–9. See also discussion in Rose Parfitt, "Theorizing Recognition and International Personality" in Florian Hoffman and Anne Orford (eds), *The Oxford Handbook of International Legal Theory* (forthcoming).

63 Bhandar, above n 58, 228. See also discussion in Parfitt, above n 62.

64 United Nations Universal Declaration of Human Rights, adopted by the United Nations General Assembly on 10 December 1948, at www.un.org/en/documents/udhr/ (accessed 6 October 2015).

65 Ellen Messer, "Anthropology and Human Rights" (1993) 22 *Annual Review of Anthropology* 221, 222–3.

66 On 22 December 2004, the General Assembly adopted Resolution A/RES/59/174 for a Second International Decade, which commenced on 1 January 2005 and concluded in December 2014.

accomplished was assessed.[67] Achievements include the adoption of the Declaration in September 2007,[68] the establishment of the Permanent Forum on the Rights of Indigenous Peoples, the Expert Mechanism on the Rights of Indigenous Peoples, the Special Rapporteur on the Rights of Indigenous Peoples, and the World Conference on Indigenous Peoples.[69] In Australia, this decade was marked by the momentous national apology to Indigenous Australians in February 2008.[70] The UN General Assembly Final Report of the Second Decade reports the achievement of some of the initial goals for the Decade, but acknowledges "a substantial gap . . . between the formal recognition of Indigenous peoples and the implementation of policies on the ground".[71] While proposing the declaration of a Third Decade of the World's Indigenous People,[72] the Report identifies the need to "[r]ecognize Indigenous peoples as distinct peoples and not as marginalized and vulnerable groups in both the sustainable development goals and the post-2015 development agenda".[73] Pursuit of the latter, however, arguably necessitates the formulation of "pan-indigenous, pan-national, and pan-regional identities";[74] furthermore, it entails a seemingly untroubled engagement with a paradoxical notion of indigeneity that is culturally and geographically specific, yet simultaneously inclusive and delocalised – an engagement requiring some greater scrutiny.

Despite – or perhaps as a result of – the creation of the 'Indigenous' by the machinery of modernity, including rights discourses, this international concept of indigeneity is defined by a unique and unassailable attachment to the past. Article 9 of the Declaration affords Indigenous peoples and individuals the right to belong to an Indigenous community or nation in accordance with the traditions and customs of the community or nation concerned.[75] This community – simultaneously defined by its *indigeneity* and its *traditions and customs* – is one to which the Indigenous peoples of signatory nation states possess a right to belong.

67 United Nations Final Report of the Second International Decade of the World's Indigenous People GA, 69th Session, August 2014, UN Doc A/69/271 at http://undesadspd.org/indigenouspeoples/seconddecade.aspx (accessed 6 October 2015; "*Final Report of the Second International Decade*").

68 *Declaration*, above n 56.

69 See Communication from the United Nations Permanent Forum on Indigenous Issues Chairperson on a Third International Decade of the World's Indigenous Peoples at http://undesadspd.org/IndigenousPeoples/tabid/70/articleType/ArticleView/articleId/201/Communication-from-the-UNPFII-Chairperson-on-a-Third-International-Decade-of-the-Worlds-Indigenous-Peoples.aspx (accessed 6 October 2015).

70 Apology to Australia's Indigenous Peoples, House of Representatives, Parliament House, Canberra (13 February 2008). See full text and video at http://australia.gov.au/about-australia/our-country/our-people/apology-to-australias-indigenous-peoples (accessed 6 October 2015).

71 Final Report of the Second International Decade, above n 67.

72 Ibid., paragraph 53(a).

73 Ibid.

74 Messer, above n 65, 237.

75 Preamble to the *Declaration*, above n 56.

In order to receive the recognition and rights afforded by the international community, peoples defining themselves as Indigenous must "evoke the language of historical continuity, on which they stake their claim to collective identity".[76] Furthermore, speaking of indigeneity as defined by its historicity, Niezen remarks upon the relative newness of this concept in contrast to its reliance upon a "primordial identity", comprised of "people with primary attachments to land and culture, 'traditional' people with lasting connections to ways of life that have survived 'from time immemorial'".[77] Indeed, Sieder and Witchell have described "the distinctive criteria for indigenous populations" as including both "primordialism and cultural difference".[78] The demand for such performance arguably effects the same diminution and homogenisation of identities as other rights discourses, despite their affirmation and celebration of 'difference'.[79] Furthermore, recognition on the basis of *difference* may necessitate the creation and calcification of difference *as such*, rather than facilitate the acknowledgment of fluid subjectivities.

The articulation and promulgation of rights within the "authoritative document[s]" of international agreement, including human rights discourses, have been the subject of ongoing critique; indeed, it has been argued, "[t]he vision of human rights as limitation or empowerment-before-the-law is ideologically hegemonic".[80] Advocating a radical (re)concepualisation of human rights, as distinct from their performance in compliance with the apparently 'authoritative documents' of international law, Wall suggests that these documents confound "the multiplicity of rights-positions by implicitly claiming to write the totality of the human through her rights".[81] Similarly, Douzinas argues that where human rights "construct the individual person as a subject (of law)", such rights have become "tools of public power and individual desire".[82] Elsewhere, Butler speaks of the "language and context" of 'rights' and protection against discrimination,

76 Rachel Sieder and Jessica Witchell, "Advancing Indigenous Claims through the Law: Reflections on the Guatemalan Peace Process" in Jane K Cowen, Marie-Bénédicte Dembour and Richard A Wilson (eds), *Culture and Rights: Anthropological Perspectives* (2001) 201, 205; see also 207, 212.

77 Niezen, above n 26, 3.

78 Sieder and Witchell, above n 76, 205.

79 See Karen Engle, "From Skepticism to Embrace: Human Rights and the American Anthropological Assocation from 1947 to 1999" (2001) 23 *Human Rights Quarterly* 536; Annelise Riles, "Anthropology, Human Rights and Legal Knowledge: Culture in the Iron Cage" (2006) 108(1) *American Anthropologist* 52; Ellen Messer, "Anthropology and Human Rights" (1993) 22 *Annual Review of Anthropology* 221. Cf Fitzpatrick, above n 30, 218.

80 Illan Wall, *Human Rights and Constituent Power: Without Model or Warranty* (2012) 4. See also Costas Douzinas, *Human Rights and Empire: The Political Philosophy of Cosmopolitanism* (2007); Costas Douzinas, *The End of Human Rights: Critical Legal Thought at the Turn of the Century* (2000).

81 Wall, above n 80, 2.

82 Costas Douzinas, *Human Rights and Empire: The Political Philosophy of Cosmopolitanism* (2007) 7–8.

the former pertaining to individuals, the latter to a group or class. Accordingly, she asserts, "we have to present ourselves as bounded beings – distinct, recognizable, delineated, subjects before the law, a community defined by some shared features", in order to secure legal protections and entitlements.[83]

As a singular conception of identity, purporting to embrace a diversity of experience yet finite in its application, 'indigeneity' is ultimately a cultural and political performance.[84] Where international instruments define indigeneity in terms of "historic continuity, distinctiveness, marginalization, self-identity, and self-governance",[85] claimants must conform to and perform a mode of being that does not disrupt the articulated bounds of such recognition.[86] Nonetheless, whereas these requirements of universality define the claimant, as a determined and therefore *recognisable* legal subject, the paradoxical demand for distinctiveness necessitates a responsivity to that which is beyond the law. Indeed, while the Declaration, as an 'authoritative' document, is determinate, its potential interpretations and applications are manifold, in accordance with the "constituent conditions of society or community itself".[87] Fitzpatrick describes the dual claim of human rights, to "an operative universality whilst being, and inevitably being, a particularity".[88] Indeed, he argues, "[a] right . . . generatively trajects beyond any conditioned or conditional determinacy"; furthermore, "this perspective would open on to a human rights ever beyond ultimate affirmation, an ever-resistant human rights".[89] Accordingly, the 'human' of human rights can never be "enduringly settled"; yet, in order to realise human rights at all, "an inclusive determinacy remains imperative".[90] For my purposes, therefore, rights afforded the human being who is recognised as 'Indigenous', while violently determinative in the moment of her *recognition*, are otherwise infinitely responsive and, therefore, may be radically "intercultural".[91] That is, in the context of the "decolonial", where individuals and communities identifying as 'Indigenous' might 'delink' from

83 Judith Butler, *Precarious Life: The Powers of Mourning and Violence* (2004) 24–5. See also Brenna Bhandar, "Re-covering the Limits of Recognition: The Politics of Difference and Decolonisation in John Borrows' *Recovering Canada: The Resurgence of Indigenous Law* (2007) 27 *Australian Feminist Law Journal* 125, 138.

84 Soguk, above n 34, 5; see also Steven Robins, Comment on Adam Kuper, "The Return of the Native" (Current Anthropology Forum on Anthropology in Public, June 2003) 44(3) *Current Anthropology* 398, 398–9.

85 Dove, above n 43, 192.

86 This proposition is articulated in Australian law in *Mabo and Others v Queensland (No. 2)* (1992) 175 CLR 1, 29 ("*Mabo*") in which Brennan J held that in recognising the native title of Indigenous peoples, the court is constrained.

87 Fitzpatrick, above n 23, 125, citing Jacques Derrida, *Politics of Friendship* (George Collins trans., 1997 edn) 231.

88 Ibid., 125.

89 Ibid., 128.

90 Ibid., 127.

91 Ibid., 128.

the "occidentalized universalism" of hegemonic rights discourses, such discourses might be responsive to "an 'intercultural' plurality".[92]

(Mis)recognising indigeneity

Operating as an intercultural space, it has been suggested that indigeneity is not enunciative of particular and individualised identities but, rather, is derivative of varied and variable acts of recognition. For Healy, as for Langton, (Australian) 'Aboriginality' is not representative of Aboriginal people, but of "what happens interstitially" between Aboriginal and non-Aboriginal people.[93] In this space, selves are constructed and construed as persons able to claim rights within a legal and political discourse – which is a recognition of iterative performance, of a broader body politic unified by common struggle, as individuals defined by traditional tribal affiliations and affinities to land and waters, and as a multiplicity, which may be alternately or simultaneously autochthonous and urban, dynamic and fixed, partial and whole, spiritual and embodied, "ancient and modern".[94] These selves are responsive to different purposes and different contexts; indeed, "all identities are historically developed and are ultimately political and cultural performances".[95] Accordingly, the Indigenous self may be variably manifest, depending upon the context of recognition. It may appear, singularly or simultaneously, as fixed in a romanticised historical moment, as a pathetic lament for a dying race,[96] as an abrasive political insurgency, and as spiritually

92 Fitzpatrick, above n 23, citing Menga, above n 25, 256–8.

93 Chris Healy, *Forgetting Aborigines* (2008) 7; Marcia Langton, Well I Heard it on the Radio and I saw it on the Television: An Essay for the Australian Film Commission on the Politics and Aesthetics of Filmmaking by and about Aboriginal People and Things (1993) Australian Film Commission 31. See also Peter Sutton, *The Politics of Suffering: Indigenous Australia and the End of the Liberal Consensus* (2009) 147, who suggests that [m]ost Aboriginal people in 2009 move in what is sometimes called an intercultural space, that is also an inter-ethnic social space, and an economic and political space, where nobody's relationships are entirely with the members of a single race.

94 Stephen Muecke, *Ancient and Modern: Time, Culture and Indigenous Philosophy* (2004).

95 Soguk, above n 34, 5.

96 See Greg Lehman, "The Palawa of Tasmania" in Göran Burenhult (ed.), *Traditional Peoples Today: Continuity and Change in the Modern World* (1994) 85, 86. Lehman writes of the popular social Darwinian conception of Australian Aborigines as a "doomed race", prevalent in the 19th century: Aborigines were not dying because of things settlers had or had not done – their passing, it was claimed, was the working out of a law of nature. Western civilization was merely supplanting Aboriginal savagery. The most anyone could do was "smooth the dying pillow" of the condemned with various welfare measures . . . It was not until the early part of the 20th century that European Australians began to accept that Aboriginal people were not conveniently going to disappear. See also RD Keynes (ed.), *Charles Darwin's Beagle Diary* (2001) at http://darwin-online.org.uk/content/frameset?itemID=F1925&viewtype=text&pageseq=1 (accessed 6 October 2015). During his voyage, stopping in Australia in 1836, Darwin remarked, in portentous terms, upon the decreased numbers of Indigenous peoples, flora and fauna (401–2, emphases added):

enlivened poiesis. It is the intersubjectivity of this performance that is constitutive of indigeneity.

Langton conceives of Australian Aboriginality as akin to French sociologist Emile Durkheim's "social *thing*" – not a mere racial labelling but a dynamic dialogue, created via history and "the intersubjectivity of black and white in a dialogue".[97] Indeed, she proposes a manifestly ambiguous, indeterminate, and mutable indigeneity, itself "a process of dialogue, of imagination, of representation and interpretation".[98] Accordingly, both Aboriginal and non-Aboriginal are understood not as objects but subjects,[99] and 'Aboriginality' or 'Aboriginalities' as created via an "infinite array of intercultural experiences".[100] These experiences are reflected in three broad categories: Aboriginal interactions with other Aboriginal people and culture, non-Aboriginal stereotyping and mythologising, and constructions generated in the course of intercultural dialogue, in the pursuit of "satisfactory forms of mutual comprehension".[101]

This final notion of mutual comprehension aligns with optimistic accounts of intercultural recognition forwarded by both Taylor and Gadamer, of a "politics of recognition" achievable via a "fusion of horizons".[102] Indeed for Taylor, this is a moral imperative: by virtue of some "sense of our own limited part in the whole human story", he advocates an essential ethic of mutual respect.[103] In colonised states, however, the pursuit of such mutual comprehension is fraught, relations being indelibly stained by the blood of colonisation. Aspirations to mutuality in this context, in a reconciliatory mode, necessarily engage with problematic notions of "true identity".[104] In the conditions of the (post)colonial

> A few years since this country abounded with wild animals; now the Emu is banished to a long distance & the Kangaroo is become scarce; to both the English Greyhound is utterly destructive; it may be long before these animals are altogether exterminated, but *their doom is fixed.* The Natives are always anxious to borrow the dogs from the farmhouses; their use, offal when an animal is killed, & milk from the cows, are the peace offerings of the Settlers, who push further & further inland. The thoughtless Aboriginal, blinded by these trifling advantages, is delighted at the approach of the White Man, who seems *predestined to inherit the country of his children.*

97 Langton, above n 93, 31; see also 33.

98 Ibid., 33. See also discussion in Yin C Paradies, "Beyond Black and White: Essentialism, Hybridity and Indigeneity" (2006) 42 *Journal of Sociology* 355, 356.

99 Ibid., 32.

100 Ibid., 81.

101 Ibid.

102 Hans-Georg Gadamer, *Wahreit und Methode* [Truth and Method] (1975) 289–90, cited in Charles Taylor, "The Politics of Recognition" in Amy Guttman (ed.), *Multiculturalism: Examining the Politics of Recognition* (1994) 25, 67.

103 Taylor, above n 102, 73; see discussion 66–73.

104 Andrew Schaap, "Political Reconciliation Through a Struggle for Recognition" (2004) 13 *Social Legal Studies* 523, 524. See also Bhandar, above n 83, 151, who problematises this notion of a fusion of horizons as "configured within a liberal paradigm of identity/difference", since "preservation of difference based on cultural, ethnic or racialized identities . . . raises the spectre of essence and essentialized identities as the basis for inclusion in community".

state, this engagement, it has been argued, "leads to reduction and violent appropriation of the other".[105] I will now examine the disparity between aspirations to such a 'politics of recognition' for the Indigene, via a discussion of Hegel's dialectic of recognition, and the difficulty inherent within the realisation of such mutual recognition in a (post)colonial context, by way of Fanon.

The notion of indigeneity as created via recognition may be conceived in terms of Hegel's dialectic, in which selves are constituted via mutual recognition. This proposition is most succinctly encapsulated in Hegel's much quoted assertion: "Self-consciousness exists in and for itself when, and by the fact that, it so exists for another; that is, it exists only in being acknowledged".[106] The self is created (only) via the recognition of another. Indeed, for Hegel, "the only proportionate 'object' for a Self-Consciousness is another self . . . Self-Consciousness necessarily moves from the 'I' to the 'We'".[107] The drive to achieve self-consciousness via the recognition of the other is, in fact, a desire to possess or destroy the other.[108] Yet, the other as object of desire is revealed to be, in turn, *another* self-consciousness, which cannot be possessed.[109] Each is dependent upon the other for the creation of its own self: "[t]he road to interiority passes through the other".[110] In this way, Hegel is able to argue that "[a] self-consciousness, in being an object, is just as much 'I' as 'object'", such that "different independent self-consciousnesses" are united as " 'I' that is 'We' and 'We' that is 'I'".[111]

Hegel then speaks of the life-and-death struggle between these two self-consciousnesses, each of which seeks to express itself as more than object via the elimination of the other by staking its own life: "Thus the relation of the two self-conscious individuals is such that they prove themselves and each other through a life-and-death struggle".[112] Obviously, however, mutual elimination is pointless, as is the death of one self-consciousness, since one requires the other to recognise it.[113] This is resolved when the one who would have killed the other spares the life of the other, and becomes Lord and the other Bondsman, the latter becoming "thing-like and dependent".[114] Yet, such recognition is inadequate, since the Lord

105 Schaap, above n 104, 524–5.

106 Hegel, above n 16, §178, 111. See also Sartre, Jean-Paul, *Being and Nothingness* (Hazel E Barnes trans., 1969 edn). Sartre writes, at 223: "The Other is a thinking substance of the same essence as I am, a substance which will not disappear into primary and secondary qualities, and whose essential structure I find in myself."

107 Howard P Kaintz, *Hegel's Phenomenology of Spirit* (1994) 44.

108 Hegel, above n 16, §174, 109.

109 Ibid., §168, 106.

110 Robert R Williams, *Hegel's Ethics of Recognition* (2000) 49; the translation of Sartre makes this point in precisely the same terms: Sartre, above n 106, 236.

111 Hegel, above n 16, §177, 110.

112 Ibid., 113–14.

113 Hegel, above n 16, §188.

114 Ibid., Analysis of §189, 521.

will fail to achieve the recognition he requires and, obviously, since he has become a 'thing', neither will the Bondsman.[115] Ultimately, it is revealed: "The *truth* of the independent consciousness is accordingly the servile consciousness of the bondsman".[116] This revelation, in addition to self-recognition "through dealing with sensory objects in manual labour",[117] causes the Bondsman to become "conscious of what he truly is" – an independent self.[118]

Fanon has critiqued Hegel's dialectic in a (post)colonial context, describing Hegel's Lord as comparable to the coloniser, the Bondsman to the colonised. For the latter, liberation is impossible while the Bondsman remains ensnared within a colonial hegemony.[119] Fanon asserts that an Hegelian notion of subjectivity, as constituted by recognition, would not empower the colonised but reinforce racial demarcations,[120] where reciprocity of recognition is absent. The colonised, he argues, cannot escape objectification:

> At the foundation of Hegelian dialectic there is an absolute reciprocity which must be emphasized. It is in the degree to which I go beyond my own immediate being that I apprehend the existence of the other as a natural and more than natural reality. If I close the circuit, if I prevent the accomplishment of movement in two directions, I keep the other within himself. Ultimately, I deprive him even of this being-for-itself.[121]

For Fanon, the coloniser does not seek recognition from the colonised, but work: "[H]ere the master laughs at the consciousness of the slave".[122] In the absence of a mutual struggle for recognition, the colonised must lapse into perpetual objectification. The law, as the force of the coloniser, enacts and enforces this objectification. Both nationally and internationally, I will argue, the law prefigures an indigeneity that appears before it. An examination of this figuring reveals a particular mode of recognition – "the knowing look of recognition [that] overdetermines the other and so constitutes the death of his or her possibilities".[123]

115 Hegel, above n 16, §192–3, 116–17.
116 Ibid., §193, 117.
117 Kaintz, above n 107, §190, 58–9. At Footnote 41, Kaintz asserts: A number of points are packed into this statement: The Slave is a self-consciousness in principle, although in the present relationship the slave takes on the aspect of an object-consciousness; as a self-consciousness, just like the Master, the slave has superseded consciousness's mere relationship-of-desire to objects. The slave negates objectivity just enough to be a "self-consciousness in principle".
118 Hegel, above n 16, §195, 118.
119 Fanon, above n 17; see also Frantz Fanon, *The Wretched of the Earth* (Richard Philcox trans., with commentary by Jean-Paul Sartre and Homi K Bhabha, 1963 edn).
120 Ibid., 168–73, especially footnote 8, 172.
121 Fanon, above n 17, 169.
122 Ibid., footnote 8, 172.
123 Schaap, above n 104, 531, discussing Yar, above n 10, 62.

Rather than seeking recognition from an indifferent coloniser, Fanon asserts that self-determination for the colonised requires individual and collective self-affirmation.[124] He exhorts the colonised to abhor the creation of self-consciousness via an Hegelian recognition and, rather, to seek liberation in an existential self-recognition: "I can recapture my past, validate it, or condemn it through my successive choices . . . . I am my own foundation".[125] Furthermore, he argues, "man" has one duty alone: "That of not renouncing [his] freedom through [his] choices".[126] Denouncing the construction of humanity via the "Negro mission" or the "white burden",[127] Fanon advocates the realisation of a self that is extrinsic to the totalising encapsulation of Otherness: "The Negro is not. Any more than the white man".[128] That is, the 'Negro' ultimately resists encapsulation, as does the 'white man'. As Bhabha has affirmed, "[Fanon's] existentialist evocation of the 'I' restores the presence of the marginalized".[129] Escape from such encapsulation, as an existentialist embrace of freedom of choice, evokes the "language of a revolutionary awareness":[130]

> That familiar alignment of colonial subjects – Black/White, Self/Other – is disturbed with one brief pause and the traditional grounds of racial identity are dispersed, whenever they are found to rest in the narcissistic myths of negritude or white cultural supremacy. It is this palpable pressure of division and displacement that pushes Fanon's writing to the edge of things – the cutting edge that reveals no ultimate radiance but, in his words, 'exposed an utterly naked declivity where an authentic upheaval can be born'.[131]

Such upheaval would entail that which has elsewhere been described as a rejection of "the subjectifying gaze and assimilative lure of colonial recognition", thus initiating the very process of decolonisation via a celebratory self-regard.[132] Coulthard identifies "emancipatory potential" in such politics, a redeployment of culture and tradition as a "radical alternative to the structural and psycho-affective

124 Fanon, above n 17, 172; 180–1.

125 Ibid., 177; 180. Paralleling the Hegelian notion of self-consciousness via life and death struggle for recognition, in Hegel, above n 13, 107, Fanon writes, at 169–70: It is solely by risking life that freedom is obtained; only thus is it tried and proved that the essential nature of self-consciousness is not *bare existence*, is not merely immediate form in which it at first makes its appearance, is not its mere absorption in the expanse of life.

126 Ibid., 179.

127 Ibid., 178.

128 Ibid., 180.

129 Homi Bhabha, *The Location of Culture* (1994) (Routledge Classics edn, 2004) 58.

130 Ibid., 59.

131 Ibid., 58, citing Fanon, above n 17, 2.

132 Glen S Coulthard, "Subjects of Empire: Indigenous Peoples in the 'Politics of Recognition' in Canada" (2007) 6 *Contemporary Political Theory* 437, 453–4.

facets of colonial domination".[133] Liberation, it has been suggested, is to be found not in recognition by the coloniser, but in the "transformative praxis" of the colonised.[134] Such transformation, I would suggest, may have its genesis, at least in part, in Indigenous literature, where literature is evocative of liberated subjectivities, unconstrained by the bounds of legal recognition. As a Derridean indeterminacy, to which the law is compelled to respond,[135] Indigenous literature disturbs the objectifying Hegelian recognition of the Indigene before the law, with the expression of subversive indigeneities and, specifically, Indigenous Law. The Indigene therefore disrupts the determinacy of her own legal recognition, initiating a revolutionary Derridean event[136] or rupture, and the entry of, in Rushdie's words, "newness" . . . [into] . . . the world".[137]

In the Australian context, the reductionism of an Hegelian recognition in a (post)colonial context has led to that which anthropologist Stanner described as "a cult of forgetfulness": "We have been able for so long to disremember the aborigines that we are now hard put to keep them in mind even when we most want to do so".[138] Such forgetfulness constitutes indigeneity within a shifting dynamic, contingent upon non-Indigenous acts of remembrance and (mis)recognition. Healy has described Aboriginality as an "intercultural space . . . constituted by strange and transient patterns of remembering and forgetting", in which ephemereal notions of Aboriginality may elide actual Aboriginal persons.[139] Speaking of the mythologising that is characteristic of colonial nation building, Healy identifies an insidious culture of forgetfulness,[140] generated in the amnesic forging of national narratives, defined not by a genocidal past but an identification with a settler culture that is "new and flourishing and promising".[141] Describing this national forgetting, he instances a set of stamps commemorating the bicentenary of British settlement in Australia, in which the violence of arrival is replaced by extraordinarily peaceful, exoticised imagery.[142] Aborigines appear on the shoreline alongside the 'distinctive' flora and fauna of the country –

133 Coulthard, above n 132, 456.
134 Ibid., discussing Fanon's distinction between the Hegelian master/slave (Lord/Bondsman) relation and his own rendering in a colonial context, in Fanon, above n 17, footnote 8, 172.
135 Derrida, above n 14.
136 Ibid., above n 21, 234.
137 Bhabha, above n 129, 303, citing Salman Rushdie, "In Good Faith" in *Imaginary Homelands: Essays and Criticism 1981–1991* (1991) 393, on *The Satanic Verses* and how "newness enters the world".
138 William Edward Hanley Stanner, *After the Dreaming: The Boyer Lectures 1968* (1972) 25.
139 Healy, above n 93, 4–5.
140 Ibid.
141 Nicholas Thomas, *Possessions: Indigenous Art/Colonial Culture* (1999), cited in Healy, above n 93, 83.
142 Healy, above n 93, 108–9.

kangaroos, wallabies, cockatoos, goannas – receiving the 'tall ships' with apparent awe and wonder. Aborigines are then absent in the subsequent stamps in the series depicting the triumphant raising of the British flag. Citing Leela Gandhi on the postcolonial condition, Healy suggests that this forgetting is indicative of "the urge for historical self-invention or the need to make a new start" – to forget violence and dispossession and forge a new national pride, cleansed of the colonial past.[143]

Such sentiments were evinced in the brief rise during the 1990s of the nationalist, populist, and protectionist political party, One Nation, and its discourse of historical closure,[144] and widespread critique of the party as an aberrant anachronism, not in keeping with the "safe and peaceful" present – itself a further denial of the historical mechanisms that were formative of the party.[145] Both actions, Healy argues, seal the historical archive by forgetting the pain of the past in order to emerge whole in an unblemished – and endemically amnesic – present. Furthermore, the erasure and replacement of Aboriginality in strategic geographical and psychological *places* – for example, the shoreline and the memory of a colonial encounter in that place – have been described as a palimpsestic recreation of place.[146] Such forgetting, however, may be more indicative of that which Schaap describes as the continued "colonial logic of cultural appropriation", within the "postcolonial legal-politics of reconciliation".[147] Within this logic, indigeneity is erased and replaced with a "repressive authenticity",[148] sanitised of Indigenous alterity. As a space of social engagement rather than racial or cultural demarcation, Healy conceives of Aboriginality as "no more *about* actual Aboriginal people than it is *about* actual non-Aboriginal people".[149] Rather, "Aboriginality directs me towards what happens interstitially"[150] – that is, in an in-between or undecidable space. As such, Aboriginality is not static, but [dis]located in this oscillating dynamic, in the "space of memory and the vernacular".[151] The law is one such interstitial space, in which both indigeneity and non-indigeneity are constituted. As the space in which the force of the state is enacted, however, the constitution of indigeneity within the law is violently

143 Healy, above n 93, 22.

144 Ibid., 119–24; see also Tony Birch, " 'Black Armbands and White Veils': John Howard's Moral Amnesia" (1997) 25 *Melbourne Historical Journal* 8; Geoffrey Gray and Christine Winter (eds), *The Resurgence of Racism: Howard, Hanson and the Race Debate* (1997).

145 Ibid., 124.

146 Mark Harris, "Mapping Australian Postcolonial Landscapes: From Resistance to Reconciliation?" (2003) 7 *Law/Text/Culture* 71, 73; 86.

147 Schaap, above n 104, 536.

148 Harris, above n 146, 75; 83.

149 Healy, above n 93, 7.

150 Ibid.

151 Ibid., 131.

determinative. As the Indigenous subject appears before the law, the law is called to recognise her.[152] In so doing, particular stereotypes of indigeneity are invoked, in order to preserve the integrity of a law founded upon the arrogations of colonial sovereignty.

152 I here acknowledge the work of Judith Butler, and her conception of Kafka's "subject before the law" as a juridical construction. She asserts:

> Juridical power inevitably "produces" what it claims merely to represent . . . In effect, the law produces then concedes the notion of "a subject before the law" in order to invoke that discursive formation as a naturalized foundational premise that subsequently legitimates that law's own regulatory hegemony . . . Perhaps the subject, as well as the invocation of a temporal "before," is constituted by the law as the fictive foundation of its own claim to legitimacy.
>
> (Butler, above n 11, 2–3).

Chapter 2

The legal Indigene

Performing indigeneity

The performance and (mis)recognition of indigeneity is most patently illustrated in Australian native title law, described as a violent narrative of *terra nullius*.[1] Povinelli identifies, within the law, the "aporia of the cultural difference the court iterates and faces" in identifying Aboriginality *while* remaining non-discriminatory *while* upholding the common law.[2] The alterity of indigeneity, including Indigenous Law, is recognised within limits, and only in response to the performance of "authentic difference" and "ancient prenational meanings".[3] For the Indigenous claimant, the articulation of the self as this fetishised object of recognition must be contained within "whatever language and moral framework prevails at the time of enunciation".[4] The "real" (traditional, authentic) Aboriginal subject must not be repugnant in any sense that would shatter the skeleton of common law principle,[5] or would "provoke . . . an experience of alterity. The cunning recognition lies exactly in this play of the parentheticals: Be (not) Real; Be (not) Alterior".[6] Povinelli proposes that those customs and traditions considered repugnant to "a public sense of moral decency" are rejected – these are "the limits of recognition".[7] In these conditions, she asks, "how do jurists and other nonindigenous citizens discern a real indigenous subject from a . . . diluted subject?"[8] The response may

1 Ambelin Kwaymullina, "Living Together in Country: Creation, *terra nullius* and 'the trouble with tradition'", in Simon Young, *The Trouble with Tradition: Native Title and Cultural Change* (2008) xvi. The term "*terra nullius*" refers to the acquisition of sovereignty in a land considered "desert uninhabited": William Blackstone, *Commentaries on the Laws of England* (1830, 17th edn), Book II, Chapter I, 7, cited in *Mabo* (1992) 175 CLR 1, 33. I will return to consider this legal premise in Part III (Law).

2 Povinelli, above n 12 (Ch 1), 181.

3 Ibid., 6.

4 Ibid.

5 *Mabo* (1992) 175 CLR 1, 29.

6 Povinelli, above n 12 (Ch 1), 176; see also 181.

7 Ibid., 3.

8 Ibid., 4.

be that they need not, since the law demands this performance of the Indigenous subject, recast as "native title claimant/holder".[9]

Itself a construction of the common law, native title calculates and constrains indigeneity, such that the claimant must "prove an unbroken connection with the 'ancient tribe'".[10] Judicial interpretations of section 223 of the *Native Title Act* 1993 (Cth), which details the requirement of "traditional connection" upon which native title decisions most frequently turn, have required that rights and interests claimed in relation to land and waters be "possessed under the traditional laws acknowledged, and the traditional customs observed, by the Aboriginal peoples".[11] In the decision of *Bennell*, in which native title was claimed, among other areas, over parts of the Perth (Western Australia) metropolis, claimants were required to prove the sustained existence of "a single normative community", with members "continuing to acknowledge and observe at least some of the traditional laws and customs relating to land that were acknowledged and observed [at settlement] in 1829".[12] In the Full Federal Court decision, their Honours clarified the requirement of continuity in section 223, as referring to "laws and customs", as opposed to "community", the latter having been adopted by the trial judge.[13] In this context, they declared a "normative system" to be "the source of rights and interests", affirming the concomitant necessity to prove that the normative system in question "has had a continuous existence and vitality since [British] sovereignty"[14] – despite the emphatic absurdity of such a requirement in a region so manifestly affected by colonisation. This insistence upon the performance of 'tradition' is, in essence, to deny Indigenous cultural vitality – "that the totality of a relationship between people and place is something more than a collection of specific acts or activities".[15] Furthermore, this "over-specificity" is itself, it has been argued, an elaboration of "the intellectual accoutrements of colonialism".[16]

Interests recognised and attributed to Indigenous peoples within Australian native title law are derived from Indigenous Law and society and a relation to "country", and may be variously exclusive, collective, cultural, and spiritual. Indigenous authors have articulated "country" as an all-encompassing term, not confined to "the notion of landscape as a feature to be viewed", but as "lived in".[17] Both corporeally and culturally, Indigenous peoples are able to proclaim:

9 Schaap, above n 104 (Ch 1), 536.

10 Judith Grbich, "Tracing the Figure of the Native in Postcolonial Theory and Native Title Law: Enlightenment, Aesthetics and Charles Harpur" (2005) 22 *The Australian Feminist Law Journal* 127, 129.

11 *Bennell v Western Australia* (2006) 230 ALR 603, 628 ("Bennell").

12 Ibid., 635; 724.

13 *Bodney v Bennell* (2008) 249 ALR 300, 311.

14 Ibid.

15 Kwaymullina, above n 1, xxi.

16 Young, above n 1, 353.

17 Muecke, above n 94 (Ch 1), 60.

"I am my country".[18] Kwaymullina describes "[the] continent, named Australia by Captain Matthew Flinders" as "a land of many countries – and for every country, there is a people":

> We are the Nyungar, Palkyu, Martu, Gumilaroi, Worrimia, Bardi, Indjarbandi, Palawa, Tanganekald, and Meintangk, and we are many others. We were formed with the hills and the valleys, the water and the sky, the trees and the plants, the crows and the kangaroos, created by the ancestors who gave meaning and life to our world. And for each of us, our country is not just where we live, but who we are.[19]

Non-Indigenous recognition of such relation is grounded within a patently different system of reference – that of the common law. The common law indicia of property constitutive of Australian land law are founded upon the doctrine of tenure, and the notion that all interests in land are held of the Crown, *plenum dominium*. As such, interests conferred under this doctrine are not communal (though fragmented) but exclusive – specifically, the right to use and enjoy, the right to alienate and the right to exclude.[20] In contrast, Indigenous interests in land are defined by Indigenous Law and custom – both 'traditional' and contemporary – which may be proprietary, or may be something entirely unknown to the law.[21] Despite the triumph of *Mabo*,[22] in which the court held that Crown interests amounted to radical title rather than absolute ownership, thereby revealing the continued existence of native title,[23] recognition of the latter

18 Bob Morgan, "Country – A Journey to Cultural and Spiritual Healing", in Morgan, Mia and Kwaymullina, above n 1, 201, 204.

19 Ambelin Kwaymullina, "Introduction: A Land of Many Countries", in Morgan, Mia and Kwaymullina above n 1, 6, 7.

20 *Milirrpum v Nabalco Pty Ltd* (1971) 17 FLR 141.

21 See Kwaymullina, above n 1; Young, above n 1; see also *Bennell* (2006) 230 ALR 603, 629.

22 (1992) 175 CLR 1.

23 Radical title, as opposed to absolute Crown ownership (*plenum dominium*), is a power acquired with sovereignty, akin to a constitutional power, to deal with and make grants and interests in land. See *Mabo* (1992) 175 CLR 1, 48 (Brennan J). I will return to a discussion of radical title in Part III (Law). It has also been described as being "more in the nature of a political notion and in that sense a legal fiction. But property rights of any kind are not fictional": *Wik Peoples v Queensland* (1996) 187 CLR 1, 234 (Kirby J). I will return to this notion of the legal fiction in more detail in Part III (Law).

In *Mabo* (1992) 175 CLR 1, 48, Brennan J remarked upon the nature of radical title:

> The Crown was treated as having the radical title to all the land in the territory over which the Crown acquired sovereignty. The radical title is a postulate of the doctrine of tenure and a concomitant of sovereignty. As a sovereign enjoys supreme legal authority in and over a territory, the sovereign has power to prescribe what parcels of land and what interests in those parcels should be enjoyed by others and what parcels of land should be kept as the sovereign's beneficial demesne.

within the common law doctrine of tenure remains an exceedingly complex and difficult task. Notwithstanding its perceived role as a fundamental step toward a more egalitarian conception of nationhood, native title law is not concerned with the lived reality of Indigenous interests in land and waters, but with their recognition as an incident of the common law.[24] Justice Brennan remarked, in *Mabo*, upon the constraints of such recognition:

> In discharging its duty to declare the common law of Australia, this Court is not free to adopt rules that accord with contemporary notions of justice and human rights if their adoption would fracture the skeleton of principle which gives the body of our law its shape and internal consistency.[25]

While the need to acknowledge native title within an existing "skeleton of principle" provides a critical nexus between the common law and Indigenous interests, the obliteration of Indigenous subjectivity and Law within the confines of the common law must be acknowledged as an act of continued colonisation or "post-colonial repression".[26] The very recognition of Indigenous interests in land and waters within the law demands conformity to occidental legal categorisations – "heritage, native title, environment, and cultural property", such that Indigenous relations to country are "conceived as divisible into separate and severable portions".[27] It has been suggested that such categories are reflective of the broader formulation of legal forms, themselves constructive of the limits of realisable possibilities.[28] Indeed, Godden suggests, "the legal ordering provides an authoritative imagining of the real".[29] For Young, the restrictiveness of native

Continuing at 48, Brennan J held that since the land acquired at sovereignty was not "desert and uninhabited, truly a terra nullius", the Crown did not take "absolute beneficial title (allodial title)". Consequently: if the land were occupied by the indigenous inhabitants and their rights and interests in the land are recognized by the common law, the radical title which is acquired with the acquisition of sovereignty cannot itself be taken to confer an absolute beneficial title to the occupied land. Nor is it necessary to the structure of our legal system to refuse recognition to the rights and interests in land of the indigenous inhabitants.

24 Native title in Australia is described as *sui generis*, rendering it distinct from common law interests. Its recognition, however, is ultimately dependant upon a common law frame of reference, and its basic tenets. See Part III (Law) for further discussion.

25 (1992) 175 CLR 1, 29.

26 Lee Godden, "Indigenous Heritage and the Environment: 'Legal categories are only one way of imagining the real'" (August 2002) 19(4) *Environmental and Planning Law Journal* 258, 258, citing Rosemary J Coombe, "The Properties of Culture and the Politics of Possessing Identity", in Jonathan Locke Hart *et al.*, *Explorations in Difference: Law, Culture and Politics* (1996) 252.

27 Ibid.

28 Ibid., 259, citing Peter Fitzpatrick, "Law and Societies", (1984) 22 *Osgood Hall Law Journal* 115, 122.

29 Ibid., 266. Godden here does not appear to invoke a Lacanian reading of the Real, but refers to Clifford Geertz, *Local Knowledge: Further Essays on Interpretative Anthropology* (1983) 163–74 who, discussing the parameters of Western cultural and legal parameters, asserts that "[l]egal categories are only one way of imagining the real".

title law rests upon "an unexpressed bias towards western patterns of social organisation and land use", which "works some revival, in its dismissal of the possibility of Aboriginal 'ownership', of the theoretically defunct notion that Australia was 'land belonging to no one'".[30] Furthermore, Webber argues, native title should not be understood as "simply another kind of interest affecting land, slipped into the structure of Australian property law".[31] Native title has been described by Pearson as "a recognition space",[32] in which Indigenous interests and the common law overlap. Ultimately, however, this suggestive overlap fails to acknowledge the non-Indigenous framing of indigeneity and Indigenous interests within a non-Indigenous law, the necessity of the performance of such indigeneity on the part of the Indigenous subject, acting within the common law, the cultural violence of this imposition, and the radical alterity of ambivalent and variegated indigeneities.

Unsettling indigeneity

Contained within the bounds of non-Indigenous legal recognition, Soguk has described indigeneity as persisting in "a condition of marginality in modernity", encapsulated within "modern 'relations of ban'",[33] within the confines of colonial and neocolonial institutional and economic frameworks: "What has been banned is delivered over to its own separateness and, at the same time, consigned to the mercy of the one who abandons it – at once excluded and included, removed and at the same time captured".[34] The notion of 'ban', derived from "an old Germanic term", is elaborated by Agamben as "[t]he relation of exception" – a potentiality "in which law refers to life and includes it in itself by suspending it".[35] For Agamben, the relation is descriptive of "bare life", "the life of *homo sacer* (sacred man), who *may be killed and yet not sacrificed*".[36] The banned person is not "simply set outside the law and made indifferent to it but rather *abandoned* by it, that is, exposed and threatened".[37] Furthermore, the "bandit" occupies a "liminal status", defined as a "wolf-man" or "werewolf, who is precisely *neither man nor beast*, and who dwells

30 Young, above n 1, 353.

31 Jeremy Webber, "Beyond Regret: Mabo's Implications for Australian Constitutionalism" in Duncan Ivison, Paul Patton and Will Sanders (eds), *Political Theory and the Rights of Indigenous Peoples* (2000) 60, 61.

32 Noel Pearson, "Concept of Native Title at Common Law" in Galarrwuy Yanupingu (ed.) *Our Land is our Life: Land Rights Past Present and Future* (1997) 150, 151.

33 Soguk, above n 34 (Ch 1), 3, citing Giorgio Agamben, *Homo Sacer: Sovereign Power and Bare Life* (1998).

34 Agamben, above n 33, 110; see especially 104–11; see discussion in Soguk, above n 34 (Ch 1), 3–8.

35 Ibid., 28. Agamben derives this reading of the "ban" from Jean-Luc Nancy, "Abandoned Being" in Jean-Luc Nancy, *The Birth to Presence* (Brian Holmes trans., 1993 edn) 36, especially 44.

36 Ibid., 8.

37 Ibid., 29.

paradoxically within both while belonging to neither".[38] Citing Indigenous marginalisation in terms of Agamben's "modern 'relations of ban' in which indigeneity still remains captive to the logic and fortunes of the territorial nation-state system and global capitalism", Soguk describes the historical dispossession of Indigenous peoples as a "specific politics of encounter", which reduced such peoples to a condition of "bare life":[39]

> '[P]olitically unqualified', indigenous peoples came to be subjected to regimes of ban – power relations that denied them any historical political status while also holding them in the thrall of the expansionist orders. Ultimately . . . the 'relations of ban' operate as mechanisms of domination and control over indigenous communities while declaring them to be autonomous or even sovereign. This paradoxical situation – domination and denial – works as a 'ban' or a 'bar' on autonomous indigenous agency . . . indigenous subjectivities are regularly called into question or negated altogether.[40]

Soguk reads the Indigenous subject as analogous to *homo sacer* – constituted as the "remainder or excess",[41] existing in a "political space of exception".[42] Furthermore, he suggests that Indigenous peoples have been historically incorporated into "Europe's colonizing imaginaries as an exception",[43] such that the alterity of indigeneity is sublimated to an imperial order, evinced in its legal, political, and cultural institutions. These matrices of power impose a ban denying Indigenous peoples sovereignty and self-determination, effecting an existence of "bare life" such that the very nature of indigeneity itself, Soguk argues, has been subject to erasure.[44]

38 Agamben, above n 33, 105, 110. At 105, Agamben speaks of the "liminal status" of the "bandit", defined as a "wolf-man" or werewolf: What had to remain in the collective unconscious as a monstrous hybrid of human and animal, divided between the forest and the city – the werewolf – is, therefore, in its origin the figure of the man who has been banned from the city . . . The life of the bandit, like that of the sacred man [homo sacer], is not a piece of animal nature without any relation to law and the city. It is, rather, a threshold of indistinction and of passage between animal and man, *physis* and *nomos*, exclusion and inclusion: the life of the bandit is the life of the *loup garou*, the werewolf, who is precisely *neither man nor beast*, and who dwells paradoxically within both while belonging to neither.

39 Soguk, above n 34 (Ch 1), 3.

40 Ibid.

41 Ibid., 6.

42 Prem Rajaram, "Dystopic Geographies of Empire" (October–December 2006) 31(4) *Alternatives* 475, 480, cited in Soguk, above n 34 (Ch 1), 6.

43 Soguk, above n 34 (Ch 1), 7.

44 Ibid., 3. Citing Indigenous marginalisation as "an expression of what Giorgio Agamben would call modern 'relations of ban' in which indigeneity still remains captive to the logic and fortunes of the territorial nation-state system and global capitalism", Soguk proceeds to speak of these relations of ban as mechanisms of domination and control over indigenous communities while declaring them to be autonomous or even sovereign. This paradoxical situation – domination and denial – works as a "ban" or a "bar" on autonomous indigenous agency . . . indigenous subjectivities are regularly called into question or negated altogether.

I would suggest, however, that Soguk's reading of indigeneity as analogous to Agamben's *homo sacer* fails to acknowledge the very strangeness or alterity of indigeneity, which marks it as exceptional and therefore unsettling, incapable of erasure. Accordingly, comparison may be made between the Indigene and *homo sacer* only where both function as sites of confluence between the determinate and indeterminate. As Fitzpatrick has asserted, the bareness of the life of *homo sacer* is itself demonstrative of "the subsistent legal quality of . . . inclusion/exclusion".[45] While *homo sacer* is of the sacred, "occup[ying] a meditative domain in between the profane and the transcendent beyond", so too is law: "[Law] determinantly combines what is determinately here with responsiveness to what is ever beyond, even if that determination is only and ever 'for the time being'".[46] Indeed, for Nancy, "[t]he law of abandonment is the other of law, which constitutes the law".[47] Reading Nancy on this point, Pryor affirms this notion of abandonment as constitutive – as that which "cannot be represented" and is "entirely other", and yet is "an 'inevitable' condition for our thought".[48] He further suggests that "constitutive abandonment . . . is the name and law of the always withdrawing character of law's presence".[49] Within legal and social identity, I would suggest, indigeneity is thus constituted as alterity – a persistent "unquiet movement".[50] It is the Other that the law must contain and, simultaneously, to which the law must remain ever responsive.[51] Indeed, it is the very violence of historical impositions upon Indigenous peoples, via the law, that is revealing of this unique capacity for indigeneity to unsettle. I will return to these mutually suffusing dimensions[52] in the context of the Indigenous subject before the law – an encounter in which both the conditioned law and the unconditional subject surpass one another, thereby mutually constituting one another.[53]

Characterised both by an excess and lack, inclusion and exclusion, presence and absence, indigeneity has been described as ambivalent – present in an ability to claim rights, absent insofar as such claims are necessary.[54] International and national definitions of Indigenous peoples simultaneously locate indigeneity in the colonial and precolonial, "suggest[ing] *both* an indigenous continuity and its colonial

45 Peter Fitzpatrick, "Bare Sovereignty: *Homo Sacer* and the Insistence of Law", in Andrew Norris (ed.), *Politics, Metaphysics and Death: Essays on Giorgio Agamben's Homo Sacer* (2005) 49, 51.
46 Ibid., 53; see also 62; see also Fitzpatrick, above n 30 (Ch 1), 44–5.
47 Nancy, above n 35, 44.
48 Benjamin S Pryor, "Law in Abandon: Jean-Luc Nancy and the Critical Study of Law" (2004) 15 (3) *Law and Critique* 259, 279.
49 Ibid., 282.
50 Fitzpatrick, above n 30 (Ch 1), 5.
51 Fitzpatrick, above n 45, especially 52; see also Fitzpatrick, above n 30 (Ch 1).
52 Fitzpatrick, above n 30 (Ch 1), 102.
53 Derrida, above n 14 (Ch 1); see also Fitzpatrick, above n 30 (Ch 1).
54 Colin Perrin, "Approaching Anxiety: The Insistence of the Postcolonial in the Declaration on the Rights of Indigenous Peoples" in Eve Darian-Smith and Peter Fitzpatrick (eds), *Laws of the Postcolonial* (1999) 19, 29.

interruption".[55] This ambivalence has been described as the "problem of 'placing' indigenous peoples",[56] whose precise identity remains so uncertain as to require formal declaration. Discussing "the *act* of 'constructing' indigenous peoples"[57] in the 1993 Draft UN Declaration on the Rights of Indigenous Peoples,[58] Perrin describes this ambivalence:

> [W]e cannot be sure if the thing declared was already extant prior to its declaration, and is therefore simply declared; or whether it is inaugurated in its declaration – the status of the thing declared is therefore undecidable.[59]

The "compulsive repetition" of the markers of indigeneity – the "mysterious and unknowable character of their bonds to blood and soil",[60] a bond which "no-one should be permitted to destroy"[61] – reveals, he suggests, an anxiety surrounding the unresolvable nature of indigeneity. Such anxiety "signals the proximity of indigenous peoples not simply as a lack *of* modernity, but as a lack *in* modernity", a discomforting irresolution evoked by Perrin as "the 'appearance' of a certain absence in reality", which leads to "referential panic".[62]

One of the most cited international definitions of Indigenous populations, the 'working definition' contained within the Martinéz Cobo Report to the UN Sub-Commission on the Prevention of Discrimination of Minorities in 1986, identifies and, arguably, exoticises the Indigenous, locating it firmly in the past. This report defines Indigenous populations as descendants of those with an "historical continuity with pre-invasion and pre-colonial societies", who "consider themselves distinct from other sectors of the societies now prevailing in those territories, or parts of them".[63] Such definitions evoke a primordial Indigenous subject, described by Povinelli as "that imaginary prenational subject haunting the actions of every

55 Perrin, above n 54, footnote 49, 37.
56 Ibid., 20.
57 Ibid., 26.
58 UN Doc E/CN.4/Sub.2/1993/29/Annex I. The Articles in this draft Declaration, to which Perrin refers, do not differ significantly from the finally adopted Declaration, above n 56 (Ch 1).
59 Perrin, above n54, 26.
60 Ibid.
61 JR Martinéz Cobo, *Study of the Problem of Discrimination against Indigenous Populations* (UN Doc. E/CN.4/Sub.2/1983/21/Add.8 1983) 67, discussed in Perrin, above n 54, 25.
62 Perrin, above n 54, 28 (emphases added), citing Martin Heidegger, "What is Metaphysics?" in Martin Heidegger (D Farrell-Krell, ed.), *Basic Writings* (1993) 101. In Perrin, at 37, footnote 44, the author also makes reference to this anxiety as an experience in which one is "ill at ease", a translation of *unheimlich*, "rendered elsewhere as 'the uncanny' – the strangely or disturbingly familiar". I will return to this notion throughout this book.
63 Cobo, above n 61. Note, however, discussion in Erica-Irene Daes, "An Overview of the History of Indigenous Peoples: Self-Determination and the United Nations" (2008) 21 *Cambridge Review of International Affairs* 7, 9: "[T]here is not an international consensus on who indigenous peoples are: the term cannot be defined precisely or applied all-inclusively".

actual Aboriginal person . . . captured in the most banal public and private queries to Aboriginal persons: 'Tell us what it was like before us'".[64] Recognition of rights of persons able to present themselves as the embodiment of this image reveals a double inscription – that of a performed identity,[65] and that of an actual subjectivity. Indeed, Perrin argues, it is "the enunciative moment of 'construction'" of Indigenous peoples that reveals the ambivalence and undecidability of indigeneity.[66]

Consequently, resort is made to stereotype, "a form of knowledge and identification that vacillates between what is always 'in place,' already known, and something that must be anxiously repeated".[67] For Bhabha, stereotype is the "major discursive strategy" of colonial discourse, animated by the constructed opposition or ambivalence between "ideological construction of otherness" and self.[68] He suggests that the force of ambivalence constitutive of the stereotype ensures its currency and strategies, "produc[ing] that effect of probabilistic truth and predictability which . . . must always be in *excess* of what can be empirically proved or logically construed".[69] In so doing, the discursive construction of alterity "denies an 'original' identity or a 'singularity' to objects of difference".[70] In a legal context, I will argue, (mis)recognition of indigeneity in *excess* is recognition of a legal artifice, a fiction in which the ambivalence of indigeneity may be, albeit temporarily, contained, and to which it must persistently be returned. An interstitial figure, the Indigene appears and performs before the law; yet, the shadow behind this figure haunts the law, persisting in the moment of indecision – the moment in which justice might appear.[71]

64 Povinelli, above n 12 (Ch 1), 55.
65 Soguk, above n 34 (Ch 1), 5.
66 Perrin, above n 59, 26.
67 Bhabha, above n 129 (Ch 1), 94–95.
68 Ibid., 94.
69 Ibid., 95.
70 Ibid., 96.
71 Derrida, above n 14 (Ch 1), 240–1.

Chapter 3

The literary Indigene

A strange play

> [L]iterature itself makes law, emerging in that place where the law is made. Therefore, under certain determined conditions, it can exercise the legislative power of linguistic performativity to sidestep existing laws from which, however, it derives protection and receives its conditions of emergence . . . Under these conditions literature can *play the law*, repeating it while diverting or circum-venting it.[1]

In approaching the relations between law, literature, and indigeneity, I begin with the proposition that the law is, in Derrida's terms, intangible – in order to reach the law, one must not and cannot enter it, one must remain *before* the law.[2] Yet, the law itself is not pure sovereignty but is constituted by that which is not law – the Derridean unconditional, that which is beyond, "*the law of the law*".[3] The text and force of the law are derived from that which they not; iterations of the law are constituted via an interminable responsiveness.[4] For Derrida, this unconditional beyond may, at times, be occupied by literature; indeed, "literature itself makes law".[5] The responsiveness of the law to the unconditional of literature emerges in the very moment in which the law is formulated, the undecidable moment occupying the space between calculable law and the singularity of a case. It is from this position that alterity emanates, disrupting and deconstructing calculable law. I will elaborate a conceptualisation of indigeneity, and of Indigenous literature, as existing and persisting in this undecidable, 'in-between', space – that which, according to Derrida, "remains caught, as a ghost at least, but an essential ghost, in every decision, in every event of decision".[6] While the law must ultimately cut, categorise and determine indigeneity in order to recognise it, I will suggest

1 Derrida, above n 15 (Ch 1), 216.
2 Ibid.
3 Ibid., 191; see also 205.
4 See Fitzpatrick, above n 30 (Ch 1).
5 Derrida, above n 15 (Ch 1), 216.
6 Derrida, above n 14 (Ch 1), 253.

that the literary expression of indigeneity can "exercise the legislative power of linguistic performativity", to "*play the law*, repeating it while diverting or circumventing it".[7] That is, a reading of literature as a "subversive juridicity"[8] reveals the literary nature of law itself, iteratively productive of new meaning in each reading, each instant of decision. It is in this instant that subversive and revolutionary indigeneities may be revealed.

A precise definition of 'literature' remains elusive – indeed, according to Derrida, literature cannot be defined, or even "identified with any other discourse".[9] Furthermore, for Attridge, a failure to define literature is "a *necessary* failure", where its "unsettling, intoxicating, moving, delighting powers" are enabled by this very evasion of definition.[10] Yet, theories abound.[11] For Eagleton, while literature may not be defined, the literary work may be conceived as a strategy.[12] That is, as a "strategic labour", which is not merely reflective of "reality", but itself generates the historical or ideological subtext to which it is a response, or "strategic reply".[13] This subtext, of which the law is an integral part, does not exist apart from the text – "certainly not as some 'common-sense' external reality'", but is "projected backwards . . . from the work".[14] As such, literary works are not "secondary and derivative" but, rather, engaged with and constitutive of 'reality'.[15] In this way, *reading* is also "a strategic enterprise", an interpretative intervention through which "[t]he work can reformulate its own norms and conventions as it evolves".[16] The "workings of the text", described as "strategies", connect the work and its reader, "as the cooperative activity which brings the literary work into being in the first place".[17] Accordingly, the work may be conceived as an "unfolding project . . . not an *object* but a *practice*" or, indeed, an "event", which might equally allow for resolution or irresolution.[18]

The notion of literature as *event* is explicitly engaged by Attridge, who describes the "singular events of literature", whereby literature becomes literature only in the performative act of reading or hearing it.[19] This singular act, furthermore, involves an encounter and response:

7 Derrida, above n 15 (Ch 1), 216.
8 Ibid.
9 Jacques Derrida, "'This Strange Institution Called Literature': An Interview with Jacques Derrida" in Jacques Derrida (Derek Attridge, ed.), *Acts of Literature* (1992) 33, 47.
10 Attridge, above n 20 (Ch 1), 1.
11 For a comprehensive treatment of theories and philosophies of literature, see Eagleton, above n 19 (Ch 1). See also Attridge, above n 20.
12 Eagleton, above n 19, 169.
13 Ibid., 170.
14 Ibid.
15 Ibid., 173.
16 Ibid., 185, 187.
17 Ibid., 186.
18 Ibid., 186–7, 224 (emphases added).
19 Derek Attridge, "The Singular Events of Literature" (2010) 50(1) *British Journal of Aesthetics* 81, 83. See also Attridge, above n 20 (Ch 1), especially 58.

> [T]he event of literature always involves the emergence within the reader's set of assumptions, routines, and expectations of an element of foreignness, something unanticipated, not immediately graspable, at a tangent to ingrained habits of thought and feeling.[20]

This 'event', or singularity, of literature is further described as "transformative difference"[21] – reading Attridge, Pereira describes this difference as "the ability to welcome otherness in the existent cultural field – and not just as mere uniqueness".[22] That is, for Attridge, a "shifting and opening-up of settled modes of thinking and feeling", which constitutes "a powerful and repeatable *event* of mental and emotional restructuring".[23] This notion of singularity draws upon the work of Derrida, who describes the singularity of the literary work not in terms of its uniqueness, but its iterability. Literature emerges not in the creation of a unique text, but in the performance of the text (read or heard), which is iteratively productive of new meaning as it is experienced.[24] The event of a text elicits a response or countersignature – indeed, a "proliferation of countersignatures" – which are, in turn, "equally singular . . . irreducible, irreplaceable, 'new'".[25] I would suggest that such conceptions of the literary work, as cooperative strategy or singular 'event', particularly characterise the literature I describe as 'Indigenous'. Frequently departing from conventional literary form and language and presenting subversive historicities and juridicities, these works mutually engage the work and reader in "a potentially unending process"[26] of interpretation and reinterpretation and, therefore, the implicit and explicit creation and legislation of meaning.[27] Furthermore, the singular experience of such literary works enables, as described by Derrida, the 'proliferation of countersignatures' in readers, and is thereby iteratively productive of new meaning.

For Derrida, however, the literary text and its reader stand in a particular relation, whereby the author is "authoriz[ed] to say everything [or anything: *tout dire*]", while acknowledging the right of the reader to "absolute non-response".[28]

20 Attridge, above n 19, 83.
21 Attridge, above n 20 (Ch 1), 136.
22 Pedro Schacht Pereira, Review of Derek Attridge, *The Singularity of Literature* (2004) in (2007) 104(4) *Modern Philology* 560, 563.
23 Attridge, above n 20 (Ch 1), 28–29.
24 Ibid., 136. Attridge argues that the literary work emerges in a performance in which the authored signature, alterity, and inventiveness of the work as an exploitation of the multiple powers of language are experienced and affirmed in the present, in a creative, responsible reading.
25 Derrida, above n 9, 69–70.
26 Eagleton, above n 19 (Ch 1), 187.
27 Aristodemou, above n 4 (Ch 1), 3.
28 Jacques Derrida, "Passions: An Oblique Offering" in Jacques Derrida (Thomas Dutoit, ed.), *On the Name* (David Wood, John P Leavey, Jr, and Ian McLeod, trans., 1995 edn) 3, 28–29.

This reader, or "literary subject",[29] existing within that which Derrida describes as "a hyperbolic condition of democracy",[30] has a "responsibility *without limits*" – that is, an "unlimited, undecided" responsibility, which may include non-response.[31] In contrast, "the calculable, responsible citizen-subject",[32] whose response and *responsibility* are constrained, is described as "a subject having-to-respond [devant-repondre], having-to-tell [devant-dire] the truth, having to testify according to the sworn word ('the whole truth, nothing but the truth'), before the law [devant la loi]".[33] The imperatives of this latter responsibility, and the positioning of the subject *before* the law, would appear to present a determinate, impenetrable law. This distinction between the legal and literary subject, however, and the apparent constraint of the legal text, are scrutinised in the following Derridean analysis.

In his study of Kafka's 'parable', "Before the Law", Derrida describes the impenetrability of the law, akin to a guarded gate. Appearing before the law, the subject must not disturb the text of the law: he must not touch the law, "*must not* have a rapport with the law", must not and cannot enter the law.[34] Though the gate is open, the law is ever inaccessible to the countryman outside.[35] The parable begins:

> Before the Law stands a doorkeeper. To this doorkeeper there comes a countryman and prays for admittance to the Law. But the doorkeeper says that he cannot grant admittance at the moment . . . From hall to hall there is one doorkeeper after another, each more powerful than the last.[36]

The relation is one of prohibition, the law being an 'original' text, which must not be changed or disfigured, which "guards itself, maintains itself" and "leaves the reader before [itself]".[37] Yet, to be before the law is to be before a law "still

29 Jonathan Culler, "Derrida and the Singularity of Literature" (2005) 27(2) *Cardozo Law Review* 869, 874.

30 Derrida, above n 28, 29.

31 Culler, above n 29, 874. More fully, Culler defines this notion of responsibility as not limited to what you consciously intended, or to the responsibility to or for members of your group or nation; it can extend to animals and the inanimate world. It is unlimited, undecided.

This is to be distinguished from a Levinasian notion of responsibility: Emmanuel Levinas, *Totality and Infinity: An Essay on Exteriority* (Alphonso Lingis trans., 1969 edn). See also Jacques Derrida, *Adieu to Emmanuel Levinas* (Pascale-Anne Brault and Michael Naas, trans., 1999 edn).

32 Ibid., 874.

33 Derrida, above n 28, 29.

34 Ibid., above n 15 (Ch 1), 203–204.

35 Ibid., 184; 203.

36 Franz Kafka, "Before the Law" in Franz Kafka (Nahum N Glatzer, ed.), *The Complete Short Stories of Franz Kafka* (Willa and Edwin Muir trans., 2005 edn) 3, 3. Cited and discussed in Derrida, above n 15 (Ch 1), 183.

37 Derrida, above n 15 (Ch 1), 211.

undetermined, before the law as before a law still nonexisting, a law still ahead, still having to and yet to come".[38] It is the countryman who must institute the law, by a "pure performative act".[39] The Indigenous subject is created within the text of the law: ancient, primordial, existing (in the context of native title law) within the "terminology of 'tradition'" – the latter itself "used as a synonym for 'Aboriginal', 'ancestral', 'historical' or 'long-held'".[40] This determinate subject is created by and remains *within* the law, apparently impenetrable, yet an indeterminate indigeneity remains *outside* the law, *before* the law, *beyond* the law. Derrida writes:

> We are *before* this text that, saying nothing definite and presenting no identifiable content beyond the story itself, except for an endless *différance*, till death, nonetheless remains strictly intangible . . . inaccessible to contact, impregnable and ultimately ungraspable, incomprehensible – but also that which we have not the *right* to touch.[41]

Further, Derrida proposes, the law is, itself, akin to literature, "its possibility and its impossibility, its readability and unreadability, its necessity and prohibition, and the questions of relation, of repetition and of history".[42] The prohibitions of the text – the doorkeepers – proliferate in an infinite *mise-en-abyme*, each text guaranteed and legitimised by the next "more powerful guardian".[43] While this determinate law contains the Indigenous subject, as a static, primordial figure, I will suggest that Indigenous literature, alongside other postcolonial writing, surpasses the containment of the colonial legal narrative, venturing "outside the source that is presupposed by its very existence".[44] Illuminating the ancestral tracks or songlines – "the Aboriginal Law handed down through the ages since time began"[45] – and articulating "[t]he voice that is silent or elusive",[46] the aesthetic of such writing is an evocation of the unconditional of indigeneity, emerging in the undecidable moment. For Derrida, it is literature that emerges in "that place where the law is made".[47] Indeed, two laws here emerge – one that is able to contain and secure fixity, the other intangible and responsive, partaking of the unconditionality of literature.

38 Derrida, above n 14 (Ch 1), 270.
39 Ibid.
40 Young, above n 1 (Ch 1), 240.
41 Ibid., above n 15 (Ch 1), 211.
42 Ibid., 196.
43 Ibid., 214.
44 Patricia Tuitt, *Race, Law, Resistance* (2004) 76.
45 Alexis Wright, *Carpentaria* (2006) 3.
46 Ibid., "Politics of Writing" (Summer 2002) 62(2) *Southerly* 10, 14.
47 Derrida, above n 15 (Ch 1), 216.

In his seminal text, "Force of Law",[48] Derrida conceives of justice as traversing both of these laws, and as both essential and impossible.[49] Furthermore, he envisages justice as constitutive of a just or "judged legitimate" enforcement of law – "not only as instrument in the service of law but the practice and even the fulfillment, the essence of law", as opposed to "the violence that one always judges unjust".[50] As such, justice is that which "exceeds or contradicts law" or "has no relation to law".[51] Derrida describes the moment in which justice may appear or be experienced as a passage or aporia:

> *Aporía* is a nonpath. From this point of view, justice would be the experience of what we are unable to experience . . . . But . . . I believe there is no justice without this experience, however impossible it might be, of aporia. Justice is an experience of the impossible.[52]

Derrida elaborates upon this notion of the impossibility of justice, equating law and justice, respectively, with the calculable and incalculable.[53] Moreover, he suggests, "justice is the possibility of deconstruction",[54] manifest in aporetic experiences, "moments in which the *decision* between just and unjust is never insured by a rule".[55] Yet, law and justice are not distinct but mutually constitutive,[56] such that the enactment and enforcement of the law must pass through "the test and ordeal of the undecidable".[57] For justice to be rendered, it must be enacted in a calculated legal decision, "that cuts and divides".[58] Derrida maintains that "justice, as the experience of absolute alterity, is unpresentable, but it is the chance of the event and the condition of history".[59] As such, "incalculable justice *commands* calculation".[60] He describes this force as "the 'mystical'" – the "revolutionary moment of law" which, while founding law, is itself "an instance of nonlaw".[61]

48 Derrida, above n 14 (Ch 1), 228.
49 Ibid., 244. See also discussion in Stewart Motha, "Mabo: Encountering the Epistemic Limit of the Recognition of 'Difference'" (1998) 7 *Griffith Law Review* 79, 89.
50 Ibid., 234.
51 Ibid., 233. Derrida elsewhere nuances his conception of the relation between law and deconstruction, law and justice: Jacques Derrida, James Adner, Kate Doyle, and Glenn Hendler, "Women in the Beehive: A Seminar with Jacques Derrida" (2005) 16(3) *A Journal of Feminist Cultural Studies* 139, 149. I will discuss this in greater detail in Part II (Indigeneity) and will return to it throughout this book.
52 Derrida, above n 14 (Ch 1), 233.
53 Ibid., 244.
54 Ibid., 243.
55 Ibid., 244; see also 250.
56 Ibid., 251.
57 Ibid., 252.
58 Ibid.
59 Ibid., 257.
60 Ibid.
61 Ibid., 269.

The rendering of justice in native title law, for instance, demands that justice be calculated and meted out by the law. Yet, there must always be a moment of indecision, in which indigeneity – as an unconditioned, unresolvable, radical alterity – appears, and is suppressed. While the law constructs an indigeneity that appears before it, an Other, unresolved, persistently pressing and potentially subversive indigeneity remains, appearing in a moment of justice. Where justice "must always concern singularity, individuals, irreplaceable groups and lives, the other or myself *as* other, in a unique situation"[62] it is, for Derrida, "an experience of the impossible".[63] The law can only accommodate such singularities, such alterity, for a moment.

In Kafka's parable, the countryman encounters difficulties he "has not expected; the Law, he thinks, should surely be accessible at all times and to everyone".[64] Ultimately, when he has grown old and wearied, nearing death, still awaiting admittance to the law, the countryman finally asks of the doorkeeper:

> 'Everyone strives to reach the Law . . . so how does it happen that for all these many years no one but myself has ever begged for admittance?' The doorkeeper recognizes that the man has reached his end, and to let his failing senses catch the words roars in his ear: 'No one else could be admitted here, since this gate was made only for you. I am now going to shut it'.[65]

While each gate to the law is made for a singular individual, as for the countryman, each must ultimately be shut.[66] The law must "exceed all fixity of determination . . . to remain pervaded by the relation to what is beyond", yet it must remain within "responsive range".[67] To fail to close the gate would be to permanently admit alterity into the law – to, as Justice Brennan maintained in *Mabo*, "fracture the skeleton of principle which gives the body of our law its shape and internal consistency".[68]

62 Ibid., 245.
63 Ibid., 244.
64 Kafka, above n 36 (Ch 3), 183.
65 Ibid., 184.
66 Derrida, above n 15 (Ch 1), 184.
67 Fitzpatrick (2004), above n 18 (Ch 1), 224.
68 *Mabo* (1992) 175 CLR 1, 29. See also Bhandar's argument in the Canadian context, who asserts that the "frozen rights approach" to recognition situates Aboriginal legal rights and practices, both spatially and temporally, as separate and distinct from the contemporary, post-colonial order in order to avoid any disruptions of the 'present'. The recognition and acceptance of differences between communities (within the boundaries of one nation state) in political organization, economic ideologies and practices, land and resource use, would *bend the overarching structure of the nation state out of shape and radically alter its boundaries* (Bhandar, above n 83 (Ch 1), 142, emphasis added).

This repetitious process of construction and deconstruction has been described as the "inexorable combining" of the "two dimensions [that] form the horizon of the law, a moving horizon",[69] which must exhibit both determinacy and "extraordinary responsiveness".[70] For Fitzpatrick, the law "must ever respond to society, historical change", and is therefore "intrinsically dependant and derivative, quite lacking in any content of its own".[71] It is via such oscillation that the law is simultaneously closed and open: the countryman is, at once, both "before the law" and "prior to the law".[72] Fitzpatrick writes: "What is always involved with law, then, is the creative reaching out to a possibility beyond its determinate existence, a beyond where law 'finds itself' in being integrally tied to, and incipiently encompassing of, its exteriority".[73] Nevertheless, the "aleatory margin" of the law must always remain "homogenous with calculation, within the order of the calculable".[74] Indeed, in so doing, law necessarily contains and construes "its borrowed contents" within its own distinctive "force and meanings".[75] Yet there is always, in law, a fleeting moment in which alterity may enter. Indigeneity may be understood as simultaneously manifest in the Derridean unconditioned, the 'law of the law', and the conditioned, contained within positivist law. Indeed, I would suggest, indigeneity – as expressed in Indigenous literature – opens out a suppressed dimension of law, "the dimension enabling law to bring possibility into normatively determinate existence".[76] Where a legal case "is not only unseen but has to be so", such that "judicial discourse shows itself to be the true discourse of fiction",[77] the call for decision causes the law to reach beyond its own determinacy, thereby opening the law to a multitude of Indigenous imperatives.

Puncturing the horizon

> You fellas, whitefellas, put us in the back all the time, like we've got no language for the land. But we've got the story for the land.[78]

69 Fitzpatrick (2004), above n 18 (Ch 1), 223.

70 Ibid., 224.

71 Fitzpatrick, above n 18 (Ch 1), 216.

72 Derrida, above n 18, 216.

73 Fitzpatrick (2004), above n 18 (Ch 1), 221.

74 Jacques Derrida, "Psyche: Inventions of the Other" in Lindsay Waters and Wlad Godzich (eds), *Reading de Man Reading* (Catherine Porter trans., 1989 edn) 55, cited in Fitzpatrick (2004), above n 18 (Ch 1), 224.

75 Fitzpatrick (2004), above n 18 (Ch 1), 225.

76 Ibid., 220.

77 Jean-Luc Nancy (Simon Sparks, ed.), *Finite Thinking* (2003) 156–157, cited in Fitzpatrick (2004), above n 18 (Ch 1), 221.

78 Eileen Unkari Crombie, "We are the Kupa Pita Kungka Tjuta, the Senior Aboriginal Women of Coober Pedy, South Australia", cited in Milroy and Milroy, above n 1 (Ch 1), 24.

Literature, it has been suggested, "unsettles the law"[79] such that it is able, in a "fleeting moment", to "play the law".[80] In this moment, Derrida writes, literature "is on both sides of the line that separates law from the outlaw, it splits the being-before-the-law, it is at once, like the man from the country, 'before the law' and 'prior to the law'".[81] That is, the "writings which preface the law",[82] prior to the doorkeeper, "without history, genesis, or any possible derivation", in the realm of the "law of the law".[83] Literature, therefore – for Derrida – occupies a place of "subversive juridicity", which "supposes also a power to produce performatively the statements of the law, of the law that literature can be, and not just of the law to which literature submits".[84] It is, accordingly, "the name for a neutrality before decision, conceptuality, prior to the oppositions between actual and virtual, serious and non-serious, real and fictional".[85] This place *before the law* is, Derrida further suggests, a recovery of "language without language, language beyond language . . . [an] interplay of forces which are mute but already haunted by writing, where the conditions of a performative are established, as are the rules of the game and the limits of subversion".[86] As discussed earlier, Derrida describes literature as "stand[ing] on the edge . . . almost beyond",[87] as that which "allows one to *say everything*, in *every way*",[88] and furthermore, as allowing not only a reconceptualisation of the law, but a defiance or lifting of it, a capacity "to think the essence of the law in the experience of this 'everything to say' . . . to overflow the institution".[89] Accordingly, he emphasises a notion of the literary work as "singular, which is to say irreducible, irreplaceable . . . neither imitation, nor reproduction, nor metalanguage".[90] The unconditional aesthetic of the literary text is that which performs the unanticipated "as if", an event that arrives and "punctures the horizon, *interrupting* any performative organization, any convention, or any context that can be dominated by conventionality".[91] Where the law derives its content from that

79 Hanafin, Gearey and Brooker, above n 3 (Ch 1), 2.

80 Derrida, above n 15 (Ch 1), 216.

81 Ibid.

82 Ibid., 217, citing Franz Kafka, *The Penguin Complete Novels of Franz Kafka* (Willa and Edwin Muir trans., 1983 edn) 161.

83 Ibid., 191.

84 Ibid., 216.

85 Culler, above n 29 (Ch 3), 873.

86 Derrida, above n 15 (Ch 1), 216.

87 Ibid., n 9 (Ch 3), 47.

88 Ibid., 36.

89 Ibid.

90 Ibid., 69–70. See also Attridge, above n 20 (Ch 1), 29, who describes the literary experience as "a *singular* encounter, and an encounter with singularity":

> The otherness that is brought into being by an act of inventive writing . . . implies a wholly new existent that cannot be apprehended by the old modes of understanding, and could not have been predicted by means of them; its singularity, even if it is produced by nothing more than a slight recasting of the familiar and thus of the general, is irreducible.

91 Derrida, above n 21 (Ch 1), 234. I will return to this notion of the "as if" in Part II (Indigeneity).

which is extrinsic to it – *before* and *beyond* it – in each moment of decision, literature ruptures and reformulates the narrative of the law. It is in this moment that indigeneity is glimpsed, toward which the law is momentarily compelled.

Indigenous literature has been understood as a means of critique and intervention, perhaps even as strategy, in Eagleton's terms,[92] bringing "specific critical understandings of agency, subjectivity, difference and representation to bear in scrutinising the intersection of a range of prevailing 'knowledges' about Indigenous Australians, and the theoretical and lived implications of those knowledges", a process described as "Indigenous intellectual activism".[93] Tuhiwai Smith has suggested that Indigenous peoples "across the world have other stories to tell", which serve to question and critique the "assumed nature" of occidental academic ideals and practices "through the eyes of the colonized".[94] Furthermore, Indigenous author Alexis Wright describes literature as an act of "wresting words from silence and ideas from obscurity"[95] within the context of an unresponsive nation which, in her novel *Carpentaria*, "chants, *but we know your story already*".[96] Such literature, it has been suggested, is reflective of both a "history of defining Aboriginality in Australia and the experience of 'being Aboriginal' ".[97] Irrespective of the diversity of Indigenous cultural expression, both nationally and internationally, Heiss asserts that Indigenous literatures express a "shared sense of Aboriginality . . . regardless of the geographical location or socio-economic experience".[98] Accordingly, she maintains, such unity is generative of a "distinct Aboriginal literary discourse", identifiable "within the Australian literary canon".[99]

Where such aspirations to cultural 'purity' in "(pan)-Indigeneity" have been described as potentially empowering, it must be recalled that such "boundary construction" or "policing" may falsely construe "Indigenous and non-Indigenous identities as 'mutually impermeable and incommensurable' ",[100] a " 'prison-house'

92 Eagleton, above n 19 (Ch 1).

93 Michele Grossman, "After Aboriginalism: Power, Knowledge and Indigenous Australian Critical Writing" in Michele Grossman (ed.), *Blacklines: Contemporary Critical Writing by Indigenous Australians* (2003) 1, 9. See also Anita Heiss and Peter Minter, "Aboriginal Literature" in Anita Heiss and Peter Minter (eds), *Macquarie PEN Anthology of Aboriginal Literature* (2008) 1. At 2, the authors remark: For [Australian] Aboriginal people, the use of English became a necessity within the broader struggle to survive colonisation. From the early days, writing became a tool of negotiation in which Aboriginal voices could be heard in a form recognisable to British authority . . . . [The works in this anthology] reveal modes of performativity that are central to literary writing. They also demonstrate one of the persistent and now characteristic elements of Aboriginal literature – the nexus between the literary and the political.

94 Tuhiwai Smith, above n 31 (Ch 1), 2.

95 Wright, above n 46 (Ch 3), 12.

96 Ibid., above n 45 (Ch 3), 1.

97 Heiss, above n 45 (Ch 1), vi.

98 Ibid., 21.

99 Ibid., 17.

100 Paradies, above n 98 (Ch 1), 356, citing Paul Gilroy, *Small Acts: Thoughts on the Politics of Black Cultures* (1993) 65.

of identity".[101] Moreover, such formulations may not be expressive of *actual* identities but, rather, of the insatiable demands of "prevailing discourses".[102] Particularly within the context and confines of identity politics, Indigenous authors have frequently sought to bind identity for use as a weapon in pursuit of particular recognition, revealing a tension between differing uses of Indigenous expression. Indeed, Butler has critiqued the use of stable categories of identity for "strategic purposes", where "strategies always have meanings that exceed the purposes for which they are intended".[103] Attempting to limit such essentialism, Grossman has proposed writing as a vital political role for Indigenous artists and intellectuals, "the enduring imperative" being to "negotiate the tensions between 'representation' and 'representativeness'".[104] Negotiation of these dual registers may be conceived as that between the Derridean conditioned and unconditioned – while an interior indigeneity may be unconditioned, it must be conditioned in order to be represented. Many literary evocations of indigeneity, however, deliberately attempt to eschew such static representations, via the adoption of narrative modes and literary forms that are disruptive of conventionality, including untranslated language and unexplained Indigenous knowledge.[105] Such disruptions may indeed evoke a pan-indigeneity, but may also evoke particular communal, geographical or temporal specificities, and, most particularly for my purposes, may be expressive of Indigenous Law.

Indigenous Australians frequently assert storytelling as a cultural responsibility – Mozzie Fishman in Wright's novel, *Carpentaria*, avows: "Nothing must stop our stories, understand?"[106] Indigenous creation stories, which have been identified as originating in specific locations,[107] may be contrasted with the narratives of

101 Ien Ang, *On Not Speaking Chinese: Living Between Asia and the West* (2001) 11; Darlene Oxenham, Kim Collard, Pat Dudgeon, Darren Garvey, Marion Kickett, Tracey Kickett, Jeannie Roberts and Jules Whiteway, *A Dialogue in Indigenous Identity: Warts 'n' All* (1999) 70; Joan Wallach Scott, "Multiculturalism and the Politics of Identity" (1992) 61 *October* 18, all cited in Paradies, above n 98 (Ch 1), 356.

102 Paradies, above n 98 (Ch 1), 356.

103 Butler, above n 11 (Ch 1), 4.

104 Grossman, above n 93, 8.

105 In the context of Native American Indian literatures, Gerald Vizenor has usefully remarked upon such opacity: There can never be "correct" or "objective" readings of the text or the tropes in tribal literatures, only more energetic, interesting, and "pleasurable misreadings". Gerald Vizenor, "A Postmodern Introduction", in Gerald Vizenor (ed.), *Narrative Chance: Postmodern Discourse on Native American Indian Literatures* (1993) 3, 5, discussing Vincent Leitch, *Deconstructive Criticism* (1983) 59. Cf Mudrooroo, *The Indigenous Literature of Australia: Milli Milli Wangka* (1997) 16, in which the author laments the replacement of Indigenous "activist literature" with a "literature of understanding", more amenable to a non-Indigenous readership. This view has been explicitly contested: Graham Huggan, *The Postcolonial Exotic: Marketing the Margins* (2001) 163.

106 Wright, above n 45 (Ch 3), 194.

107 Kwaymullina, above n 19 (Ch 2).

the European explorers and settlers, described by Milroy and Milroy as "the story nomads", who "wander about in other people's stories, mucking them up and changing the endings . . . [arriving] too late to understand what the story is about".[108] They write:

> The first thing the *story nomads* do when they arrive somewhere is to begin to order the 'landscape' to establish their 'view' of country, what they want to see in their field of vision, and what they want to exclude. What they really do is *dis*order country, removing it from its own story.[109]

For Milroy and Milroy, the "story nomads" are "perpetual travellers" who, by "dis(re)membering stories . . . create limited knowledge systems"[110] – a movement reminiscent of Healy's notion of a non-Indigenous culture of forgetfulness.[111] This inversion of pejorative descriptions of Indigenous peoples as nomadic adroitly repositions British colonisers as global wanderers, on voyages animated by a pursuit of the fantastical 'Great Southern Continent', rather than a receptiveness to the ancient and inhabited country upon which they alighted. For Indigenous peoples, however, the life-giving stories of country are a birthright, deserving of protection.

The perpetuation of Indigenous stories is expressive not only of the energy of political and environmental protest, but of a law of alterity – Indigenous Law. Indigenous Law has been described as (literally) grounded in the landscape, expressed in stories passed from generation to generation.[112] Narratives of the Dreaming have been described as "the stories without which there could be no others; the ongoing creation of the world", which "do not exist in people", but Indigenous peoples "exist in them . . . 'not written down, but . . . written on the land'".[113] Indigenous poet George Tinamin describes the fundamental relationship between the land, the Law laid down by the ancestors of the Dreaming, and the Aboriginal community in his poem, "One Land, One Law, One People":

> This is not a rock, it is my grandfather.
> This is a place where the dreaming
> comes up, right up from inside the ground.[114]

108 Milroy and Milroy, above n 1 (Ch 1), 29.
109 Ibid., 32.
110 Ibid., 29.
111 Healy, above n 93 (Ch 1), 4–5.
112 See Morgan, Mia and Kwaymullina, above n 1 (Ch 1); Kwaymullina, above n 1 (Ch 2).
113 Ambelin Kwaymullina, "Seeing the Light: Aboriginal Law, Learning and Sustainable Living in Country" (2005) 6(11) *Indigenous Law Bulletin* 12, 14, citing David Mowaljarlaiand and Jutta Malnic, *Yorro Yorro, Everything Standing Up Alive: Spirit of the Kimberley* (2001) 82.
114 George Tinamin, "One Land, One Law, One People", in Lorraine Mafi-Williams (ed.), *Spirit Song: A Collection of Aboriginal Poetry* (1993) 4.

Many Australian Indigenous communities have identified themselves as connected in kinship to the creatures of the Dreaming, now manifest in the terrain.[115] Author and artist Nellie Green describes the notion of Aboriginality as "intrinsically linked to the sense of belonging or the homelands of Indigenous people".[116] Such spiritual and corporeal connections to country, as expressions of identity, are frequently articulated in Indigenous literature, in which Indigenous people have been described as "a living, breathing, thinking, physical manifestation of [their] land".[117] Moreover, in such articulations, country is defined not merely by geography, but as spiritually enlivened: "It is the whole of reality, a living story that forms and informs all existence. Country is alive, and more than alive – it is life itself".[118] Such affinity is exemplified in the Indigenous imperative to 'care for country' as a necessity for human prosperity: "If you don't look after country, country won't look after you."[119] Indigenous Law is derived from the ancestors, and therefore from country itself – according to Kwaymullina, "[t]he ancestors created all life, and gave life and knowledge and law. Each country has its own people who hold the stories of these great events".[120] Collard affirms this relation, in describing the ancestral Rainbow Serpent of the Dreaming:

> [T]he Waakal is the Creator, the keeper of the freshwater sources. He gave us life and our trilogy of belief in the boodjar – the land – as our mother and nurturer of the Nyungar *moort* – family and relations – and our *katitjin* Law – knowledge so that we could weave the intricate tapestry known as the 'web of life'.[121]

Stories, and the telling of stories, are descriptively and spiritually expressive of country and of its Law, such that Indigenous peoples are able to describe the land

115 See Silas Roberts, first Chairman of the Northern Land Council, cited in Deborah Bird Rose, *Nourishing Terrains: Australian Aboriginal Views of Landscape and Wilderness* (1996) 26, available at www.environment.gov.au/heritage/ahc/publications/commission/books/nourishing-terrains.html (accessed 6 October 2015).

116 Nellie Green, "Chasing an Identity, An Aboriginal Perspective on Aboriginality" in Kerry Reed-Gilbert (ed.), *The Strength of Us as Women: Black Women Speak* (2000) 47, cited in Heiss, above n 45 (Ch 1), 19.

117 Kwaymullina, above n 171, 9.

118 Ibid.

119 April Bright Yinirrakun, "Burn Grass" in Deborah Bird Rose (ed.), *Country in Flames: Proceedings of the 1994 Symposium on Biodiversity and Fire in North Australia*, Biodiversity Series, Paper No 3, Department of the Environment, Sport and Territories and the North Australia Research Unit (ANU), Canberra (1995). This obligation, in addition to the right to speak for country, have been articulated by the High Court of Australia in the course of establishing 'connection' for the purposes of proving native title: *Western Australia v Ward* (2002) 213 CLR 1, 64–65 ('*Ward*').

120 Kwaymullina, above n 19 (Ch 2), 8.

121 Len Collard, "Kura, Yeye, boorda 'from the past, today and the future'", in Morgan, Mia and Kwaymullina, above n 1 (Ch 1), 59, 62.

as "a big book", and country as "a living story".[122] Indeed, the life-giving stories of country literally *are* country, "what brings [it] into being and keeps it alive".[123] Speaking of the European incursion into *Trowuna*, or Tasmania, Lehman laments an ignorance of Indigenous Law on the part of the colonisers:

> [T]he sons of England did not know *tunapri manta* [old knowledge, law]. This is our knowing that comes from the old stories, handed down for a thousand generations. It gives us our Law and a way to know the world that works for everyone. But the sealers and soldiers would not learn.[124]

Watson speaks of the redemptive capacity of Indigenous Law, and an Indigenous imperative to decolonise spaces in order to restore "the jurisdiction of Aboriginal peoples and their distinct laws".[125] Where this jurisdiction is expressed in Indigenous oral and written stories, this literature acts to uniquely recuperate suppressed Indigenous Law by, Watson suggests, "[d]reaming back to Country".[126]

Within Indigenous literature, non-Indigenous law is frequently depicted as utterly other to Indigenous Law, the latter evoked as an inherent force manifest within the land, explicable as a persistent and life-giving source of potential. Throughout this book, I will consider this antinomy within the context of Benjamin's "Critique of Violence",[127] which opposes mythical violence as lawmaking, and divine violence as law-destroying.[128] Although Benjamin's vision was situated within a Marxist tradition, this book will extend this analysis, comparing these antagonists to non-Indigenous law and Indigenous Law, the latter potentially comprehensible as a force of divine violence that would bloodlessly annihilate the former. This may be compared with the imperative of disruption in decolonisation, described by Fanon as necessarily violent.[129] Indeed, he insists, "for the [colonized] there is no compromise, no possible coming to terms; colonization and decolonization are simply a question of relative strength".[130] Rather than liberation via direct violence, however, I would identify within Indigenous writing an aesthetic of transformative

122 Kwaymullina, above n 113 (Ch 3), 14.

123 Carter, Paul, *The Road to Botany Bay: An Essay in Spatial History* (1987) 346.

124 Greg Lehman, "A Snake and a Seal", in Morgan, Mia and Kwaymullina, above n 1 (Ch 1), 132, 135.

125 Irene Watson, "De-colonising the Space: Dreaming back to Country", in Morgan, Mia and Kwaymullina, above n 1 (Ch 1), 82, 92.

126 Ibid.

127 Benjamin, above n 24 (Ch 1), 277. Benjamin asserts, at 295: "Justice is the principle of all divine end making, power the principle of all mythical law making".

128 Ibid., 297.

129 See Fanon, above n 119 (Ch 1), 1. Fanon describes the violence of such liberation: "National liberation, national reawakening, restoration of the nation to the people or Commonwealth, whatever the name used, whatever the latest expression, decolonization is always a violent event".

130 Ibid., 61.

potential, a Benjaminian "pure violence", which "does not posit, [but] . . . 'deposes'", as "not performative but afformative",[131] capable of "break[ing] through the cycle of laws and their decay".[132] Such writing provides a moment of potentiality, in which to "dislocate old laws and structures, and articulate new imaginaries which may in turn become laws".[133] Indeed, in the novels I will discuss in this book, Indigenous Law is depicted as a regenerative force of law – of divine violence, I will suggest. Via imaginary scenes of apocalyptic destruction and Edenic restoration, these texts express and recuperate an Indigenous Law that troubles and recontextualises non-Indigenous law, and its apparent "monopoly of legal knowledge".[134]

131 Werner Hamacher (Dana Hollander trans.), "Afformative, Strike: Benjamin's 'Critique of Violence'" in Andrew Benjamin and Peter Osborne (eds), *Walter Benjamin's Philosophy: Destruction and Experience* (2000) 108, 115, footnote 12:

> [A]fformative, or pure, violence is a 'condition' for any instrumental, performative violence and, at the same time, a condition which suspends its fulfilment in principle . . . . The afformative is the ellipsis which silently accompanies any act and which may silently interrupt any speech act.

132 Ibid., 113.

133 Aristodemou, above n 4 (Ch 1), 11.

134 Peter Goodrich, *Law in the Courts of Love: Literature and Other Minor Jurisprudences* (1996) 2.

Chapter 4

Positioning

To speak of the Other

> "There is no more dangerous pastime than transposing proper names into common nouns, translating, and using them as sociological evidence". All transcendental logic is, at its heart, imperialistic.[1]

Engaging with questions of indigeneity or indeed, more broadly, of those defined by others as the "irretrievably heterogeneous", colonised subaltern,[2] the non-Indigenous scholar must articulate and constantly affirm her position: as one among those attempting to "align themselves with the subaltern", or one among those who maintain that "this attempt becomes at best only a refined version of the very discourse it seeks to displace".[3] Research, according to Tuhiwai Smith, must be approached not as "an innocent or distant academic exercise" but as an invested exercise, politically and socially embedded.[4] In the pursuit of an intellectual positioning on questions concerning the subaltern, Spivak, in her seminal essay, "Can the Subaltern Speak?", reminds the reader of the ever-present "possibility that the intellectual is complicit in the persistent constitution of Other as the Self's shadow".[5] Spivak reveals the "asymmetrical obliteration of the trace of the Other" inherent within the "palimpsestic narrative of imperialism",[6] by which the colonial subject is constituted. That is, the subjugation of 'other' knowledges, "disqualified . . . located low down on the hierarchy, beneath the required level of cognition

1 Jay Maggio, "Can the Subaltern Be Heard? Political Theory, Translation, Representation, and Gayatri Chakravorty Spivak" (2007) 32(4) *Alternatives* 419, 420, citing Spivak, above n 33 (Ch 1), 306; and Spivak, above n 55 (Ch 1), 334.

2 Spivak, above n 33 (Ch 1), 284.

3 Bill Ashcroft, Gareth Griffiths and Helen Tiffin, "Issues and Debates", in Bill Ashcroft, Gareth Griffiths and Helen Tiffin (eds), *The Post-Colonial Studies Reader* (1995, 2nd edn) 9, 11.

4 Tuhiwai Smith, above n 31 (Ch 1), 5.

5 Spivak, above n 33 (Ch 1), 280.

6 Ibid., 281.

or scientificity".[7] The subaltern, ever situated within a dominant discourse, is a "vanishing point",[8] an "inaccessible blackness",[9] "simultaneously invoked and foreclosed",[10] defined by erasure.[11] While the subaltern, even the 'hybrid' subject, inhabits this void, she is defined by the non-subaltern and is – according to Spivak – only able to speak via the non-subaltern ventriloquist. Referring to Said's notion of Orientalism, Spivak asserts that the coloniser himself is constructed in relation to the colony: "The colonizer constructs himself as he constructs the colony. The relationship is intimate, an open secret that cannot be part of official knowledge".[12] Questioning the role of academia in issues surrounding the subaltern, Spivak asks whether, indeed, there remains "a liberating place for the intellectual desires of studying the subaltern",[13] where the intellectual herself may indeed be "complicit" in the "constitution of Other".[14] For Spivak, it seems, the subaltern may never be able to speak: "One cannot 'intervene benevolently'".[15] Harris applies Spivak's assertions to the law of native title in Australia, in which Indigenous knowledges are manifestly disqualified. Indeed, where it has been argued that "Australia is a white country with a black history",[16] Harris considers the native title process itself to be a "product of neo-colonialist thought, where Indigenous Australians have 'no history and cannot speak'".[17]

While most readings of Spivak suggest an inescapable descent into neo-colonialism, Maggio has proposed a more optimistic interpretation, advocating "a reading of culture(s) based on the assumption that all actions, to a certain extent, offer a communicative role".[18] This approach entails a "more open-ended view of discourse and communication", enabling cross-cultural understanding.[19] Maggio refers to Benjamin's account of translation as "the 'movement' between one hermeneutic moment and another",[20] whereby the translation may "elevate" or

7 Michel Foucault, *Power/Knowledge: Selected Interviews and Other Writings 1972–77* (Colin Gordon *et al.* trans., 1980 edn) 82, cited in Spivak, above n 33 (Ch 1), 281.
8 Maggio, above n 1, 427.
9 Ibid., 427, citing Bart Moore-Gilbert, *Postcolonial Theory* (1997) 91.
10 David Huddart, "Making an Example of Spivak" (April 2001) 6 *Angelaki: Journal of Theoretical Humanities* 35, 38, cited in Maggio, above n 1, 427.
11 Maggio, above n 1, 427.
12 Spivak, above n 55 (Ch 1), 203.
13 Maggio, above n 1, 420.
14 Spivak, above n 33 (Ch 1), 280.
15 Maggio, above n 1, 427, citing Bart Moore-Gilbert, above n 9, 89.
16 AAP (2002) "Native Title Near Impossible to Prove: Lawyer" (12 December 2002) *Sydney Morning Herald*, cited in Mark Harris, "Mythologising 'Recollections of Squatting in Victoria': Law's Intersection with Colonial Memory" (2003) 1 *Law, Social Justice & Global Development Journal* at www2.warwick.ac.uk/fac/soc/law/elj/lgd/2003_1/harris (accessed 6 October 2015).
17 Harris, above n 16, 12, citing Spivak, above n 33 (Ch 1), 287.
18 Maggio, above n 1, 421.
19 Ibid., 421.
20 Ibid., 432, citing Samuel Weber, "A Touch of Translation: On Walter Benjamin's 'Task of the Translator'" in Sandra Bermann and Michael Wood (eds), *Nation, Language and the Ethics of Translation* (2005) 65, 66.

at least "echo" the original, acting as "a kind of 'midway' point in intellectual dialogue".[21] Furthermore, Benjamin elsewhere asserts, "[t]ranslation passes through *continua* of transformation, not abstract ideas of identity and similarity".[22] Indeed, for Spivak, the translator must " 'inhabit' the host language" – that is, "attempt to find the presuppositions of the language and of the cultures that are communicating".[23] Maggio maintains that the inaccessibility of the other may be overcome via an attempt to " 'translate' the other, rather than seeking an imaginary knowledge", explained as "a desire to 'understand,' rather than to 'know' ", where knowledge implies domination.[24] Such translation would apply not merely to that which is written, but to "the cultural practices of daily culture, the 'repetitive tasks people do every day' ".[25] In advocating an approach to the subaltern via translation, Maggio maintains that the translator must be ever aware that his work is neither "equivalent with the 'original' ", nor a "wholly 'imaginative' translation":

> The translator is certainly trying to 'capture' an aspect of the original and convey that, but is not trying to 'represent' (*vertreten*) or 're-present' (*dartelling*) the original . . . . [W]ith the case of the subaltern, one must first decide to recognize the language of communication as a valid mode. In other words, we must . . . try hard to listen to people in all their forms of communication. The subaltern speaks *all the time:* We are simply unable to hear them.[26]

Maggio reads Spivak's account of Hindu *sati* – widow self-immolation – as a search for a "deliberate act of speaking" on the part of the subaltern, the " 'true' subaltern into which the careful Western can tap".[27] In the alternative, he advocates a more nuanced attentiveness to the various speech acts of the subaltern, as expressed in everyday acts.

21 Maggio, above n 1, citing Walter Benjamin, *Illuminations* (1968) note 109, 75–7. Benjamin, at 77, writes:

> The task of the translator consists in finding that intended effect [*Intention*] upon the language into which he is translating which produces in it the echo of the original. Unlike a work of literature, translation does not find itself in the centre of the language forest but on the outside facing the wooded ridge; it calls into it without entering, aiming at that single spot where the echo is able to give, in its own language, the reverberation of the work in the alien one.

22 Walter Benjamin, "On Language as such and the Language of Man", cited in Bhabha, above n 129 (Ch 1), 303.

23 Maggio, above n 1, 434, citing Gayatri Chakravorty Spivak, "Translating into English" in Sandra Bermann and Michael Wood, *Nation, Language, and the Ethics of Translation* (2005) 93, 85.

24 Ibid.

25 Joe Moran, *Reading the Everyday* (2005) 22, cited in Maggio, above n 1, 435. See also Keiichi Omura, Comment on Adam Kuper, "The Return of the Native" (Current Anthropology Forum on Anthropology in Public, June 2003) 44(3) *Current Anthropology* 389, 395–6.

26 Maggio, above n 1, 437.

27 Ibid., 430.

As a non-Indigenous researcher and writer, my search for the subaltern voice and the position from which I speak are of fundamental significance to my discussion of the ways in which indigeneity is and has been defined. The legitimacy and capacity for non-Indigenous people to speak on Indigenous issues, particularly language, culture, and history, is highly contested. Indeed, the very word 'research' has been maligned by Indigenous authors, as "probably one of the dirtiest words in the indigenous world's vocabulary . . . stir[ring] up silence . . . bad memories . . . a smile that is knowing and distrustful".[28] For Tuhiwai Smith, research represents a site of contestation and "struggle between the interests and ways of knowing of the West and the interests and ways of resisting of the Other".[29] Furthermore, according to Heiss, "[t]here are strong and original arguments coming from people who believe that white writers should not write about Aboriginal issues, especially sacred matters".[30] This may include the bases of Indigenous relations to country and Indigenous Law, fundamental to claims to native title.

Indigenous author Laughton is dismissive of non-Indigenous attempts to construe Indigenous issues: "I reckon that is our business and we should be the ones writing it; and receiving the appropriate recognition and status as the custodians and experts on that history".[31] Nyoongar writer, van den Berg, maintains, "[i]t does not matter how many of the 'experts' on Aboriginal issues write about the Indigenous people, they are still outsiders looking in".[32] Bropho asserts:

> When a white author decides to write a book he hears direct from the Aboriginal person broken words which the white man calls 'broken English', he hears it and then he twists it around and his mind is taking up the sounds of that and he's putting the flavour of the white mind into those words that go into the lines and become chapters in that book.[33]

While it has been argued that non-Indigenous perspectives are and will necessarily remain partial,[34] my work should not be construed as an attempt to speak for the 'Other' – in the words of Indigenous academic Birch, "by capturing and controlling definitions of 'the other' in the colonial imagination".[35] In reading Indigenous writings, I seek not to capture or control but, akin to Maggio's notions

28 Tuhiwai Smith, above n 31 (Ch 1), 1.
29 Ibid., 2.
30 Heiss, above n 45 (Ch 1), 10.
31 Kenny Laughton, email to the author (17 October 1998) in Heiss, above n 45 (Ch 1), 11.
32 Rosemary van den Berg, email to the author (12 August 1999) in Heiss, above n 45 (Ch 1), 12.
33 Robert Bropho, personal interview (4 March 1998) in Heiss, above n 45 (Ch 1), 11.
34 Cathy Craigie, personal interview (9 October 1997) in Heiss, above n 45 (Ch 1), 12.
35 Tony Birch, "'Real Aborigines': Colonial Attempts to Re-Imagine and Re-Create the Identities of Aboriginal People" (1993) 4 *Ulitarra* 13.

of translation, to be transformed into new understanding – that is, to receive the communications of the Other on her own terms.[36]

It must also be borne in mind that Indigenous literature itself, as one expression of indigeneity, is frequently articulated within and through the dominant ideology.[37] Though it may be disruptive of conventional literary forms, such writing is sufficiently recognisable within occidental conceptualisations of 'literature' to allow broad dissemination into a non-Indigenous community. Such dissemination is not devoid of power. As Bhabha asserts, "there is always, in Said, the suggestion that colonial power and discourse is possessed entirely by the coloniser, which is an historical and theoretical simplification".[38] The adoption of writing as a tool in the articulation of indigeneity is a unique weapon; its discussion and analysis by non-Indigenous readers is, arguably, a response to this force.[39] Such dialogue may indeed constitute a form of communication and translation, as envisaged by Maggio, rendering subaltern speech audible. In the context of the decolonial, Fitzpatrick describes the aforementioned notion of " 'interculturality', through which a culture involves a 'basic and constant translation' . . . and through which we both appropriate and absorb another culture whilst maintaining a '*responsivity*' to it, including what remains 'alien' of it".[40] Much Indigenous writing speaks of a dramatic dissolution of non-Indigenous law by Indigenous Law, and relates stories of "people with ancient ties to their land . . . people who had been colonised, people who had suffered at the hands of other people . . . about [Indigenous] lives, [Indigenous] lands, and the agelessness of [Indigenous] culture".[41] In this book, I endeavour to speak not for Indigenous Australians but, in a mode of cross-cultural translation or " 'intercultural' plurality",[42] to be ever more attentive to Indigenous voices.

36 See Maggio, above n 1, 421.

37 Margery Fee, "Who can Write as Other?" from "Why C.K. Stead Didn't Like Kerry Hulme's *The Bone People* or Who Can Write as the Other" (1989) 1 *Australian and New Zealand Studies in Canada*, in Ashcroft, Griffiths and Tiffin, above n 3, 169, 171.

38 Homi Bhabha, "The Other Question: The Stereotype and Colonial Discourse" in Mandy Merck *The Sexual Subject: A Screen Reader in Sexuality* (1992) 312, 318. Bhabha, at 318, writes:

> It becomes difficult . . . to conceive of the *historical* enunciations of colonial discourse without them being either functionally overdetermined or strategically elaborated or displaced by the *unconscious* sense of latent Orientalism. Equally, it is difficult to conceive of the process of subjectification as a placing *within* Orientalist or colonial discourse for the dominated subject without the dominant being strategically placed within it too.

39 See, for instance, David Campbell, "Voice of the New Tribes" *The Guardian* (4 January 2003) at www.theguardian.com/books/2003/jan/04/artsfeatures.fiction (accessed 6 October 2015). Native American author, Sherman Alexie, is quoted: "I have enormous cultural power now . . . Because of my ethnicity, my age, the times we live in, I have power".

40 Fitzpatrick, above n 23 (Ch 1), 128, citing Menga, above n 25 (Ch 1), 256–8 (Menga's emphasis).

41 Wright, above n 46 (Ch 3), 12.

42 Fitzpatrick, above n 23 (Ch 1), 128, citing Menga, above n 25 (Ch 1), 256–8.

Synopsis

The remainder of this book is divided into three principal parts – Indigeneity, Law, Literature – the initial engagement serving to frame the latter.[43] This introductiory part has elaborated my principal concerns, theoretical and philosophical points of departure, and positioning as a non-Indigenous researcher. I will now provide an orientation to the remaining chapters of the book.

Part II, *Indigeneity*, will engage more fully with the question of indigeneity, as a global and local identity and discourse. In the Australian context, I will examine and problematise non-Indigenous literary and legal conceptions of Indigenous subjectivity, and the construction of 'indigeneity' as an impermeable and "impossible object" of identification.[44] Furthermore, I will situate the articulation and recognition of identity within the tension between the mobilisation of 'indigeneity' as a tool in the politics of land rights and management, by both Indigenous and non-Indigenous parties,[45] and the more subversive expression of identities in Indigenous literature. This will include an engagement with pervasive and persistent debates surrounding the very term, "Indigenous", and its articulation and deployment in domestic and international fora.[46] I will preface this with an examination of notions of identity itself, as articulated within an Hegelian dialectic of recognition and subsequent critique thereof, particularly in the (post)colonial context. In so doing, I will consider the liberatory force of Indigenous literary expression where the Indigene, while apparently rendered the *property* of a colonising law, remains indeterminately resistant to her *proper* recognition by the law.[47]

Anticipating engagements with the colonial gaze in Part II, this discussion will extend to an examination and critique of the legal narrative in terms of Derrida's notion of the archive. That is, the archive as a source of original a thority and

43 With respect to "framing", I here refer to Jacques Derrida, "The Parergon", in Jacques Derrida, *The Truth in Painting* (Geoff Bennington and Ian McLeod trans., 1987 edn) 37, 54. Derrida describes the parergon, not as limiting, but as an opening out, the "supplementary work", inscrib[ing] something which comes as an extra, exterior to the proper field . . . but whose transcendent exteriority comes to play, abut onto, brush against, rub, press against the limit itself and intervene in the inside only to the extent that the inside is lacking.

44 Povinelli, above n 12 (Ch 1), 6.

45 Fabienne Bayet-Charlton, "Overturning the doctrine: Indigenous Peoples and Wilderness – Being Aboriginal in the Environmental Movement", in Michele Grossman (ed.), *Blacklines: Contemporary Critical Writing by Indigenous Australians* (2003), discussed in Grossman, above n 93 (Ch 3), 13.

46 Roger Sandall, *The Culture Cult: Designer Tribalism and Other Essays* (2001); Peter Sutton, above n 93 (Ch 1); Barnard, above n 36 (Ch 1); Adam Kuper, "The Return of the Native" (Current Anthropology Forum on Anthropology in Public, June 2003) 44(3) *Current Anthropology* 389. See also replies in this issue and (April 2004) 45(2) *Current Anthropology* 263 and Discussion: The Concept of Indigeneity (2006) 14(1) *Social Anthropology* 17–32. This debate is discussed at length in Part II (Indigeneity).

47 Jean-Luc Nancy, "Identity and Trembling" in Nancy, above n 35 (Ch 2), 9, 10; see particular engagement in Bhandar, above n 83 (Ch 1), especially 141–2.

as a technology or prosthesis for memory, which remains nonetheless perpetually haunted by an origin to which it seeks to return yet cannot.[48] That is, it seeks to return to the origin, which exists only "at the limit of the condition originated, cannot be contained within it and goes ever beyond it".[49] Indeed, for Fitzpatrick, the perpetual movement between determinacy and indeterminacy ensures that "always 'something happens' and that 'means that the origin is not and was never present'".[50] Following Derrida, I will argue that this movement, "the movement of deconstruction",[51] is evoked by the emergence of indigeneity *with-in* the law. This will then be carried forward to a comparative examination of indigeneity within a Levinasian ethics of alterity, to conclude, following Derrida once again, with a discussion of the necessarily violent determination of the Indigene before the law.[52]

Part III, *Law*, will further consider the vexed relation between law and justice via a more fulsome discussion of the mythic violence of a determinate law, as opposed to the divine violence of an indeterminate indigeneity, as it is expressed in literature. This will extend my introductory discussion of the notion of literature as strategy[53] and, further, of that which Fitzpatrick has described as the "constituent correspondence between law and literature".[54] In the course of considering this correspondence, I will examine Sherman Alexie's text, "The Trial of Thomas Builds-the-Fire", in which the author presents Native American counternarratives within the context of legal orthodoxy and, further, from which I draw the Derridean conception of a disruptive and irreducible "idea of justice".[55] This liberatory notion is compared to juridical renderings of "justice *as law*",[56] and the capacity for such literary narratives to escape and, indeed, (re)constitute legal narratives is discussed. The appearance of the Indigene before the law in this text is illustrative of the aforementioned antinomy within the law, as simultaneously violent and nonviolent, destructive and responsive.

In the remainder of Part III, I will embark upon an examination of the legal depiction of the Indigene through a reading of Australian native title case law, legislation, and broader jurisprudence. This analysis will be prefaced by an engagement with the 'colonial gaze' of the historical legal archive, the construction of the legal Indigene within scientific classificatory terms consistent with the

48 Jacques Derrida, *Archive Fever: A Freudian Impression* (Eric Prenowitz trans., 1995 edn).

49 Peter Fitzpatrick, *Modernism and the Grounds of Law* (2001) 90.

50 Nancy, above n 35 (Ch 2), 162, cited in Fitzpatrick, above n 30, 34.

51 Derrida, above n 14 (Ch 1), 254.

52 Emmanuel Levinas, *Totality and Infinity: An Essay on Exteriority* (Alphonso Lingis trans., 1969 edn), Jacques Derrida, "Violence and Metaphysics: An Essay on the Thought of Emmanuel Levinas" in Jacques Derrida, *Writing and Difference* (1967) 97.

53 Eagleton, above n 19 (Ch 1).

54 Fitzpatrick (2012), above n 18 (Ch 1), 193.

55 Derrida, above n 14 (Ch 1), 254.

56 Ibid., 240 (emphasis added).

European voyages of 'discovery' of earlier centuries, and the ensuing foundational jurisprudence in accordance with which the Indigene, and Indigenous land and waters, were situated within the law. This discussion examines the ramifications of this historic construction for contemporary Australian native title law. I will then focus upon juridical engagements with the requirements of acknowledgment and observance of 'traditional' laws and customs that constitute the 'origin and content' of native title in case law, and the requirement for continuous or 'substantially uninterrupted' connection to land and waters claimed. As part of a broader discussion, I will particularly consider *Bennell*[57] and *Yorta Yorta*,[58] both of which contain extended analyses of connection to country. This examination will be framed by a discussion of Benjamin's opposing notions of violence, as elaborated in his "Critique of Violence",[59] in the context of the "legitimate fictions"[60] with which the law must engage in its construal of the Indigenous legal subject.

Part IV, *Literature*, will further consider the notion of the literary work as strategy,[61] and as a 'singular' event,[62] in a broader examination of the literature relating to law and literature, and of the law conceived as a narrative – encapsulated within that which has been termed the "Law and Literature project".[63] This section will situate the non-Indigenous legal narrative alongside other modes of storytelling. Further, it will examine Indigenous literature as a part of a broader, longer oral tradition, principally concerned not with the aesthetic but with epistemological transfer – across generations, stories are repeated and contextualised, but retain an integral constancy. In this way, knowledge and Law relating to land 'management' and sustainable practices, frequently expressed in stories, are considered a fundamental part of Indigenous socialities.[64] Ultimately, I will examine the role of literature as a source of law – as a part of the "cultural sphere" of which both law and literature are a product.[65] Indeed, I will suggest, the common law of Australia may be understood as a narrative, inaugurating sovereignty and violently preserving it,[66] while constructing social meaning to the exclusion of (present and prior) Indigenous meanings. Where this law suppresses

57 (2006) 230 ALR 603. I will also examine the Full Federal Court decision in this matter, *Bodney v Bennell* (2008) 249 ALR 300.
58 *Members of the Yorta Yorta Aboriginal Community v Victoria* (2002) 214 CLR 422 ("Yorta Yorta").
59 Benjamin, above n 24 (Ch 1); see also discussion thereof in Derrida, above n 14 (Ch 1).
60 Derrida, above n 14 (Ch 1), 240.
61 Eagleton, above n 19 (Ch 1).
62 Attridge, above n 20 (Ch 1).
63 Aristodemou, above n 4 (Ch 1), 4.
64 See Langton, above n 26 (Ch 1), 79.
65 Aristodemou, above n 4 (Ch 1), 10.
66 See Benjamin, above n 24 (Ch 1), 277, in which Benjamin asserts, at 295: "Lawmaking is power making and, to that extent, an immediate manifestation of violence." See also Derrida, above n 14 (Ch 1), 228.

and expels Indigenous Law, the latter is expressed within a paradigm of resistance, in Indigenous literature which, as a subversive jurisprudence, ruptures the colonial narrative of the law and enables its recontextualisation and (re)constitution.

I will then consider the situation of indigeneity, as expressed in Indigenous literature, within a postcolonial paradigm, and resistance to postcolonial categorisation by Indigenous peoples. That is, within a notion of the postcolonial as Bhabha's reading of a Derridean *différance*, "an alternative to . . . cultural specification in the fundamentally non-relational terms of *pure* 'incommensurability' or 'untranslatability'".[67] Bhabha's notion of hybridity expresses "a difference 'within', a difference without binary terms", which describes a "process of cultural 'enunciation' or 'performance'", such that "[s]pecific individuals are here always derivative, a result".[68] I am interested to consider the emergence, proliferation, and purposes of Indigenous literature as an iterative performance of identity as *différance* and, as such, as a means of altering and recreating both the reader and writer.[69] I will situate Indigenous literature within broader discussions of literature as a thing greater than a mere "supplement to political struggle"[70] – indeed, as uniquely transformative. This will include an examination of the notion of law and literature as mimetic texts, and of the ways in which literary representations might subvert the putative 'truths' of juridical narratives. Finally, I will examine the rendering of indigeneity as a radical newness, expressed in the liberating alterity of the Deleuzian simulacrum.[71]

The above analyses will be integrated with a close reading of two Indigenous authored texts, Kim Scott's *That Deadman Dance*[72] and Alexis Wright's *Carpentaria*.[73] I will engage here with Benjamin's antinomic notions of mythical and divine violence in "Critique of Violence",[74] and Derrida's "Force of Law",[75] in which Derrida envisages the law as "the element of calculation" as contrasted with justice,

67 Peter Hallward, *Absolutely Postcolonial: Writing between the Singular and the Specific* (2001) 24, citing Bhabha, above n 129 (Ch 1), 207, 224.

68 Ibid.

69 See Fanon, above n 17 (Ch 1), 179: "In the world in which I travel, I am endlessly creating myself. And it is by going beyond the historical, instrumental hypothesis that I will initiate my cycle of freedom". See also Thomas Docherty, *Aesthetic Democracy* (2006) in which Docherty asserts that in reading a text, the reader is *interpreted* by the text as much as she *interprets* it – we are shaped by aesthetics as well as shaping them. The reader and text are mutually determinative. Furthermore, Costas Douzinas and Adam Gearey, *Critical Jurisprudence: The Political Philosophy of Justice* (2005) 341, argue that "[r]eading fuses the horizon of the interpreter with the symbolic world projected by the text".

70 Gary Boire, "Ratione Officii: Representing Law in Postcolonial Literatures" (1994) 27(4) *Mosaic: Journal for the Interdisciplinary Study of Literature* 199; see also Fitzpatrick (2004), above n 18 (Ch 1).

71 Gilles Deleuze, *Difference and Repetition* (Paul Patton trans., 2004 edn).

72 Kim Scott, *That Deadman Dance* (2011).

73 Wright, above n 45 (Ch 3), 3.

74 Benjamin, above n 24 (Ch 1), 277.

75 Derrida, above n 14 (Ch 1), 228.

which is "incalculable",[76] as that which "exceeds or contradicts law".[77] I will conclude that the incalculable of Indigenous writing speaks from beyond the determinate narratives of the law, presenting the unpresentable of Indigenous subjectivities and Indigenous Law.[78]

76 Derrida, above n14 (Ch 1), 244.
77 Ibid., see also 250.
78 Ibid., 255. Here, Derrida describes justice as the "unpresentable", citing Kierkegaard for whom, in Derrida's words, "the instant of decision is a madness". Furthermore, at 257, Derrida writes: "Justice, as the experience of absolute alterity, is unpresentable, but it is the chance of the event and the condition of history".

Part II

Indigeneity

Chapter 5

Situating indigeneities

> It seems that the law as such should never give rise to any story. To be invested with its categorical authority, the law must be without history, genesis, or any possible derivation. That would be the law of the law . . . [W]hen one tells stories on this subject, they can concern only circumstances, events external to the law and, at best, modes of its revelation.1

The relations between law and literature, and their conception and evocation of indigeneity, may be understood, in Derridean terminology, to be aporetic.[2] Juridical and literary conceptions of indigeneity are expressive of subjectivities that are, respectively, constrained within the limits of legal recognition, yet are uniquely transformative of it. The alterity of indigeneity is necessarily inaccessible to non-Indigenous law – an "experience of aporia . . . impossible . . . a nonpath".[3] Yet, it is an alterity to which the law is perpetually called to respond, in the "madness" of the "instant of decision".[4] The literary expression of indigeneity reveals the antinomic nature of law[5] – as "irresolute", "in-between" the determinate

1 Jacques Derrida, "Before the Law" in Jacques Derrida (Derek Attridge, ed.), *Acts of Literature* (1992) 181, 191.

2 See Jacques Derrida, "Force of Law: The Mystical Foundation of Authority" in Jacques Derrida (Gil Anidjar, ed.), *Acts of Religion* (2002) 228. This Derridean concept is usefully expounded, in the context of recognition of Indigenous difference, by Stewart Motha, "Mabo: Encountering the Epistemic Limit of the Recognition of 'Difference'" (1998) 7 *Griffith Law Review* 79, 89. Motha writes: "Derived from the Greek word for 'passage' (*poros*), 'aporia' indicates the 'impassable' or, for our purposes, the impossibility of reaching the 'experience of the "other"'".

3 Derrida, above n 2, 244.

4 Ibid., 255. See also Peter Fitzpatrick, *Modernism and the Grounds of Law* (2001) 78, who describes the " 'madness' in the moment of decision" as a violence that "threatens [law] from within": "So this violence 'threatens the entire juridical order itself', yet 'that which threatens law already belongs to it'" (citing Jacques Derrida, "Force of Law: The Mystical Foundations of Authority" in Drucilla Cornell (ed.), *Deconstruction and the Possibility of Justice* (Mary Quaintance trans., 1992 edn) 3, 33, 35).

5 See Jacques Derrida, *Of Hospitality* (Rachel Bowlby trans., 2000 edn) 79–81.

and "what is ever beyond",[6] the calculable and incalculable[7] and, I argue, as a violence both mythic and divine.[8] Derrida describes this distinction as that between law and justice. Whereas the former may be apparent in "the exercise of justice as law . . . a system of regulated and coded prescriptions",[9] he also describes a radically contrasting "infinite, incalculable" justice,[10] which is aporetic, "the experience of what we are unable to experience".[11] To ensure a "just and responsible decision", therefore, Derrida suggests that such a decision "must preserve the law", yet also sufficiently "destroy or suspend it" in order to "reinvent it in each case".[12] This justice, he argues, "if such a thing exist, outside or beyond law, is not deconstructible . . . . *Deconstruction is justice.*"[13]

For Derrida, justice, or the possibility of justice (as deconstruction), appears "outside or beyond law", where law is conceived as determinate, "the element of calculation".[14] The law, however, must be destroyed, suspended and reinvented in each case: "Each case is other, each decision is different and requires an absolutely unique interpretation, which no existing, coded rule can or ought to guarantee absolutely."[15] Accordingly, where the law "claims to exercise itself in the name of justice and . . . justice demands for itself that it be established in the name of a law that must be put to work", it must remain open to this indeterminacy, in the "instant of decision".[16] Conceived as comprising these two facets, however, Derrida elsewhere equates law itself with deconstruction, where law may be conceived as "affirmation" rather than negation: "As soon as you affirm a desire, you perform something which is the Law".[17] Indeed, he argues, "deconstruction cannot be transgression of the Law", since "[d]econstruction *is* the Law"[18] Law, for Fitzpatrick, may be accordingly conceived as "the place where contained presence impossibly combines with uncontained responsiveness", such that "perhaps deconstruction connects more compendiously with law than with justice".[19]

6 Fitzpatrick, above n 4, 36.
7 Derrida, above n 2.
8 Walter Benjamin, "Critique of Violence" in Walter Benjamin, *Reflections: Essays, Aphorisms, Autobiographical Writings* (1978) 277. See also discussion thereof in Derrida, above n 2, 265. I will return to Benjamin's particular antinomy in Part III (Law).
9 Derrida, above n 2, 250.
10 Ibid., 250.
11 Ibid., 244.
12 Ibid., 250–1.
13 Ibid., 243.
14 Ibid., 244.
15 Ibid., 251.
16 Ibid., 251, 255.
17 Jacques Derrida, James Adner, Kate Doyle and Glenn Hendler, "Women in the Beehive: A Seminar with Jacques Derrida" (2005) 16(3) *A Journal of Feminist Cultural Studies* 139, 149.
18 Ibid.
19 Fitzpatrick, above n 4, 76.

The disruptive indeterminacy or alterity of justice – as "*the law of the law*"[20] – is that which is beyond law, "always without law",[21] and is also that which constitutes law, which provides its substance. Derrida describes "a law, perhaps the very essence of law", that is "prior to all *determined* law, *qua* natural law or positive law, but not prior to law *in general*".[22] Indeed, as de Ville suggests, "[f]or Derrida, justice is, as it is for Benjamin, an 'anterior law' and not of the order of knowledge", yet "[d]iffering from Benjamin . . . justice for Derrida is indissociable from law and yet without sovereignty".[23] De Ville has usefully articulated this duality in terms of a "tension, differential [sic] relation or aporia . . . between incalculable justice or singularity 'reconceptualised' as a general economy on the one hand and law as a restricted economy on the other".[24] Accordingly law, for Derrida, should be understood "in a double sense", as institutionalised law ("*le droit*"), and as "the law itself (*la loi*)".[25] De Ville suggests that Derrida does not oppose two forms of violence as does Benjamin but envisages these dimensions as mutually suffusing:[26] "[T]here is no pure moment of undecidable justice but always a *differantial* relation between (undecidable) justice and (decidable) law", which must be " 'negotiated' in singular instances".[27] Furthermore, in the relation between "justice in itself (if it exists) and justice as law", de Ville, reading Derrida, distinguishes between, respectively, "justice as the perfect gift, beyond reason and law" and justice as "a binding stricture or mastery of forces".[28]

The law, therefore, is conceived as constituted by "the movement between determination and responsiveness".[29] While this movement must be fixed, if only temporarily[30] – "there is always a return to determination"[31] – alterity persists as the indeterminate evocation of justice *with-in* law. That is, as the evocation of the "always something, something 'other,' infinitely disrupting what is . . . *within* –

20 Derrida, above n 1, 191. See also Derrida, above n 5, 79, where he describes the unconditionality of hospitality as "*The* law", which is "above the laws" and is "thus illegal, transgressive, outside the law, like a lawless law, *nomos* and *animos*, law above the laws and law outside the law". See also Jean-Luc Nancy, *Corpus* (2000), cited in Peter Fitzpatrick, "Juris-fiction: Literature and the Law of the Law" (2004) 35 (1–2) *ARIEL* 215, 221.

21 Nancy, cited in Fitzpatrick, above n 20, 221.

22 Jacques Derrida, *Politics of Friendship* (George Collins trans., 1997 edn) 231, cited and discussed in Peter Fitzpatrick, "Making Difference: Modernity and the Political Formations of Death" in Charles J Ogletree Jr and Austin Sarat (eds), *The Road to Abolition: The Future of Capital Punishment in the United States* (2009) 319, 333.

23 Jacques de Ville, *Jacques Derrida: Law as Absolute Hospitality* (2011) 158.

24 Ibid., 147.

25 Ibid., 39.

26 See my earlier discussion and reference to, among other works by the same author, Fitzpatrick, above n 4, 102.

27 De Ville, above n 23, 152, citing Jacques Derrida (Gil Anidjar, ed.), *Acts of Religion* (2002) 257.

28 Ibid., 148.

29 Fitzpatrick, above n 4, 6.

30 Fitzpatrick, above n 20, 225.

31 Fitzpatrick, above n 4, 33; see also 34.

what is seemingly known and what is held to", rendering the "placid . . . normality of the contained word [of the law]" illusory.[32] In this part, I will elaborate a conception of indigeneity as this alterity – an impossibility or 'nonpath' existing beyond the law, yet simultaneously constitutive of law as a persistent and spectral ambivalence *with-in* it.

Part I introduced a concern with the 'question' that is indigeneity, as articulated and animated within literary and juridical narratives. Where these narratives create and legislate meanings, indigeneities are articulated within the various spaces of recognition afforded by such narratives. Furthermore, it elaborated a conception of literary narratives as disruptive and deconstructive of colonial legal narratives and, moreover, the commensurate relation between law and literature.[33] The generative capacity of the literary was examined via a reading of indigeneity within Indigenous authored literature, as an undecidability.[34] That is, indigeneity conceived as that which evades categorical stasis, whether literary or legal, evocative of a Deleuzian radical openness or newness, a Derridean unconditional or a Benjaminian divine violence. This part will further examine some of these rich evocations, once more situating indigeneity in the undecidable 'in-between'.[35] Where I have described Derrida's depiction of law as operating in two, mutually suffusing[36] modes – the determinate and indeterminate, calculable and incalculable, conditional and unconditional – I will also situate indigeneity between these, conceived as the impossible of deconstruction, which "always finds itself and moves itself between these two poles".[37] Specifically, where the Indigenous person may

32 Peter Fitzpatrick, "Why the Law Is Also Nonviolent" in Austin Sarat (ed.), *Law, Violence and the Possibility of Justice* (2001) 142, 145 (emphasis added).

33 Derrida, above n 1.

34 Derrida, above n 2, 228. At 251–2, Derrida speaks of the undecidable as the experience of simultaneous obedience and disobedience to the law which, in a "reinstituting act of interpretation", instantiates the law in every decision:

> [T]he undecidable is not merely the oscillation between two significations or two contradictory and very determinate rules, each equally imperative . . . The undecidable is not merely the oscillation or tension between two decisions. Undecidable – this is the experience of that which, though foreign and heterogeneous to the order of the calculable and the rule, must [*doit*] nonetheless . . . deliver itself over to the impossible decision while taking account of law and rules.

35 See Part I (Narratives), especially at 23.

36 Fitzpatrick, above n 4, 102. Fitzpatrick usefully articulates the mutuality of these modes, or dimensions:

> [L]aw's responsive indeterminacy and its enduring determinacy cannot be separated from each other either entirely or in calculated proportion. *Each suffuse[s] the other to its full extent.* The responsive cannot be purely beyond and thence be merely inaccessible. It must be positioned in possibility, oriented toward determinability . . . Nor can a determinate position be at all set or complete. The assertion of position is made and must continue to be made in relation to the infinitely responsive. (emphasis added)

37 Derrida, above n 2, 251.

appear both before the law as a determinate configuration of Indigenous subjectivity, whether strategically or forcibly,[38] and beyond such law as an alterity to which it must respond, it is in the movement between these that indigeneity appears as an evocation of the justice Derrida equates with deconstruction.[39]

To begin Part II, I will extend my earlier discussion of the construction of a determined, legally recognisable Indigenous subject, the performance of which is productive of mere "subjects of empire".[40] While remaining ever responsive to possibility, to the 'beyond', the incorporation of external content within a determined law is always, necessarily, "mediated through law itself".[41] That is to say, as previously, "law will itself endow its borrowed contents with its own force and meanings", which "often differ markedly from their source".[42] In so doing, I argue, the variegated indigeneities appearing before this law are constrained in the creation of a preconceived Indigenous legal subject. Povinelli argues that this constraint is made manifest in the required performance of failed authenticity on the part of the Indigenous person before the law – a demonstration of the necessary elements of a legally prescribed 'traditional' indigeneity, which requires the performance of an unachievable embodiment of indigeneity.[43]

Accordingly, I will then move to a consideration of this positioning of the Indigene as an "impossible object" of identification,[44] and the tension between dynamic, literary indigeneities and legal or political Indigenous identities. This analysis will include an engagement with debate surrounding the very term, 'Indigenous', where its expression is necessarily altered in the strategic pursuit of legal and political recognition. Where such recognition is predicated upon the performance of universal and objective criteria, the singularity of indigeneity is necessarily "excluded by justice *as law*, inasmuch as justice as law seems to imply

38 For discussion of this tension, see Wendy Brown, "Suffering the Paradoxes of Rights" in Wendy Brown and Janet Halley (eds) *Left Legalism/Left Critique* (2002) 420.

39 Derrida, above n 2, 243.

40 Glen S Coulthard, "Subjects of Empire: Indigenous Peoples and the 'Politics of Recognition' in Canada" (2007) 6 *Contemporary Political Theory* 437, 439.

41 Fitzpatrick, above n 20, 225.

42 Ibid.

43 Elizabeth Povinelli, *The Cunning of Recognition: Indigenous Alterities and the Making of Australian Multiculturalism* (2002) 6, 48.

44 Ibid., 6. My analysis here references indigeneity as a preconceived and therefore "impossible object" of performance but, simultaneously, as impossible in the Derridean sense: in the words of Fitzpatrick, as "always beyond attainment" and which, "[t]o be made possible, in the sense of becoming existent, and given operative force . . . must be 'cut' into, reduced, and in a certain sense denied" (Fitzpatrick, above n 4, 74, citing Derrida, above n 4, 24). See also discussion of imposed romanticisation of Indigenous history, in the context of Canada, in Bradley Bryan, "Property as Ontology: On Aboriginal and English Understandings of Ownership" (2000) 13(1) *Canadian Journal of Law and Jurisprudence* 3. At 17–18, Bryan asserts: "[I]f a cultural group learns to operate within a romanticized past, its endeavors into its own cultural practices will always be cluttered with ideals that are impossible."

an element of universality, the appeal to a third party who suspends the unilaterality or singularity of the idioms".[45] Instituted as a superior imperial law, the creation and governance of native title law in Australia remains, I argue, "caught . . . in an ultimacy of exclusion and denial . . . fixedly restrained in [its] responsive dimension".[46] As such, indigeneity persists as the impossible, which cannot be recognised by mere 'calculation', but fleetingly enters the law in the moment of indecision. Part III will engage more specifically with such moments in case law examples.

The analysis of (mis)recognition in the present part will entail some further engagement and critique of the notion of the subject as created within an Hegelian dialectic of recognition. An Hegelian mutuality would envisage the realisation of indigeneity via recognition, according to which "[e]ach is for the other the middle term, through which each mediates itself with itself and unites with itself".[47] That is, a notion of recognition whereby the object is not seized, negated and consumed but, rather, "is a mediated self-consciousness made possible by and conditioned on allowing the other to be what it is, a letting the other go free".[48] While I will suggest that in the postcolonial context, recognition of indigeneity by the law is obscured by the figure of a prescribed Indigenous legal subject, and thereby rendered the *property* of the law,[49] this subjectivity, it will be revealed, is not fixed but transient, where indigeneity perpetually moves between a determinate law and an indeterminate justice. In this way, indigeneity is conceived as ultimately resistant to determinate legal classification and, therefore, to its *proper* recognition.[50]

45 Derrida, above n 2, 245, discussed in Motha, above n 2, 90 (emphasis added).

46 Fitzpatrick, above n 4, 181. This fixity is exemplified in the allusion to the skeletal principles of law in *Mabo and Others v Queensland (No. 2)* (1992) 175 CLR 1, 29 ("*Mabo*"), discussed previously.

47 Georg Wilhelm Friedrich Hegel, "Self-Consciousness: The Truth and Self-Certainty: Independence and Dependence of Self-Consciousness: Lordship and Bondage", in *Phenomenology of Spirit* (AV Miller trans., with analysis and forward by JN Findlay, 1977 edn) 111, 112.

48 Robert R Williams, *Hegel's Ethics of Recognition* (2000) 57; Hegel, above n 47, 111. Note that Williams rejects Levinas's critique of the Hegelian dialectic, via Derrida, arguing that "[t]he absolution of *relata* that Levinas wants, claims Derrida, is already there in Hegel. Derrida is correct": 411; generally, see 398–412. See also Simon Critchley, *The Ethics of Deconstruction: Derrida and Levinas* (1992). This extensive debate is beyond the scope of my engagement here, where I am principally concerned with legal recognition of the Indigene in a specifically postcolonial context.

49 Jean-Luc Nancy, "Identity and Trembling" in Jean-Luc Nancy, *The Birth to Presence* (Brian Holmes trans., 1993 edn) 9, 10.

50 Ibid., 10. See particular engagement in Brenna Bhandar, "Re-Covering the Limits of Recognition: The Politics of Difference and Decolonisation" in John Borrows's *Recovering Canada: The Resurgence of Indigenous Law* (2007) 27 *Australian Feminist Law Journal* 125, especially 141–2. I also note here Fitzpatrick's "analytic of exclusion" (which I here extend to the postcolonial subject) that is, in contrast to an Orientalist subjectification, persistently ambivalent: The picture to be presented . . . is one in which the overall modality is one of exclusion *and* inclusion, and this ambivalence both grounds and destabilizes occidental "identity" (Fitzpatrick, above n 4, footnote 14, 222–3).

I will then examine the colonial legal narrative, and its creation, in terms of Derrida's conception of the archive, which contains an originary trace of the *arkhē* that haunts the law and to which the law seeks to return, yet cannot.[51] For Fitzpatrick, the "incessant violence" of the law resides in its "fully occupying the place of the origin", where "the law comes from nowhere and is not beholden to anything before it"[52] and, further, "[i]t is in this original 'nothingness' that law is needful of and impelled to the violence of determining decision".[53] Indeed, Derrida describes the "origin of authority, the founding or grounding . . . the positing of the law" as "a violence without ground . . . its ultimate foundation . . . by definition unfounded".[54] Yet, while the violence of a "revolutionary origin . . . 'appears savage' in its unrestrained illegality", it "is not exterior to the order of *droit* . . . [but] threatens it from within", as the " 'madness' in the moment of decision".[55] While determinate law perpetually seeks a self-justificatory purity of origin and linearity of precedent, the law is nonetheless revealed to be necessarily (re)instantiated in each instance of judicial decision. For Derrida, "for a decision to be just and responsible", it must, as previously mentioned, simultaneously "preserve the law [*loi*] and also destroy or suspend it enough to have [*pour devoir*] to reinvent it in each case".[56] It is this "movement of deconstruction at work in the law"[57] that is revealing of the transgressive alterity that exists *with-in* it.

I will conclude with a comparative analysis of this Derridean alterity – transgressive, yet constitutive – and a Levinasian ethics of alterity. Levinas's work, most particularly *Totality and Infinity*,[58] provides a radical critique of Western philosophy, particularly that of Heidegger which, he argues, "marks the apogee of a thought in which the finite does not refer to the infinite".[59] He rejects Heidegger's

51 Jacques Derrida, *Archive Fever: A Freudian Impression* (Eric Prenowitz trans., 1995 edn). I will examine the colonial narrative, and the legal construction of indigeneity within it, in greater detail in Part III (Law).

52 Fitzpatrick, above n 4, 80–1.

53 Fitzpatrick, above n 32, 157. See also Derrida, above n 1, 194, in which he suggests that the law is necessarily without origin: "The law, intolerant of its own history, intervenes as an absolutely emergent order, absolute and detached from any origin". See also discussion in Jacques de Ville, "On Law's Origin: Derrida Reading Freud, Kafka and Lévi-Strauss" (2011) 7(2) *Utrecht Law Review* 77, 87. De Ville cites and affirms Derrida's position, suggesting that for law as such (pure morality) to have authority, according to Kant, it is required that it does not have a history. The law (as such) must present itself as "an absolutely emergent order, absolute and detached from any origin".

54 Derrida, above n 2, 242. See also discussion on the question of "founding", in Jacques Derrida, *Who's Afraid of Philosophy? Right to Philosophy 1* (2002). At 22, Derrida writes: [A] self-foundation could not be a present event. It cannot *exist*, in the strong sense of this word that implies *presence*, at the moment of installation or institution.

55 Fitzpatrick, above n 4, 77–8 citing Derrida, above n 4, 33–5.

56 Derrida, above n 2, 251. See also Fitzpatrick, above n 4, 80–1.

57 Ibid., 254.

58 Emmanuel Levinas, *Totality and Infinity: An Essay on Exteriority* (Alphonso Lingis trans., 1969 edn).

59 Emmanuel Levinas, "Philosophy and the Idea of Infinity" in Emmanuel Levinas, *Collected Philosophical Papers* (1957) (Alphonso Lingis trans., 1998 edn) 47, 52.

preoccupation with a totalising conception of the self as Being[60] and, instead, asserts a metaphysical relation of the self to the Other, to whom the former must remain "infinitely inadequate".[61] Indeed, discussing Levinas's transcendental ethics, Derrida describes "the metaphysics of desire" as "a metaphysics of infinite separation".[62] For Derrida, however, alterity cannot retain its infinite "non-violent purity", but must be ultimately determined in the violence of the concept.[63] Accordingly, and in the continued context of Derrida's analysis in "Before the Law",[64] I argue that while the transgressive alterity of indigeneity remains ever *beyond* the law, as the undecidable that is justice and is constitutive of law itself, the Indigene must be nonetheless determined *before* the law, in a violent act of (mis)recognition.

An imperial orientation

Derrida conceives of law, in its determinate manifestation, as "legitimacy or legality, a stabilizable, statutory and calculable apparatus [*dispositif*], a system of regulated and coded prescriptions".[65] This law is exemplified in the law of the coloniser, concerned to determine the ontological substance of indigeneity as a totality. Indeed, the imperial law of the coloniser has been described as "the apotheosis of legality", in accordance with which a "deathly disregard of the other marks an extremity of legal determination".[66] Recognition and determination of the Indigenous legal subject in fixity is demonstrative of the *gewalt* of this law – translated as "both violence and legitimate power, justified authority".[67] Determinate law, however, derives its content from that which is extrinsic to it – that which Derrida describes as justice, "infinite, incalculable, rebellious to rule and foreign to symmetry, heterogeneous and heterotropic".[68] That is, justice as an evocation of the unconditional, which imports a specific meaning for Derrida.

In his (in)famous assertion that "nothing exists outside context" ["*il n'y a pas de hors-texte*"],[69] Derrida conceives of "the frame or border of the context" as "always entail[ing] a clause of *non-closure* [*non-fermature*]", such that "[t]he outside penetrates and thus determines the inside".[70] Indeed, he has compared this notion to his

60 Martin Heidegger, *Being and Time* (John Macquarie and Edward Robinson trans., 1962, 7th edn).
61 Jacques Derrida, "Violence and Metaphysics: An Essay on the Thought of Emmanuel Levinas" in Jacques Derrida, *Writing and Difference* (1967) 97, 115.
62 Ibid.
63 Ibid., 185.
64 Derrida, above n 1, 181.
65 Ibid., above n 2, 250.
66 Fitzpatrick, above n 4, 181.
67 Derrida, above n 2, 234.
68 Ibid., 250.
69 Jacques Derrida, *Of Grammatology* (Gayatri Spivak trans., 1976 edn) 163, cited in Critchley, above n 48, 25.
70 Critchley, above n 48, 32, citing Jacques Derrida, *Limited Inc* (1990) 281–2; *Limited Inc* (1988) 152–3.

previous references to 'supplementarity' and 'parargonality', where "[t]hese concepts come close to blurring or dangerously complicating the limits between inside and outside, in a word, the framing of a context".[71] Accordingly, the context is interrupted and therefore *opened* by "an unconditional affirmation that intervenes in this context and motivates deconstruction", where the unconditional is conceived as "independent of every determinate context"[72] and "announces itself as such only in the *opening* of context".[73] This unconditional disrupts and deconstructs the context that is determinate law; indeed, as discussed at the outset, Derrida equates deconstruction with justice.[74] Accordingly, deconstruction occurs "in the interval that separates the undeconstructibility of justice from the deconstructibility of law".[75] It is the unconditionality and impossibility of justice, therefore, that is constitutive of determined law. Derrida writes: "[J]ustice demands for itself that it be established in the name of a law that must be put to work [*mis en oeuvre*] (constituted and applied) by force 'enforced'".[76] This necessity, the "*il faut*", belongs to both law and justice "by exceeding each one in the direction of the other", such that "in their very heterogeneity, these two orders are undissociable".[77] Fitzpatrick has aptly described the relation between "these consequent dimensions of law" as "one of apposition, where apposition could comprehend . . . things being proximate and applied to each other along with their being parallel and opposed"[78] and, following Derrida, as "neither one nor two".[79] This part will

71 Derrida (1988), above n 70, 151. See also reference to "supplementarity" in Derrida (1976), above n 69, and "parergonality" in Jacques Derrida, "The Parergon" in Jacques Derrida, *The Truth in Painting* (Bennington Geoff and McLeod Ian trans., 1987 edn) 37, 54. Also referenced in Ch 4, footnote 43.

72 Ibid.

73 Ibid., 152.

74 Derrida, above n 2, 243.

75 Ibid.

76 Ibid., 251. See also Fitzpatrick, above n 32. In summarising his argument in response to Robert Cover, "Violence and the Word" (1986) 95 *Yale Law Journal* 1601, Fitzpatrick writes, at 167: Such a violence also provided force and sustained focus as the word [of the law] moved, as it always had to move, beyond the confines of its determined "completeness". This movement meant that the word had to be not just violently determining, but also nonviolently responsive to what lay beyond it "for the time being," and that nonviolent responsiveness in its turn could not have effect except in the violence of determination.

77 Derrida, above n 2, 257. See also Jacques Derrida, "On Forgiveness" in Jacques Derrida, *On Cosmopolitanism and Forgiveness* (Mark Dooley and Michael Hughes trans., 1997 edn) 27, 44–5, cited and discussed in Fitzpatrick, above n 22, 332. Derrida writes:

> These two poles, *the unconditional and the conditional*, are absolutely heterogeneous, and must remain irreducible to one another. They are nonetheless indissociable . . . It is between these two poles, *irreconcilable but indissociable*, that decisions and responsibilities are to be taken.

78 Fitzpatrick, above n 4, 104. See also Fitzpatrick, above n 32, 146; 167, on the apposition of violence and nonviolence *within* the law.

79 Jacques Derrida, "The Law of Genre" in Jacques Derrida (Derek Attridge, ed.), *Acts of Literature* (1992) 221, 231, cited in Fitzpatrick, above n 32, 167.

dwell upon the situation of indigeneity within the *open* context of a determinate law. That is, the indeterminacy of indigeneity conceived as *with-in* the law – subject to its determinacy, yet simultaneously constitutive of it.

The creation of the Indigenous subject as a recognisable identity before a determinate law and, more broadly, within a contemporary liberal rights framework, entails the production of an abstraction – "socially produced and negotiated"[80] – the performance of which attracts legal entitlements. As "mystical abstractions",[81] all such identities "fail to correspond fully with any particular social subject or group",[82] being legally recognisable rather than embodied subjectivities. Indeed the very construction of a universal legal subject, it has been suggested, denotes "the kernel only of an embodied human being", "a pure logical cipher, whose only role is to be the abstract support of universal norms and only quality, to possess legal rights and duties".[83] This disembodied, abstracted, 'reasonable man' of liberal jurisprudence is possessed only of "the ability to reason and calculate", in the absence of any particularity or specificity.[84] Such is the logic of the Kantian autonomous subject, which founds modern jurisprudence, whose universal law appears unable to countenance alterity.[85] Indeed, speaking of a Levinasian "jurisprudence of alterity", Smith suggests that "[v]iolence begins in the subsumption of the particular to the universal, and pretensions otherwise only allow the roots of injustice to grow deeper".[86] From an anthropological perspective, Geertz asserts that occidental conceptions of the self, as "a bounded, unique, more or less integrated motivational and cognitive universe", are culturally specific to the West.[87] Instead, individual identity has been described as "a contingent and highly mutable combination of many positions . . . only some of which are generalizable and shared with others".[88] Yet, in the pursuit of universality, it has been asserted that the law predetermines the legal subject within "a circular

80 Povinelli, above n 43, 55.

81 Costas Douzinas, *The End of Human Rights: Critical Legal Thought at the Turn of the Century* (2000) 238.

82 Povinelli, above n 43, 55.

83 Douzinas, above n 81, 267.

84 Alan Norrie, *Crime, Reason and History* (1993) 23, cited in Douzinas, above n 81, 237–8.

85 Immanuel Kant, *Critique of Practical Reason* (Lewis White Beck trans., 1956 edn). See discussion in Douzinas, above n 81, 188–95. For Kant, particularities are subsumed within a generality or universalism: Immanuel Kant, *Critique of Judgment* (JC Meredith trans., 1964 edn) 18.

86 Nick Smith, "Questions for a Reluctant Jurisprudence of Alterity" in Desmond Manderson (ed.), *Essays on Levinas and Law: A Mosaic* (2009) 55, 57–8.

87 Clifford Geertz, "From the Native's Point of View: On the Nature of Anthropological Understanding" in Paul Rabinow and WM Sullivan (eds), *Interpretive Social Science* (1979) 225, 229, cited in Iver B Neumann, "Self and Other in International Relations" (1996) 2(2) *European Journal of International Relations* 139, 140.

88 Costas Douzinas, "Identity, Recognition, Rights or What Can Hegel Teach Us About Human Rights?" (Sept 2002) 29(3) *Journal of Law and Society* 379, 402.

relationship": "The law presupposes the existence of subjects and its rules define their capacities, powers, immunities and duties . . ."[89] It is this presupposition that denies the particularity of the subject before the law, who is encapsulated within the "equalizing" or "universalizing logic of the law", which "always fails the uniqueness of the other".[90]

This static notion of universality, however, is contested, most particularly in the context of the law. Fitzpatrick has argued that "the claim to the universal can never be achieved in its own terms".[91] That is, "[i]t can never be 'truly' universal and thence all-inclusive because of its dependence on what must remain ever beyond it".[92] That which is beyond, he continues, "marks the place of the postcolonial and institutes its 'ambivalence'".[93] As previously outlined, the law, in its aspiration to generality and universality, is also dependent upon that which is extrinsic to it, in "unrestrained responsiveness . . . result[ing] in its not having any enduring content of its own".[94] This antinomic quality of law enables the mutual constitution of the general and particular, determinate and indeterminate, conditional and unconditional. Derrida describes "[t]hese two regimes of law, of *the* law and the laws", as "both contradictory, antinomic, and inseparable . . . incorporat[ing] one another at the moment of excluding one another . . . dissociated at the moment of enveloping one another".[95] In seeking to secure completeness and coherence, the law persists in perpetually repressing an alterity within itself, reasserting its universality in an "implosive ambivalence" that is repressive of "what transgressively opposes yet constitutes it".[96] In describing this "exteriority which is yet of the law, this law of the law", Fitzpatrick cites Blanchot, for whom this law "entails . . . 'a responsibility . . . towards the Other'".[97] This Other, to an extent that I will later qualify, may be conceived as the alterity that is indigeneity, to which the law is responsible and by which it is constituted, and yet also as that which the law simultaneously denies, in the assertion of a static Indigenous legal subject.[98] While the application of the law may "move beyond the assertion of particular power and receptively [respond] to possibility",[99] determinate legal recognition entails a specific application of the general –

89 Douzinas, above n 81, 233.
90 Ibid., above n 88, 403.
91 Fitzpatrick, above n 20, 217.
92 Ibid.
93 Ibid.
94 Fitzpatrick, above n 20, 225.
95 Derrida, above n 5, 79–81.
96 Fitzpatrick, above n 20, 216, citing Gary Boire, 'Ratione Officii': Representing Law in Postcolonial Literatures" (1994) 27(4) *Mosaic* 199, 202, 204, 207, 211.
97 Ibid., 223, citing Maurice Blanchot, *The Unavowable Community* (Pierre Joris trans., 1988 edn) 43.
98 I make this qualified claim in the context of Derrida's limited recourse to Levinas's ethics of alterity, in Derrida, above n 2, 250.
99 Fitzpatrick, above n 20, 226.

"law's 'generality must be specific'"[100] – a movement inevitably occasioning the violent determination of the subject before it. For Indigenous peoples, this entails the recognition of a particularised conception of indigeneity, which must be performed in order to prove entitlement.

In examining various (mis)recognitions of indigeneity, it is necessary to broadly distinguish notions of identity and subjectivity. Following Venn, I would suggest for the present purposes that the latter refers to the dynamic of an internal self, in accordance with which an individual acts and reacts in the world.[101] This definition relates to my articulation of 'indigeneity' in Part I, which included the notion of Indigenous subjectivity.[102] This should be distinguished from 'identity', which refers to those aspects of the subject denotative of appreciable *difference* – that is, categorisations "correlated to particular performative practices and routines of action".[103] Moreover, identity refers to those aspects of the subject that are recognisable as indicative of a particular (preconceived) identity. This would extend to those markers of indigeneity recognised by Australian law, such as an identifiable genealogy in determinations of Aboriginality,[104] or the sufficiency and vitality of an Indigenous "normative system" of "rights and interests" in determining native title.[105] It is the tension between Indigenous subjectivities and identities with which I am, here, principally concerned.

In the context of the pursuit of cultural and economic attachments and entitlements, the identity ascribed to Indigenous peoples has been described as "a narrow target, which is easily over- or undershot".[106] Niezen describes such constraints:

> Today the term is both a fragile legal concept and the indefinite, unachievable sum of the historical and personal experiences of those gathered in a

100 Franz Neumann, The Democratic and the Authoritarian State: Essays in Political and Legal Theory (1957) 28, cited in Fitzpatrick, above n 20, 226.

101 See Couze Venn, *The Postcolonial Challenge: Towards Alternative Worlds* (2006) 79, in which he defines subjectivity as a self, the product of an interiorization of attitudes, values, expectations, memories, dispositions, instantiated in inter-subjective relations and activities that, though historically specific and self-reflective processes of recognition, constitute a particular named person, a singularity.
See also Sarah E Roberts-Cady, "Rethinking Justice with Levinas" in Manderson, above n 86, 241, who describes a Levinasian approach to subjectivity, to which I will return in this part: "Subjectivity is a kind of response to otherness; I find myself involved with others in the very moment of finding myself".

102 See Chapter 1, footnote 26.

103 Venn, above n 101, 79.

104 See *Shaw v Wolf* (1998) 163 ALR 205, in which the definition of "Aboriginality" was examined at length. See also legislative definition, in *Aboriginal and Torres Strait Islander Act* 2005 (Cth) s 4(1), in which "Aboriginal person" is defined as "a person of the Aboriginal race of Australia", and "Torres Strait Islander" as "a descendant of an indigenous inhabitant of the Torres Strait Islands".

105 *Bodney v Bennell* (2008) 249 ALR 300, 311.

106 Michael R Dove, "Indigenous People and Environmental Politics" (2006) 35 *Annual Review of Anthropology* 191, 194.

room who share, at the very least, the notion that they have all been oppressed in similar ways for similar motives by similar state and corporate entities.[107]

For Paradies, these "powerful tropes" are marshalled in the construction of a "distinct, coherent and thus relatively homogeneous pan-Indigenous social and political community", and an associated "communal shared identity".[108] While such an identity may enable legal and political recognition, such constructions necessarily define and confine indigeneity, thereby "interpellat[ing] every Indigenous person . . . through a plethora of stereotyped images . . . that coalesce around specific fantasies of exclusivity, cultural alterity, marginality, physicality and morality".[109] Such fantasies evoke an unachievable image of indigeneity, to which the Indigenous person is required to aspire, *yet fail* to embody. Indeed for Povinelli, this failure is, itself, the very identity that Indigenous peoples are called to perform. She writes: "To be truly Aboriginal, indigenous persons must . . . occupy a place in a semiotically determined social space", in which 'tradition' resides in the past tense.[110] Notions of "customary law", "ancient tradition", and "traditional culture" are recognisable to the settler state, yet only as "residual", located in "the now fragmentary bodies, desires, and practices of Aboriginal persons" – traditions to be lamented as lost.[111]

The sustained performance of this static cultural identity, Povinelli argues, entails a "discursive passage into being", whereby indigeneity exists only in the difference between the actual Indigenous subject and "the full presence promised by the phrase 'indigenous tradition' and thus the identity 'indigenous'".[112] Indigeneity is thereby always already constituted as a failure, identifiable in the "scars" or "lacerated bod[ies]" that are indicative of "the ancient customs that define(d) their difference".[113] In this context, determinate legal and political recognition of indigeneity involves a recognition of and response to this scarring, and an assessment of "[w]hat institutional suturing was and is necessary to keep this lacerated body functional".[114] Confinement to this position entails the 'forgetting' discussed in Part I, whereby indigeneity is encountered not as a contemporary alterity, but as constructed in accordance with a putative past 'authenticity' and

107 Ronald Niezen, *The Origins of Indigenism: Human Rights and the Politics of Identity* (2003) 4.

108 Yin C Paradies, "Beyond Black and White: Essentialism, Hybridity and Indigeneity" (2006) 42 *Journal of Sociology* 355, 356.

109 Ibid., 357.

110 Povinelli, above n 43, 48.

111 Ibid.

112 Ibid., 49.

113 Ibid., 48.

114 Ibid., 49.

judicial allegiance to the founding myths of a determinate colonial sovereignty,[115] contingent upon non-Indigenous acts of remembrance and forgetting.[116]

This constrained positioning, however, is only ever " 'for the time being', a determinative bringing of what is beyond into the normatively determinate".[117] Indeed, Fitzpatrick argues, "[w]ithin the determinate, within the realized law there would still subsist the unrealized possibility of its opening to, or falling into, being otherwise", such that "[t]his possibility always remains anterior to the law iterably made determinate", an "incipience . . . [that] remains within that law".[118] While the "universalising and neutralizing rhetoric" of the law frequently and historically "serves particular imperial interests by elevating them to some absolute condition",[119] the law remains ever open and receptive to possibility.[120] In my examination of Australian native title jurisprudence, and the construction of the Indigene within it, I am particularly concerned with the appearance of alterity within a determinate law, where the latter elevates such imperial interests.[121] In the context of postcolonial nations, the responsive dimension of law is principally concerned "to orient the movement of law imperially",[122] thereby subordinating alternative constructions and orders to itself. Such orientation and subordination is evident in the determinate configuration of indigeneity within contemporary legal and political discourses.

Subjects of empire

The subordination of Indigenous alterity to the violent exercise of non-Indigenous sovereignty is evident in national and international "discourse[s] of recognition",[123] which entail the pursuit of legal and political recognition and postcolonial reconciliation. Both implicit and explicit within these discourses is the fundamental "assumption that adequate recognition of the other's true identity *will* bring about reconciliation".[124] That is, according to Schaap, reconciliation as the advent of a "shared horizon", enabling the recognition of past injustices and the formation

115 Brenna Bhandar, " 'Spatialising History' and Opening Time: Resisting the Reproduction of the Proper Subject" in Scott Veitch (ed.), *Law and the Politics of Reconciliation* (2007) 93, 107. See also Peter Fitzpatrick, "No Higher Duty: Mabo and the Failure of Legal Foundation" (2002) 13 *Law and Critique* 233.

116 Chris Healy, *Forgetting Aborigines* (2008) 4–5. I will return to this duality in Chapter 7, in the context of the archive.

117 Fitzpatrick, above n 20, 225.

118 Ibid., 226.

119 Ibid., 225, citing Boire, above n 96.

120 Ibid., 226.

121 Fitzpatrick, above n 115, 238.

122 Ibid.

123 Andrew Schaap, "Political Reconciliation Through a Struggle for Recognition?" (2004) 13 *Social Legal Studies* 523, 524.

124 Ibid.

of "a new civic friendship".[125] Yet, such notions of 'true' or 'distinct' identity are dependent upon an "ideal of authenticity",[126] to which an individual is perpetually tethered, and which "must be recovered and restored to its proper place".[127] This notion of the proper is evocative of Nancy's conception of the interior creation of identity *within* the self, as difference *proper*[128] – a notion to which I will return in this part.

The inauguration of indigeneity, as both a local and a global marker of identity, entailed the creation of an international movement described as "indigenism" – a movement "that aspires to promote and protect the rights of the world's 'first peoples'", numbering an "estimated three hundred million people from four thousand distinct societies".[129] The now "improper antecedents" to the term – "barbarian", "savage", "primitive" – have been replaced, and its ownership, according to Niezen, is "changing hands".[130] Indeed, whereas 'indigenous' was previously a "technical term", applied to "the original and culturally distinct occupants of state or colonial territory", it has now been appropriated as a tool for empowerment: "It has acquired a 'we'".[131] While the first reference to the term at international law[132] appeared at a time when Indigenous peoples were commonly identified by scholars as "primitives",[133] the international social, political, and legal identity now afforded Indigenous peoples, it is asserted, is "embodied in those who sit together at [UN] indigenous conferences and working group meetings".[134] Moreover, where Indigenous identity has been, arguably, forged via collective dispossession – "the runny eyes, the angry, frustrated faces, the lost knowledge, the desecrated land and the hopelessness"[135] – this discourse

125 Schaap, above n 123, 524.

126 Ibid., 526, 527. Cf Derrida's discussion of forgiveness that, he argues, should not be reduced to "some political therapy of reconciliation": Derrida, above n 77, 45. See also Borrows's problematisation of "reconciliation" in Australia: John Borrows, "Practical Reconciliation, Practical Re-Colonisation?" (May 2004) 2(27) *Land, Rights, Laws: Issues of Native Title* (Native Title Research Unit, AIATSIS).

127 Ibid., 527.

128 Nancy, above n 49, 10.

129 Niezen, above n 107, 4.

130 Ibid., footnote 3, 224.

131 Ibid. See also Steven Robins, Comment on Adam Kuper, "The Return of the Native" (Current Anthropology Forum on Anthropology in Public, June 2003) 44(3) *Current Anthropology* 398.

132 International Labour Organization (ILO) Convention (No. 107) *Concerning the Protection and Integration of Indigenous and Other Tribal and Semi-Tribal Populations in Independent Countries* (1957), accompanied by the ILO Recommendation (No. 104) (1957).

133 Niezen, above n 107, 4.

134 Ibid., 4. See also Sharon Helen Venne, *Our Elders Understand Our Rights: Evolving International Law Regarding Indigenous Peoples* (1998), especially 68–94.

135 Mick Dodson, "Linking International Standards with Contemporary Concerns of Aboriginal and Torres Strait Islander Peoples" in Sarah Pritchard (ed.), *Indigenous Peoples, the United Nations, and Human Rights* (1998) 18, cited in Niezen, above n 107, 56.

of survival is contested.[136] While acknowledging that "the pain of loss and disempowerment give [Aboriginal people] common cause with the indigenous nations of the world", Lehman maintains that "the politics of survival are not our culture" but, rather, "a measure of the days we live in".[137] In this context, Indigenous identity is now also forged via the pursuit of legal recognition of individual and collective rights, in a variety of international and national fora. Despite the fervour of aspirations to recognition in the context of contemporary liberal identity politics, however, I will suggest that the alterity of indigeneity remains unrecognisable to a determinate law; further, in appearing before the law, indigeneity is subsumed by the "impossible object" of a preconceived authenticity.[138] Where the Indigenous person seeks legal recognition by elaborating "local imaginaries and translocal economic, political and social facts", she is met only with a "law of recognition that places a limit on exactly this type of creativity".[139]

In the Canadian context, Coulthard has argued that "recognition has emerged as the hegemonic expression of self-determination within the Indigenous rights movement".[140] Yet, he opposes the recognition described by Taylor, that is "'granted' . . . or 'accorded' . . . to a subaltern group or entity by a dominant group or entity", thereby failing to "modify, let alone transcend, the breadth of power at play in colonial relationships".[141] The politics of recognition, he argues, subsume individual and collective identification within the production of revivified "Indigenous subjects of empire".[142] The production of such subjects is reflective of the creation of colonial subjects, whose very history was erased in their reconstitution within empire. In the context of colonial Africa, for example, it has been suggested that the erasure of African history via the machinery of British colonial law "did not simply redeem native subjects, but actively constituted them."[143] The colonised are brought into being as historical fragments, "relegated to a timeless past without a dynamic, to a 'stage' of progression", to be "brought

136 See Greg Lehman, "Being Black" in Goran Burenhult (ed.), *Traditional Peoples of Today – The Illustrated History of Human Kind* (1994) 89; Jim Everett, "Aboriginality in Tasmania" (2000) 12 *Siglo* 2. Everett describes Aboriginality as a "philosophical set of rules that are manifested in customary cultural practices, set in a belief of the Great Spirit which comprises our Spiritual All".

137 Ibid., 89.

138 Povinelli, above n 43, 6.

139 Ibid., 7.

140 Coulthard, above n 40, 438.

141 Ibid., 442–3, citing, respectively, Charles Taylor, *Reconciling the Solitudes: Essays on Canadian Federalism and Nationalism* (1993) 148; and Charles Taylor, "The Politics of Recognition" in Amy Guttman (ed.), *Re-Examining the Politics of Recognition* (1994) 25, 41.

142 Ibid., 439.

143 Ravit Reichman, "Undignified Details: The Colonial Subject of Law" (2004) 35(1–2) *ARIEL* 81, 97.

into History by the active principle embodied in the European".[144] Indeed, as Fitzpatrick asserts, the very creation of "the native and the native law and custom" by European colonists constituted an antithesis to the simultaneous creation of occidental law and custom.[145] Accordingly, the law of postcolonial nation states reconfigures the Indigene as its subject, who is (only then) capable of legal recognition.

The Indigenous subject thereby constructed has been described as "a national noumenal fantasy",[146] which an Indigenous person must perform in order to receive legal recognition. Povinelli describes the Australian nation notionally "stretch[ing] out its hands to ancient Aboriginal laws (as long as they are not 'repugnant')", demanding the performance of "an authentic difference in exchange for the good feelings of the nation and the reparative legislation of the state".[147] Such demands, she writes, are generative of "impossible desires" in the Indigenous claimant: "*to be* this impossible object and to transport its ancient prenational meanings and practices to the present".[148] Where a determinate law demands this embodiment, the appearance of an actual Indigenous person is preconstituted as a failure of authenticity. That is, in terms of Nancy's challenge to the Hegelian dialectic of mutual recognition, the Indigene is (mis)recognised as the "difference *proper*",[149] which is the difference constitutive of the Indigenous legal subject, conceived not by the Indigenous person but by a determinate and imperially oriented law.[150] The alterity of indigeneity therefore remains unrecognisable since, Povinelli argues, the law "always already constitutes indigenous persons as failures of indigeneity as such".[151] Accordingly, the Indigene remains encapsulated within the "strategic 'domestication' of the terms of recognition".[152]

Contrary to an Hegelian conception of pure intersubjectivity, as discussed in Part I, whereby "[s]elf-consciousness exists . . . only in being acknowledged",[153]

144 Peter Fitzpatrick, *The Mythology of Modern Law* (1992) 110. Fitzpatrick here cites Frantz Fanon, *Black Skin, White Masks* (Charles Lam Markmann trans., 1967 edn), who elaborates a history of this violent fragmentation. Fitzpatrick writes:

> Such an ultimate negation by imperialism was profoundly identified by Fanon as the fragmentation of a life once lived and the consequent rigidification of the fragments, the dynamic of which is now external to them.

145 Ibid., cited and discussed in Reichman, above n 143, 97.

146 Povinelli, above n 43, 55. Povinelli's use of the term "noumenal" here is, presumably, a reference to Kant's notion of the "noumenon", which he defined as "object in itself", as distinct from a phenomenon, perceived via the senses: Immanuel Kant, *Critique of Pure Reason* (John Miller Dow Meiklejohn trans., 1855 edn) 185.

147 Ibid., 6.

148 Povinelli, above n 43, 6.

149 Nancy, above n 49, 10.

150 Fitzpatrick, above n 115, 238.

151 Povinelli, above n 43, 39.

152 Coulthard, above n 40, 451, citing Isabelle Schulte-Tenckhoff, "Reassessing the Paradigm of Domestication: The Problematic of Indigenous Treaties" (1998) 4(2) *Review of Constitutional Studies* 239.

153 Hegel, above n 47, 111.

others have presented recognition in the context of colonised nations as a relation of domination, "contiguous with the deployment of power".[154] Drawing upon the work of Sartre and Levinas, Yar has argued that recognition necessarily demands a violent reduction of the Other:

> To 'recognize' the other, to render her known, understood, interpretable, is to rob her of her alterity or difference, to appropriate and assimilate her into a sameness with my own subjectivity. As such, this represents the abrogation of a primordial ethical responsibility, the respect for others in their alterity.[155]

Recognition of a subject by "the Big Other of legal and social institutions" has been described not as a dialogue, but "a monologue in which aspects of self are recognized or not".[156] Yar draws attention to the work of Althusser in this respect, where the latter describes the interpellation of the subject "into trans-subjective structures of meaning by the 'big other' of ideological apparatuses".[157] While liberal ideology purports to enable the unencumbered articulation of myriad identities, such articulations are facilitated via the assertion of rights – which, to be recognised by the law, are necessarily circumscribed. Existentialist critics of the Hegelian dialectic, such as Sartre and Fanon, advocate the self-liberation of the other, as discussed previously. Sartre argues that "Hegel does not even conceive of the possibility of a being-for-others which is not finally reducible to a 'being-as-object'".[158] Realisation of self-consciousness via the Hegelian dialectic, in which the self requires recognition "defined by [his] own need", diminishes the Other, rendered a mere reflection of the self.[159] Via this objectification, her alterity is "lost, discarded, violated, consumed"; moreover, Yar describes the encounter as "specular, cognitive and representational anthropophagy . . . an imperialism whereby I colonize the other person as part of the circuit of my own self-conscious identification".[160] For Fanon, escape from the encapsulation of colonial (mis)recognition requires

154 Schaap, above n 123, 531. See also Fanon, above n 144, 179. Fanon here articulates his much quoted self-affirmation: I should constantly remind myself that the *real* leap consists in introducing invention into existence. In the world through which I travel, I am endlessly creating myself. I am part of Being to the degree to which I go beyond it.

155 Majid Yar, "Recognition and the Politics of Human(e) Desire" (2001) 18(2–3) *Theory, Culture & Society* 57, 62.

156 Douzinas, above n 88, 385.

157 Yar, above n 155, 61, citing Louis Althusser, "Ideology and Ideological State Apparatuses (Notes towards an Investigation), in Slavoj Žižek (ed.), *Mapping Ideology* (1994) 100, 128. Yar writes:

> In Althusser's work the logic of the subject's coercive objectification reappears via the interpellative insertion of the individual into trans-subjective structures of meaning by the "big other" of ideological apparatuses.

158 Jean-Paul Sartre, *Being and Nothingness* (Hazel E Barnes trans., 1969 edn) 225, 238.

159 Yar, above n 155, 63.

160 Ibid.

that the colonised initiate her own process of decolonisation, via a process of self-creation and self-recognition.[161]

Such self-recognition in the context of a fraught identity politics, however, is a troubled endeavour. Within the context and confines of the identity politics and rights discourses of postcolonial nations, differing expressions of Indigenous identity have been articulated in the pursuit of differing interests. Whereas literary presentations frequently depict more varied, dynamic indigeneities, I have suggested that Indigenous people may adopt alternate, static conceptions of the Indigenous in the strategic pursuit of legal and political rights and interests. Such seeming caprice has been generative of some criticism and, moreover, has opened the very notion of indigeneity to debate. I will return to this particular debate shortly, following some consideration of these various uses, and the inherent "paradoxes of rights".[162]

Strategic engagement with rights discourses as a political tool, and the associated assertion of particularised identities, have been problematised elsewhere, particularly in the work of Brown, who describes rights as inherently paradoxical, simultaneously reinforcing existing normative contexts while appearing to empower particular social and cultural groups.[163] She suggests that "rights for the systematically subordinated tend to rewrite injuries, inequalities, and impediments to freedom", yet "the absence of rights in these domains leaves fully intact these same conditions".[164] Furthermore, Brown argues that an assertion of identity founded upon an inscription of "suffering, injury, or inequality" necessarily "lock[s] us into the identity defined by our subordination",[165] thereby "shoring up a fictional identity".[166] Where rights articulate that which the subordinated is denied, they appear as that which "we cannot not want", thereby entrapping individuals and groups within a dominant narrative, in which the particular voice of the marginalised is silenced.[167] The pursuit of legal and political entitlements entails the assertion of rights founded not upon particular and varied Indigenous conceptions of indigeneity, but upon those assumed by the state.[168] Within such

161 See Fanon, above n 144, 179.

162 Brown, above n 38, 420.

163 Ibid., 420, 422–3.

164 Ibid., 431–2.

165 Ibid., 423.

166 Ibid., 429. See also Wendy Brown, Regulating Aversion: Tolerance in the Age of Identity and Empire (2006) 38–47.

167 Ibid., 430. Brown writes: "That which we cannot not want is also that which ensnares us in the terms of our domination".

168 This constraint is evident in the Australian law of native title. Consider this constraint also in the international context of the *United Nations Declaration on the Rights of Indigenous Peoples*, adopted on 7 September 2007, taking note of the recommendation of the Human Rights Council contained in its Resolution 1/2 of 29 June 2006, by which the Council adopted the text of the Declaration. See http://social.un.org/index/IndigenousPeoples/DeclarationontheRightsofIndigenousPeoples.aspx accessed 6 October 2015 ('Declaration on the Rights of Indigenous Peoples').

paradox, however, Brown identifies a unique capacity for political agitation, where paradox presents a challenge to "received authority, goes against the doxa".[169] This capacity may be compared to a Deleuzian analysis of the simulacrum as a challenge to the *doxa* of 'common sense' in the law, to which I will return in detail in Part IV, which is productive of both rebellion and uncanniness, thereby opening new spaces of discourse. Citing the work of Butler, Brown presents the paradox of rights as a challenge to normative conditions, where the marginalised voice exists simultaneously within and without "the universal":

> Speaking and exposing the alterity within the norm (the alterity without which the norm would not 'know itself') exposes the failure of the norm to effect the universal reach for which it stands, exposes what we might underscore as *the promising ambivalence of the norm.*[170]

This 'promising ambivalence' may be usefully utilised by marginalised groups, including Australian Indigenous peoples, in the exposure of the ambivalences of the law. Specifically, where the law requires the performance of particularised Indigenous norms, the exposure of such norms as unachievable demands, via the expression of alternate indigeneities within Indigenous literature, reveals the requirements of the law to be paradoxical.

169 Brown, above n 38, 431.

170 Judith Butler, *Excitable Speech: A Politics of the Performative* (1997) 91, cited in Brown, above n 38, footnote 14, 434.

Chapter 6

An impossible object

Return of the native

Despite the exposure of such paradox, strategic conformity to and performance of the cultural norms of indigeneity specified within the law (such as those pertaining to native title), in the pursuit of entitlement to land and waters or to social and political rights, subjects Indigenous claimants to accusations of cultural fraud. In a broadly assimilationist argument, Sandall has criticised that which he terms "the culture cult" – a fetishised pursuit of tradition, evinced in an "aggressive ethnic assertiveness".[1] Sandall depicts Australian Indigenous peoples as victims of a Rousseauian romantic primitivism: "[i]lliterate, vocationally disabled, unpresentable outside the ethnographic zoos they live in . . . Australia's contribution to the New Stone Age".[2] Citing the "Hindmarsh Island Affair",[3] Sandall blithely dismisses those Indigenous cultural interests claimed in the case as "imaginative lying", "liberating fictions" and manipulations on the part of opponents to the building of the bridge, identifying a putative "traditional cost in terms of cruelty, pain and disease" to be borne by those advocating a "romantic primitivism".[4] While presenting a clear and, perhaps, compelling critique of governmental policy failures in Indigenous communities, and of the vulnerability of indigeneities to modern fetishisation, Sandall's approach to Indigenous claims to cultural specificity is, I would suggest, more indicative of an inverse romanticisation of modernity.

1 Roger Sandall, *The Culture Cult: Designer Tribalism and Other Essays* (2001) 17, citing Ernest Gellner, *Spectacles and Predicaments* (1979).

2 Ibid., 17. See also Peter Sutton, "The Politics of Suffering: Indigenous Policy in Australia since the Seventies" (10 April typescript) revised version of the Inaugural Berndt Foundation Biennial Lecture, University of Western Australia (23 September 2000).

3 *Kartinyeri v Commonwealth* (1998) 195 CLR 337. This case concerned the validity of the *Hindmarsh Island Bridge Act 1997* (Cth), enacted in response to opposition to development of a bridge between Hindmarsh Island (Kumarangk), situated in the Murray River delta in South Australia, and the mainland. The development was "opposed on environmental grounds and on Aboriginal heritage grounds, particularly by a group of Ngarrindjeri women claiming to be the custodians of secret 'women's business' concerning the creation and renewal of life for which the island had traditionally been used" (337). The court ultimately held that the Act was constitutionally valid.

4 Sandall, above n 1, 9.

In a more nuanced argument, Sutton has asserted that "[o]bjectifying and putting values on 'culture' is . . . a Western idea"[5] and, further, that "[t]raditional culture, as something to be preserved even at high cost, has been overrated".[6] Denouncing "propaganda images of idyllic, art-producing, close-to-the-earth remote settlements in picture-postcard locations", Sutton poignantly distinguishes that which has been euphemistically termed 'Aboriginal disadvantage' from that which he describes as the "politics of suffering".[7] In discussing internal Indigenous conflict and violence, Sutton argues that the romanticisation of Indigenous culture does little to remedy colonial racist stereotypes. He writes:

> [T]o idealise and romanticise the classical Aboriginal past as nothing but a time of peace and harmony also does no justice to the evidence and no service of historical truthfulness towards the very people one may admire and respect.[8]

Sutton speaks of a waning cultural relativism, including "comprehensive recognition of Aboriginal customary law", as "the poignant failure of a great idea".[9] He denounces the view that a fractured or broken customary law can "rise like a phoenix from its own ashes and come back to restore law and order among the people" and, rather, argues that Indigenous identity, customary law and practice are now mediated by "large-scale social integration", which may render the loss of customary law traditions irreversible.[10] Nonetheless, discussing liberal aspirations to a notion of political reconciliation between Indigenous and non-Indigenous Australia, Sutton alludes to the persistent cultural difference of "non-literate [Indigenous] friends . . . [who] do not tire of criticising white man's law for being on paper and open to change, whereas theirs is in their minds and landscapes and is unchanging and thus superior".[11] Despite Sutton's assertion of an apparently irreversible movement toward cultural homogeneity, demonstrable cultural difference persists. I would argue that it is the negotiation and assertion of such difference within legal and political discourses that elicit non-Indigenous accusations of cultural artifice.

Beyond Australia, similar contestation – specifically over the meaning and application of the term 'Indigenous' – reached a particular crescendo in a

5 Peter Sutton, *The Politics of Suffering: Indigenous Australia and the End of the Liberal Consensus* (2009) 63.
6 Ibid., 65.
7 Ibid. See especially Chapter 3, "The Trouble with Culture", 87. See also discussion in Larissa Behrendt, "The Relevance of the Rights Agenda of Practical Reconciliation" in Rosemary Hunter and Mary Keyes (eds), *Changing Law: Rights, Regulation and Reconciliation* (2005) 137, 144.
8 Ibid., 91.
9 Ibid., 144.
10 Ibid., 157–8.
11 Sutton, above n 5, 199.

controversial article published in 2003, entitled "The Return of the Native".[12] This article brought renewed vigour to contestation over the term, and was followed by strident defences of the notion of indigeneity, and its social, political and legal uses.[13] Anthropologist Kuper roundly critiqued the concept of indigeneity as a fabrication, "the rhetoric of the indigenous-peoples movement",[14] a divisive romanticisation in which "people have been obliged to reformulate their ethnic identities" in the pursuit of resources.[15] Kuper identifies in Indigenous land claims an appeal to "essentialist ideologies of culture and identity",[16] reliant upon "obsolete anthropological notions and on a romantic and false ethnographic vision".[17] Describing "loaded terms 'native' and 'indigenous'" as regressive euphemisms for "primitive",[18] Kuper proceeds to argue that assertions of originary status via descent in land claims are flawed where human societies are historically mixed, such that the claims of Indigenous peoples are indefensible against those of later immigrants.[19] Ultimately, he laments that "[a] drift to racism may be inevitable where so-called cultural identity becomes the basis for rights".[20]

These assertions elicited several animated responses, at first instance, in which the meanings and uses of the concept of indigeneity were, once again, deconstructed. Suzman supports Kuper's equation of the 'indigenous' with the 'primitive', and the notion that Indigenous rights narratives are punctuated by "the novel invocation or reconceptualization of [Western] concepts such as 'history', 'culture', and 'tradition'".[21] Furthermore, he maintains, the frustrations of minority cultures, such as Southern Africa's San people, are derived not from an incapacity to "pursue their 'traditional culture' but because they are impoverished, marginalized, and exploited by the dominant population".[22] Omura

12 Adam Kuper, "The Return of the Native" (Current Anthropology Forum on Anthropology in Public, June 2003) 44(3) *Current Anthropology* 389.

13 See Comments on Adam Kuper, "The Return of the Native" (Current Anthropology Forum on Anthropology in Public, June 2003) 44(3) *Current Anthropology*. See also Justin Kenrick and Jerome Lewis, "Indigenous Peoples' Rights and the Politics of the Term 'Indigenous'" (2004) 20 *Anthropology Today* 4; Alan Barnard, "Indigenous Peoples: A Response to Justin Kenrick and Jerome Lewis" (2004) 20 *Anthropology Today* 19; Alan Barnard, "Kalahari Revisionism, Vienna and the 'indigenous peoples' Debate" (2006) 14(1) *Social Anthropology* 1; Discussion: "The Concept of Indigeneity" (2006) *Social Anthropology* 14(1) 17. For an overview of this ongoing debate, see Jaimal Sandhu, "'Caliban Rediscovered? On the Rise of the Global Indigenous Movement" (2012) 1 *Burgmann Journal* 27.

14 Kuper, above n 12, 390.

15 Ibid., 394.

16 Ibid., 395.

17 Ibid.

18 Ibid., 389.

19 Ibid., 392.

20 Ibid.

21 James Suzman, Comment on Adam Kuper, "The Return of the Native" (Current Anthropology Forum on Anthropology in Public, June 2003) 44(3) *Current Anthropology* 389, 399.

22 Ibid., 400.

asserts that claims "based on the [Euro-American] assumptions of ties of blood and soil" bear little resemblance to "the reality of indigenous peoples' societies",[23] which should be assessed on daily practice rather than through the lens of "Euro-American essentialist ideology".[24] Furthermore, despite the acknowledged contribution of "the indigenous peoples movement" to recognition of collective rights and empowerment, Omura critiques this movement for a reliance upon essentialism, at risk of "amplif[ying] the differences among ethnic groups and thus exacerbat[ing] ethnic frictions".[25] In the absence of some reformulation of such constructions, "the 'primitive'" will indeed "be restored to life under the veil of the 'indigenous'".[26]

In opposition, Plaice argues that Kuper's position, though perhaps the only tenable one in the opposition between relativist arguments for diversity and aspirations to an appreciation of human commonality, fails not only to address past inequalities and "blatantly racist politics", but to safeguard against the perpetuation of such politics and "the seemingly inevitable erosion of diversity".[27] Ramos vigorously refutes Kuper's claims, asserting that the latter's "discomfort with the term 'indigenous'" as a euphemism for primitivism "is to blame the conquered for the conqueror's bad language".[28] Furthermore, Robins suggests that it is Kuper himself who "seems to expect indigenous peoples to conform to their primordial identity narratives", where many Indigenous groups draw upon "the resources of global civil society to reconstitute themselves as 'traditional communities'".[29] Accordingly, he suggests that "anthropology should not strive to reduce subaltern voices and histories to a sanitized and standardized version of the anthropologist's 'truth'", lest we regress to "good old-fashioned ethnographic authority".[30]

Asch and Samson have identified this "equation of 'primitive' and 'indigenous'" in Canadian Indigenous claims, "applied by the state to minimize recognition of indigenous rights" in the course of adherence to precedent, according to which the Indigenous party must prove "it was sufficiently 'organized' prior to European settlement to bring the case'".[31] In response to Kuper's critique of the defence of

23 Keiichi Omura, Comment on Adam Kuper, "The Return of the Native" (Current Anthropology Forum on Anthropology in Public, June 2003) 44(3) *Current Anthropology* 389, 395.
24 Ibid., 396.
25 Ibid., 395.
26 Ibid.
27 Evie Plaice, Comment on Adam Kuper, "The Return of the Native" (Current Anthropology Forum on Anthropology in Public, June 2003) 44(3) *Current Anthropology* 396, 397.
28 Alcida Rita Ramos, Comment on Adam Kuper, "The Return of the Native" (Current Anthropology Forum on Anthropology in Public, June 2003) 44(3) *Current Anthropology* 397, 397.
29 Robins, above n 131 (Ch 5), 398.
30 Ibid., 399.
31 Michael Asch and Colin Samson, Discussion of Adam Kuper, "The Return of the Native" (April 2004) 45(2) *Current Anthropology* 261, 261.

Indigenous peoples on the grounds of primitiveness and original occupation, these authors affirm that "indigenous rights . . . arise as a consequence of the recognition that people lived in societies prior to European settlement and the acknowledgment that certain rights flow from this fact".[32] Furthermore, they assert, "it is the opponents and not advocates of indigenous rights who found their position on such racist stereotypes".[33]

Kenrick and Lewis cite an alternative definition of indigenous to that which they describe as "Kuper's caricatured and essentialist definition" – that of Saugestad, "who suggests that the term 'indigenous' is following a similar path to that travelled by 'ethnic' and that we need to understand it in a relational rather than an essentialist way".[34] According to Kenrick and Lewis, such an approach would focus upon issues of power and dispossession and the relation between these, in the context of which the Indigenous describes not "some quintessential primitive" but the dispossessed, and Indigenous rights "a strategy for resisting dispossession that employs a language understood by those wielding power".[35] This relational approach bears upon the ways in which such resistance is enacted, where attempts to seek recognition of rights to particular lifestyles and land use must be articulated "within structures of authority that systematically discriminate against them".[36] Assertion of Indigenous rights is, in the authors' opinion, "part of an emerging international political process", and an acknowledgment that equality must be founded upon "recognition and negotiation of difference rather than simply on enforcing cultural homogeneity alongside ever-increasing economic inequality".[37] Turner suggests that "Kuper's caricature of indigenous movements as motivated by atavistic fantasies about 'primitive' *Naturvölker* serves only to deflect attention from the real historical and social basis of indigenous struggles".[38] In contrast to Kuper's attachment to notions of descent in identifying indigeneity, Turner proposes a definition of Indigenous identity and "relative historical priority of occupancy of a territory" derived from "kinship, affinal, and adoptive relations", as opposed to the "legal calculus of patrilineal descent and limited numbers of collateral degrees employed by the governments of some modern

32 Michael Asch, *Home and Native Land: Aboriginal Rights and the Canadian Constitution* (1984); *Calder et al v Attorney General of British Columbia* (1973) 34 DLR (3d) 145; *R v Van der Peet* (1996) 137 DLR (4d) 289, all cited in Asch and Samson, above n 31 (Ch 5), 261.

33 Asch and Samson, above n 31, 262.

34 Justin Kenrick and Jerome Lewis, Discussion of Adam Kuper, "The Return of the Native" (April 2004) 45(2) *Current Anthropology* 263, 263.

35 Ibid., 263.

36 Ibid.

37 Elizabeth Povinelli, "The State of Shame: Australian Multiculturalism and the Crisis of Indigenous Citizenship" (Winter 1998) *Critical Inquiry* 575; Deborah Bird Rose, "Indigenous Ecologies and an Ethic of Connection" in Nicholas Low (ed.), *Global Ethics and Environment* (1999) 175, both cited in Kenrick and Lewis, above n 34, 263.

38 Terry Turner, Discussion of Adam Kuper, "The Return of the Native" (April 2004) 45(2) *Current Anthropology* 264, 265.

nation-states".[39] Ultimately, Kuper responded with a reassertion of his initial conclusion, that "essentialist ideologies of culture and identity", upon which he suggests Indigenous land claims are premised, are "obsolete" and "romantic", and "may have dangerous political consequences".[40]

This discussion was followed by an extended response from Barnard, published in 2006, and a further discussion.[41] Barnard argues that "[t]here is no, and can be no, theoretically-unproblematic *anthropological* definition of 'indigenous'". Rather, he suggests, it is "a legal concept", which may be a "useful tool for political persuasion".[42] Indeed, he suggests, "[t]he legitimate claims of 'indigenous peoples' appeal not to objective elements of anthropological theory, but to common identities objectified by participants".[43] Further discussion ensued, examining distinctions between essentialist and relational concepts of indigeneity. Kenrick suggests that, while claims to the 'indigenous' in the international sphere may tend to essentialism, they challenge the presentation of a "eurocentric perspective as universal"; moreover, he argues, while essentialist, the international discourse of indigeneity may be the only discourse available to counter colonial hegemony,[44] including in the courtroom.[45] While cautioning against the reductionism of a distinctive "indigenous difference", Plaice similarly supports its adoption in the pursuit of social justice.[46] Thuen also defines 'indigeneity' as a necessary "image self-constructed by the subordinate under restrictions set by the superordinate discourse".[47] Wolfe describes the imposition of a "repressive authenticity" in claims to indigeneity, where such claims are "addressed" to the coloniser,[48] whereas Zips argues that "the common denominator of 'indigeneity'" facilitates the pursuit of "equality, procedural justice and a universal right of self-determination",[49] which should not be denied to those "forming a new alliance around a term that they certainly did not invent".[50]

Such vehement contestation is indicative of a unique investment of "political capital" in the term[51] that, for Indigenous peoples, provides unprecedented

39 Turner, above n 38.

40 Adam Kuper, Reply to Discussion of Adam Kuper, "The Return of the Native" (April 2004) 45(2) *Current Anthropology* 265, 266.

41 Barnard (2006), above n 13; Discussion: "The Concept of Indigeneity" (2006) *Social Anthropology* 14(1) 17.

42 Barnard (2006), above n 13, 7–8.

43 Ibid., 13.

44 Justin Kenrick, "Discussion: The Concept of Indigeneity" (2006) *Social Anthropology* 14(1) 17, 19.

45 Ibid., 20, citing Marc Pinkoski and Michael Asch, "Anthropology and Indigenous Rights in Canada and the United States: Implications in Steward's Theoretical Project" in Alan Barnard (ed.), *Hunter-Gatherers in History, Archaeology and Anthropology* (2004) 187; Povinelli, above n 37.

46 Evie Plaice, "Discussion: The Concept of Indigeneity" (2006) *Social Anthropology* 14(1) 17, 23.

47 Trond Thuen, "Discussion: The Concept of Indigeneity" (2006) *Social Anthropology* 14(1) 17, 24.

48 Patrick Wolfe, "Discussion: The Concept of Indigeneity" (2006) *Social Anthropology* 14(1) 17, 27.

49 Werner Zips, "Discussion: The Concept of Indigeneity" (2006) *Social Anthropology* 14(1) 17, 27–8.

50 Ibid., 28.

51 Dove, above n 43 (Ch 1), 193.

opportunities for activism and economic empowerment. Furthermore, the demands of Indigenous peoples at both national and international levels have been described as "a manifestation of claims for recognition and distributive justice over goods that International Law has assigned exclusively to states", which may include but are not limited to 'rights'.[52] Álvarez Molinero describes the claims of the Lubicon Cree, an Indigenous nation in Alberta, Canada, who appealed to international law, demanding not mere recognition of rights but "a recognition of their identity as subjects with capacities, necessities and values far beyond the limits offered by the State".[53] In seeking those rights afforded Indigenous peoples at an international level, such as are contained within the Declaration on the Rights of Indigenous Peoples, Indigenous communities are frequently compelled to fashion themselves in accordance with specific demands and conceptions of authenticity.[54] Yet, in the context of Indonesia, Li has suggested that the very articulation of indigeneity "opens up room to maneuver that might otherwise be unavailable, even if some of the elements employed in this articulation are essentialized".[55] Although such "strategic essentialism"[56] has been critiqued as bearing little or no resemblance to actual contemporary societies,[57] its use as a tool by minority communities speaks more of the ideological demands of non-Indigenous political and legal institutions than of the integrity of those communities themselves. Moreover, as Robins argues, such "essentialist constructions of identity are not necessarily incompatible with an active embrace of the contradictions of modernity", where land claims require the performance of a certain 'authenticity' so as not to be dismissed as "false and opportunistic".[58]

52 Natalia Álvarez Molinero, "From the Theory of Discovery to the Theory of Recognition of Indigenous Rights: Conventional International Law in Search of Homeopathy" in Saladin Meckled-García and Başak Çali, *The Legalization of Human Rights: Multidisciplinary Perspectives on Human Rights and Human Rights Law* (2006) 165, 166.

53 Ibid., 173.

54 See Dove, above n 43 (Ch 1), 194, citing Jean E Jackson, "Culture, Genuine and Spurious: The Politics of Indianness in the Vaupés" (1995) 22(1) *American Ethnologist* 3; Jean E Jackson, "The Politics of Ethnographic Practice in the Columbian Vaupés" (1999) 6(2–3) *Identities* 281; Laura Pulido, "Ecological Legitimacy and Cultural Essentialism" in Daniel Richard Faber (ed.), *The Struggle for Ecological Democracy: Environmental Justice in the United States* (1998) 293; Tania Li, "Ethnic Cleansing, Recursive Knowledge, and the Dilemma of Sedentarism" (2002) 173 *International Journal of Social Sciences* 361.

55 Dove, above n 43 (Ch 1), 199, citing Tania Li, "Articulating Indigenous Identity in Indonesia: Resource Politics and the Tribal Slot" (2000) 42(1) *Comparative Studies in Society and History* 149.

56 Ramos, above n 28, 398, citing Gayatri Spivak's concept of 'strategic essentialism' in the context of "situated activist logics". See also Steven Robins, "Whose 'Culture'? Whose Survival?" in Alan Barnard and Justin Kenrich (eds), *Africa's Indigenous Peoples* (2001); Sidsel Saugestad, Discussion of Adam Kuper, "The Return of the Native" (April 2004) 45(2) *Current Anthropology* 263, 264; Kuper, above n 40, 265.

57 Kuper, above n 12, 395. More generally, on the question of essentialism in the "identity politics" of postcolonial resistance, see Venn, above n 101 (Ch 5), 77–8.

58 Robins, above n 131 (Ch 5), 398.

This paradoxical positioning of indigeneity – as, at once, both recognisably authentic and inauthentically opportunistic – diminishes the Indigenous subject or community to that of an "impossible object" of identification.[59] While the law remains responsive to indigeneities in moments of judicial indecision, thereby revealing the violence of preconstituted norms,[60] the determinate limits of "the skeleton of principle"[61] of the law persist through the violence of their continued (re-)instantiation. The limits imposed by these norms have particular ramifications for Indigenous peoples attempting to claim rights to land, waters and resources on their own terms.

The proper Indigene

In Australia, Povinelli describes the national recognition of indigeneity as operating simultaneously as a "formal meconnaissance[62] of a subaltern group's *being* and of its *being worthy* of national recognition", and as "a formal moment of being inspected, examined, and investigated".[63] Her invocation of the Lacanian term, "meconnaisance", is here intended to emphasise a knowing misrecognition,[64] by which the actual Indigenous subject is violently rejected as incapable of recognition – indeed, as *repugnant.* This notion of repugnancy is an historical reference to repugnancy clauses in colonial legislation, which "excluded practices that were anathema to 'justice, equity and good conscience'".[65] Indeed, in *Mabo*, Justice Brennan held that the incidents of native title rights may be recognised only where the laws and customs of the claimants in question "are not so repugnant to natural justice, equity and good conscience that judicial sanctions under the new regime must be withheld".[66] The assertion of such limitations is reflective of that which Kerruish describes as "a Kantian idiom" in judicial decision-making – a perceived

59 Povinelli, above n 43 (Ch 5), 6.
60 Brown, above n 38 (Ch 5), 420.
61 *Mabo* (1992) 175 CLR 1, 29, discussed in greater detail in the previous chapters.
62 Povinelli, above n 43 (Ch 5), footnote 14, 246.
63 Ibid., 39.
64 Ibid., footnote 14, 246. I do not intend to invoke a detailed Lacanian reading here, but to draw attention to Povinelli's use of the term, which she clarifies in terms of misrecognition:

> I mean "meconnaissance" in the technical Lacanian sense in which misrecognition is not ignorance. Misrecognition represents a certain organization of affirmations and negations, to which the subject is attached. Hence it cannot be conceived without correlative knowledge. If the subject is capable of misrecognising something, he surely must know what this function has operated upon. There must surely be, behind his misrecognition, a kind of knowledge of what there is to misrecognise
>
> (Jacques Lacan (Jacques Alain-Miller, ed.), *The Seminar of Jacques Lacan: Book I, Freud's Papers on Technique, 1953–1954* (John Forrester trans., 1988 edn) 167).

65 Ravit Reichman, "Undignified Details: The Colonial Subject of Law" (2004) 35(1-2) *ARIEL* 81, 97, citing Kenneth Roberts-Wray, "The Adaptation of Imported Law into Africa" (1960) 4(2) *Journal of African Law* 66, 77. See also discussion in Fitzpatrick, above n 144 (Ch 5), 110.
66 See *Mabo* (1992) 175 CLR 1, 160, 162 (Dawson J); 61 (Brennan J).

sense of entitlement and, indeed, obligation to decide matters in certain ways.[67] That is, Kerruish suggests, Kant's application of "this idiom . . . to formal logic's having, as the condition of its success, to abstract from all objects of knowledge and their differences".[68] Such rigidity was evidenced in the 1998 Australian Federal Court decision, *Shaw v Wolf*, in which the definition of 'Aboriginal person' was the subject of explicit and extended examination.[69] While Justice Merkel acknowledged the irony of judicial enquiry into Aboriginality, where "the most dispossessed, dispersed and alienated Aboriginals might find it hardest to establish their descent and identification for the purposes of the Act", he was nonetheless compelled to "determin[e] a practical and realistic approach" to the definition of Aboriginality within the parameters of the Act in question – the *Aboriginal and Torres Strait Islander Commission Act 1989* (Cth).[70] Accordingly, in considering Indigenous laws and customs, as expressions of indigeneity, determinate law is confined to the limits of its own prescribed forms.

In this way, the encapsulation of self or community within the confines of a legally recognisable construction of indigeneity, albeit 'strategically', for the purposes of reclamation of land and waters or the assertion of political or cultural rights, may, in fact, be emphatically disempowering for Indigenous peoples. Where notions of indigeneity are evocative of particular tropes of authenticity – including tradition, custom, laws, and knowledge thereof – those unable to conform to such ideals may be excluded, as insufficiently 'Indigenous'. Indeed, those individuals and groups most dispossessed may encounter the greatest difficulty establishing their 'Indigenous' credentials for the purposes of legal recognition.[71] In terms of principal language spoken, identification with a particular clan, tribal or language group, and familial arrangements, Paradies cites statistics that "suggest that many Indigenous Australians fail to conform to the fantasy of cultural alterity".[72] This difficulty extends to native title claims, in which the requirement to demonstrate the continuation of authentically 'traditional' beliefs, laws, and customs presents an exceedingly challenging task for those most affected by the assimilative effects of colonisation.[73] The appearance of indigeneity before the law is always already circumscribed in the privileging of the 'traditional' over the modern Indigene, such that "the modern must always be displaced or expelled by the jurisdiction

67 Valerie Kerruish, "Imperatives of Extinguishment: Kartinyeri v The Commonwealth of Australia" (2008) 3 Jahrgang DILEMMATA: Jahrbuch der Altonaer Stiftung für philosophische Grundlagenforschung 1, 21.

68 Ibid., footnote 44, citing Immanuel Kant, *Immanuel Kant's Critique of Pure Reason* (1929, Norman Kemp Smith trans., 1982 edn, uncountable reprint of the 1933 (2nd) edn) 18; Immanuel Kant, *Kritik der reinen Vernunft* (1781/87, 1st and 2nd edns, Felix Meinder, PhB 37a, 1956) 15.

69 *Shaw v Wolf* (1998) 163 ALR 205, 208.

70 Ibid.

71 Ibid.

72 Paradies, above n 108 (Ch 5), 356; 358. See also *Shaw v Wolf* (1999) 163 ALR 205, 208.

73 See, for example, *Bennell v Western Australia* (2006) 230 ALR 603, 609 ("*Bennell*").

of the court".[74] In this context, indigeneity and Indigenous Law are (mis)recognised, where "[l]egality and sovereignty are pre-judged as always already British".[75]

Such circumscription is evidenced in Australian native title jurisprudence. In *Bennell v Western Australia*[76] the claimants were required, as a matter of fact, to establish the continuity of the Noongar community since settlement of the land and waters in question in 1829.[77] In order to claim "connection", in accordance with the requirements of s 223(1) of the *Native Title Act*,[78] the applicants were required to assert that

> members of that community had continued, and still continue, to define themselves as Noongars, to share a body of beliefs and to acknowledge and observe some traditional laws and customs, including in relation to land and waters.[79]

At trial, Justice Wilcox held that a determination of native title depends upon the establishment of "the identity of the community whose laws and customs governed the use and occupation of the land within the claim area at the relevant date of settlement", and the present existence of that community, which must continue "to acknowledge and observe those laws and customs, albeit perhaps in an attenuated or somewhat changed form".[80] While this requirement was clarified on appeal,[81] the claimants were still required to demonstrate the "continuous existence and vitality since [British] sovereignty" of a "normative system" of rights and interests.[82] The capacity to self-define as Indigenous and, moreover, as sharing beliefs, laws and customs that may be described as 'normative', may be a difficult task for those most dispossessed, frequently living in diasporic, urban communities. Recognition of an(other) in this context eschews the mutuality of recognition in Hegel's dialectic, in an Orientalist construction of alterity – a predetermination of the other, which renders the recognition of alterity impossible.[83]

74 Judith Grbich, "Tracing the Figure of the Native in Postcolonial Theory and Native Title Law: Enlightenment, Aesthetics and Charles Harpur" (2005) 22 *The Australian Feminist Law Journal* 127, 128.

75 Ibid.

76 (2006) 230 ALR 603.

77 *Bennell* (2006) 230 ALR 603, 604.

78 *Native Title Act* 1993 (Cth).

79 *Bennell* (2006) 230 ALR 603, 604.

80 Ibid., 609.

81 On appeal, this requirement was clarified as referring to "laws and customs", as opposed to "community" (see *Bodney v Bennell* (2008) 249 ALR 300, 311).

82 *Bodney v Bennell* (2008) 249 ALR 300, 311.

83 This assertion and, arguably, radical counter to Hegel, draws upon Levinas's principal distinction between the "other" (*l'autre*) and the "Other" (*Autrui*), the former being that which is reduced to the Same: Levinas, above n 58 (Ch 5), 24–6. I will engage with this distinction at some length in Chapter 8.

In the postcolonial context and subsequent discourses of recognition, the Indigenous subject is conceived not as liberated, but perpetually enmeshed within the proprietorial confines of legal recognition.

The notion of the *proper*, or prescribed (legal) identity, is the performance of an identity capable of legal recognition. This recognition is not of an Other, but of that which the law has (pre)designated. Presenting a challenge to the Hegelian dialectic of recognition, Nancy has described identity as created via the always already (mis)construed identity of the other. Indeed, in creating identity, he asserts, the self creates the other: "[I]dentity *makes difference*", thereby "relegat[ing] the other to a self (or to an absence of self) that is different".[84] In this way, identity – "the Self that identifies itself" – makes "difference *proper*";[85] that is, the difference from the self, which yet remains the *property* of the self. Reading Nancy on this point, Bhandar argues that this "proper(tied) nature of identity and difference" is embodied within "an ontological 'economy of the same' in which difference is not really difference at all, but a presupposed, assumed counterpart to the self-same subject".[86] In the context of legal recognition, the subject is always already construed *as difference*, yet as difference that is *proper* to the law – that is, as the property of the law. For Nancy, the "true *plural* is excluded": "The path of self-consciousness can easily lead through desire and recognition of the other, but it is *traced beforehand* as the circular process of the Self of this consciousness".[87]

Bhandar describes the (mis)recognition of Indigenous subjectivity before the law in colonial settler contexts, the former defined in terms of "Anglo-European norms of private property ownership and colonial sovereign power".[88] Perpetually constrained by an allegiance to a 19th-century "ghostly subject", the Indigene is "confined by the spectre of a racialised, propertied being".[89] Bhandar elsewhere applies similar criticism to the situation of the Aboriginal subject before the law in the Canadian courts, in which recognisable difference is limited to that which may be contained within "the boundaries of the liberal democratic capitalist state".[90] Assuming the 'frozen rights' approach to Aboriginal claims – that is, a consideration of claims to traditional rights in accordance with evidence of precolonial occupation – the law configures the Aboriginal subject, and her capacity and right, without recourse to the claimant's own articulations of subjectivity.

84 Nancy, above n 49 (Ch 5), 10.

85 Ibid.

86 Bhandar, above n 50 (Ch 5), 142. Bhandar's notion of a restricted economy of recognition here draws upon Derrida's analysis of the Hegelian dialectic: Jacques Derrida, "From Restricted to General Economy: A Hegelianism without Reserve" in Jacques Derrida, *Writing and Difference* (2002) 317.

87 Nancy, above n 49 (Ch 5), 11 (second emphasis added).

88 Brenna Bhandar, "Plasticity and Post-Colonial Recognition: 'Owning, Knowing and Being'" (2011) 22(3) *Law and Critique* 227, 236.

89 Ibid.

90 Bhandar, above n 50 (Ch 5), 142.

Although the Canadian requirement for continuity is more concerned with occupation than custom and tradition,[91] Canadian Aboriginal title remains subject to the "inherent limit" that it "cannot be used in a manner that is irreconcilable with the nature of the attachment to the land which forms the basis of . . . [this title]",[92] thereby continuing to privilege the maintenance of putatively originary rights. Echoing the words of Justice Brennan in his decision in *Mabo*, who refused the adoption of those "notions of justice and human rights" that "would fracture the skeleton of principle of the common law which gives the body of our law its shape and internal consistency",[93] Bhandar argues that the *actual* recognition of difference in Canadian courts – necessary to the process of decolonisation – "would bend the overarching structure of the nation state out of shape and radically alter its boundaries".[94] Both of these statements are reflective of the limits of a law that, in its recognition of indigeneity, is productive of mere misrecognition. Indigeneity is thereby subsumed within the "repressive authenticity"[95] of a presupposed legal subjectivity.

In the foregoing analysis of the determinate Indigenous legal subject as a misrecognition and appropriation of indigeneity, I have sought to emphasise the ways in which indigeneity, as alterity, is subordinated to the mythic violence that founds and preserves the law.[96] Specifically, the ways in which indigeneity, and Indigenous Law, are subordinated to the (re)instantiation of Australian law, founded as it is upon the fiction of *terra nullius* and the assertion British sovereignty. Motha describes this reinstantiation in the *Mabo* decision, which "reinforced the founding violence of [the law's] origin by shielding certain aspects of the common law from deconstruction . . . by invoking the amorphous notion of a 'skeletal principle'".[97] Defined and confined by the discourses that informed her 'discovery', the Indigene nonetheless remains a haunting alterity, both disruptive and constitutive of the legal archive.[98] Derrida conceives of this archive ontologically,

91 See *Delgamuukw v British Columbia* (1997) 153 DLR (4th) 193.

92 Ibid., 240–1. See also Lisa Strelein, " 'Beliefs, Feelings and Justice' – Delgamuukw v British Columbia: A Judicial Consideration of Indigenous Peoples' Rights in Canada" (1998) *Land, Rights, Laws: Issues of Native Title* (Issues Paper No 22).

93 (1992) 175 CLR 1, 29.

94 Bhandar, above n 50 (Ch 5), 142. I will return to this notion of "bending" in chapter 9, in the course of a discussion of the Freudian notion of the "*unheimlich*" or "unhomely".

95 Mark Harris, "Mapping Australian Postcolonial Landscapes: From Resistance to Reconciliation?" (2003) 7 *Law/Text/Culture* 71, 75; 83.

96 Benjamin, above n 8 (Ch 5). See also discussion thereof in Derrida, above n 2 (Ch 5), 265.

97 Motha, above n 2 (Ch 5), 92. This reference to 'skeletal principle' is to *Mabo* (1992) 175 CLR 1, 29 (Brennan J), cited in Part I. I reiterate it here:

> In discharging its duty to declare the common law of Australia, this Court is not free to adopt rules that accord with contemporary notions of justice and human rights if their adoption would fracture the skeleton of principle which gives the body of our law its shape and internal consistency.

98 See Derrida, above n 51 (Ch 5), 91.

as a source of law and authority, constitutive of the past itself, "which retrospectively, or retroactively gives it so-called final truth".[99] Indeed, in the case of law, it has been suggested that "precedent is the process by which the past gets produced by the present, so that it can then be cited as the producer of the present".[100] In this context, I will now turn to examine the constitution of the Indigene *with-in* the legal archive as both a legal and political act, and as a simultaneous act of remembrance and forgetting.[101]

99 Jacques Derrida, "Archive Fever in South Africa" in Carolyn Hamilton, Verne Harris, Michèle Pickover, Graeme Reid, Razia Saleh and Jane Taylor (eds), *Refiguring the Archive* (2002) 38, 42.

100 Stanley Fish, Doing What Comes Naturally: Change, Rhetoric, and the Practice of Theory in Literary and Legal Studies (1989) 514, cited in Fitzpatrick, above n 4 (Ch 5), 90.

101 See Verne Harris, "A Shaft of Darkness: Derrida in the Archive" in Hamilton *et al.*, above n 99, 75, 165, who counters conventional conceptions of the archive as a repository for memory. I will discuss this further in the following section. See also discussion in Karin van Marle, "Constitution as Archive" in Scott Veitch (ed.), *Law and the Politics of Reconciliation* (2007) 215, 216–17.

Chapter 7

The legal archive

An originary indigeneity

While indigeneity persists as an alterity to which the law remains responsive, it is nonetheless an originary alterity that the law must forget, "absorbing the dimensions of the origin" within itself, "leaving law bereft of any originating reference exterior to it".[1] In this way, the legal archive may be understood not as a repository of memory, but as a site of simultaneous remembrance and forgetting. The apparent completeness and authority of the archive act to constitute the past, necessitating a forgetting of the law that results in its becoming a mere technology, a *prosthesis* for memory, where its originary impetus is now indistinct. Where the legal Indigene is constructed by the law, this construction is also haunted by the spectral visitation[2] of an originary Indigene – a truth, which always "slips away".[3] Indigeneity persists within Australian law as its threatening origin, a ghost in every decision, an ungraspable and undecidable alterity, which renders the positioning of indigeneity uncertain, unsettling and uncanny – in Freudian terms, *unheimlich*.[4] Indeed, as Biber has suggested, native title claims elicit the terror of the unhomely via the "necessity to reach into a dark and unknown place – Freud's 'locked cupboard of history' – to locate and seize the principles it will apply".[5]

1 Fitzpatrick, above n 4 (Ch 5), 70.
2 Derrida, above n 51 (Ch 5), 84.
3 Ibid., 91.
4 This concept of the "uncanny" refers to Sigmund Freud, "The 'Uncanny'", in Albert Dickson (ed.), *The Pelican Freud Library: Art and Literature*, Vol. 14 (1990). In this essay, Freud articulates a circular or continuous conception of the *heimlich* ("homely") or *heimisch* ("native") and the *unheimlich* ("unfamiliar", "strange" or "unhomely"), whereby an experience of uncanniness occurs when the latter is evoked within the space of the former (201). See also discussion in Homi Bhabha, *The Location of Culture* (1994) (Routledge Classics Edition, 2004) 9; Katherine Biber, "Being/Nothing: Native Title and Fantasy Fulfilment" (2004) 3 *Indigenous Law Journal* 1, 12. I will return to consider this concept in the following chapters.
5 Biber, above n 4, 13.

The archive is described by Derrida in terms of Greek etymology,[6] as the *arkhē*, a place of convergence, a name that coordinates two principles: "the *commencement* and the *commandment*".[7] That is,

> the principle according to nature or history, *there* where things *commence* . . . [and] . . . the principle according to law, *there* where men and gods *command*, *there* where authority, social order are exercised, *in this place* from which *order* is given – nomological principle.[8]

Derrida further describes the *arkhē* as inaugurating, as "the originary, the first, the principial, the primitive . . . the commencement", which follows the "even more, *even earlier*", "the *arkhē* of the commandment".[9] As a founding, or instituting source of law, the archive documents "speak the law: they recall the law and call on or impose the law".[10] The archive is physically entrusted to the "archons", who possess the hermeneutic power "in the jurisdiction of this *speaking the law*".[11] This notion of the place of jurisdiction is a reference to the *arkheion*, "a house, a domicile, an address",[12] where "discernible acts of interpretation occur".[13] The *archons* are guardians of the archive and, further, are "accorded the hermeneutic right and competence . . . the power to interpret the archives", which "recall the law and call on or impose the law".[14]

Shetty and Bellamy describe Derrida's conception of the archive as "a 'thinking' of the law that approaches it not so much discursively as ontologically" and, further, as "a juridical concept, an attempt at a general theory of how the law becomes institutionalized *as law*".[15] An understanding of the archive is concerned with "the place and the law according to which the archontic becomes instituted"[16] – that is, a theory of "the law which begins by inscribing itself there and of the right which authorizes it".[17] Yet, when considering "the moment *proper* to the archive", or "the instant of archivisation", Derrida is concerned with the archive not as "so-called live or spontaneous memory (*mnēmē or anamnēsis*), but rather a certain

6 See Sandhya Shetty and Elizabeth Jane Bellamy, "Postcolonialism's Archive Fever" (Spring 2000) 30(1) *Diacritics* 25, 28.
7 Derrida, above n 51 (Ch 5), 1.
8 Ibid.
9 Ibid., 2.
10 Ibid.
11 Ibid.
12 Ibid.
13 Shetty and Bellamy, above n 6, 28.
14 Derrida, above n 51 (Ch 5), 2.
15 Shetty and Bellamy, above n 6, 27.
16 Derrida, above n 51 (Ch 5), 3.
17 Ibid., 4.

hypomnesic and prosthetic experience of the technical substrate".[18] That is, the inauguration or originary moment of archivisation as mediated by the technical apparatus of the archive itself and, further, of the archive not as conceptual but notional, yet as that which leaves an impression, "an unknowable weight".[19]

The British assertion of sovereignty on "[t]his continent, named Australia by Captain Matthew Flinders",[20] entailed the institution of a legal archive that is, in Derrida's terms, guarded by the authority of British sovereignty. The acts of those British subjects determined to colonise and prosper in the "great southern continent"[21] were authorised by this sovereign, thereby inaugurating a distinct legal narrative. Derrida alludes to the "institutional implementation" of the archive – that is, "the law which begins by inscribing itself there and of the right which authorizes it".[22] That is, once again, a notion of the "origin of law" as "arriving from outside the law":

> The foundation of all states occurs in a situation that one can thus call revolutionary. It inaugurates a new law; it always does so in violence . . . this founding or revolutionary moment of law is, in law, an instance of nonlaw . . . But it is also the whole history of law.[23]

The claim to sovereignty simultaneously entails the creation of the legal archive, its bounds and limits articulated, authored and *authorised* by the sovereign. This is, for Derrida, "the institution of limits *declared* to be insurmountable", evidenced in "a politics of the archive"; indeed, he asserts, "[t]here is no political power without control of the archive, if not of memory".[24]

This political power and control are of unique significance in considering the instantiation of the Australian legal archive, authorised by the false premise of *terra nullius* and the claim to British sovereignty.[25] In native title jurisprudence the

18 Derrida, above n 51 (Ch 5), 25.

19 Ibid., 29. On the paradox of inauguration, see Pierre Legendre, "*Le Désir Politique de Dieu: Étude sur les montages de L'État et du Droit* (1988) 160, cited in Yifat Hachamovitch, 'The Ideal Object of Transmission: An Essay on the Faith which Attaches to Instruments (*de fide instrumentorum*)' (1991) 2(1) *Law and Critique* 85, 100: "[T]he inaugural inaugurates nothing at all; it consists in saying that which must be said, in making that which must be made, in putting texts in their place and in putting into play *our relation to the gods*."

20 Ambelin Kwaymullina, "Introduction: A Land of Many Countries", in Sally Morgan, Tjalaminu Mia and Blake Kwaymullina (eds), *Heartsick for Country: Stories of Love, Spirit and Creation* (2008) 6, 6.

21 The discovery of this land was, for the initial British explorers, a disappointment. See Paul Carter, *The Road to Botany Bay: An Essay in Spatial History* (1987) 23: "The chief discovery of the *Endeavour* was its discovery of nothing or, rather, of the non-existence of a great southern continent . . ."

22 Derrida, above n 51 (Ch 5), 4.

23 Derrida, above n 2 (Ch 5), 269.

24 Ibid., 4. I will return to this notion of memory.

25 *Mabo* (1992) 175 CLR 1. I will return to a more fulsome analysis of the legal premise of *terra nullius* in Part III (Law).

fiction of this premise is made most explicit where, I will argue, the very title recognised is derived not from "effective indigenous law"[26] but is a creation of the common law, "utterly subordinated and thoroughly complected by [the radical title of sovereign power]".[27] I will not engage here with substantive questions of sovereignty and its founding in Australia,[28] but draw attention to the elision of indigeneity entailed in its assertion.[29] The tenuous foundation of the common law in Australia, it is suggested, contains "the panic-tinged scent of the phantasm in legal foundation but also the arbitrary sacrifice of indigenous peoples shoring up that foundation".[30] Indeed, for Derrida, the "founding origin of law . . . defers the problem of justice", which "will have been posed and violently resolved . . . buried, dissimulated, repressed".[31] Where justice has been described as "the movement of deconstruction . . . in the law",[32] however, and deconstruction as "a deconstruction of the phantasm . . . of any putatively pure origin",[33] the unconditionality that literature reveals in the common law is demonstrative of the persistence of an Indigenous alterity within the legal archive, as an *impression* that haunts the archival narrative of Australian law. While legal constructions of the Indigenous subject and the requirements of 'traditional' connection enshrined within the law constrain Indigenous communities in their attempts to articulate Indigenous Law, the legal archive is revealed to be a mere palimpsest, its originary ghosts perceptible beneath the apparently inviolate constructions of contemporary jurisprudence.

An essential ghost

The compilation of this legal narrative, institutionalised as an archive, may be understood in terms of Derrida's notion of the "archontic principle" of the archive as one of "consignation . . . of gathering together".[34] The creation of the archive

26 Fitzpatrick, above n 115 (Ch 5), 243.
27 Ibid., 248.
28 For a discussion of the perplexing foundation of sovereignty, and in particular "Kant's injunction against enquiry into such matters", see ibid., 233.
29 See William P MacNeil, " 'It's the vibe!': The Common Law Imaginary Down Under" in Leslie J Moran, Emma Sandon, Elena Loizidou and Ian Christie (eds), *Law's Moving Image* (2004) 31.
30 Fitzpatrick, above n 115 (Ch 5), 242, citing Judith Grbich, "The Scent of Colonialism: Mabo, Eucalyptus and Excursions within Legal Racism" (2001) 15 *Australian Feminist Law Journal* 119, 123–4.
31 Derrida, above n 2 (Ch 5), 252.
32 Ibid., 254.
33 Michael Naas, *Derrida from Now On* (2008) 191. Naas here cites Jacques Derrida, *Monolingualism of the Other, or The Prosthesis of Origin* (Patrick Mensah trans., 1998 edn), in which Derrida writes, at 46:

> [T]he first impulse of what is called "deconstruction" carries it toward this "critique" of the phantasm or of the axiom of purity, or toward the analytical decomposition of a purification that would lead back to the indecomposable simplicity of the origin.

34 Derrida, above n 51 (Ch 5), 3.

is conceived as a (violent) act of unification, whereby material documents are gathered in one place, "this place of election where law and singularity intersect in *privilege*".[35] That is, the privilege of the *archons*, who govern the archive.[36] This is a gathering into singularity, of "the One", of "the Unique", which is "the law of the *consignation* which orders the archive".[37] For Derrida, the gathering of this singularity, the One, establishes the bounds of the archive and its authority, but in so doing, incorporates the other, whereby the one is "the condition of the other. And the Other is the condition for the One".[38] He writes:

> The One guards against/keeps some of the other. It protects *itself* from the other, but, in the movement of this jealous violence, it comprises in itself, thus guarding it, the self-otherness or self-difference (the difference from within oneself) which makes it One . . . the One as the Other.[39]

In this way, the archive is a place of haunting, such that the archive itself is conceived as spectral, "a trace always referring to another whose eyes can never be met".[40] It gestures toward truth, but only as a trace, "repressed or suppressed".[41] Derrida describes the archive as akin to a delusion in psychoanalysis, as "the hallucinatory haunting of the archaeologist".[42] In order to "decipher" or "read" the truth of the archive, "one must take into account a *prosthesis*, this 'distorted substitute'".[43] Yet, "a part of truth remains, a piece or a grain of truth breathes at the heart of the delusion, of the illusion, of the hallucination, of the hauntedness".[44] Indigeneity, I continue to argue, persists as this spectre or haunting, as that which "remains caught, as a ghost at least, but an essential ghost, in every decision, in every event of decision".[45] This haunting is, for Derrida, productive of "*mal d'archive*", or "archive fever", an impassioned search for origin.

35 Derrida, above n 51 (Ch 5), 3.

36 See also Franz Kafka, "The Problem of Our Laws" in Franz Kafka (Nathum Norbert Glazer, ed.), *The Complete Stories of Franz Kafka* (Willa Muir and Edwin Muir trans., 2005 edn) 437.

37 Derrida, above n 51 (Ch 5), 78.

38 Ibid., 79. See also useful discussion in Gilbert Leung and Matthew Stone, "Otherwise than Hospitality: A Disputation on the Relation of Ethics to Law and Politics" (2009) 20 *Law and Critique* 193, 201–3.

39 Ibid., 78. This notion also appears in the work of Jean-Luc Nancy, as *transimmanence*, described as "the amorphous line between immanence and transcendence, interiority and exteriority", such that "the other elusively distinguishes itself from the same while simultaneously haunting the same from within": Leung and Stone, above n 38, 201, citing Jean-Luc Nancy, *The Sense of the World* (1997) 55.

40 Ibid., 84.

41 Ibid., 87.

42 Ibid.

43 Ibid., citing Sigmund Freud, "Delusions and Dreams in Jensen's 'Gradiva' (1906–07)" in Sigmund Freud, *The Standard Edition of the Complete Psychological Works of Sigmund Freud* (James Strachey trans., 1953–1974 edn) 80.

44 Ibid., 87.

45 Derrida, above n 2 (Ch 5), 253.

Archive fever may be understood as a simultaneous imperative to remember and forget – to recall an originary truth, yet to forget it – since the archive is formed via the destruction of origin in anticipation of the future. Indeed, comparing the archive to the Freudian death drive, Derrida describes the former as an "archiviolithic force" that "leaves nothing of its own behind", such that "the archive takes place at the place of originary and structural breakdown of the said memory".[46] In this way, the alterity of indigeneity is subsumed within the determinate parameters of the legal Indigene, remaining only as a ghost appearing in moments of justice. It is a 'ghost', or spectre, since it is not conditional or determinate, but unconditional and, indeed, impossible. It is, however, an 'essential' ghost, since the very construction of the legal Indigenous subject is contingent upon its haunting by the alterity that is indigeneity.

In speaking of *mal d'archive*, translated as archive sickness or fever, Derrida describes a search or passion for an origin, "an irrepressible desire to return to the origin, a homesickness, a nostalgia for the return to the most archaic place of absolute commencement".[47] To be consumed by archive fever is, moreover, "to burn with passion . . . never to rest, interminably, from searching for the archive right where it slips away" and further, "to run after the archive, even if there's too much of it, right where something in it anarchives itself".[48] Where the archive is conceived as a gathering in singularity, archive fever is a desire to locate the instituting impetus of the archive, the truth of commencement, the source of law and authority. Yet, the violence of the archive is in its "*superrepression* (suppression and repression) . . . the possibility of putting to death the very thing . . . which *carries the law in its tradition*, the archon of the archive . . . and the subject of the law".[49] For the objects of this passionate violence – in the context of this book, Indigenous people – this 'superrepression' entails a forgetting of indigeneity itself, as a complex expression of myriad subjectivities and 'life-ways', and of Indigenous Law,[50] and a persistent constraint on attempts to pursue claims to country and associated cultural and political identities.

46 Derrida, above n 51 (Ch 5), 11; generally, 10–20. At 11, he writes:

> [T]his archiviolithic force leaves nothing of its own behind. As the death drive is also, according to the most striking words of Freud himself, an aggression and a destruction (*Destruktion*) drive, it not only incites forgetfulness, amnesia, the annihilation of memory, as *mnēme* or to *anamnēsis*, but also commands the radical effacement, in truth the eradication, of that which can never be reduced to *mnēme* or to *anamnēsis*, that is, the archive, consignation, the documentary or monumental apparatus as *hypomnēma*, mnemotechical supplement or representative, auxiliary or memorandum . . . the archive takes place at the place of originary and structural breakdown of the said memory.

47 Ibid., 91.

48 Derrida, above n 51 (Ch 5), 91.

49 Ibid., 79.

50 Marcia Langton, "The 'Wild', the Market and the Native: Indigenous People face New Forms of Global Colonization" in William M Adams and Martin Mulligan (eds), *Decolonizing Nature: Strategies for Conservation in a Post-Colonial Era* (2003) 79, 80.

Van Marle has discussed the relation between the archive and memory, and between memory and forgetting, in the context of the archive in post-Apartheid South Africa. She argues that the archive is not, as conventionally understood, concerned with the preservation of memory, but is productive of forgetting. She writes: "Derrida emphasizes the fact that the archive is not simply a recording of the past, but that it constitutes the past".[51] Nevertheless, "[t]his constitution of the past is done with a future in mind, 'which retrospectively, or retroactively gives it so-called final truth'".[52] The archive is comprised of "subjective constructions with their own histories of negotiations and contestations"; yet, in the pursuit of a putatively objective and neutral production of history, it was "vested with 'the power to speak the truth' . . . and thus became the place of commencement despite the fact that it held only selections of the past".[53] Whereas the archive is conventionally conceived as closed and finite, Derrida reveals a contingency and contextuality that must be forgotten, appearing as a mere trace. The archive is constructed from memory, yet its instantiation requires a forgetting of its origins. Harris emphasises this duality:

> This notion of the archive, as Derrida has shown in Archive Fever . . . is bullshit. There is no remembering without forgetting. There is no remembering that cannot become forgetting. Forgetting can become a deferred remembering. Forgetting can be a way of remembering.[54]

Where this simultaneous urge – remembrance and forgetting – exemplifies the modern project, and its construction of an authoritative and universal legal archive, indigeneity has persisted as "the emblematic primitive against which the European order defined its modernity".[55] Following Derrida I would suggest, however, that this forgetting and the violence it entails for those constructed by the law is not fixed but momentary, where the archive is haunted by the alterity of its origin. As previously discussed in terms of the universal, Fitzpatrick has identified the origins of modernity not within itself, but within that which is other to it, whereby "the powerful pretensions of modernity" collapse in the face of an originary alterity:

> The claim to universality would bring the origin ever within, but what it would thereby bring within cannot be known and contained and so, it contests the universality, the completeness and coherence of modernity. The origin, then, is rendered both proximate and threatening.[56]

51 Van Marle, above n 101 (Ch 6), 216–17.
52 Derrida, above n 99 (Ch 6), 42, cited in van Marle, above n 101 (Ch 6), 216–217.
53 Ibid.
54 Harris, above n 101 (Ch 6), 75. See also discussion in van Marle, above n 101 (Ch 6), 216–17.
55 Stephen Muecke, *Ancient and Modern: Time, Culture and Indigenous Philosophy* (2004) 138.
56 Fitzpatrick, above n 4 (Ch 5), 44.

Further, as Fitzpatrick argues, "the sustaining force . . . of the origin does not come from its being a stilled or set template"; rather, the origin "is at the limit of the condition originated, cannot be contained within it and goes ever beyond it".[57] In this way, the threat of an originary alterity persists, where the authority of the archive is constituted by a simultaneous remembrance and forgetting. The Indigenous subject oscillates between the "colonial desire for a 'reformed, recognisable Other'", and a "fear of the Other's immutable difference".[58] In so doing, the construction of the Indigene as a legal subject is perpetually disrupted by the alterity of indigeneity as a spectre *with-in* the law itself, as its very origin.

The desire for an origin, *mal d'archive* – that is, for the place of institution – may be conceived as a simultaneous desire for the Other and for the truth of the Other. That is, the Other as an absolute Other to the law, within a Levinasian ethics, constituted by desire. Although a Levinasian ethics of alterity is commonly characterised as a "transcendental mode of thinking", whereby the Other is absolutely irreconcilable and unassimilable with the Same, Derrida's approach here may be more akin to Nancy's notion of 'transimmanence', whereby "[t]he self is a self only because it is in intimate relation with the other, a self which is transimmanently 'one as the other'".[59] Levinas gestures toward this, describing subjectivity as "the other in the same . . . the restlessness of the same disturbed by the other".[60] In discussing the two modes of law that frame this part – determinate and indeterminate, conditional and unconditional – and the movement of indigeneity between these, before and beyond the law, I will now consider an application of Levinas's ethics of alterity, and a Derridean response.

57 Fitzpatrick, above n 4 (Ch 5), 89–90.

58 Rod Macneil, "Time after Time: Temporal Frontiers and Boundaries in Colonial Images of the Australian Landscape" in Lynette Russell (ed.), *Colonial Frontiers: Indigenous-European Encounters in Settler Societies* (2001) 47, 51–2, citing Homi Bhabha, "Of Mimicry and Man: The Ambivalence of Colonial Discourse" (1984) 28 *October* 125.

59 Leung and Stone, above n 38, 202.

60 Ibid.

Chapter 8

Indigeneity as Other

Desiring indigeneity

> Desire is desire for the absolutely Other.[1]
>
> The law, colonial or otherwise . . . is . . . a site of desire, both authoritarian and resistant, a site where desire is actualized.[2]

Within the (*open*) context of the Indigene before the law, I have described the alterity of indigeneity as existing in a particular tension with the law, as that which animates it and, ultimately, constitutes it. While the law strives to determine indigeneity as a finite, knowable object, suitable for legal recognition, indigeneity remains beyond the law, as the unknowable origin in opposition to which its legal manifestation was and is constructed. Any decision enacted by the law must always pass through "the test and ordeal of the undecidable"; to be fixed otherwise would render it a mere "programmable application" or "continuous unfolding of a calculable process".[3] Where the law must always pass through this undecidability, whereby a rule is "given, received, confirmed, preserved or reinvented", the legal Indigene is necessarily (re)created at each moment of decision. In this way, the 'test and ordeal' is "never past or passed . . . surmounted or sublated", but remains as a haunting presence *with-in* the law.[4] I have described this presence, or 'impression', as an evocation of justice, conceived as incalculable[5] – that which "exceeds or contradicts law"[6] – and as the "revolutionary moment of law", which simultaneously founds law and is "an instance of nonlaw".[7] It is this infinite

1 Levinas, above n 58 (Ch 5), 34.
2 Gary Boire, "Symbolic Violence: Law, Literature, Interpretation: An Afterword" (2004) 35 (1–2) 231, 236.
3 Derrida, above n 2 (Ch 5), 252.
4 Ibid., 253.
5 Ibid., 244.
6 Ibid., 233.
7 Ibid., 269.

notion that Derrida equates with justice, as distinct from a determinate law, and that may be akin to a Levinasian alterity.

In distinguishing law and justice, Derrida proposes a notion of the latter as "up to a certain point . . . closer to Levinas's".[8] That is, to a Levinasian evocation of justice as equated to the relation with the Other: "la relation avec autrui – c'est a dire la justice [the relation with the other – that is to say, justice]".[9] Derrida describes this relation as a "heteronomic relation to the other [*autrui*], to the face of the other that commands me, whose infinity I cannot thematize and whose hostage I am".[10] This reading follows Levinas's ethical assertion that justice "consist[s] in putting the obligation with regard to the other before obligations to oneself, in putting the other before the same", as an example of the Platonic good, situated above Heideggerian Being.[11] Where, for Derrida, the law "claims to exercise itself in the name of justice", and justice "demands for itself that it be established in the name of a law",[12] the responsibility of the law to justice – that is, to the alterity that is justice – is demonstrative of a constitutive relation between law and justice, law and alterity. In this way, Levinas's rendering of the liberating trauma of the encounter with alterity, whereby the self is created in relation to the infinite Other, may contribute to an understanding of Derrida's notion of momentary justice.

For my purposes, this alterity may be conceived as indigeneity. More fully, in Levinasian terms, whereas the law determines the Indigene as an other (*l'autre*), rendered a static concept and thereby subsumed by the imperatives of an imperially oriented law,[13] the alterity of indigeneity also remains its Other (*Autrui*), for which the law is ethically responsible.[14] As such, indigeneity persists as a spectral haunting within the law, "a ghost . . . but an essential ghost",[15] to which the law is compelled

8 Derrida, above n 2 (Ch 5), 250.

9 Ibid., citing Levinas, above n 58 (Ch 5), 89. In this edition, translated as "the relation with the Other, that is, to justice" (89). See also, at 71: "We call justice this face to face approach, in conversation".

10 Ibid.

11 Levinas, above n 58 (Ch 5), 53.

12 Derrida, above n 2 (Ch 5), 251.

13 Fitzpatrick, above n 115 (Ch 5), 238.

14 Derek Attridge, "Introduction: Derrida and the Questioning of Literature" in Jacques Derrida (Derek Attridge, ed.), *Acts of Literature* (1992) 1, 5–6. Attridge here describes Derrida's approach to "responsibility" as being beyond a Levinasian notion of "ethics", as "not something we simply 'take'" but, rather, as a demand to think or read "otherwise":

> [W]e find ourselves summoned, confronted by an undecidability which is also always an opportunity and a demand, a chance and a risk. Highlighted in Derrida's readings of literary texts are those aspects which make the most demands on us, which are the most difficult to write about in the conventional discourse of criticism because they shake the foundations of that discourse. And Derrida's argument is that it is those aspects which mark literarure *as* literature . . . [since] the "literary" aspects of these texts not only trouble the "philosophical" grounds of the critical discourse but are what make this discourse possible.

15 Derrida, above n 2 (Ch 5), 253.

to respond. Furthermore, it remains resistant to absorption into the Same of the law, appearing not in the recognisable performance of the determinate Indigenous subject before the law but, as I continue to suggest, in literary modes of expression. Such alterity perpetually interrupts the legal narrative, as the movement of deconstruction that is justice. I will return to this suggestion, via a re-engagement with Derrida's "Before the Law",[16] following a brief elucidation of Levinasian ethics.

Ethics, for Levinas, has been described as "the positive movement which takes itself beyond the disdain or disregard of the other . . . beyond the appreciation or possession, understanding and knowledge of the other", which is "*desire*".[17] Rejecting Kant's universality of reason as a foundation of ethics, where "[a] universal thought dispenses with communication . . . renouncing singularity",[18] Levinas conceives of a particular notion of ethics that is not concerned with moral principle, but is the "calling into question [*mise en question*] of the Same – which cannot occur [*se faire*] within the egoistic spontaneity of the Same . . . [but] is brought about [*se fait*] by the Other [*l'Autre*]."[19] That is, a calling into question of the violence of Western philosophy as an ontology, which entraps the Other as concept – as *knowledge*. For Levinas, "the known is understood and so *appropriated* by knowledge", such that "the *other* of thought becomes the characteristic *property* of thought as knowledge".[20] This notion of entrapment may be considered alongside the previous discussion of a preconceived Indigenous subject as *proper* to the law, always already grasped and known by it. Accordingly, Levinas writes, "cognition consists in grasping the individual . . . not in its singularity . . . but in its generality", which results in "their being taken in hand, their domestication, their possession".[21] It is this violence that Levinas identifies in Western ontology, and which he seeks to counter with the notion of metaphysical transcendence in desire for the Other. This Other simultaneously disrupts and constitutes the law, calling its totalising conceptions into question.

Davis provides a useful analysis of Levinas's critique, for whom Western philosophy is "an egology",[22] the "hidden purpose" of which is "always to find a means of offsetting the shock of alterity", thereby "asserting the primacy of the self, the Same, the subject or Being".[23] Accordingly,

16 Derrida, above n 1 (Ch 5), 181.
17 Ibid., above n 61 (Ch 5), 114.
18 Levinas, above n 58 (Ch 5), 72.
19 Ibid., 43.
20 Emmanuel Levinas, "Ethics as First Philosophy" in Sean Hand (ed.), *The Levinas Reader* (1989) 75, 77.
21 Levinas, above n 59 (Ch 5), 50.
22 Levinas's use of this term – "egology" – is derived from Edmund Husserl. In Levinas, above n 59 (Ch 5), 50, he asserts: "Every philosophy is – to use Husserl's neologism – an egology", citing Edmund Husserl, *The Crisis of European Sciences and Transcendental Phenomenology* (David Carr trans., 1970 edn) 255. See also Levinas, above n 58 (Ch 5), 44.
23 Colin Davis, *Levinas: An Introduction* (1996) 40.

> the Other is acknowledged only in order to be suppressed or possessed; as in the workings of the Hegelian dialectic, the characteristic gesture of philosophy is to acknowledge the Other in order to incorporate it within the expanding circles of the Same.[24]

In this way, the totality of Heideggerian Being is described as "flawless and all-encompassing", such that "[t]otality has no outside, the subject receives nothing, learns nothing, that it does not or cannot possess or know".[25] Being, as conceived by Heidegger, is described by Levinas as "a singularity across a neuter . . . which illuminates freedom without putting it into question".[26] That is, it conceals singularity within a totality, which refuses the infinite.[27] In contrast, Levinas advocates the preservation of "the Other as Other",[28] in its absolute alterity.

In preserving a "relation whose terms do not form a totality",[29] the self and Other are suspended in a particular tension, in which neither must disturb the independence of the other. To repeat from earlier, this relation is one of desire, which is "equal only to excess. No totality will ever encompass it . . . the metaphysics of desire is a metaphysics of infinite separation".[30] Further, "metaphysical desire does not seek to consume, as do Hegelian desire or need".[31] While relationship necessitates the introduction of the Other "into the self's sphere of familiarity", this relation cannot encapsulate the Other: a "failure of understanding is essential if the radical otherness of the Other is to be preserved".[32] To know the Other would be to diminish it, "reducing it to nothing, removing it from its alterity".[33] Indeed, as Davis suggests, for Levinas the Other is preserved only where it is not rendered "an object of knowledge or experience", since "knowledge is always *my* knowledge, experience always *my* experience", so reducing the Other to the total sum of personal encounter.[34] The relation between self and Other requires the

24 Davis, above n 23, 40.
25 Ibid.
26 Levinas, above n 59 (Ch 5), 51.
27 Ibid.
28 Davis, above n 23, 41.
29 Levinas, above n 58 (Ch 5), 39.
30 Derrida, above n 61 (Ch 5), 115. Derrida describes desire as "permit[ting] itself to be appealed to by the absolutely irreducible exteriority of the other to which it must remain infinitely inadequate". Further, at 119, he writes: "Metaphysics begins when theory criticizes itself as ontology, as the dogmatism and spontaneity of the same, and when metaphysics, in departing from itself, lets itself be put into question by the other in the movement of ethics."
31 Ibid., 124.
32 Davis, above n 23, 41.
33 Levinas, above n 58 (Ch 5), 44.
34 Davis, above n 23, 41. See also Derrida, above n 61 (Ch 5), 118; Emmanuel Levinas, *Entre Nous* (1951, MB Smith trans., 1991 edn) 8, in which Levinas affirms this reductionism: "[W]ith regard to beings, understanding carries out an act of violence and of negation . . . [which] denies the independence of beings: they are mine."

maintenance of an irreducible distance between these – "that of conversation, of goodness, of Desire".[35] Levinas proceeds further, to distinguish this discourse from "a prefabricated internal logic", insisting upon the necessity of "the strangeness of the interlocutors", whose relation is defined by the absolute foreignness of one to the other.[36] Such foreignness is experienced as liberating, "refractory to every typology, to every genus, to every characterology, to every classification"; further, as radically transformative, as "a *pure* 'knowledge' or 'experience,' a *traumatism of astonishment*".[37] In this way, the Other cannot be conceptualised, and remains necessarily unrecognisable. In contrast to the dialectic of recognition proposed by Hegel in which, Levinas argued, the other is subsumed in the realisation of the self-consciousness of the self, the latter proposes "a relationship with the other that does not result in a divine or human totality . . . but the idea of infinity".[38] This infinite Other may, to some extent, be comparable to the indeterminacy of indigeneity as it appears in Indigenous literature, which deconstructs yet constitutes the law.

Within this ethics of alterity, the relation and responsibility to the Other is conceived as asymmetrical. Levinas distinguishes his argument from "the telos of intersubjective and social relationships" envisaged by Hegel in reciprocal recognition, asserting rather that if the asymmetry of self and other "is transcended, the resulting reciprocity implies a coequality that in turn implies that self and other are leveled and totalized", such that "the other is neutralized by ontological universality and totality".[39] For Levinas, the notion of a symmetrical "equality before the law" emerges only from the permanent "unequal, asymmetrical moral responsibility for others".[40] This asymmetrical relationship, between self and other, is " 'interrupted' by a 'third' person" – that is, "justice, in the form of law, equality, and reciprocity", which "demands that responsibilities be thought in a new way".[41] In this way, any attempt to conceive of the other in terms of " 'universal' categories of comparison" necessarily diminishes her.[42] Rather, justice, in accordance with a Levinasian ethics, requires "political simultaneousness . . . thinking the universal together with the unique and unsubsumable particular, creating systems while critiquing systems, fighting for symmetry only because of the asymmetry of my

35 Levinas, above n 58 (Ch 5), 39. See also 51: "To approach the Other in conversation . . . is . . . to *receive* from the Other beyond the capacity of the I", which is "to have the idea of infinity".

36 Ibid., 73.

37 Ibid.

38 Ibid., 52. See also Derrida, above n 61 (Ch 5), 129: "[T]he other is the other only if his alterity is absolutely irreducible, that is, infinitely irreducible; and the infinitely Other can only be Infinity".

39 Williams, above n 48 (Ch 5), 411. Williams here problematises Levinas's rejection of Hegel's reciprocity.

40 Roberts-Cady, above n 101 (Ch 5), 240.

41 Ibid., 245.

42 Ibid., 252. This assertion also recalls my earlier citation of Neumann's proposition that the "generality" of law "must be specific": Neumann, above n 100 (Ch 5), 28, cited in Fitzpatrick, above n 20 (Ch 5), 226.

responsibilities".[43] That is, for Levinas, a "call to justice" that requires a conception of "the abstraction of law" alongside "the uniqueness of every face . . . to think the equality of every citizen together with their inequality".[44]

Indigeneity may be understood as that which traverses these two poles – symmetrical and asymmetrical, abstract and unique. Accordingly, useful comparisons may be made to the two aforementioned modes of law – determinate and indeterminate – as articulated by Derrida. Where, for Derrida, "[t]he imperative of deconstruction is the duty to be open to alterity", Williams suggests that "[t]his turn to an introduction of the other as the condition and criterion of ethics means that Derridean deconstruction must be supplemented with Levinas".[45] Although for Levinas, the Other is conceived as absolute, removed from the violent imperatives of the force of law,[46] I have described indigeneity as perpetually in-between the decidable and undecidable of the law.[47] That is, as that which must be inevitably and violently conceptualised by the law at each moment of judicial decision, yet simultaneously as a disruptive alterity, to which the law is ethically compelled to respond in the moment of undecidability.[48] Indeed, as Williams argues, "[t]he event of the face provides the ethical norm and imperative for deconstruction, as well as the criterion of practical decision that suspends Derridean undecidability".[49]

Before the law

For Derrida, however, Levinas's ethics necessarily fails in its attempt to escape the determinative nature of law, and of the concept, as "Ethics of Ethics beyond

43 Roberts-Cady, above n 101 (Ch 5), 249.
44 Ibid., 240.
45 Williams, above n 48 (Ch 5), 400.
46 See Derrida, above n 61 (Ch 5), 185.
47 Derrida, above n 2 (Ch 5).
48 See also Simon Critchley, *Ethics-Politics-Subjectivity: Essays on Derrida, Levinas and Contemporary French Thought* (1999), in which Critchley argues that Derridean deconstructive justice is defined as ethical, in a specifically Levinasian sense; and moreover, that it contains an element of pragmatism. At 102, he writes:

> The undeconstructable condition of possibility for deconstruction is a commitment to justice, defined in terms of an ethical relation to the other, a response to suffering that provokes an infinite responsibility and the attempt to minimize cruelty. Such an ethical conception of justice can never be fully instantiated in the public realm, nor can it be divorced from the latter; rather, justice regulates public space, making politics critical, Utopian and radically democratic.

Furthermore, see Jacques Derrida, "Autoimmunity: Real and Symbolic Suicides – A Dialogue with Jacques Derrida" in Giovanna Borradori, *Philosophy in a Time of Terror: Dialogues with Jürgen Habermas and Jacques Derrida* (2003) 85, 120, cited and discussed in Fitzpatrick, above n 22 (Ch 5), 332. Derrida writes: "Political, juridical, and ethical responsibilities have their place, if they take place, only in this transaction – which is each time unique, like an event – between these two hospitalities, the unconditional and the conditional".
49 Williams, above n 48 (Ch 5), 400, discussing Critchley, above n 48 (Ch 5).

all laws", or "the Law of laws" and, furthermore, as "the infinite concept, hidden within the protest against the concept".[50] In "Violence and Metaphysics", an essay engaged with *Totality and Infinity*, Derrida contrasts this "infinitely-other" with the determined and "foreseen" horizon of the concept, which "is always a horizon of the same, the elementary unity within which eruptions and surprises are always welcomed by understanding and recognized".[51] Questioning the possibility of an infinite Other which, for Derrida, must be ultimately conceptualised in language, he argues that entry into discourse always necessitates the violence of the concept,[52] and therefore remains ontological, rather than ethical. Furthermore, Levinas's notion of ethics – "an Ethics without law and without concept . . . maintains its non-violent purity only before being determined as concepts and laws".[53] In this way, he continues, "this Ethics of Ethics can occasion neither a determined ethics nor determined laws without negating and forgetting itself".[54]

Whereas, for Levinas, ethics has been described as "a movement of *desire* . . . that cannot be reduced to a *need* that returns to self", for Derrida – and the deconstructive account of indigeneity *with-in* the law I am here proposing – deconstruction occurs in "repetition and alterity", the "double gesture of deconstructive reading: the figure of the chiasmus".[55] That is, "[d]econstruction opens a reading by locating a moment of alterity within a text".[56] For my purposes, this text is the text of the law, in which indigeneity emerges as 'a moment of alterity'. In the (con)text of the Indigenous subject before the law, this chiasmic reading may be elucidated via a further Derridean reading of Kafka's literary text, "Before the Law".[57] Through this 'parable', I will suggest that the movement of indigeneity between the two poles of law – determinate and indeterminate – is demonstrative of a law that must be constituted by the Other, yet also violently determined. Accordingly, indigeneity emerges within the law as the "origin of *différance* . . . the law of the law",[58] which is indeed alterity, but must be 'cut' and 'divided' with the force of law, in order to (re)enact the law.[59]

Derrida describes law and literature as distinct, yet as potentially sharing the same conditions of possibility.[60] The law, lacking substance and essence of its

50 Derrida, above n 61 (Ch 5), 138.
51 Ibid., 118.
52 Ibid., 185.
53 Ibid., 138.
54 Ibid.
55 Critchley, above n 48 (Ch 5), 28.
56 Ibid.
57 Derrida, above n 1 (Ch 5), 181.
58 Ibid., 181, 205. See also Derrida, above n 61 (Ch 5), 122, 128.
59 Derrida, above n 2 (Ch 5). See also Derrida, above n 5 (Ch 5), 79–81. Derrida describes

> *the* unconditional law of hospitality [that] needs the laws, it *requires* them. This demand is constitutive . . . And vice versa, conditional laws would cease to be laws . . . if they were not guided, given inspiration, required, even, by the law of unconditional hospitality.

60 Derrida, above n 1 (Ch 5), 191.

own, is "structurally related to what Derrida terms *différance* or, in its non-metaphysical sense, 'literature'".[61] Where *différance* is conceived as "a chain or systematic play of differences", the signified concept is that which "Derrida – borrowing from Levinas – calls a 'trace', a past that has never been present".[62] Accordingly, the law is "always to come, always promised, because it is immanent, finite, and thus already past" such that "[e]very 'subject' is caught up in this aporetic structure in advance".[63] That is, every subject appearing before the law appears, rather, before an as yet undetermined law, which must yet be determined in violence.[64] Returning to my earlier analysis of the non-closure of the law, as context, this context is paradoxically conditioned by the unconditional, which arises *with-in* the conditional or determinate context.[65] Critchley provides a useful analysis:

> Derrida's argument is not that the unconditioned is present or existent somewhere outside all context, but rather that it arises as the interruption, or non-closure, of any determinate context; it is an injunction, or law, that 'transcends this or that determination of a given context' . . . Thus, there are only contexts; nothing exists outside context; and yet, Derrida claims, the context contains a clause of non-closure whereby an unconditioned injunction comes to interrupt the conditioned context.[66]

The door to the law, in Kafka's parable, in fact "open[s] on nothing, before nothing, the object of no possible experience".[67] This follows Levinas's idea of the infinite, which cannot be "grasped" as a concept but "is the radically, absolutely other".[68] Yet, the apparently "inaccessible transcendence of the law" is 'filled' by that which is extrinsic to it – the "man", who appears *before* it, by whose performative act the law is instituted, "who produces it, founds it, authorizes it in an absolute performative whose presence always escapes him".[69] Derrida writes: "The man from the country had difficulty in grasping that an entrance was singular or unique when it should have been universal, as in truth it was. He had difficulty with literature".[70] Indeed, for Levinas, the subject is always already constituted by the Other – not via a dialectic resulting in resolution, but by the face and

61 Attridge, above n 14, 182.
62 Critchley, above n 48, 37, citing Jacques Derrida, *Margins of Philosophy* (A Bass trans., 1982 edn) 12, 21.
63 Derrida, above n 2 (Ch 5), 270.
64 Ibid.
65 Critchley, above n 48, 37, citing Jacques Derrida, *Limited Inc* (1990) 281.
66 Ibid., 40, citing Jacques Derrida, *Limited Inc* (1990) 281.
67 Derrida, above n 1 (Ch 5), 211–12.
68 Levinas, above n 59 (Ch 5), 54.
69 Derrida, above n 2 (Ch 5), 270.
70 Derrida, above n 1 (Ch 5), 213.

language of alterity. Whereas Levinas envisages an Other that cannot and, indeed, *must* not be known, Derrida describes a movement between the determinate and indeterminate, such that alterity haunts the law as its very condition.[71] Both law and literature are engaged in a simultaneity, in which the "singular crosses the universal" and "the categorical engages the idiomatic".[72] That is, the law remains ever open to the unconditional, yet simultaneously requires the violence of the concept, in order to enter into force. Fitzpatrick suggests that a Derridean notion of justice "imports an unlimited responsiveness to the singularity of the other", yet "[t]o be effective, to be made possible, justice must be given operative force and for this it must, in a sense, be denied".[73] That is, "[t]he limitless expanse of justice . . . must be 'cut' into, reduced and rendered expressible", such that "justice can only be made just in a way that is unjust".[74] Accordingly, law necessarily "codifies, prescribes and determines",[75] but this determinate law is animated and, moreover, constituted by the unconditional and indeterminate.

The movement between these poles is reflected in Derrida's concern with the 'as if'. Derived from the second formulation of Kant's categorical imperative – "Act as if the maxim of your action were by your will to turn into a universal law of nature" – the "as if", for Derrida, imports "narrativity and fiction into the very core of legal thought".[76] Indeed, Naas describes this movement as that between "the *comme si* [as if] of speculative fiction" and "the *comme ça* [as so, as such] of an inflexible law".[77] Elsewhere, Derrida describes literature as "aim[ing] toward the filling of a lack (a hole) in a whole that should not itself in its essence be missing (to) itself" and, further, as "the *exception to everything* . . . a part that, within *and* without the whole, marks the wholly other, the other incommensurate with the whole".[78] Whereas the "rationality" and "the authority of law" appear "alien to all fiction and imagination . . . [the law] still seems *a priori* to shelter these parasites".[79] The imperative to respond to that which is beyond the universality of law is conceived as a responsibility, to which we are "summoned, confronted by an undecidability which is always an opportunity and a demand, a chance and a risk", and which enables entry into discourse at all.[80] It is this singularity, or alterity, that is both before and beyond the law: "the Other is the condition

71 Derrida, above n 51 (Ch 5), 79.
72 Derrida, above n 1 (Ch 5), 213.
73 Fitzpatrick, above n 4 (Ch 5), 74.
74 Ibid., 74, citing Derrida, above n 1 (Ch 5), 24. See also Ibid., 140.
75 Ibid., 74.
76 Derrida, above n 1 (Ch 5), 190.
77 Naas, above n 33 (Ch 7), 188.
78 Jacques Derrida, "Outwork, Prefacing", in Jacques Derrida, *Dissemination* (Barbara Johnson trans., 1981 edn) 1, 56. See also Jacques Derrida, "This Strange Institution Called Literature: An Interview with Jacques Derrida" in Jacques Derrida (Derek Attridge, ed.), *Acts of Literature* (1992) 33.
79 Derrida, above n 1 (Ch 5), 190.
80 Attridge, above n 14, 5–6.

for the One".[81] Indigeneity, while determined by the context of the law, interrupts this narrative with its indeterminacy, as the "undecidable [that] brings justice into law".[82]

In Part III, I will dwell further upon this Derridean notion of justice, as it momentarily appears within the law, and a reading of Indigenous literature as a presentation of the unpresentable of indigeneity, including Indigenous Law.[83] This will entail a detailed consideration of the construction of the legal Indigene within the archive of Australian law, and juridical engagements with the restrictive statutory requirements of native title, which reduce Indigenous claims to specific and technical interpretations of 'tradition'.[84] These analyses will be read through Benjamin's "Critique of Violence"[85] and Derrida's "Force of Law", and a conception of literature as a radical and transformative counter to bounded, conditioned conceptions of indigeneity.

81 Derrida, above n 51 (Ch 5), 79. See also Derrida, above n 61 (Ch 5), 121–2, 128. Speaking of the face as the "expression of infinity" that is the Other, Derrida describes the face as not 'of this world'", but as "the origin of the world". Further, at 130: "As speech and glance the face is not in the world, since it opens and exceeds the totality. This is why it marks the limit of all power, of all violence, and the origin of the ethical."

82 Fitzpatrick, above n 4 (Ch 5), 75.

83 Derrida, above n 2 (Ch 5), 257. Derrida writes: "Justice, as the experience of absolute alterity, is unpresentable, but it is the chance of the event and the condition of history".

84 See especially Simon Young, *The Trouble with Tradition: Native Title and Cultural Change* (2008). See also Povinelli, above n 43 (Ch 5), 55–6.

85 Benjamin, above n 8 (Ch 5), 277.

Part III

Law

Chapter 9

Juridical indigeneities

> I want to insist at once to reserve the possibility of a justice, indeed of a law [*loi*] that not only exceeds or contradicts law but also, perhaps, has no relation to law, or maintains such a strange relation to it that it may just as well demand law as exclude it.[1]

The search for, and articulation of, indigeneity[2] within Australian native title jurisprudence entails a unique positioning of the Indigenous person as a subject of justice. That is, as a subject to whom justice is due, within contemporary Australian discourses on 'reconciliation',[3] but also as the subject of a Derridean justice, identifiable in discourses on "the undecidable, the incommensurable or the incalculable, on singularity, difference and heterogeneity".[4] It also entails a positioning of the Indigene as the product of, and as productive of, violence – in Benjaminian terms, of the mythic violence that founds law and constructs the Indigenous subject before the law, and of the divine and "sovereign" violence that perpetually destroys it.[5] Within this schema, justice may be conceived accordingly – as the "justice *as law*"[6] of a mythic violence. It is the juxtaposition of these two dimensions of law – mythic and divine, determinate, and indeterminate – that is

1 Jacques Derrida, "Force of Law: The Mystical Foundation of Authority" in Jacques Derrida (Gil Anidjar, ed.), *Acts of Religion* (2002) 228, 233.

2 See my previous definition of "indigeneity", as denoting Indigenous subjectivities, "life-ways" and Law, in Part I (Narratives).

3 See, for instance, www.reconciliation.org.au/ (accessed 6 October 2015). This is a non-government, not-for-profit foundation, focused upon national reconciliation. Among other things, it promotes the annual "Reconciliation Week", the Indigenous Governance Program, and the Reconciliation Action Plan (RAP) Program, launched in 2006, which aims to "close the gap" on life expectancy between Indigenous and non-Indigenous children.

4 Derrida, above n 1, 235.

5 Walter Benjamin, "Critique of Violence" in Walter Benjamin, *Reflections: Essays, Aphorisms, Autobiographical Writings* (1978) 277, 300. See also Derrida, above n 1, 265.

6 Derrida, above n 1, 240 (emphasis added). Discussed in Stewart Motha, "*Mabo*: Encountering the Epistemic Limit of the Recognition of 'Difference'" (1998) 7 *Griffith Law Review* 79, 90.

made manifest in the appearance of the Indigene before the law, most particularly before the law of native title. Furthermore, it is these dimensions, conceived in this book as the forces of non-Indigenous law and Indigenous Law respectively, which organise this part, and the following.

An enquiry into the question that is indigeneity, and the appearance of the Indigenous person before the law, is necessarily and simultaneously concerned with "the question of justice, of the possibility of justice"[7] and its relation, if any, to law.[8] Indeed, for Derrida, law and justice are opposed: "[L]aw is not justice . . . [but] the element of calculation".[9] In the course of the same argument, however, he also considers law and justice to be mutually dependent, yet remaining, necessarily, opposed[10] and furthermore, as I have previously articulated, equates law itself with deconstruction.[11] In the present context, I am concerned with explicit evocations of justice in common law renderings of native title in Australia, where determinations are exacted in the name of a conditional justice, and the deconstructive movement within this law appears as an evocation of an unconditional justice.[12]

The momentous High Court decision in *Mabo* turned upon an acknowledgment of the injustice and fiction of the doctrine of *terra nullius*, and the corrective realignment of the common law with the history of colonial settlement in Australia.[13] Such correction and the assertion of justice it entailed, however, were subject to the limitations of a determinate law, where the court had already declared itself constrained, "not free to adopt rules that accord with contemporary notions of justice and human rights if their adoption would fracture the skeleton of principle

7 Derrida, above n 1, 245.
8 Ibid., 233.
9 Ibid., 244.
10 Ibid., 251.
11 Jacques Derrida, James Adner, Kate Doyle and Glenn Hendler, "Women in the Beehive: A Seminar with Jacques Derrida" (2005) 16(3) *A Journal of Feminist Cultural Studies* 139, 149.
12 Ibid., 254.
13 *Mabo and Others v Queensland (No. 2)* (1992) 175 CLR 1 ("*Mabo*"). At 58, Brennan J remarked:

> The common law of this country would perpetuate injustice if it were to continue to embrace the enlarged notion of terra nullius and to persist in characterizing the indigenous inhabitants of the Australian colonies as people too low in the scale of social organization to be acknowledged as possessing rights and interests in land. Moreover, to reject the theory that the Crown acquired absolute beneficial ownership of land is to bring the law into conformity with Australian history.

At the time of the *Mabo* decision, the then Prime Minister Paul Keating remarked upon this historical correction, published in Paul Keating, "The Redfern Park Speech" in Michelle Grattan (ed.), *Essays on Australian Reconciliation* (2000) 60, 62:

> *Mabo* is an historic decision. We can make it an historic turning point, the basis of a new relationship between indigenous and non-Aboriginal Australians. The message should be that there is nothing to fear or to lose in the recognition of historical truth, or the extension of social justice, or the deepening of Australian social democracy to include indigenous Australians. There is everything to gain.

which gives the body of our law its shape and internal consistency".[14] Indeed, the very authority of Australian law – the declaration of British sovereignty in Australia on the basis of a denial of Indigenous occupation – rests upon its foundation in this arrogation of sovereignty, arising from the fiction of *terra nullius*. The ensuing development of Australian law, while liberated from its historical predecessor, is nonetheless constrained where a departure would "fracture . . . [this] skeleton of principle".[15] While, in his *Mabo* judgment, Justice Brennan laboured to rectify that which he perceived as past injustice, incompatible with "contemporary notions of justice and human rights", the osseous foundation of the law nonetheless remains indestructible,[16] thereby presenting a fundamental distinction between law, as right (*droit*), and as justice.[17]

Such constraint may be contrasted with my earlier description of the responsive dimension of the law, and its reception of alterity, in accordance with which, as Fitzpatrick suggests, the law must "accommodate, give way to, and give a way to, what comes from beyond it".[18] This 'beyond' would, in my analysis, encompass Derrida's conception of an unconditional justice, which "exceeds or contradicts law".[19] Furthermore, it may be understood in terms of Benjamin's critique, as a divine and "sovereign violence".[20] Benjamin's use of the word 'sovereign' here requires some clarification. Martel has suggested that whereas 'sovereignty' is conventionally used to describe the sovereignty of a nation state, translation of the German word, *waltende*, as used by Benjamin, is uncertain. He suggests a distinction between Benjamin's evocation of *waltende* and state sovereignty:

> [W]altende has connotations of ruling and order . . . but it also suggests a form of rule that is not exactly the same as sovereignty . . . and therefore is not identical to the mythological structures that form our current conceptions of politics. The alternative thus may have some features in common with sovereignty as we understand it, but it is of a different order, a different form of representation.[21]

14 Mabo (1992) 175 CLR 1, 29.
15 Ibid., 30.
16 Ibid.
17 See Derrida, above n 1. At 240, Derrida cites Montaigne's distinction between "laws [*lois*], that is to say law [*droit*] . . . [and] justice": Michel de Montaigne, *The Essayes of Montaigne* (John Florio trans., 1933 edn) 970. See also Jacques de Ville, *Jacques Derrida: Law as Absolute Hospitality* (2011) 39. Reading Derrida, de Ville distinguishes between "law in the sense of a legal system (*le droit*), and the law itself (*la loi*)".
18 Peter Fitzpatrick, "Why the Law Is Also Nonviolent" in Austin Sarat (ed.), *Law, Violence and the Possibility of Justice* (2001) 142, 154.
19 Derrida, above n 1, 233; see also 250.
20 Benjamin, above n 5, 300.
21 James R Martel, *Divine Violence: Walter Benjamin and the Eschatology of Sovereignty* (2012) 61.

For my purposes, Benjamin's evocation of "sovereign violence" is here, and throughout this book, conceived as being within the order of the divine, which must be always in excess of a state 'sovereignty' and its law. Accordingly, I argue that where the law must remain ever responsive to that which lies beyond its own 'shape and internal consistency', in order to retain its relevancy and applicability to contemporary contexts,[22] it is indigeneity that enters the law of native title in such expansive moments. Indeed, the deconstruction that Derrida equates with justice,[23] and with law,[24] arising in these moments, is well captured in Biber's description of the native title claim as "powerful *in spite of the law*".[25] That is, in terms of my continuing argument, powerful despite the violence of the element of law that must remain determinate and, in Benjaminian terms, mythic. In this part, I focus upon the authority and perpetuation of a law conceived, in Benjaminian terms, as 'mythic', and its violent determination of indigeneity, and the "legitimate fiction[s]"[26] necessary to the authority and determination of this law, demonstrable in the law of native title. I will then consider the relationship between these and questions of justice.

Part II considered constructions and evocations of indigeneity within antinomic[27] yet mutually constitutive dimensions of law, whereby the moment of judicial decision "singularly and inextricably combines the dimensions of determination and responsiveness . . . [and] cannot be reduced to either".[28] In so doing, I examined the resort to preconceived notions of the Indigene within a determinate law, concerned to 'calculate' indigeneity in an 'imperial' orientation.[29] This entailed an analysis of the required performance, on the part of an Indigenous person before the law, of a universal and objective 'indigeneity', in accordance with the exercise of "justice *as law*".[30] That is, justice as the application of a determinate law, according to which the Indigene is always already a preconceived and thereby subordinated subject. In this way, recognition of indigeneity by the law of the (post)colonial state is rendered impossible. Such determinacy is exemplified in the law of native title, to which the present part will ultimately turn. Nonetheless this very law, it was revealed, is constituted by that which is beyond it, necessitated

22 See generally Derrida, above n 1; Peter Fitzpatrick, *Modernism and the Grounds of Law* (2001); Peter Fitzpatrick, "No Higher Duty: Mabo and the Failure of Legal Foundation" (2002) 13 *Law and Critique* 233, especially 237–8.

23 Derrida, above n 1, 243.

24 Derrida, Adner, Doyle and Hendler, above n 11, 149.

25 Katherine Biber, "Being/Nothing: Native Title and Fantasy Fulfilment" (2004) 3 *Indigenous Law Journal* 1, 14.

26 Derrida, above n 1, 240.

27 See Jacques Derrida, *Of Hospitality* (Rachel Bowlby trans., 2000 edn) 79–81, who describes "[t]hese two regimes of law, of *the* law and the laws" as simultaneously "antinomic, and inseparable".

28 Fitzpatrick (2002), above n 22, 237.

29 Ibid.

30 Derrida, above n 1, 240 (emphasis added).

by the rendering of "fresh judgment" in each instance of judicial decision.[31] The "violence, the irreducible 'madness,' of the act of the decision", is transgressive and therefore indeterminate, uncontainable within a static law; yet, it "is inextricably and repetitively *in* law".[32]

By way of these antinomic renderings of indigeneity, this part will begin with a discussion of the mythic violence of a determinate law, as opposed to the notion of indigeneity as evocative of a divine violence. This will entail a close reading of Benjamin's "Critique of Violence", and the application of this text to the positioning of the Indigenous subject *before* the law, and of Indigenous literature *beyond* the law. I will then consider the question of justice in this context, and its different manifestations, illustrated via a reading of the work of Native American (Spokane/C'oeur d'Alene) author, Sherman Alexie – specifically his short story, "The Trial of Thomas Builds-the-Fire", from his 1993 collection, *The Lone Ranger and Tonto Fistfight in Heaven*.[33] This text depicts antithetical yet simultaneous evocations of justice in a non-Indigenous North American courtroom, and the challenge for Native Americans in, as Dix suggests, "mak[ing] their little narratives stick when confronted still by the metanarrative of US power".[34] In this story, the protagonist articulates competing conceptions of justice – "real justice" and the "idea of justice"[35] – and appeals to the 'truth' and emancipatory potential of the latter. I will consider this appeal in the context of Derrida's allusions to an irreducible 'idea' of justice, in contrast to the 'justice as law' of the courtroom.[36] This engagement will also consider the notion of literature as strategy,[37] discussed in Part I. These analyses will lead into a discussion of the fictions engaged by the law in its construal of the Indigenous subject, including those of discovery and assertion of sovereignty, and subsequently of native title.

The remainder of Part II will consider the aforementioned opposing dimensions of violence and justice in their application to the law of native title. I will focus first upon the historical and contemporary instantiation and preservation of a determinate law, as an expression of mythic violence. Following and extending several concerns of the previous chapters, I will examine the construction of the common law narrative as reflected in the authoritative archive of precedent, and its creation of a determinate Indigenous legal subject. In so doing, I will trace various constructions of indigeneity in historical perspective, via the colonial gaze of the first European explorers and settlers to Australia, and the inauguration and elaboration of particular conceptions of land and waters, flora and fauna in

31 Derrida, above n 1, 251.

32 Fitzpatrick, above n 18, 156; 144.

33 Sherman Alexie, "The Trial of Thomas Builds-the-Fire", in Sherman Alexie, *The Lone Ranger and Tonto Fistfight in Heaven* (1993) 100.

34 Andrew Dix, "Escape Stories: Narratives and Native Americans in Sherman Alexie's *The Lone Ranger and Tonto Fistfight in Heaven*" (2001) 31 *The Yearbook of English Studies* 155, 167.

35 Alexie, above n 33, 100.

36 Derrida, above n 1, 254; 240.

37 Terry Eagleton, *The Event of Literature* (2012).

accordance with a dichotomy between nature and culture, and of Indigenous peoples and cultures within this narrative.

I will then delve into a discussion of specific legal renderings of these dimensions, in Australian jurisprudence. This will entail an examination of the modes and mechanisms of legal construction of indigeneity, as informed by these historical narratives. I will examine the Australian statutory formulation and common law interpretation of native title, most particularly focusing upon the requirements of acknowledgment and observance of 'traditional' laws and customs that constitute the 'origin and content' of native title,[38] and the requirement for continuous or "substantially uninterrupted"[39] connection to land and waters claimed. This discussion will be broad, but will devote particular attention to the articulation of these requirements in the High Court of Australia decisions in *Bennell*[40] and *Yorta Yorta*.[41] My reflections here will be situated within the context of the aforementioned 'colonial gaze', through which indigeneity, for the purposes of legal claims, is arguably reduced to an objectified cultural specificity. Perpetuated by the national mythologising discussed in the introduction to this book, and the attendant "remembering and forgetting" of indigeneity entailed,[42] this objectification relegates the Indigene to the past, proof of her claims to country determined by proof of her membership of a fictitious "ancient tribe",[43] as evidenced by the continued

38 *Mabo* (1992) 175 CLR 1, 58. Brennan J asserts:

> Native title has its origin in and is given its content by the traditional laws acknowledged by and the traditional customs observed by the indigenous inhabitants of a territory. The nature and incidents of native title must be ascertained as a matter of fact by reference to those laws and customs.

39 *Akiba and Another (on behalf of the Torres Strait Islanders of the Regional Seas Claim Group) v Queensland and Others* (No 2) (2010) 270 ALR 564 ("Akiba"), [544]–[552]:

> The criterion in s 223(1)(b) of the NT Act that the members of the native title claim group of each island community have a connection with their marine estates by their laws and customs required that the claim group demonstrate a substantially uninterrupted acknowledgment of those laws and customs from the time of annexation.

This case considered *Bodney v Bennell* (2008) 249 ALR 300, especially 324–325; *Western Australia v Ward* (2002) 213 CLR 1 ('*Ward*'); *Members of the Yorta Yorta Aboriginal Community v Victoria* (2002) 214 CLR 422 ("*Yorta Yorta*"); *Neowarra v Western Australia* [2003] FCA 1402; *Sampi v Western Australia* [2005] FCA 777. See also proposed amendments contained within the Native Title Amendment (Reform) Bill 2014 (Cth), Schedule 1, 14, which provides a presumption of connection, to be inserted after s 61 of the *Native Title Act 1993* (Cth) as s 61AB. See also proposals for reform in the Australian Law Reform Commission Review of the Native Title Act 1993 Issues Paper 45 (IP 45) (March 2014) ('*ALRC IP 45*') at www.alrc.gov.au/publications/native-title-ip-45 (accessed 6 October 2015).

40 *Bennell v Western Australia* (2006) 230 ALR 603 ("*Bennell*"). I will also examine the Full Federal Court decision in this matter, *Bodney v Bennell and Others* (2008) 249 ALR 300 ("*Bodney v Bennell*").

41 *Yorta Yorta* (2002) 214 CLR 422 ("*Yorta Yorta*").

42 Chris Healy, *Forgetting Aborigines* (2008) 4–5.

43 Judith Grbich, "Tracing the Figure of the Native in Postcolonial Theory and Native Title Law: Enlightenment, Aesthetics and Charles Harpur" (2005) 22 *Australian Feminist Law Journal* 127, 128 citing the *Native Title Act 1993* (Cth) s 223(1).

observance and acknowledgment of law and custom deemed 'traditional' before (non-Indigenous) law.

Overall, this discussion should be understood within the context of my previous analysis of the legal archive in Derridean terms, where "archive fever" is conceived as an impassioned yet futile search for origin.[44] That is, a search for an intangible origin that haunts the archive as a trace, existing only "at the limit of the condition originated".[45] In terms of the law, the perpetual movement between determinacy and indeterminacy, decision and indecision, renders the origin ungraspable and, perhaps, spectral. Indeed, Benjamin has elsewhere poetically described the origin as "an eddy in the stream of becoming, and in its current it swallows the material involved in the process of genesis".[46] That is, an origin can never be truly known; rather, as Martel notes, "we can be attuned to its coming and going, its appearance, disappearance and reappearance in new guises".[47] In terms of the law, Derrida's analysis of the archive reveals not an ungraspable origin, but a vacuous one, and furthermore, according to Fitzpatrick, "[t]here is nothing here before the law or, reversing the perspective, what is before the law is nothing".[48] The law is necessarily instantiated in each moment of decision, yet the putative authority of the law is derived from its recourse to precedent. The legal construction of the Indigene, historically contrived via Enlightenment scientific and imperial narratives, is exemplified in this body of precedent. The foundation and authority of this law, following Goodrich, may be conceived as a practice of forgetting historical injustices, which are "hidden within the phantasms of precedent, incorporated in the imaginary of a system or body of law".[49] While the contemporary recognition of indigeneity before the law appears to be violently constrained within legal narratives, in the enactment of a preserving, mythic violence, the actual vacuity of the law nonetheless reveals an alterity that incipiently exists *with-in* it, thereby constituting it.

Juridical violence

> If justice is the criterion of ends, legality is that of means.[50]

In his seminal essay, "Critique of Violence", Benjamin summarises "the task of a critique of violence . . . as that of expounding its relation to law and justice".[51] That is, as "the question whether violence . . . is a means to a just or an unjust

44 Jacques Derrida, *Archive Fever: A Freudian Impression* (Eric Prenowitz trans., 1995 edn).
45 Fitzpatrick (2001), above n 22, 90.
46 Walter Benjamin, *The Origin of German Tragic Drama* (1998) 45, cited in Martel, above n 21, 19.
47 Martel, above n 21, 19.
48 Fitzpatrick, above n 18, 157. See also Derrida, above n 44; Fitzpatrick (2001), above n 22, 80–1.
49 Peter Goodrich, *Law in the Courts of Love: Literature and Other Minor Jurisprudences* (1996) 124.
50 Benjamin, above n 5, 278.
51 Ibid., 277.

end".[52] The notion of justice and its pursuit through the mechanism of law is, at least in contemporary scholarship, fraught.[53] Nonetheless, it is a pursuit that has had longevity,[54] the ethical distance between law and justice having been thoroughly identified.[55] While the relationship between violence and justice has been similarly examined,[56] I wish to briefly draw attention to the instability of these terms, and the antinomies within them, before elaborating upon their application to the determination and articulation of indigeneity both before and beyond the law. To begin, I will consider the relation between violence and the law where, it has been argued, the law is "violently determining", yet also exhibits a "nonviolent responsiveness",[57] the latter being productive of an unconditional justice.[58]

The violence of the law – law and its interpretation, it has been argued, "tak[ing] place in a field of pain and death"[59] – is conventionally understood to be an exercise in the threat and application of force in response to transgression.[60] This entails the justification of violence in its role in the preservation and "restoration of the concordant world" where this violence, in accordance with "occidental myth", is presumed to be "the preserve of the law".[61] In this context, "law is not poetry" but, rather, possesses " 'world-destroying' capacity".[62] Accordingly, "[t]he force of law", it has been argued, "is remarkable principally for its multivalent violences

52 Benjamin, above n 5, 277.

53 Austin Sarat, "Situating Law Between the Realities of Violence and the Claims of Justice: An Introduction" in Sarat, above n 18, 3, 6. See the engagements with these themes in this volume in general.

54 See, for instance, Marianne Constable, "The Silence of the Law: Justice in Cover's 'Field of Pain and Death'" in Sarat, above n 18, 85. Constable suggests, at 91, that "[s]ince Plato . . . it seems, the history of jurisprudence has been, at least in part, the history of a quest for justice".

55 Sarat, above n 53, 6–7 citing Drucilla Cornell, "Post-Structuralism, the Ethical Relation, and the Law" (1988) 9 *Cardozo Law Review* 1587; Drucilla Cornell, *The Philosophy of the Limit* (1992); Costas Douzinas and Ronnie Warrington, "The Face of Justice: A Jurisprudence of Alterity" (1994) 3 *Social and Legal Studies: An International Journal* 23; Thomas Keenan, "Deconstruction and the Impossibility of Justice" (1990) 11 *Cardozo Law Review* 1680.

56 See, for instance, Sarat, above n 18; James B Brady and Newton Garver (eds), *Justice, Law, and Violence* (1991).

57 Fitzpatrick, above n 18, 146; 167.

58 See, for instance, Jacques Derrida, "The University Without Condition" in Jacques Derrida, *Without Alibi* (2002) 202, 206, 234.

59 Robert M Cover, "Violence and the Word" in Bruce B Lawrence and Aisha Karim, *On Violence: A Reader* (2007) 293, 293.

60 Generally, see Jan Narveson, "Force, Violence, and Law" in James B Brady and Newton Garver, *Justice, Law, and Violence* (1991) 149, 150; Mark C Taylor, "Desire of Law Law of Desire" (1990) 11 *Cardozo Law Review* 1269. At 1271, Taylor equates the law with force insofar as it is responsive: "law and transgression are interpreted as force and counter-force".

61 Fitzpatrick, above n 18, 143.

62 Constable, above n 54, 90, 85, citing Cover, above n 59, originally published in (1986) 95 *Yale Law Journal* 1601, reprinted in Martha Minnow, Michael Ryan and Austin Sarat (eds), *Narrative, Violence, and the Law: The Essays of Robert Cover* (1992) 203, 205.

. . . with which it struggles to institute and replicate itself as the central discourse of official power".[63] These include "an inherent theatricality, a hegemonic realignment of indigenous systems of law, and a deployment of both physical and symbolic violence", all of which have been aptly described as the "chameleon-like strategies of colonial law".[64] It has also been argued, however, that the law is both violent and nonviolent – that is, in accordance with my previous discussion of the antinomic nature of law, it exhibits a violence that is both "determining force and responsive expectancy".[65] For my purposes, I am concerned not with the corporal violence inflicted by the word of the law, but with a determinate law that violates the alterity of Indigenous subjectivities and Law, in the context of colonised nations. While this law must exert a force that "cuts and divides", it is also necessarily responsive to that which annihilates its order, in the 'madness' of judicial (in)decision.[66]

Benjamin elaborates two opposing conceptions of violence, as derived from "positive law" and "natural law", the latter being outside of the former, a threat to the law "by its mere existence outside the law".[67] As discussed throughout this book, Benjamin describes these conceptions as "mythic" and "divine", the latter confronting and annihilating the former:

> If mythical violence is lawmaking, divine violence is law-destroying; if the former sets boundaries, the latter boundlessly destroys them; if mythical violence brings at once guilt and retribution, divine power only expiates; if the former threatens, the latter strikes; if the former is bloody, the latter is lethal without spilling blood.[68]

He further conceives of a dual "function of violence in lawmaking", where "[j]ustice is the principle of all divine end making, power the principle of all mythical lawmaking".[69] For Benjamin, "lawmaking" pursues its ends and establishes law via the exercise of violence and is, moreover, "intimately bound to it".[70] As such, he describes it as "power making, and, to that extent, an immediate manifestation of violence".[71] Whereas mythical violence is "bloody power over mere life for its

63 Gary Boire, "Symbolic Violence: Law, Literature, Interpretation: An Afterword" (2004) *ARIEL* 35 (1–2) 231, 236.

64 Ibid., 236.

65 Fitzpatrick, above n 18, 144.

66 Derrida, above n 1, 252, 255. See also Fitzpatrick, above n 18. At 154, Fitzpatrick writes: "[I]n the violence of its making and of its sustained remaking, the decision must also and inextricably be nonviolently responsive".

67 Benjamin, above n 5, 278, 281.

68 Ibid., 297.

69 Ibid., 295.

70 Ibid.

71 Ibid.

own sake" – that is, for the sake of its own establishment and preservation – divine violence is "pure power over all life for the sake of the living"[72] – that is, for the sake of those remaining in the wake of the divine expiation of mythic law, where this expiation "purifies the guilty, not of guilt . . . but of law".[73] In this context, it has been suggested, Benjamin refers to the guilt of idolatry, and "the law and political authority that such guilt produces".[74] I will return to this notion of idolatry in the following part, in the context of a discussion of a Benjaminian notion of sovereignty. Suffice it to say at this point, however, that it is these antithetical conceptions of violence, or force,[75] and their differing manifestations of power and justice, which particularly animate my reading of indigeneity, and representation and expression of the latter in law and literature.

The determinate law of native title is, I suggest, exacting in its requirements of the Indigenous claimant, setting boundaries and exercising power and force in the pursuit of its own preservation – that is, for 'its own sake'. Indigenous authored literature, by contrast, depicts and, arguably, evokes a boundless divine violence that is destructive of this law; moreover, it is a display of bloodless 'pure power', roused not for its own sake, but for the sake of human subjects – 'the living'. In the literary texts to which I have already alluded, and which form the basis of my analysis in Part IV, I argue that Indigenous Law is depicted as a manifestation of this divine violence, destructive of the determinate law of the coloniser, and further as a source of unconditional justice for Indigenous peoples.

According to Benjamin's schema, Derrida conceives of justice as the "justice, *as law*" of a mythic violence, which "assumes the generality of a rule, a norm or a universal imperative", and as the justice of a divine violence, "as the experience of absolute alterity", as "unpresentable".[76] This latter justice exceeds the former, as an "excess of justice over law and calculation" and an "overflowing of the unpresentable over the determinable".[77] In contrast, Derrida argues, "[t]he justice of law, justice as law is not justice" and, moreover, the authority and foundation of laws rests upon a mere belief in them, rather than their justice:

> The very emergence of justice and law, the instituting, founding, and justifying moment of law implies a performative force, that is to say always an interpretative force and a call to faith . . .[78]

72 Benjamin, above n 5, 297.
73 Martel, above n 21, 52.
74 Ibid., 52, citing Werner Hamacher, "Guilt History: Benjamin's Sketch 'Capitalism as Religion'" (2002) Fall-Winter *Diacritics* 81.
75 Ibid., 51.
76 Derrida, above n 1, 245, 257.
77 Ibid.
78 Ibid., 240, 241.

For Derrida, for a law to be just, it must preserve, suspend and perpetually (re)create itself, in a "fresh judgment".[79] Each legal decision must pass through "the moment of suspense of the undecidable", between a divine and mythic violence, such that this suspenseful moment "remains caught" within the law, as its "essential ghost".[80] It is this spectral haunting that is evoked in the appearance of indigeneity before the law, allowing the entry of an indeterminate justice into a determinate law.

According to Benjamin's critique, and Derrida's response, the aforementioned contrary elements are engaged in a perpetual " 'dialectic' and its 'law of oscillation' ", whereby "law-imposing violence must become law-preserving, must turn against its original positing character, and, in this collusion with itself, must disintegrate".[81] That is to say, the law is perpetually engaged in a "circular succession of imposing forces of law",[82] such that every new law is "destined in its turn to decay".[83] Elsewhere, this cycle of laws, as the very "history of law", has been compared to "a child's kaleidoscope, 'which with every turn of the hand dissolves the established order into a new array' ".[84] Fitzpatrick clarifies this cyclical duality: "[The law] is neither simply destroyed nor simply conserved but is ever being destroyed and conserved – destroyed in its responsiveness and conserved in its being repeatedly determined".[85] The law is ceaselessly engaged in this cycle, whereby the laws that are determined and conserved must, in time, be destroyed and overturned by newly determined laws. These latter laws are, in fact, derived from the response of the law to the not (yet) law, that which confronts the law.[86] This confrontation perpetuates a regeneration of law and, perhaps, its redemption,[87] where the entry

79 Derrida, above n 1, 251.

80 Ibid., 253.

81 Werner Hamacher (Dana Hollander trans), "Afformative, Strike: Benjamin's 'Critique of Violence'" in Andrew Benjamin and Peter Osborne (eds), *Walter Benjamin's Philosophy: Destruction and Experience* (2000) 108, 109.

82 Ibid.

83 Benjamin, above n 5, 300, also cited in Hamacher, above n 81, 109. At 300, Benjamin writes:

> [A]ll law-preserving violence, in its duration, indirectly weakens the lawmaking violence represented by it, through the suppression of hostile counter-violence . . . This lasts until either new forces or those earlier suppressed triumph over the hitherto lawmaking violence and thus found a new law, destined in its turn to decay.

84 Ari Hirvonen, "The Politics of Revolt: On Benjamin and Critique of Law" (2011) 22(2) *Law and Critique* 101, 103, citing Walter Benjamin, "Central Park" in Walter Benjamin, *Selected Writings* (Vol. 4) (2006) 164.

85 Fitzpatrick, above n 18, 167. This is a response to Cover's conception of the relation between violence and the word: Cover, above n 59.

86 See Benjamin, above n 5. At 284, Benjamin identifies a violence that is not yet law, but nonetheless threatens law for its potentially 'lawmaking' capacity:

> The state . . . fears [criminal] violence simply for its lawmaking character, being obliged to acknowledge it as lawmaking whenever external powers force it to concede them the right to conduct warfare, and classes the right to strike.

87 See Ann Curthoys, Ann Genovese and Alexander Reilly, *Rights and Redemption: History, Law and Indigenous People* (2008).

of alterity into the law is productive of 'newness' in the world, created not by recognition of the same, but by the appearance of the unrecognisable.[88] I will return, once again, to these points.

The madness of the decision

For Derrida, a further layer of complexity is assumed within this cycle. He suggests that the violence that "threatens law" is "not an accident arriving from outside the law" but, rather, "already belongs to it, to the right to law [*au droit au droit*], to the origin of law".[89] Furthermore, the violence of this 'non-law' may be described as a "*founding* violence . . . able to justify, to legitimate (*begründen*), or transform the relations of law (*Rechtsverhältnisse*)".[90] I have elaborated upon this notion of origin in Part II, in my discussion of Derrida's conception of the archive, which contains an originary and haunting trace to which the law persistently seeks to return.[91] For Derrida, the origin is ceaselessly reconstituted in this movement between judicial decision and indecision, such that an alterity that may appear to be extrinsic to overt manifestations of determinate law is, in fact, necessarily a part of that which the law draws upon in constituting itself. Yet, the law maintains the fiction of self-sufficiency of origin; indeed, it has been suggested, "[t]hat which most immediately must not be questioned or controverted is law's self-constituting origin – an origin replete with legal matter, with the question of validity, with rights and right".[92]

This may be understood as a demonstration of Derrida's "paradox of iterability", which "requires the origin to repeat itself originarily, to alter itself so as to have the value of origin".[93] Indeed, Fitzpatrick has argued that while law must distinguish itself from "a transgressive violence beyond", it is this violence that, "in its being transgressive, emanates from and is in thrall to that determined norm that is the law".[94] The threat of the 'beyond' is, "*in* law, what suspends law" and "interrupts the established law to found another".[95] The inauguration of new law is always violent, not necessarily insofar as it may consist of tangible violence, but as "an instance of nonlaw".[96] The nonviolence of a responsive law, however, can only become effective law "in the violence of determination".[97] This moment

88 Gilles Deleuze, *Difference and Repetition* (Paul Patton trans., 2004 edn) 172. In Part IV (Literature), I discuss the notion of indigeneity as a radical openness or newness.
89 Derrida, above n 1, 269.
90 Ibid., 268.
91 Derrida, above n 44.
92 Peter Fitzpatrick, " 'Enacted in the Destiny of Sedentary Peoples': Racism, Discovery and the Grounds of Law" (2000) 1(1) *Balayi* 11, 23.
93 Derrida, above n 1, 277–8, cited and discussed in Fitzpatrick (2001), above n 22, 78.
94 Fitzpatrick, above n 18, 144.
95 Derrida, above n 1, 269 (emphasis added).
96 Ibid.
97 Fitzpatrick, above n 18, 167.

of "madness" is an unconditional "event", which "exceeds calculation, rules, programs . . . [and] anticipations".[98] While this confronting alterity "exists even beyond the sphere of law" and is therefore nonviolent insofar as it is conceived as a "pure violence . . . beyond the law",[99] it is nonetheless necessary, to impel the law to the violence of decision.[100] The law is destroyed and newly instituted in each act of judicial interpretation, "by a reinstituting act of interpretation, as if, at the limit, the law [*loi*] did not exist previously – as if the judge himself invented it in each case".[101]

The suspension required in this act, the 'as if',[102] is a (legal) fiction that constitutes the law itself; that is, the apparently determinate law is perpetually (re)created in each moment of decision, its absoluteness founded upon its very contingency. Indeed, Fitzpatrick has suggested that the legal fiction, which may initially appear to be "an apotheosis of autonomously determinant law", actually reveals the paradoxical dependence of law, as "the most dependent yet the most independent thing" – ever responsive to societal change, yet retentive of a "primal power" to assume and absorb the legal fiction.[103] The very capacity of the law to accommodate the fiction of the legal Indigene in native title law – that is, of an individual with a demonstrable and historically constant connection to those cultural and societal norms defined as 'traditional' (and therefore 'Indigenous') – necessarily allows for a (re)writing of this fiction in each moment of judicial decision. In this way, in this moment, the law remains open to the potentiality of intervening (Indigenous) narratives.[104]

In the context of this book, I argue, the appearance of the Indigene before the law and the rupture to this law that is entailed within the counternarratives of Indigenous literature, are productive of a suspension of the mythical force of the law, of a revolutionary chance or moment,[105] and of an unconditional justice that may manifest in the emergence of alternative (legal and political) representations.

98 Derrida, above n 1, 253; 255; 257.

99 Hamacher, above n 81, 113; 126, footnote 12. At 113, Hamacher writes:

> Pure violence does not posit, it "deposes"; it is not performative, but afformative. If the pure violence of de-posing exists even beyond the sphere of law, this pure, and thus nonviolent, non-instrumental violence may at any time – if not universally at any time – break through the cycle of laws and their decay.

100 See Jacques Derrida, "Violence and Metaphysics: An Essay on the Thought of Emmanuel Levinas" in Jacques Derrida, *Writing and Difference* (1967) 97, 185, on the violence of the concept in ultimate determination, as discussed in Part II (Indigeneity).

101 Derrida, above n 1, 251, cited and discussed in Sarat, above n 53, 3, footnote 37.

102 I will return to this notion of the "as if" and the legal fiction in the following section.

103 Fitzpatrick (2001), above n 22, 88.

104 See Curthoys *et al.*, above n 87, 166.

105 Derrida, above n 1, 269; Martel, above n 21, 52; see also discussion in Fitzpatrick (2001), above n 22, 77–8. I evoke the notion of the "revolutionary" here to describe the moment of judicial indecision and the elicitation of Indigenous alterity, as opposed to its more frequent use in the description of Marxist struggle.

Indeed, this rupture may be conceived as a suspension of the law of native title, and the evocation of Indigenous Law. In Freudian terms, this suspension may be understood as the *unheimlich* or "unhomely moment"[106] that, while disruptive, is necessary to the perpetuation of a (legal) order.[107] Derrida describes these unhomely moments as "terrifying . . . because they are in themselves . . . uninterpretable or undecipherable", and the moment of revolution as *unheimlich*, as the "*mystical*" that "is, in law, what suspends law . . . to found another".[108] Furthermore, he elsewhere describes the subversive capacity of literature and "the imperious necessity of what it tells, its law", which renders it uncanny.[109] Biber articulates "the panic of the unhomely moment" in the context of native title and the common law of Australia, and the circularity of the *unheimlich*:

> The unhomely moment does not destabilize the symbolic order; it is necessary to the perpetuation of the order. It sets a new limit and requires new ways of bending and stretching to accommodate it.[110]

While the court of law seeks to limit this 'bending and stretching' in order to maintain the "skeleton of principle",[111] I argue that the alterity of indigeneity that confronts the law is already an intrinsic, yet deconstructive, element of the law itself. Appearing both before and beyond the law, the unstable figure of the Indigene disrupts her own (pre)determination by inciting the uncanny,[112] and the "irreducible 'madness'"[113] that is judicial (in)decision.

Within the law of native title, the intangible yet pervasive 'beyond' is revealed, at times, to be Indigenous Law, made manifest in the common law via the

106 See discussion in Homi Bhabha, *The Location of Culture* (1994) (Routledge Classics Edition, 2004) 9, who suggests that "[t]he unhomely moment creeps up on you stealthily as your own shadow and suddenly you find yourself . . . taking the measure of your dwelling in a state of 'incredulous terror'", cited in Biber, above n 25, 12.

107 As briefly discussed in Part II (Indigeneity), in his essay, "The Uncanny", Freud explores the concept of uncanniness as a literary aesthetic, fuelled by psychological impulses. He suggests that the experience of "uncanniness" is a frightening one because it is an evocation of the unfamiliar; moreover, of the unfamiliar within a familiar space. In order to define the circularity of these antitheses, Freud uses German definitions: *heimlich* ("homely") or *heimisch* ("native") as opposed to *unheimlich* ("unfamiliar", "strange" or "unhomely"). He asserts that these definitions are not polarities, but part of a continuum or circularity: Sigmund Freud, "The 'Uncanny'", in Albert Dickson (ed.), *The Pelican Freud Library: Art and Literature*, Vol. 14 (1990) 201. I will return to this concept in Part IV (Literature).

108 Derrida, above n 1, 269.

109 Jacques Derrida, "Before the Law" in Jacques Derrida (Derek Attridge, ed.), *Acts of Literature* (1992) 181, 199.

110 Biber, above n 25, 12.

111 *Mabo* (1992) 175 CLR 1, 29, discussed in greater detail in Part I.

112 I will return to this suggestion in the context of a close reading of Kim Scott, *That Deadman Dance* (2010), in Part IV (Literature).

113 Fitzpatrick, above n 18, 156.

constrained language of 'tradition' – that is, "traditional laws" and "traditional customs".[114] Such narratives and (Indigenous) Law, however, are recognisable to the common law only where they are not "repugnant to natural justice",[115] thus invoking a highly constrained notion of justice, whereby "[t]he laws of some peoples are ever contingent, the laws of others ever expansionary and surpassing".[116] In this way, the responsiveness of the law, though apparently directed by notions of 'natural justice', resolves itself in acquisitiveness, rendering indigeneity the *property* of the law.[117] The purpose of the elevation of "law's determinant dimension over the responsive", it has been argued, is to "appropriate, and to do so exclusively", thereby "recogniz[ing] indigenous laws, but always in a filtering and qualifying process of its own".[118] Accordingly, the "mythic", law-preserving violence[119] of a determinate law, I would argue, reasserts the sovereignty of its own (fictitious) narrative.

This very narrative, however, is instantiated within a circularity whereby "[l]aw . . . is created by that which it creates".[120] While determinate constructions hinder the Indigenous claimant, my argument follows Derrida in suggesting that the law is nonetheless radically, if minutely, altered in each "event"[121] of decision, such that this alterity persists as the unconditional *with-in* the law. Indeed, where Derrida imagines a law that is constituted both by that which is beyond it, and a simultaneous imperative to contain such excesses, this responsiveness allows for the possibility that "different versions of the past" may indeed become a part of the "official record".[122] While the law, to be effectual, must maintain prescribed boundaries, the archive may be demonstrative of the redemptive potentiality of intervening narratives – stories to which the law has responded, if momentarily, and "now exist within the carapace of the wider legal archive".[123] The rupture or 'event' entailed in such interventions, I argue, is an exemplar of Benjamin's

114 *Mabo* (1992) 175 CLR 1, 58 (Brennan J); *Native Title Act 1993* (Cth) s 223.

115 Ibid., 160, 162 (Dawson J); 61 (Brennan J).

116 Fitzpatrick (2002), above n 22, 250.

117 Jean-Luc Nancy, "Identity and Trembling" in Jean-Luc Nancy, *The Birth to Presence* (Brian Holmes trans., 1993 edn) 9, 10. See earlier discussion of this manoeuvre, in Part II (Indigeneity).

118 Fitzpatrick (2002), above n 22, 238.

119 Benjamin, above n 5. See also discussion thereof in Derrida, above n 1, 265.

120 Fitzpatrick, above n 18, 157. At 167, Fitzpatrick clarifies this argument:

> [T]he word [of the law] is neither simply destroyed nor simply conserved but is ever being destroyed and conserved – destroyed in its responsiveness and conserved in its being repeatedly determined. See also Hamacher, above n 81, 113.

121 Derrida, above n 1, 253; above n 58, especially 234. See my discussion of this in Part I (Narratives).

122 Curthoys *et al.*, above n 87, 227.

123 Ibid., 166. Indeed, in Australia, the *Evidence Amendment Act 2008* (Cth) s 29(2), which impacts directly upon native title hearings, provides that a witness may "give evidence wholly or partly in narrative form", thereby explicitly allowing for the (limited) entry of Indigenous narrative into court hearings.

'divine violence', which is "not law", but justice.[124] It is these apparent oppositions, between law and non-law, violence and nonviolence,[125] which the revelation of alterity *with-in* the law disrupts, and that are made manifest in such renderings of justice. I will now consider the nature of such justice, as distinct from the mythic violence of "justice *as law*",[126] in a literary depiction of the Indigenous subject before the law.

124 Derrida, above n 1, 254.
125 See Fitzpatrick, above n 18.
126 Derrida, above n 1, 240 (emphasis added).

Chapter 10

Justice as law

An idea of justice

> Imagination is the politics of dreams; imagination turns every word into a bottle rocket.[1]

In Sherman Alexie's short story, "The Trial of Thomas Builds-the-Fire",[2] the (Native American, Spokane) defendant, Thomas, explicitly and implicitly challenges the capacity of the court to deliver and, indeed, to conceive of 'justice'. The story is concerned with the antinomic manifestations of justice I have earlier described – as both determinate and responsive,[3] mythic and divine[4] – and the impact of one upon the other. Convicted on the basis of an apparently fictitious crime,[5] Thomas presents his testimony via storytelling. Indeed, the text itself is comprised of a series of short stories, as told by Thomas to the waiting courtroom; furthermore, Thomas himself is described as existing only within the context of a series of interweaving narratives, through which he is "transported": "The only appeal I have is for justice", Builds-the-Fire reportedly said as he was transported away from this story and into the next".[6] Thomas begins his testimony:

1 Sherman Alexie, "Imagining the Reservation" in Sherman Alexie, *The Lone Ranger and Tonto Fistfight in Heaven* (1993) 149, 152.

2 Alexie, above n 33 (Ch 9).

3 See, for instance, Fitzpatrick (2001), above n 22 (Ch 9), especially 6; Fitzpatrick, above n 18 (Ch 9), 144.

4 Benjamin, above n 5 (Ch 9).

5 Alexie, above n 33 (Ch 9), 93, quotes Franz Kafka, "The Trial", in the epigraph to the story: "Someone must have been telling lies about Joseph K., for without having done anything wrong he was arrested one fine morning." Further, at 93–4, Alexie explains Thomas's incarceration:

> Thomas was in the holding cell because he had once held the reservation postmaster hostage for eight hours with the idea of a gun and had also threatened to make significant changes in the tribal vision. But that crisis was resolved years ago as Thomas surrendered voluntarily and agreed to remain silent.

6 Ibid., 102–3.

> "Your Honor", he said. "I don't believe that the exact nature of any charges against me have been revealed, let alone detailed".
>
> There was a hush in the crowd, followed by exclamations of joy, sadness, etc. Eve Ford, the former reservation postmaster held hostage by Thomas years earlier, sat quietly in the back row and thought to herself, *He hasn't done anything wrong.*
>
> "Well, Mr. Builds-the-Fire", the judge said. "I can only infer by your sudden willingness to communicate that you do in fact understand the purpose of this trial".
>
> "That's not true".
>
> "Are you accusing this court of dishonesty, Mr. Builds-the-Fire?"
>
> Thomas sat down, to regain his silence for a few moments.[7]

Later, following an outburst in the courtroom upon hearing Thomas's stories, the judge attempts to restore order once again, via the assertion of 'justice as law':

> "Now", the judge said. "We can go about the administration of justice".
>
> "Is that real justice or the idea of justice?" Thomas asked him, and the judge flew back into anger.[8]

The emergence of such justice, an 'idea of justice', resonates with Derrida's conception of the same: Derrida describes "an 'idea of justice' that is infinite, infinite because irreducible, irreducible because owed to the other".[9] This justice may be further construed as the emergence of the new,[10] "that which is not yet established elsewhere" – a process that, Derrida argues in another context, "forces us to *think* [institutions] differently"[11] and, furthermore, to be created anew.[12] For Derrida, "a new institution" must "access what is forbidden (repressed, made minor, marginalized, even 'unthought') elsewhere" – that is, "the exorbitant" or

7 Alexie, above n 33 (Ch 9), 95–6.
8 Ibid., 100.
9 Derrida, above n 1 (Ch 9), 254.
10 Deleuze, above n 88 (Ch 9), elaborated in the context of this book in Part IV (Literature).
11 Jacques Derrida, *Who's Afraid of Philosophy? Right to Philosophy* 1 (2002) 13.
12 See also Deleuze, above n 88 (Ch 9), 175–6; 172 on the notion of the "new", which Deleuze equates to difference and considers regenerative; see also Simone Drichel, " 'How Newness (not) Comes into the World': Eva Rask Knudsen's *The Circle and the Spiral*" (October 2006) 22(4) *Australian Literary Studies* 507, 507, 510. I will engage with these authors in Part IV (Literature).

"the external".[13] In Alexie's story, this newness is apparent in the emergence of an 'idea of justice' that interrupts the monologic narrative of the law, and is made manifest in the corporeal presence in the courtroom of Thomas Builds-the-Fire himself, and in the simultaneously truthful and fantastical revelations of his stories. Such stories, I argue, are generative of a 'newness' that I conceive as apparent in the revolutionary event of deconstruction and of justice, and thereby reveal the antinomic nature of law – as both violent and nonviolent, destructive and responsive.

While Thomas's narratives of colonial injustice remain apparently unrecognisable to the court, he nonetheless conceives of a justice that is evoked in his storytelling – an(other) justice that interrupts the putative justice of the court of law. This interruption occurs both literally (in his courtroom testimony) and figuratively (in the context of his own and Alexie's narratives). In response to a request to provide his testimony to vaguely drawn charges – "What charges should we bring him up on? . . . Inciting riot? Kidnapping? Extortion? Maybe murder? . . . We don't need his kind around here anymore"[14] – Thomas begins to tell stories. He speaks of broader Native American experiences of violence and dispossession. While his compatriots in the courtroom are encouraging – "Thomas . . . We're all listening . . . Thomas . . . We hear you"[15] – the arms of law and government are dismissive:

> "Builds-the-Fire has a history of this kind of behavior," a man in a BIA [Bureau of Indian Affairs] suit said to the others. "A storytelling fetish accompanied by an extreme need to tell the truth. Dangerous."[16]

Standing before the law, Thomas seeks to interrupt its narrative with alternative historical accounts, and with silence. From the outset, his responses (or lack thereof) disrupt the conventional narrative of the trial, as the judge (unsuccessfully) attempts to elicit Thomas's testimony within the limits of judicial procedure. The judge is dismissive of his responses:

> "Well, Mr. Builds-the-Fire, we're going to dispense with opening remarks and proceed to testimony. Are you ready to call your first witness?"
>
> "Yes, I am your Honor. I call myself as first and only witness to all the crimes I'm accused of and, additionally, to bring attention to all the mitigating circumstances".

13 Derrida, above n 11, 14–15.

14 Alexie, above n 33 (Ch 9), 94.

15 Ibid., 99.

16 Ibid., 93. Alexie's reference to the "BIA" is to a United States federal agency, the Bureau of Indian Affairs. Established in 1824, the history, present purpose and mandate of the Bureau are set out on their website: www.bia.gov/WhoWeAre/BIA/index.htm (accessed 6 October 2015).

"Whatever", the judge said. "Raise your right hand and promise me you'll tell the whole truth and nothing but the truth".

"Honesty is all I have left", Thomas said.[17]

This demand for truth recalls my earlier discussion of "the calculable, responsible citizen-subject"[18] who must, according to Derrida, tell the truth "before the law [devant la loi]".[19] In contrast, the "literary subject", or reader of literature, possesses a "responsibility *without limits*"[20] – that is, the freedom to respond or not, without constraint, within "a hyperbolic condition of democracy".[21] Alexie's depiction of this juridical demand for truth creates a literary challenge to the imperatives of the court, where Thomas refuses to respond in the prescribed form, or indeed at all. Further, this demand for truth stands in contrast to the earlier description of Thomas as one who exhibits "an extreme need to tell the truth", an apparently dangerous trait.[22] It is, in fact, Thomas's honesty that is most challenging to the historical record, and to the performance required of him as he stands before the law, accused. Thomas does not conform to the requirements of judicial procedure, but presents testimony unfamiliar to the court in both form and substance.

As he challenges the capacity of the court to deliver justice, it has been further suggested that his articulation of historical narratives "puts the notion of truth on trial".[23] Whereas the confessional nature of the legal trial purports to reveal truth, " 'free' speech does not prevail in the court of law".[24] Rather, the court is constrained in its capacity to consider alternative narratives, particularly those that would challenge the very authority of the law itself. Nonetheless, the "strategic labour"[25] of this literary work constructs an alternative reality, revealing Indigenous subjectivities that imaginatively challenge and, thereby, rearticulate historical narratives and contemporary social attitudes. Indeed, it has been suggested that the trial depicted within Alexie's text challenges the assumption that "law . . . is a system closed to politics and societal influence".[26]

17 Alexie, above n 33 (Ch 9), 95–6.

18 Jonathan Culler, "Derrida and the Singularity of Literature" (2005) 27(2) *Cardozo Law Review* 869, 874.

19 Jacques Derrida, "Passions: An Oblique Offering" in Jacques Derrida (Thomas Dutoit, ed.), *On the Name* (David Wood, John P Leavey, Jr and Ian McLeod, trans., 1995 edn) 3, 29.

20 Culler, above n 18, 874.

21 Derrida, above n 19, 29.

22 Ibid., 93.

23 Elizabeth Archuleta, " 'An Extreme Need to Tell the Truth': Silence and Language in Sherman Alexie's 'The Trial of Thomas Builds-the-Fire' " in Jeff Berglund and Jan Roush (eds), *Sherman Alexie: A Collection of Critical Essays* (2010) 44, 54.

24 Ibid., 51.

25 Eagleton, above n 37 (Ch 9), 170. See discussion of this notion in Part I (Narratives).

26 Archuleta, above n 23, 51.

Comprised of a series of stories, Thomas's testimony includes the narrative of a surviving pony from the 1858 conflict between the Spokane tribe and the American army, in which 800 horses were slaughtered.[27] His narratives challenge the court and are, moreover, politically and culturally galvanising to his Spokane audience. At the triumphant conclusion of this counternarrative – "I lived that day, even escaped Colonel Wright, and galloped into other histories" – those Native Americans present in the courtroom are newly empowered:

> Thomas opened his eyes and saw that the Indians in the courtroom sat up straight, combed their braids gracefully, smiled with Indian abandon.[28]

The judge asks whether his testimony is concluded, to which Thomas responds, "There are so many more stories to tell".[29] Having situated his equine narrator within interweaving stories, Thomas transposes the putative authority of judicial narrative and diminishes its authority by his refusal to adhere to the linguistic and performative demands of the court. Indeed, it has been suggested, "he simply becomes a conduit for the pony's narrative".[30] Both in his choice to articulate such narratives, and to maintain his silence, Thomas creates "a third space or dialogics that moves beyond the colonizer/colonized and oppressor/victimized dichotomies",[31] facilitating the interactive dynamic of narrative, rather than the oppositional dynamic of litigation. This movement recalls Derrida's notion of democracy in the singular literary work – a hyperbolic condition of democracy",[32] in accordance with which the response of the reader, as opposed to the litigant, might include non-response.[33]

Following Thomas's second story, detailing the execution of Qualchan, the 19th-century Yakama chieftain, who "had been fighting for our people, for our land"[34] and whose violent death is sanitised by a municipal decision to build a golf course in the valley in which he was hung,[35] his audience is once again enlivened:

> The courtroom burst into motion and emotion. The judge hammered his gavel against his bench. The bailiff had to restrain Eve Ford, who had made a sudden leap of faith across the room toward Thomas.[36]

27 Alexie, above n 33 (Ch 9), 96–8.
28 Ibid., 98.
29 Ibid.
30 Archuleta, above n 23, 57.
31 Ibid., 59.
32 Derrida, above n 19, 29.
33 Jacques Derrida, " 'This Strange Institution Called Literature': An Interview with Jacques Derrida" in Jacques Derrida, Jacques Derrida (Derek Attridge, ed.), *Acts of Literature* (1992) 33, especially 68–9. See also discussion in Culler, above n 18, especially 873–4.
34 Alexie, above n 33 (Ch 9), 98.
35 Ibid., 99.
36 Ibid.

These narratives elicit a physical and emotional response, both from his tribe, present in the courtroom, Eve's leap of faith echoing the "call to faith" described by Derrida as necessary to the foundation and authority of laws,[37] and from the judge: "The judge was red-faced with anger; he almost looked Indian. He pounded his gavel until it broke".[38] The court asserts its power in the course of preserving itself – that is, in Benjamin's terms, "for its own sake".[39] In contrast, Thomas's narratives exhibit a transformative or revolutionary power that may be described as being "over all life for the sake of the living"[40] – that is, for the sake of those who hear him, who are politically and, perhaps, culturally and spiritually enlivened by his utterances.

Previously silent for nearly 20 years, his "stories remain[ing] internal",[41] it has been suggested that Thomas, through his broken silence and the force of his narratives, "inspires the [Spokane] tribe to renew its identity in the face of direct threat by US authority".[42] Moreover, Dix argues, "Thomas's stories signify not because of their imaginative re-creation of the past but because of their pragmatic effect upon the listening Spokanes", such that "[f]or the moment of the trial anyway, the tribe experiences through the medium of narrative a sense of its collectivity".[43] In this way, the narratives in Alexie's literary text function to "revitalize" and "reconnect" both fictitious and actual Spokane communities, "whose stories official histories have silenced and concealed behind upscale neighbourhoods and golf courses".[44] This generation of "cultural pride" is, in Alexie's text, "somewhat distanced or ironized (italicized, as it were)", yet it nonetheless remains a source of "possible force".[45] Dix cites another of Alexie's stories in the same collection, entitled "A Drug Called Tradition", in which the characters (including Thomas Builds-the-Fire) satirise their proposed Native American storytelling, performed while taking drugs: "It'll be very fucking Indian. Spiritual shit, you know?"[46] Alexie's description of the judge in "The Trial of Thomas Builds-the-Fire" as "red faced" and therefore "almost" Indian, also satirises conventional expectations of Native American indigeneity.[47] Storytelling in this context, I would argue, is emphatically empowering to Indigenous peoples where it self-consciously disrupts existing hegemony, provocatively exposing the

37 Derrida, above n 1, 240–1.
38 Alexie, above n 33 (Ch 9), 99.
39 Benjamin, above n 5 (Ch 9), 297.
40 Ibid.
41 Alexie, above n 33 (Ch 9), 94.
42 Dix, above n 34 (Ch 9), 165.
43 Ibid., 165–6.
44 Archuleta, above n 23, 58.
45 Dix, above n 34 (Ch 9), 166.
46 Sherman Alexie, "A Drug Called Tradition" in Sherman Alexie, *The Lone Ranger and Tonto Fistfight in Heaven* (1993) 12, 14.
47 Alexie, above n 33 (Ch 9), 99.

performative markers of the Indigenous legal subject. Moreover, focusing upon Thomas's silence, rather than his narratives, Dix further suggests that Alexie's work presents an escape not "*by* or *into* stories, but, rather . . . escape *from* stories".[48] That is, an escape from dominant historical narratives and their required performances – "out of history altogether" – or, in fact, rupturing such narratives from within – ruptured via the telling of new stories that are, in the words of Alexie, "raised from the ash of older stories".[49]

At the close of these narratives, Thomas is convicted of murder. Whether or not he is guilty before the law is irrelevant where his plea is for justice – perhaps the 'idea' of justice to which he earlier alludes, as contrasted with 'real' justice, as dispensed by the judge.[50] For Thomas, it seems, the 'idea' of justice emerges in his storytelling, which he continues even as he is transported to the state penitentiary.[51] The court, however, is confined to its own (arguably fictitious) narrative;[52] indeed, as Cover suggests, "[t]he very imposition of a normative force upon a state of affairs, real or imagined, is the act of creating narrative".[53] While the law is unable to accommodate Thomas's (alternative) narratives, "and is driven to violence and obscenity to assert its own encapsulated reality",[54] his stories nonetheless persist in the broader narrative of history, including that of the legal archive itself, and as a part of Alexie's story. Furthermore, I would suggest, they evoke a Derridean "deconstructive movement" within the law and the emergence of an unconditional justice.[55] That is, in the words of Fitzpatrick, the intervention of an "outside into which . . . [law] is always receding".[56]

48 Dix, above n 34 (Ch 9), 162.

49 Alexie, above n 33 (Ch 9), 163; 98.

50 This notion of the "idea" resonates with one of Thomas's alleged crimes – that of holding "the reservation postmaster hostage for eight hours with the idea of a gun": Alexie, above n 33 (Ch 9), 93.

51 Alexie, above n 33 (Ch 9), 103:

> Thomas looked at these five men who shared his skin color, at the white man who shared this bus which was going to deliver them into a new kind of reservation, barrio, ghetto, logging-town tin shack. He then looked out the window, through the steel grates on the windows, at the freedom just outside the glass. He saw wheat fields, bodies of water, and bodies of dark-skinned workers pulling fruit from trees and sweat from thin air. Thomas closed his eyes and told this story.

52 I will return to this notion of legal fictions in the following chapters, in the course of considering the foundations of native title.

53 Robert Cover, "Nomos and Narrative" in Martha Minnow, Michael Ryan and Austin Sarat (eds), *Narrative, Violence, and the Law* (1992) 95, 102.

54 Peter Fitzpatrick, "Necessary Fictions: Indigenous Claims and the Humanity of Rights" (20 February 2010) *Human Rights and Human Welfare Working Paper No 57*, 17, at www.du.edu/korbel/hrhw/workingpapers/archive/index.html (accessed 6 October 2015).

55 Derrida, above n 1 (Ch 9), 254.

56 Fitzpatrick, above n 18 (Ch 9), 144, citing Michel Foucault, "Maurice Blanchot: The Thought from Outside" in Michel Foucault and Maurice Blanchot, *Foucault/Blanchot* (Brian Massumi trans., 1987 edn) 7, 34.

The apparent impenetrability of such hegemonic narratives, and the revelation of their ultimate vacuity, recalls, once again, Kafka's parable of the countryman before the law. The law, the countryman laments, should be "accessible at all times and to everyone",[57] yet his repeated attempts to gain admittance are delayed and, ultimately, refused. To stand before the law, Derrida argues, is to stand before a text – "impregnable and ultimately ungraspable, incomprehensible".[58] In this way, the law is imagined to be "fantastic . . . its original site and occurrence are endowed with the qualities of a fable", such that it remains "essentially inaccessible even when it, the law, presents or promises itself".[59] The origin and foundation of the law is revealed to be fantastical, while its impenetrability and, therefore, perpetuation, are ensured by a doorkeeper. While the law remains impenetrable, the narrative of the countryman remains *outside* the law; indeed, for Derrida, the countryman is "a subject of the law in appearing before it . . . but since he is *before* it because he cannot enter it, he is also *outside the law* (an outlaw). He is neither under the law nor in the law. He is both a subject of the law and an outlaw".[60]

This exclusion, however, is the revolutionary potential of the countryman and, more broadly, of narratives alternative to those of the law, as a challenge to or rupture of it. That is, the challenge of the Derridean unconditional, as an event – "*what arrives, what comes about*".[61] Martel has suggested that the justice for which the countryman (everyman) waits has already arrived, evident in the "justice and democratic practices" already existing outside of the law.[62] The perpetual expectation of the waiting countryman renders such practices illegible, the ultimate realisation of the futility of his wait only revealed to him upon his death. For Derrida, however, this justice has not arrived but perpetually haunts the law – a spectre that, I argue, interrupts the determinate narratives of the law. The countryman arrives, to stand before the law; yet the law itself is revealed to be a text, its content inscribed by the countryman himself, contingent upon his entry into it.[63] Where the "story of prohibition is a prohibited story",[64] it is a powerfully disruptive 'idea' of justice, and of law. I will now turn to consider the nature of these dominant yet fantastic (legal) narratives – their authorisation, foundation, legitimation and imposition – and their content, whether 'just' and whether legitimate, fictitious or both. In so doing, I will examine the nature of the legal fiction more broadly, and its particular relation to the aforementioned notions of justice – as an 'idea', and as law.

57 Franz Kafka, "Before the Law" in Franz Kafka (Nahum N Glatzer, ed.), *The Complete Short Stories of Franz Kafka* (Willa Muir and Edwin Muir trans., 2005 edn) 3, 3.

58 Derrida, above n 109 (Ch 9), 211.

59 Ibid., 199–200.

60 Ibid., 204.

61 Derrida, above n 58 (Ch 9), 234.

62 Martel, above n 21 (Ch 9), 70.

63 Derrida, above n 1 (Ch 9), 270.

64 Derrida, above n 109 (Ch 9), 199–200.

Legitimate fictions

> [N]ostre droict mesme a, dict-on, des fictions legitimes sur lesquelles il fonde la vérité de sa justice [and our law hath, as some say, certaine lawfull fictions, on which it groundeth the truth of justice].[65]

"What is a legitimate fiction? What does it mean to found the truth of justice?"[66] As discussed, Derrida describes the law – its accessibility or impenetrability – as akin to literature.[67] He draws upon Kant's notion of the "as if"[68] to suggest that "narrativity and fiction" may be found in "the very core of legal thought" and, furthermore, that literature emerges in "that place where the law is made".[69] While the Part IV will more fully address the juridical capacities of literature, it is to the fictitious 'core' of the law and its narratives of legitimacy that I now turn, in considering the law of native title in Australia. Founded and continuing in reliance upon a variety of historical and legal fictions, native title law arguably contains a series of "legitimate fictions", with which the law purports to "found the truth of justice".[70]

Discussing the relation between law and justice, and the authority of law, Derrida proposes a fictional source of foundation. That is, obedience to laws on the basis of "the credit granted them . . . that is their only foundation".[71] He cites Montaigne's proposal that the law contains "certaine lawfull fictions" being, for Derrida, the "supplement of a legitimate fiction . . . the fiction necessary to found the truth of justice".[72] He further cites Montaigne, who attributes artifice to the law:

> Montaigne proposed an analogy between this supplement of a legitimate fiction, that is, the fiction necessary to found the truth of justice, and the supplement of artifice called for by a deficiency in nature, as if the absence of natural law called for the supplement of historical or positive (that is to say, an addition of fictional) law . . .[73]

65 Michel de Montaigne, *Essais* 3, Ch 13, "De l'expérience" (1962), 1203 *The Essayes of Montaigne* (John Florio trans., 1933 edn) 970, cited in Derrida, above n 1 (Ch 9), 240.
66 Derrida, above n 1 (Ch 9), 240.
67 Derrida, above n 109 (Ch 9), 181. At 196, Derrida likens law and literature, in terms its "possibility and its impossibility, its readability and unreadability, its necessity and prohibition, and the questions of relation, of repetition and of history".
68 Once again, this is a reference to Kant's second formulation of the categorical imperative: "Act as if the maxim of your action were by your will to turn into a universal law of nature", cited in Derrida, above n 109 (Ch 9), 190. Refer also to my earlier discussion of this maxim in this particular context, in the previous chapters of this book.
69 Derrida, above n 109 (Ch 9), 190, 216.
70 Derrida, above n 1 (Ch 9), 240.
71 Ibid.
72 Ibid.
73 Ibid. See also discussion in Fitzpatrick, above n 54, 19.

Drawing upon the work of Rousseau, Derrida identifies the supplement as "compensatory and vicarious", that which "intervenes or insinuates itself *in-the-place of* . . . a subaltern instance", whose "place is assigned in the structure by the mark of an emptiness".[74] Accordingly, "something" may be wholly comprised of that which signifies it, since "[t]he sign is always the supplement of the thing itself".[75] This notion recalls Derrida's description of the archive as a technology or prosthesis for memory,[76] and my earlier discussion of the law as just such a technology.[77] Where the completeness of the law is, itself, a fiction – the law being comprised of and revised by that which is extrinsic to it – this fiction may indeed be described as a supplement to, and therefore wholly comprising, the law.[78] Moreover, as discussed earlier, where the law is itself "fantastic . . . endowed with the qualities of a fable", it necessarily remains perpetually inaccessible, its very narrative "the impossible story of the impossible".[79]

The particular (legal) fictions with which I am here concerned relate to the origin and perpetuation of native title, particularly in Australia. These include the declaration of *terra nullius*, the founding of British sovereignty in Australia, and the consequent positioning of Indigenous Australians. I would suggest that the maintenance of these fictions is exemplified in the law of native title. Exemplified, since native title directly pertains to questions of sovereignty and tenure, and to the recognition or extinguishment of Indigenous rights and interests, proprietary or otherwise. Furthermore, native title pertains to questions of ontological significance, where Indigenous and non-Indigenous conceptions of 'property' patently differ.[80] For many Australian Indigenous societies, it has been argued, knowledge, including law, is inseparable from the broader notion

74 Jacques Derrida, ". . . That Dangerous Supplement . . ." in Jacques Derrida (Derek Attridge, ed.), *Acts of Literature* (1992) 76, 83.

75 Ibid.

76 Derrida, above n 44 (Ch 9), 25.

77 I have, in Part II, discussed the founding of legal authority, its institution conceived as "a violence without ground", being "by definition unfounded" (Derrida, above n 1 (Ch 9), 242). See also discussion on the question of "founding", in Derrida, above n 44 (Ch 9), 22. See also discussion in Part II (Indigeneity). That is, the law being without ground or origin, (re)instantiated in each instance of judicial decision (Derrida, above n 1 (Ch 9), 251). See also Fitzpatrick (2001), above n 22 (Ch 9), 80–1; cf 88, on the law as a "mute ground" but "a ground nonetheless", which "does not disappear in its responsiveness but endures in some palpable positioning".

78 See, for instance, Derrida, above n 74. At 83, Derrida writes:
"But the supplement supplements. It adds only to replace . . . The sign is always the supplement of the thing itself." Further, at 89, Derrida continues: "Blindness to the supplement is the law".

79 Derrida, above n 109 (Ch 9), 200.

80 See, for instance, Marcia Langton, "The Estate as Duration: 'Being in Place' and Aboriginal Property Relations in Areas of Cape York Peninsula in North Australia" in Lee Godden and Maureen Tehan (eds), *Comparative Perspectives on Communal Lands and Individual Ownership: Sustainable Futures* (2010) 75; Bradley Bryan, "Property as Ontology: On Aboriginal and English Understandings of Ownership" (2000) 13 *Canadian Journal of Law and Jurisprudence* 3.

of "life-ways".[81] Such knowledge is literally manifest in the landscape, broadly described as 'country', to the extent that "Aboriginal law is 'grown' not 'made' ".[82] The landscape is spiritually animated, governing property relations through "laws of ritual engagement with ancestors and spiritual Beings"[83] – a system that differs markedly from non-Indigenous juridical emphases upon hierarchies of right and entitlement.

The purported 'discovery' and colonisation of the continent, named Australia, was dependent upon these particular (European) assumptions of sovereign and proprietorial right, and contemporaneous understandings of 'civilised' habitation and 'wilderness', 'nature', and 'culture'. [84] European divisions between notions of " 'settled and civilised', 'wild and native' "[85] arguably provided a foundation for the assumption of the legal fiction of *terra nullius* in Australia – that is, the acquisition of sovereignty in a land considered "desert uninhabited"[86] – and the consequent erasure of indigeneity. Rose describes this violent foundation as the "peculiar notion that if one cannot see traces or signs of one's own culture in the land, then the land must be 'natural' or empty of culture" and, furthermore, as the imperial gaze

81 Marcia Langton, "The 'Wild', the Market and the Native: Indigenous People face New Forms of Global Colonization" in William M Adams and Martin Mulligan (eds), *Decolonizing Nature: Strategies for Conservation in a Post-Colonial Era* (2003) 79, 80.

82 Mary Graham, "Some Thoughts about the Philosophical Underpinnings of Aboriginal Worldviews" (2008) 45 *Australian Humanities Review* 181, 192.

83 Langton, above n 81, 93. See also George Tinamin, "One Land, One Law, One People", in Lorraine Mafi-Williams (ed.), *Spirit Song: A Collection of Aboriginal Poetry* (1993) 4, cited in Part I (Narratives), who articulates this animation.

84 See also *Johnson v M'Intosh* 21 US 543, 590 (1823), in which Marshall CJ justified the use of force in the acquisition and maintenance of Indigenous territory by the equation of its Indigenous inhabitants with a putative "wilderness": "To leave [the tribes of Indians inhabiting the country] in possession of their country, was to leave the country a wilderness".

85 Lee Godden and Maureen Tehan, "Introduction: A Sustainable Future for Communal Lands, Resources and Communities", in Godden and Tehan, above n 80, 10.

86 William Blackstone, *Commentaries on the Laws of England* (1830, 17th edn), Book II, Chapter I, 7, cited in *Mabo* (1992) 175 CLR 1, 33; see also 48 (Brennan J). Subsequently confirmed in *Cooper v Stuart* [1889] 14 AC 286, 291, in which the Privy Council determined that Australia, at the assertion of British sovereignty, was "a tract of territory practically unoccupied without settled inhabitants or settled law". See also S. James Anaya, *Indigenous Peoples in International Law* (2004, 2nd edn) 29, cited and discussed in Lisa Strelein, "From *Mabo* to *Yorta Yorta*: Native Title Law in Australia" (2005) 19 *Washington University Journal of Law and Policy* 225, 228. Strelein describes the justification of legal occupation of land by " 'discovering' [European] states" as *terra nullius* on the basis of a perceived absence of political force in the existing societies. Even in territories not considered *terra nullius*, but nonetheless inhabited by Indigenous nations and governed by Indigenous law, such as the Americas and Canada, European imposition was considered legally and socially justified. See extended discussion in Strelein, above, especially 227:

> Superiority in land use and the "right" of civilized peoples to cultivate the land was the justification for taking the territories from the Indigenous peoples. Recognition was dependant upon a Eurocentric evaluation of the social and political development of Indigenous peoples and was dismissive of the Indigenous governmental structures that were in place.

of the explorer upon the landscape, "wherein one sees oneself or one sees nothing at all".[87] Legal narratives that have been historically determinative of land, waters, and, indeed, of Indigenous peoples themselves, retain these conceptions – integral to the arguably continued process of 'deep' colonisation.[88]

In the following sections, I will consider the various fictions that enable and perpetuate the law of native title in Australia and the relation of these, if any, to justice. I will proceed from the historical moment of encounter, between European nautical explorers and those peoples and nations occupying the 'discovered' continent, and descriptions of such peoples as "barbarous or unsettled and without settled law"[89] and, consequently, of the landscape as a 'wilderness'. I will also consider the subsequent declaration of the legal and historical fiction of *terra nullius*, of British sovereignty and radical title,[90] the persistent fiction of a recoverable "ancient tribe",[91] apparent in the legal requirement for evidence of unbroken – or, at the very least, "substantially uninterrupted"[92] – traditional connection to land and waters. In all these, I will consider the fiction of the Indigene herself,[93] upon which, I argue, Australian law has and continues to depend for its very foundation and perpetuation.

87 Deborah Bird Rose, "Land Rights and Deep Colonising: The Erasure of Women" (1996) 28 *Aboriginal Law Bulletin* 6, 17–18.

88 Ibid., 17–18. See also Michael Dodson, "From Lore to Law: Indigenous Rights and Australian Legal Systems" (1995) 72(2) *Aboriginal Law Bulletin* 2, who suggests that "the machinery of the Australian legal system has acted as the legitimising arm of colonialism".

89 *Mabo* (1992) 175 CLR 1, 38.

90 Ibid., 48 (Brennan J). See extended reference at footnote 23 (Ch 2).

91 Grbich, above n 43 (Ch 9), 128 citing s 223(1) *Native Title Act 1993* (Cth).

92 *Akiba* (2010) 270 ALR 564, [544]–[552]. For further references, see above, n 39 (Ch 9).

93 See related discussion of the fictitious creation of the American "Indian" in Fitzpatrick, above n 92 (Ch 9), 24: "The *über* fiction through which law created and sustained both its factual ground and its self-entitling was the figure of the Indian".

Chapter 11

The last uncharted continent

The colonial gaze

> The eye which sees is not the organic counterpart of Locke's blank mind: its gaze is not random, open-minded, equally attentive to all directions, all phenomena. On the contrary, it looks down a telescope . . .[1]

The 'discovery',[2] sovereign acquisition, and colonisation of new territories by European explorers[3] began with the voyages of Columbus to the Americas in the late 15th century[4] and included those of Cook between 1768 and 1771, who set out with the intent of "search[ing] between Tahiti and New Zealand for 'a Continent or Land of great extent'".[5] This historical moment of encounter, between European explorers and those peoples and nations occupying lands and

1 Paul Carter, *The Road to Botany Bay: An Essay in Spatial History* (1987) xx.

2 The assumptions of discovery are stridently contested in Henry Reynolds, *The Law of the Land* (1992). As has been documented elsewhere, Reynolds argues, at 9–10, that "Cook didn't really 'discover' eastern Australia", and that the legal doctrine of discovery was "above all else a means of adjudicating between competing European powers, allowing them to define spheres of influence while avoiding perpetual conflict over competing claims in the non-European world". Reynolds argues, more broadly, for a radical reconceptualisation of the prevailing legal and historical orthodoxy of Indigenous land rights. Reynolds's book, first published in 1987, and revised and republished in 1992 and 2003, provided an enormously significant contribution to scholarship in Indigenous Australian history. For a useful discussion and appraisal, see David Ritter, "Tilting at Doctrine in a Changing World: The Three Editions of Henry Reynolds' *The Law of the Land*" (2008) 32(3) *Journal of Australian Studies* 393.

3 I here follow Pratt in defining "European" as "a network of literate northern Europeans, mainly men from the lower levels of the aristocracy and the middle and upper levels of the bourgeoisie": Mary Louise Pratt, *Imperial Eyes: Travel Writing and Transculturation* (1992) 37.

4 Paul Keal, *European Conquest and the Rights of Indigenous Peoples: The Moral Backwardness of International Society* (2003) 24.

5 See the *Journal of the H.M.S. Endeavour, 1768–1771* [manuscript] National Library of Australia, MS 1. See also discussion at http://pandora.nla.gov.au/pan/44385/20040920-0000/www.nla.gov.au/collect/treasures/mar_treasure.html (accessed 6 October 2015).

waters previously uncharted by European explorers, remains integral to the legal, political and cultural narratives of settler nation states, including Australia. For those who deemed Australia the "last uncharted continent",[6] the imperial and scientific imperatives that drew British explorers and, later, settlers to the southern hemisphere necessarily informed this encounter. While the expansionist projects of empire were motivated by European political and economic ambitions, such projects temporally coincided with another European conquest – that of scientific identification and systematisation of 'nature'[7] throughout the 'discovered' world. Indeed, as Pratt asserts, this project, "[b]lanketing the surface of the globe . . . specified plants and animals in visual terms as discrete entities, subsuming and reassembling them in a finite, totalizing order of European making".[8]

These scientific expeditions, oriented toward the exploration and documentation of continental interiors, impelled "new forms of European knowledge and self-knowledge, new models for European contact beyond its borders . . . [and] new ways of encoding Europe's imperial ambitions".[9] Such ambitions were enlivened by the emergent "descriptive apparatuses of natural history", including the classification system designed by Carl Linné or, in Latin, Linneaus – "a descriptive system designed to classify all the plants on earth, known and unknown".[10] Pratt suggests that the confluence of such expeditions and classificatory modalities was generative of a new European " 'planetary' consciousness",[11] oriented toward a Eurocentric "construction of global-scale meaning".[12] Such classificatory schemas have been described as "a critical element in the rationalizing gaze of colonialism: the 'othering' of nature[13] in science, art and society . . . [as] 'the ideological practice'" enabling its plunder.[14] Indeed, the categorisations of natural science

6 Pratt, above n 3, 39.
7 See discussion in Pratt, above n 3, 37.
8 Ibid.
9 Ibid., 23–4.
10 Ibid, 15, 229 (footnote 19), in which Pratt references a facsimile edition of the 1758 edition of *The System of Nature* under its Latin title, *Caroli Linnaei Systema Naturae*, published by the British Museum in 1956. This document inaugurated the present system (taxonomy) of biological classification.
11 Ibid, 5. Schmitt also describes the "struggle over land- and sea-appropriations of the New World". Beginning in the 15th and 16th centuries, these struggles initiated the "epoch of modern international law that lasted until the 20th century", when "lines were drawn to divide and distribute the whole earth . . . to establish the dimensions and demarcations of a global spatial order", in "the first stage of the new planetary consciousness of space": Carl Schmitt, *The Nomos of the Earth in the International Law of Jus Publicum Europaeum* (GL Ulman trans. and annotation, 1950 edn) 86.
12 Ibid., 15.
13 According to Pratt, " '[n]ature' meant above all regions and ecosystems which were not dominated by 'Europeans,' while including many regions of the geographical entity known as Europe": ibid., 37.
14 William M Adams, "Nature and the Colonial Mind" in Adams and Mulligan, above n 81 (Ch 10), 16, 24, citing Cindi Katz and Andrew Kirby, "In the Nature of Things: The Environment and Everyday Life" (1991) 16 (2) *Transactions of the Institute of British Geographers* 259, 265.

arguably "locked [species] into colonial patterns of global exploitation", enabling "a rationalizing, extractive, dissociative understanding which overlaid functional, experiential relations among people, plants and animals".[15] It was with this particular 'planetary consciousness' that explorers and settlers encountered the land they imagined as the 'Great Southern Continent', and situated (Indigenous) country and its inhabitants within a universalising taxonomy. While explorers embarked upon expeditions founded upon the premises of imperial conquest and scientific discovery, however, many of these encountered "a land which defied knowing in the European way",[16] such expeditions thus failing to conform to the scientific ideologies of "the knowing and naming men of Europe".[17] Accordingly, the 'discovered' landscape was largely rendered an untameable 'wilderness' that "transcended mere strangeness to become the site of colonial fantasy", simultaneously bearing "untapped natural wealth, and the threat of that which remained unseen and unknown".[18]

It is this historical context and its associated conceptions, I argue, that inform the present law of native title and the constrained situation of the Indigene before it, Indigenous identity more broadly having been historically "submerged or lost . . . reconstituted for the purposes of the coloniser".[19] Elided by the colonial imperative – seen, described and classified – and simultaneously merged with the prosopopoeic tropes of the landscape, the Indigenous inhabitants of the 'discovered' continent of Australia were legally classified, yet were also ciphers for this legal state of *terra nullius*. Boire has proposed that the inscription of (British) law upon the new territory was a means of both disciplining the 'wilderness' space in which the explorers found themselves, as well as its inhabitants:

> For those Europeans wandering in what they believed to be either *terra nullius* or (later) a land populated by barbarians, transplanted European law became the one singular method of both political order and psychological stability. Law from back home, as it were, became a method of both writing the new land into ordered existence and, later, of reading its inhabitants out of resistance and control.[20]

Furthermore, he argues, any existing legal and political order was symbolically erased in advance of their encounter, "as a pre-condition of their impossibility"

15 Pratt, above n 3, 24, 38.
16 Julie Evans, "Beyond the Frontier: Possibilities and Precariousness along Australia's Southern Coast" in Lynette Russell (ed.), *Colonial Frontiers: Indigenous-European Encounters in Settler Societies* (2001) 151, 157.
17 Ibid., 157.
18 Rod Macneil, "Time after Time: Temporal Frontiers and Boundaries in Colonial Images of the Australian Landscape" in Russell, above n 16, 47.
19 Keal, above n 4, 49.
20 Boire, above n 63 (Ch 9), 231.

and of the imposition of "the discursive grids of Eurocentric authority".[21] Carter describes "the road to Botany Bay" as implying "a confrontation with savage nature" and further, the Indigene as "stand[ing] in for irredeemable nature".[22] He evokes the classical viewpoint of the explorer, as seen through "the ring of the telescope", in which the "Australian savage" is framed:[23]

> The Aborigines are grouped together with the "natural productions" of the country, with its fauna and flora. They find themselves, if at all, consigned to the category of miscellaneous information, sailing directions, prospects for trade, geological specimens and the climate. They inhabit the realm of the "etc.".[24]

In this context, the Indigene has been described as having been "[s]et at the margins of colonised space . . . distinguishing the modern, colonial landscape from its prehistoric, uncolonised, Aboriginal Other" and, moreover, imagined as the boundary to "a wild, untamed space" of "unexplored depths", replete with "other-worldly wonders of the uncivilised and the exotic".[25]

Both seen and unseen, encountered but subsumed by the 'wilderness', the Indigenous peoples and the "culturally managed landscape"[26] they inhabited were, to the European arrivals, unrecognisable. To the European invaders, who "could no longer feel their Mother's heart as it beat beneath the green lands of their home", Kwaymullina suggests that the country was empty and meaningless.[27] The land was conceived as "an inert possession", to be "described and catalogued . . . as an object, not as grandmother, grandfather, mother, father, sister, brother and family. And by being named as the land, country became hidden".[28] Indeed, Carter has suggested that the European explorers did not merely discover a pre-existing land but, in fact, created it: "They were choosing directions, applying names, imagining goals, inhabiting the country . . . the land itself did not precede the traveller. It was the offspring of his intention".[29] Abrogating Indigenous

21 Boire, above n 63 (Ch9), 234. See also 235–6, citing Pierre Bourdieu, "The Force of Law: Towards a Sociology of the Juridical Field" *The Hastings Law Journal* 38 (Richard Terdiman trans., 1987 edn) 814, 838:

> Colonial law emerges within and for colonial cultures as *the* necessary forceful inscription of authoritarian desire, or what Pierre Bourdieu so poetically calls "the entire [official] activity of world-making".

22 Carter, above n 1, 320–1.

23 Ibid., 350.

24 Ibid., 335.

25 Macneil, above n 18, 60–1, 47.

26 Ambelin Kwaymullina, "Introduction: A Land of Many Countries", in Sally Morgan, Tjalaminu Mia and Blake Kwaymullina (eds), *Heartsick for Country: Stories of Love, Spirit and Creation* (2008) 6, 11.

27 Ibid., 11–12.

28 Ibid., 11.

29 Carter, above n 1, xxi; 349.

perspectives with a particular notion of 'wilderness', country was and, arguably, is disembodied and emptied, in order to perpetually (re)inscribe the name of the coloniser.

This literal and figurative emptying of the landscape, consequent erasure of indigeneity and violent (re)inscription were essential to the imperial project – the 'discovery' and acquisition of territory, and concomitant assertion of sovereignty and radical title. The "authorising force" of this law has been described as authoritarian, "the 'totalising global vision' of the colonial gaze", in accordance with which "no territory can be left uncharted, no region . . . incognita or nameless or unclaimed".[30] Nonetheless this force of law, it is argued, is not absolute but, rather, "a site of desire, both authoritarian and resistant", as "a language constantly being spoken".[31] In this context, the assertion of radical title has been elsewhere described as "more in the nature of a political notion and in that sense a legal fiction", yet with palpable effects: to reiterate, "property rights of any kind are not fictional".[32] Indeed, Indigenous claims to rights and interests in the land and waters of which they have been historically dispossessed are met with the apparently impenetrable fictions of the law of the sovereign. The legal premises for the acquisition of such territory, as articulated by Blackstone, are founded upon theories of natural law and the "law of nations":[33]

> Plantations, or colonies in distant countries, are either such where the lands are claimed by right of occupancy only, by finding them desert and uncultivated, and peopling them from the mother country; or where, when already cultivated, they have been either gained, by conquest, or ceded to us by treaties. And both these rights are founded upon the law of nature, or at least upon that of nations.[34]

The validity of this right, as against the rights and interests of Indigenous occupants, was first heard in 1823 in *Johnson v M'Intosh*,[35] one of a series of cases that was subsequently foundational to native title law in the United States, Canada, and Australia. In his decision, Chief Justice Marshall held that the rights of the Indigenous claimants to sovereignty and alienation of their traditional lands were "necessarily diminished" and "denied" by "the original fundamental

30 Boire, above 63 (Ch 9), 233.

31 Ibid., 236, 243. See also 238–9 on the "splittedness" of imperial law, and its "always and already threatening condition of imposion".

32 *The Wik Peoples v Queensland & Ors*; *The Thayorre People v Queensland & Ors* (1996) 187 CLR 1, 234 (Kirby J) ("Wik").

33 See discussion of this law in Strelein, above n 86 (Ch 10). At 226, Strelein asserts:

> The law of nations, while positing equality of nations as a central tenet, was also formulated to justify colonization and to limit the recognition of Indigenous peoples.

34 Blackstone, above n 86 (Ch 10), cited in *Mabo* (1992) 175 CLR 1, 34 (Brennan J).

35 Thomas Johnson and Graham's *Lessee v William M'Intosh* 21 US 543 (1823) ("*Johnson v M'Intosh*").

principle, that discovery gave exclusive title to those who made it" and, furthermore, "[t]hus has our whole country been granted by the crown while in the occupation of the Indians".[36] Such assertions rest, at least in part, upon those of 16th-century theologian and natural law theorist, de Vitoria, who suggested that while American Indian societies were in possession of "a certain method in their affairs", their laws were not "proper laws",[37] thus recalling yet again the limitations of the law to recognition of that which is 'proper', or identical, to it.[38]

Some limited reservations to this sweeping appropriation were articulated in *Johnson v M'Intosh*, as they were in Blackstone's Commentaries, the latter suggesting that, while the acquisition of apparently "desert uninhabited" territory was "within the limits of the law of nature", the acquisition should not offend other (moral) boundaries:

> [H]ow far the seising on countries already peopled, and driving out or massacring the innocent and defenceless natives, merely because they differed from their invaders in language, in religion, in customs, in government, or in colour; how far such a conduct was consonant to nature, to reason, or to christianity, deserved well to be considered by those, who have rendered their names immortal by thus civilizing mankind.[39]

Furthermore, returning to *Johnson v M'Intosh*, Chief Justice Marshall asserted that the law itself could not dispute, and must therefore uphold, the means of its own foundation:[40]

> However extravagant the pretension of converting the discovery of an inhabited country into conquest may appear; if the principle has been asserted in the first instance, and afterwards sustained; if a country has been acquired and held under it; if the property of the great mass of the community originates in it, it becomes the law of the land, and cannot be questioned.[41]

Subsequent decisions, in the United States and beyond, affirm this fundamental constraint, and the sustained fiction necessary to its perpetuation. Indeed, "the so-called Indian cases", it has been argued, are demonstrative of the fictional premise of the doctrine of discovery where, in actuality, "[t]he fact of discovery

36 *Johnson v M'Intosh* 21 US 543 (1823) 573, 579.

37 Francisco de Vitoria, "On the American Indians" in Francisco de Vitoria (Anthony Pagden and Jeremy Lawrence, eds), *Political Writings* (1991) 231, cited in Strelein, above n 86 (Ch 10), 227.

38 Nancy, above n 117 (Ch 9).

39 Blackstone, above n 86 (Ch 10), cited in *Mabo* (1992) 175 CLR 1, 33 (Brennan J).

40 See discussion in Fitzpatrick, above n 92 (Ch 9), 23, citing *Fletcher v Peck*, 10 US (6 Cranch) 87, 142 (1810). "The law of the land, to borrow his phrase, could not for Marshall question the "momentous" national settlement which gave it being; that outcome "is not now to be disturbed"". See also discussion in Fitzpatrick (2001), above n 22 (Ch 9), especially 169.

41 *Johnson v M'Intosh* 21 US 543, 543, 591 (1823).

unadorned and the fact of settlement are cognitive perceptions and 'ground' nothing . . . No amount of plain discovery and settling can make the leap to the legal, – to entitlement, exclusivity, ultimacy, and such".[42] In the case of Australia, it has been argued that Justice Brennan's judgment in *Mabo* and, in particular, his assertions as to the non-justiciability of British sovereignty in Australia,[43] reveal the doctrine of tenure itself to be "an historical fantasy, or fictional history" and, indeed, "a legal fiction".[44] I will return to this in the following section.

For the purposes of claims to land and waters under Australian native title law, and the associated demonstration of cultural connectedness required,[45] the Indigene remains, I will suggest, conceived as a manifestation of the aforementioned historical colonial encounter, framed by European scientific and cultural notions. Such notions are reflected in the legal requirements for the recognition of native title – a doctrine that has been described as "tethered to an old colonialism that nonsensically viewed the Indigenous peoples . . . as more in the nature of curious menageries than functioning cultures".[46] Povinelli describes a landscape "emptied of all meanings derived from settlement history" as "the real, unimaginable, unrepresentable ground of 'indigenous'", of which Indigenous claimants before the law are mere "*representations*".[47] Indeed, she argues, it is against this "fantastic, unrepresentational social ground" that the Indigenous subject is measured, her entitlements assessed.[48]

Similarly, Biber describes the erasure of indigeneity that is essential to the creation of a nation that, despite the rhetoric attending native title, "can only ever be exclusively possessed", and the Aborigine as "[a]n obstacle to – and agent of

42 Fitzpatrick, above n 92 (Ch 9), 22.

43 *Mabo* (1992) 175 CLR 1, 32 (Brennan J); *Yorta Yorta* (2002) 214 CLR 422 (Gleeson CJ, Gummow and Hayne JJ, McHugh J in agreement).

44 Judith Grbich, "The Scent of Colonialism: *Mabo*, *Eucalyptus* and Excursions within Legal Racism" (2001) 15 *Australian Feminist Law Journal* 119, 121–2, discussing *Mabo* (1992) 175 CLR 1, 45. See also interesting discussion in Carter, above n 1, 64, who suggests that where it was considered that Aborigines "did not classify [the land] . . . distinguish it from other places . . . know 'it' as a 'place'", it was asked:

> [C]ould [the Aborigine] be said to understand the notion of possession at all? And if his grasp of it were so tenuous, so local, so incapable of generalization, then it was hardly a crime to take possession of it. The Whites . . . possessed a country of which the Aborigine was unaware. To talk of contracts and boundaries to an Aborigine was to talk a foreign language. Logically then, possession could go ahead without consultation.

45 In Australia, this requirement is legislatively stipulated: *Native Title Act 1993* (Cth) s 223(1).

46 Simon Young, *The Trouble with Tradition: Native Title and Cultural Change* (2008) 10. Young makes reference to the "menagerie theory" of "Indian title" in Felix Cohen, "Original Indian Title" (1947) 32 *Minnesota Law Review* 28, 58:

> [T]he theory that Indians are less than human and that their relation to their land is not the human relation of ownership but rather something similar to the relation that animals bear to the areas in which they may be temporarily confined.

47 Elizabeth Povinelli, *The Cunning of Recognition: Indigenous Alterities and the Making of Australian Multiculturalism* (2002) 59.

48 Ibid., 59.

– legitimacy . . . the impossible kernel at the heart of the nation".[49] The requirement that native title claimants prove unbroken connection to land and waters by way of "traditional laws acknowledged" and "traditional customs observed"[50] perpetually revives the (unachievable) fantasy of an "ancient tribe",[51] as it existed at the declaration of British sovereignty in Australia. Such revival, it is argued, is that of an impossible and fantastical indigeneity, bearing little resemblance to contemporary Indigenous communities and individuals, "an ancient order puncturing the present, often hybrid and degenerate, indigenous social horizon".[52] It is to this fantasy that I now turn, in discussing the requirements of native title law and the fictions this entails, including the performance of a fictitious or 'proper'[53] and 'traditional' indigeneity. Before doing so, however, an elaboration of the founding of British (land) law in this 'last uncharted continent', Australia – specifically, the claim to sovereignty and radical title, in accordance with the feudal doctrine of tenure – is now necessary.

Origin and content

The "adjustment of principle" effected in the *Mabo* decision[54] has been conceived, as I suggested in the introduction to this part, as the corrective realignment of the common law[55] with the "historical truth"[56] of colonial 'settlement'. While the court was unable to consider the validity of acquisition of sovereignty, as 'conquered' or 'ceded', as opposed to 'settled', this momentous adjustment pertained to "the precise effect of this legal history and colonial characterisation upon the land entitlements of the Aboriginal inhabitants",[57] including the acquisition of radical title. Justice Brennan provided a concise definition of radical title as, essentially, a power to alienate, acquired with sovereignty.[58] The triumph of the *Mabo* decision, as the foundation of native title in Australia, was the finding that radical title and native title are not incompatible. The former is acquired upon the assumption of sovereignty and settlement,[59] "within the familiar feudal framework of the

49 Biber, above n 25 (Ch 9), 4.
50 *Native Title Act 1993* (Cth) s 223. See also proposed statutory amendments to these requirements: Native Title Amendment (Reform) Bill 2014 (Cth).
51 Grbich, above n 43 (Ch 9), 128.
52 Povinelli, above n 47, 35.
53 I refer once again to notions of the "proper" subject, in Nancy, above n 117 (ch 9), 10.
54 Young, above n 46, 233, footnote 3.
55 *Mabo* (1992) 175 CLR 1, 58 (Brennan J).
56 Keating, above n 13 (Ch 9), 62.
57 Young, above n 46, 233, footnote 3.
58 *Mabo* (1992) 175 CLR 1, 48 (Brennan J). Generally, see discussion at 46–52.
59 *Wik* (1996) 187 CLR 1, 186 (Gummow J), citing *Mabo* (1992) 175 CLR 1, 86–7:

> Radical title is that acquired upon the assumption of sovereignty (as understood in the law of nations) or, rather, upon settlement . . . (as understood in that part of British constitutional law concerned with Imperial expansion). Radical title links international and constitutional law notions with those which support the private law of proprietary rights and interests in land.

common law",[60] including the doctrine of tenures.[61] This precedes and does not equate to absolute and beneficial Crown ownership, *plenum dominium*, which requires some subsequent act of the Crown. As a mere "logical postulate required to support the doctrine of tenure", radical title does not extinguish native title, but remains as a "burden" upon it.[62] Indeed, according to Justice Brennan, "[i]t is only the fallacy of equating sovereignty and beneficial ownership of land that gives rise to the notion that native title is extinguished by the acquisition of sovereignty".[63]

In *Wik v Queensland*, Justice Gummow described the "mediaeval notion of tenure [as] expressed by the proposition that all land was held directly or indirectly of the Crown".[64] This framework comprised "relationships of reciprocal obligation between the respective parties at each level of the feudal structure, at the peak of which stood the sovereign", such that absolute ownership or "dominium of any particular dominus 'was always a relative thing'".[65] His Honour held that the notion of absolute and beneficial Crown ownership is a comparatively recent concept, conceivably introduced to accommodate 17th- and 18th-century imperial expansion.[66] He cites Professor Jenks, writing in 1896, on the fictitious assumptions entailed within the reliance upon this framework in the (initial and continued) assertion of Crown ownership in colonised lands:

> [T]he theory had almost died a natural death when it sprang to life again in the most unexpected manner with the acquisition of the great English colonies. For if, as was the case, no subject could show a recognized title to any of the countless acres of America and Australia, at a time when those countries were first opened up by white men, it followed that, according to this relic of feudal theory, these acres belonged to the Crown. It may seem almost incredible that a question of such magnitude should be settled by the *revival of a purely technical and antiquarian fiction*.[67]

The *Mabo* decision established that, in the absence of the explicit exercise of sovereign authority, absolute Crown ownership in Australia was indeed a fiction,

60 *Mabo*, (1992) 175 CLR 1, 54 (Brennan J).
61 *Wik* (1996) 187 CLR 1, 186 (Gummow J).
62 *Mabo* (1992) 175 CLR 1, 49–50, authority from *Amodu Tijani v Secretary, Southern Nigeria* [1921] 2 AC, 403, (Viscount Haldane) *(Amodu Tijani)*, followed by the Privy Council in *Sobhuza II. v Miller* [1926] AC, 525. In *Mabo*, 56–7, Brennan J describes the circumstances of and cites the latter case, in which the title of an indigenous community, which their Lordships thought to be generally usufructuary in character, was held to survive as "a mere qualification of a burden on the radical or final title of whoever is sovereign", capable of being extinguished "by the action of a paramount power which assumes possession or the entire control of land".
63 *Mabo* (1992) 175 CLR 1, 51 (Brennan J).
64 *Wik* (1996) 187 CLR 1, 186 (Gummow J).
65 Ibid., citing SFC Milsom, *The Legal Framework of English Feudalism: The Maitland Lectures Given in 1972* (1976) 39.
66 *Wik* (1996) 187 CLR 1, 234.
67 Ibid. (emphasis added), citing Edward Jenks, *A History of the Australasian Colonies: From their Foundation to the Year 1893* (1896), 59.

where "a mere change in sovereignty does not extinguish native title to land".[68] Justice Brennan further held that, in the case of Australia, since the land acquired at sovereignty was not "desert and uninhabited, truly a terra nullius" the Crown did not take "absolute beneficial title (allodial title)".[69] This finding was made on the basis that the legal legitimacy of settled colonies, such as Australia, was previously upheld by the fiction that "customary rights could not be reconciled 'with the institutions or the legal ideas of civilized society'".[70] This fiction was revealed and the historical assertion of *terra nullius* denied; yet, the acquisition of sovereignty on this foundation and, hence, the very authority of the court, remain unchallenged.[71]

Native title has been found to inhere in land and waters not subject to the extinguishing acts of the State,[72] its origin and content identifiable in the rights and interests possessed under the "traditional laws and customs" of extant

68 *Mabo* (1992) 175 CLR 1, 56, 57; original citation from Viscount Haldane in *Amodu Tijani* [1921] 2 AC 399, 407: "A mere change in sovereignty is not to be presumed as meant to disturb rights of private owners; and the general terms of a cession are prima facie to be construed accordingly". This proposition was affirmed in *Adeyinka Oyekan v Musendiku Adele* [1957] 1 WLR 876, 880 (Ld Denning); and *Calder et al v Attorney General (British Columbia)* (1973) 34 DLR (3d) 145, 208–9 (Hall J), relying upon *Campbell v Hall* (1774) 94 ER 1045. See discussion of this history in Richard H Bartlett, *Native Title in Australia* (2000) 76–7.

69 (1992) 175 CLR 1, 48 (Brennan J).

70 Ibid., 58 (Brennan J) citing *re Southern Rhodesia* (1919) AC 211, 233–4. In this latter case, at 233–4 (cited in *Mabo* (1992) 175 CLR 1, 39 (Brennan J)), a distinction between Indigenous and non-Indigenous systems of law was explicitly drawn, and the requirement for evidence of demonstrable social organisation and rights and duties comparable to those of the British realm articulated:

> The estimation of the rights of aboriginal tribes is always inherently difficult. Some tribes are so low in the scale of social organization that their usages and conceptions of rights and duties are not to be reconciled with the institutions or the legal ideas of civilized society. Such a gulf cannot be bridged. It would be idle to impute to such people some shadow of the rights known to our law and then to transmute it into the substance of transferable rights of property as we know them.

71 See discussion in Young, above n 46, 233, especially footnote 3. This conundrum inevitably arises when the court cannot question the source of its own authority, since it would do so on the basis of such authority. See also discussion in Biber, above n 25 (Ch 9), 14. At 14, discussing the perceived (national) threat of the native title claim, Biber writes:

> The High Court will never decide to invalidate the very position from which it judges. The claim is only powerful in the fantasy space in which the Aborigine is imagined as dangerous, destructive and capable of dispossessing the colonist.

Most comprehensively, see early analysis in Kent McNeil, "A Question of Title: Has the Common Law Been Misapplied to Dispossess the Aboriginals?" (1990) 16 *Monash University Law Review* 91, 99. While it is beyond the scope of this book to fully consider the legitimacy of sovereign acquisition, I note that it has been argued that recognition of Indigenous rights and interests *beyond* the confines of the common law may be ultimately effected in the emergence of Indigenous assertions to sovereignty. See early discussion in Henry Reynolds, *Aboriginal Sovereignty: Reflections on Race, State and Nation* (1996).

72 *Mabo* (1992) 175 CLR 1, 63 (Brennan J); see also *Native Title Act 1993* (Cth) s 11, 237A, 227. The extreme vulnerability of native title to extinguishment further compounds the disadvantaged position of Indigenous traditional owners.

Indigenous societies,[73] not in the mere occupation of land.[74] For my purposes, it is worth articulating this finding, as expressed in *Mabo*, in full:

> Native title has its origin in and is given its content by the traditional laws acknowledged by and the traditional customs observed by the indigenous inhabitants of a territory. The nature and incidents of native title must be ascertained as a matter of fact by reference to those laws and customs.[75]

This definition was also refined in summary, and the requirement of connection articulated, with "native title to particular land . . . its incidents and the persons entitled thereto" being "ascertained according to the laws and customs of the indigenous people who, by those laws and customs, have a connection with the land",[76] which may be maintained in the absence of actual physical presence on the land or waters.[77] Thus established, native title remains, unless or until "the tide of history has washed away any real acknowledgment of traditional law and any real observance of traditional customs", such that "the foundation of native title has disappeared", which "cannot be revived for contemporary recognition".[78] This definition of native title, as articulated above by Justice Brennan in *Mabo*, is now expressed in statute, specifically in section 223 of the *Native Title Act 1993* (Cth).[79] While necessarily informed by common law principles, particularly those

73 *Mabo* (1992) 175 CLR 1, 58 (Brennan J); see also *Fejo v Northern Territory* (1998) 195 CLR 96, 127 (*Fejo*). See also *Native Title Act 1993* (Cth) s 223.

74 *Ward* (2002) 213 CLR 1, 92 (Gleeson CJ, Gaudron, Gummow and Hayne JJ):

> The finding that predecessors of the claimants occupied the claim area at sovereignty does not, without more, identify the nature of the rights and interests which, under traditional law and custom, those predecessors held over that area. The fact of occupation, taken by itself, says nothing of what traditional law or custom provided.

75 *Mabo* (1992) 175 CLR 1, 58 (Brennan J).

76 Ibid., 70 (Brennan J).

77 *Western Australia v Ward* (2000) 99 FCR 316; confirmed in *Ward* (2002) 213 CLR 1, 85–6, 246–7; *De Rose v South Australia (No 2)* (2005) 145 FCR 290, 306; cf *Akiba v Queensland (No 3)* (2010) 204 FCR 1, 168, 172–3, *Commonwealth v Akiba* (2012) 204 FCR 260, 301. Proposed amendments to the *Native Title Act* provide for the insertion, at s 223, of a statement that "it is not necessary for a connection with the land and waters . . . to be a physical connection": Native Title Amendment (Reform) Bill (2014), cl 18.

78 *Mabo* (1992) 175 CLR 1, 60 (Brennan J). See also a reiteration of this principle in *Members of the Yorta Yorta Aboriginal Community v Victoria and Ors* [1998] FCA 1606, [129] (Olney J):

> The facts in this case lead inevitably to the conclusion that before the end of the 19th century the ancestors through whom the claimants claim title had ceased to occupy their traditional lands in accordance with their traditional laws and customs. The tide of history has indeed washed away any real acknowledgment of their traditional laws and any real observance of their traditional customs.

79 *Native Title Act 1993* (Cth), s 223, sets out the following definition of native title:

> The expression native title or native title rights and interests means the communal, group or individual rights and interests of Aboriginal peoples or Torres Strait Islanders in relation

set out in *Mabo*, the Act is considered the point of departure for any native title proceedings begun after 1993.[80]

This origin and content, traditional law and custom, render native title *sui generis*,[81] – that is, "unique",[82] distinct from the common law, thereby distinguishing traditional law and custom from the doctrine of tenure. Indeed, recognition of native title depends upon its designation as *sui generis*,[83] where claimants are compelled to provide proof of the existence of relevant traditional laws and customs at the time of British acquisition of sovereignty,[84] and their continued existence thereafter, albeit potentially in an 'adapted' form.[85] In *Sampi v Western Australia*[86] Justice French, following *Yorta Yorta*, emphasised the necessity for rights and interests claimed to "originate in a normative system of traditional law and custom which existed at the time of colonisation or the acquisition of sovereignty by the Crown",

> to land or waters, where: the rights and interests are possessed under the traditional laws acknowledged, and the traditional customs observed, by the Aboriginal peoples or Torres Strait Islanders; and the Aboriginal peoples or Torres Strait Islanders, by those laws and customs, have a connection with the land or waters; and the rights and interests are recognised by the common law of Australia.

80 *Yorta Yorta* (2002) 214 CLR 422; *De Rose v South Australia* (2003) 133 FCR 325, [155] (Wilcox, Sackville and Merkel JJ); *Commonwealth v Yarmirr* (2001) 208 CLR 1, 39 (*Yarmirr*).

81 *Mabo* (1992) 175 CLR 1, 59, 61 (Brennan J), 89, 132–3 (Deane and Gaudron JJ); *Wik* (1996) 187 CLR 1, 215 (Kirby J); *Yarmirr* (2001) 208 CLR 1, 183–4 (Kirby J):

> It seems safer to agree with McFarlane JA in *Delgamuukw* . . . that Aboriginal rights are sui generis, difficult if not impossible to define in the terminology of traditional property law, being communal, personal and usufructory.

See also *Ward* (2002) 213 CLR 1, 161, 162 (Kirby J); 280–1 (Callinan J); *Yorta Yorta* (2002) 214 CLR 422, 490–1. This *sui generis* characterisation originated in *Amodu Tijani* [1921] 2 AC 399, 403; *Guerin v R* (1984) [1984] 2 SCR 335; *R v Sparrow* [1990] 1 SCR 1075, 1112; *Delgamuukw v British Columbia* [1997] 3 SCR 1010, [113], [190]. Cf Bartlett, above n 68, 80, who argues against this characterisation:

> The emphasis upon a unique source for native title facilitates an approach whereby it becomes a barrier to, and a limitation and weakness of, native title . . . [and] the imposition of limitations grounded in *both* [Indigenous and non-Indigenous] legal systems . . . to thereby deny giving full respect and equality of treatment to native title.

See also Young, above n46, 292, for further discussion of a "persistent [judicial] emphasis" upon the *sui generis* nature of Indigenous rights and interests.

82 *Ward* (2002) 213 CLR 1, 162 (Kirby J); *Mabo* (1992) 175 CLR 1, 89.

83 See, for instance, *Mabo* (1992) 175 CLR 1, 59; 178–9; 195; 187; 85; *Western Australia v Commonwealth* (1995) 183 CLR 373, 492; *Wik* (1996) 187 CLR 1, 215; *Yarmirr* (2001) 208 CLR 1, 121, 183–4, 198; *Ward* (2002) 213 CLR 1, 15–16, 39, 40, 193, 182, 280, 281. See also *Bodney v Bennell* (2008) 249 ALR 300, 335.

84 *Yorta Yorta* (2002) 214 CLR 422, 452–3.

85 Ibid., 552; affirmed in *De Rose v South Australia* (2003) 133 FCR 325 [164]. See also *Mabo* (1992) 175 CLR 1, 70 (Brennan J):

> It is immaterial that the laws and customs have undergone some change since the Crown acquired sovereignty provided the general nature of the connection between the Indigenous people and the land remains . . .

86 [2005] FCA 777.

in order to be "cognisable by the common law".[87] Earlier, in *Yorta Yorta*, the court defined its role in the "recognition and protection" of native title via "resort to the processes of the new legal order".[88] While the existence and content of native title, as defined by statute, are identified by reference to 'traditional law and custom', these must be nonetheless transposed into the 'legal order' of common law property in order to be recognised. In this way, the law may refuse (or be unable) to recognise "rights or interests which, in some way, are antithetical to fundamental tenets of the common law".[89]

In attempting recognition, the court has identified native title as an "intersection" between the common law and traditional laws and customs.[90] Elsewhere, native title has been described as a point of interaction,[91] or a means of "developing a dialogue"[92] between Indigenous and non-Indigenous law. Furthermore, writing extra-curially, Chief Justice French has described a notion of " 'mapping' traditional relationships to land onto the common law universe", and recognition as "a present declaration of a mapping that, from the point of view of today's common law, came into existence at the time of annexation".[93] Whether such radical difference is open to recognition within the patently different ontological framework of the common law,[94] however, or whether it is entirely desirable for it to be so, is questionable.[95] Indeed, in *Ward*, Justice Callinan remarked upon the "chasm between the common law and native title rights" and, in his view, the "ultimately futile or unsatisfactory, in my respectful opinion, attempt to fold native

87 Ibid., [961], affirmed on appeal (as established principle) in *Sampi on behalf of the Bardi and Jawi People v Western Australia* [2010] FCAFC 26, [15]. This principle was upheld in the latter case, irrespective of other differences between the trial and appeal decisions.

88 *Yorta Yorta* (2002) 214 CLR 422, 453, citing the *Native Title Act 1993* (Cth) s 3(a).

89 *Yorta Yorta* (2002) 214 CLR 422, 453, citing *Ward* (2002) 191 ALR 1, 17–18; 213 CLR 1, 66–7.

90 *Fejo* (1998) 195 CLR 96, 128; *Yorta Yorta* (2002) 214 CLR 422, 452–5.

91 Noel Pearson, "Concept of Native Title at Common Law" in Galarrwuy Yanupingu (ed.) *Our Land is our Life: Land Rights Past Present and Future* (1997) 150, 161.

92 Jeremy Webber, "Beyond Regret: Mabo's Implications for Australian Constitutionalism" in Duncan Ivison, Paul Patton and Will Sanders (eds), *Political Theory and the Rights of Indigenous Peoples* (2000) 60, 82.

93 Justice Robert French and Patricia Lane, "The Common Law of Native Title in Australia" (2002) 2 *Oxford University Commonwealth Law Journal* 15, 26–7. See also ALRC IP 45, above n 39 (Ch 9), 26.

94 See discussion of differences between Indigenous and Western ontologies of property in Bryan, above n 80 (Ch 10), 27. See also Aileen Moreton-Robinson, "I Still Call Australia Home: Indigenous Belonging and Place in a White Post Colonizing Society" in Sara Ahmed, Claudia Castañeda, Anne-Marie Fortier, Mimi Sheller (eds), *Uprootings/Regroundings: Questions of Home and Migration* (2004) 23, 36, who describes a specifically Indigenous "ontological relationship to land" as a "condition of [Indigenous] embodied subjectivity".

95 See, for instance, Ruby Langford Ginibi, "Aboriginal Traditional and Customary Laws" (1994) 1 *Law, Text, Culture* 8, 8: "Some of our laws [are] sacred and not to be spoken about to anyone, only our tribal people". This query recalls my earlier discussion, in Part I (Narratives), on the importance of speaking of, rather than for, the Other. In Part IV (Literature), I will return to this notion in discussing aspects of Indigenous literature that may be incomprehensible to a non-Indigenous reader, such as myself, and the cultural value and necessity of this exclusion.

title rights into the common law".[96]

Langton has distinguished non-Indigenous property "rights, such as the right to exclude and the right to alienate", and (Australian) Indigenous "property relations", the latter being "embedded in the texture of other social relations", derived "from an appreciation of the sacred aspects of spiritual geography".[97] She describes these relations, and the resulting systems of tenure, as *sui generis* insofar as they are deserving of explanation "in their own terms",[98] rather than those of the common law. Elsewhere, Indigenous notions of property have been described not in terms of entitlement and right, but as "embedded in seasonal significance, in kinship significance, in spiritual significance, or in terms of general cultural practice",[99] and Indigenous 'country' as "a culturally managed landscape",[100] such that the latter may be personified:

> [P]eople talk about country in the same way that they would talk about a person: they speak to country, sing to country, visit country, worry about country, feel sorry for country, and long for country. People say that country knows, hears, smells, takes notice, takes care, is sorry or happy.[101]

Accordingly, the utility and fungibility of property – integral to the common law – may not exist in such societies. For instance, a tree or rock may not be mere landscape or resource, but something else entirely: "a tree is never simply timber; indeed a tree is often something else, and can even be one's grandfather (the important thing is that it *is* one's grandfather)".[102] Indeed, in respect of the Pama community in North Australia, Langton suggests that 'things' and 'places' are conflated, as a part of a broader spiritual biogeography: "Places are discursively acknowledged as being essentially and primarily particular things in place, things that are resonances and signs of the ancestral past".[103] These analyses present Indigenous social realities that cannot be neatly encapsulated within non-

96 *Ward* (2002) CLR 1, 398–9.

97 Langton, above n 80 (Ch 10), 76.

98 Ibid. It is of interest to note the contrast between this description of Indigenous property relations as *sui generis* and arguments elsewhere where, it has been asserted, the definition of native title in Australia as *sui generis* has engendered an excessive and onerous degree of specificity: see Young, above n 46, 284; 292; 294; 310.

99 Bryan, above n 80 (Ch 10), 27.

100 Kwaymullina, above n 26, 11.

101 Deborah Bird Rose, *Nourishing Terrains: Australian Aboriginal Views of Landscape and Wilderness* (Australian Heritage Commission 1996) 7, available at www.environment.gov.au/heritage/ahc/publications/commission/books/nourishing-terrains.html (accessed 6 October 2015).

102 Bryan, above n 80 (Ch 10), 27. To reiterate, see also Tinamin, above n 83 (Ch 10), 4:

> This is not a rock, it is my grandfather.
> This is a place where the dreaming
> comes up, right up from inside the ground.

103 Langton, above n 80 (Ch 10), 87.

Indigenous proprietary institutions. Attempts to do so may amount to a form of (re)colonisation, "by actually creating a picture of society and reality that *is not there*", thereby "eradicat[ing] those culturally specific ontological grounds".[104]

Despite the apparent separation of native title and the common law, judicial opinion as to the recognition of native title has grasped at a variety of prescriptive (common law) terminologies, including "proprietary"[105] yet not "property" and, indeed, having "no parallel in the common law",[106] "personal",[107] "usufructuary",[108] affording a "permissive occupancy",[109] "possessory",[110] and "a bundle of rights".[111] In *Ward*,[112] it was further held that a consideration of the compatibility of native title within a proprietary paradigm and its requisite indicia fails to resolve the definitional difficulties within native title jurisprudence. Rather, the majority considered the common law elements of property – "[exclusive] possession, occupation, use and enjoyment" – to be an inappropriate means of classifying native title and, moreover, acknowledged a more abstract relation to land and waters, described as "speaking for country".[113] Nonetheless, it concluded that the task remaining to the judiciary was to decipher the means by which the rights and interests conferred by traditional Indigenous law and custom "can properly find expression in common law terms."[114] Indeed, more recently it has been held that recognition by the common law "means that the common law 'will, by the ordinary processes of law and equity, give remedies in support of the relevant rights and interests to those that hold them'".[115] It is the perpetual return to this objective that renders *actual* recognition of Indigenous rights and interests and, indeed, of indigeneity, a fraught endeavour. As I continue to argue throughout this book, however, such recognition may be achievable in moments of 'madness' or revolution, in which the law partakes of a constitutive alterity, prior to its return to stasis and determinacy.

While there are many points of relevance to the broader thesis of this book within Australian native title law, my particular focus is the acknowledged origin and content of native title – 'traditional' laws and customs, the attendant

104 Bryan, above n 80 (Ch 10), 5.
105 *Mabo* (1992) 175 CLR 1, 61 (Brennan J).
106 *Ward* (2002) 213 CLR 1, 397 (Callinan J).
107 *Mabo* (1992) 175 CLR 1, 61 (Brennan J); 110 (Deane & Gaudron JJ).
108 Ibid., 61; *Wik* (1996) 187 CLR 1, 130 (Toohey J), 177 (Gummow J), 215 (Kirby J); *Fejo* (1998) 195 CLR 96, 150 (Kirby J); *Yarmirr* (2001) 208 CLR 1, 121.
109 Ibid., 132–3 (Deane and Gaudron JJ).
110 Ibid., 214 (Toohey J).
111 *Fejo* (1998) 195 CLR 96, 151 (Kirby J); *Ward* (2002) 213 CLR 1, 95.
112 *Ward* (2002) 213 CLR 1.
113 Ibid., 93; 64–5.
114 Ibid., 38–9.
115 *Akiba on behalf of the Torres Strait Regional Seas Claim Group v Commonwealth* (2013) 300 ALR 1, 5, citing *Yarmirr* (2001) 208 CLR 1.

requirement for proof of 'connection' to the relevant land and waters, and the fraught recognition (and definition) of these by the common law. This highly particularised recognition, I argue, is an exemplar of Benjamin's mythic law and the enactment of a (legal) violence; moreover, it is an instance of Derrida's aforementioned "justice *as law*"[116] – that is, the 'justice' of a determinate law which, while apparently enabling claims to land and waters, actually perpetuates further dispossession. Indeed, Young has described the definition of native title and continuity requirement as, respectively, an "over-particularity" and "over-specificity", which render "a loss of tradition both a product and a cause of dispossession".[117] It is these requirements, and the arguably insurmountable burdens thereby imposed upon Indigenous claimants, that are evocative of the fictitious 'ancient tribe' to which I have earlier alluded, and the consequent foreclosure of contemporary and dynamic indigeneities.

116 Derrida, above n 1 (Ch 9).

117 Young, above n 46, 9. See also Lisa Strelein, "The Vagaries of Native Title: Partial Recognition of Aboriginal Law in the Alice Springs Native Title Case" (1999) 4(26) *Indigenous Law Bulletin* 13.

Chapter 12

Mythic indigeneity

The ancient tribe

The question of 'tradition' and continuity thereof, in relation to Australian native title, is troublesome.[1] The common law grounding of native title in 'traditional law and custom'[2] and ensuing requirement for demonstrable connection with land and waters claimed, as articulated in the *Native Title Act 1993* (Cth),[3] while apparently respectful of the integrity of Indigenous relations to country, presents a complex, twofold problem: the definitional containment of such relations within a judicial interpretation of the terms 'tradition' and 'connection', particularly where the latter is construed as 'continuing connection',[4] and the failure to recognise more encompassing notions of indigeneity, which may include forms or expressions of 'tradition' that cannot be identified in or reconciled with (European) historical and archaeological accounts, as construed by anthropological (or other) experts.[5] Indeed, in the context of the legal recognition of Indigenous traditional knowledge,

1 Young, above n 46 (Ch 11).

2 *Mabo* (1992) 175 CLR 1, 60; *Yorta Yorta* (2002) 214 CLR 422.

3 The judicial construction of this statutory requirement is aided by Brennan J's decision in *Mabo* (1992) 175 CLR 1. This mode of judicial construction was supported in *Sampi v Western Australia* [2005] FCA 777, [1079]; *Northern Territory of Australia v Alyawarr, Kaytetye Warumungu, Wakaya Native Title Claim Group* (2005) 145 FCR 442, 469–70 ("*Northern Territory v Alyawarr*").

4 *Sampi v Western Australia* [2005] FCA 777, [1079]; supported by the Full Court in *Northern Territory v Alyawarr* (2005) 145 FCR 442, 469.

5 See Ambelin Kwaymullina, "Living together in country: Creation, *terra nullius* and 'the trouble with tradition'", in Young, above n 46 (Ch 11), xvi, xx:

> Indigenous peoples are being placed in the position of having to demonstrate, not simply what Aboriginal culture is, but continuity with a Western interpretation of the minutiae of what it was at some point in the distant past. Rights to land – and future uses of land – are being constrained by a reductionist perspective that locates culture in a multitude of specific past activities, rather than looking at the holistic nature of Indigenous relationships to country.

See also discussion of the role of anthropologists as experts in native title cases in Kingsley Palmer, "Anthropologist as Expert in Native Title Cases in Australia" (2011) Australian Institute of Aboriginal and Torres Strait Islander Studies Native Title Research Unit at http://aiatsis.gov.au/sites/default/files/products/research_outputs/palmer-2011-anthropologist-expert-native-title-cases.pdf (accessed 6 October 2015).

Fitzpatrick and Joyce advocate a recognition that is "dynamically generative and relational", such that the recognition of one (traditional knowledge) need not be effected merely by its accommodation within the other (occidental law) but, rather, each may be constituted in its relation to the other.[6] In Bhabha's postcolonial account of "[t]he social articulation of difference", he suggests that the representation of such difference "must not be hastily read as the reflection of *pre-given* ethnic or cultural traits set in the fixed tablet of tradition" but, rather, "is a complex, on-going negotiation that seeks to authorize cultural hybridities".[7] Such expansive representation, and its recognition, are not yet evidenced in Australian native title law which, on the contrary, is ever more ossified.

In a book addressing this "trouble with tradition" in native title law, both in Australia and beyond, Young argues that a "restrictive 'tradition'-focused methodology" is evident both in "the formative Australian jurisprudence" and more recent case law, to the extent that it "threatens to foreclose upon any meaningful legal accommodation of change".[8] Such foreclosure is evidenced in the (in)famous judicial description of irrecoverable loss of tradition and connection, having been "washed away" by "the tide of history".[9] Some recent proposals for legislative amendment of the Act, if passed, offer a broader scope for Indigenous claims;[10] yet, I argue, ultimately even these may become instruments of a violent (mis)recognition. In this section, I will provide an overview of judicial interpretation of the current requirements and some discussion of the proposed legislative amendments, an analysis of the inevitable violence of these to indigeneities, and the potential for the reception of intervening narratives into a nonviolent law, expressed more fully *beyond* the law, in literature.

In a doctrinally significant native title (appeal) decision,[11] *Bodney v Bennell*, the court defined 'traditional' as those rights and interests that "find their origin in pre-sovereignty law and custom" and may develop thereafter, "perhaps significantly", yet remain "traditional".[12] Where such rights and interests are "the creatures of the laws and customs of a particular society that exists as a group which acknowledges and observes those laws and customs", it is necessary to prove the existence of a "normative system which possesses normative rules which give

6 Peter Fitzpatrick and Richard Joyce, "Copying Right: Cultural Property and the Limits of (Occidental) Law" in Fiona Macmillan (ed.), *New Directions in Copyright* (Vol. 4) (2007) 171.

7 Bhabha, above n 106 (Ch 9), 3.

8 Young, above n 46 (Ch 11), 3. See also Simon Young, "Tides of History and Jurisprudential Gulfs: Native Title Proof and the Noongar Western Australia Claim" (2010) 8(1) *Indigenous Law Journal* 95.

9 *Mabo* (1992) 175 CLR 1, 60 (Brennan J); see also *Yorta Yorta* (2002) 214 CLR 422, 461 (Olney J). See above, n 78 (Ch 11), for the full citation.

10 Native Title Amendment (Reform) Bill 2014 (Cth). See also ALRC IP 45, above n 39 (Ch 9).

11 See also further refinement in *Sampi on behalf of the Bardi and Jawi People v Western Australia* (2010) 266 ALR 537, discussed below at fn 353; see also *Banjima People v Western Australia (No 2)* [2013] FCA 868.

12 *Bodney v Bennell* (2008) 249 ALR 300, 301; see also 311.

rise to rights and interests in relation to land and water", such a system being "the source of the rights and interests".[13] Crucially, claimants must demonstrate that this system "has had a continuous existence and vitality since sovereignty".[14] In *Bennell*, the court rejected the emphasis of the trial judge upon continuity of society, as an indication of continuity of traditional law and custom: "It is not the society per se that produces rights and interests".[15] Indeed, it was held,

> [a]n inquiry into continuity of society, divorced from an inquiry into continuity of the pre-sovereignty normative system, may mask unacceptable change with the consequence that the current rights and interests are no longer those that existed at sovereignty, and *thus not traditional.*[16]

More recently, in *Sampi on behalf of the Bardi and Jawi People v Western Australia*, the Full Federal Court noted that the existence of a society, itself now a threshold requirement for the purpose of determining native title, depends upon whether the claimant group acknowledge "the same body of laws and customs relating to rights and interests in land and waters", irrespective of whether the group is "composed of people from different language groups or groups linked to specific areas within the larger territory which was the subject of the application".[17]

The requirement of 'connection' is attached to that of continuity, where "continuity of observance [of traditional law and custom]" is defined as "a manifestation of connection".[18] Although it has been held that a spiritual, rather than physical, connection may suffice,[19] this is not reflected in the Act.[20] Whereas the

13 *Bodney v Bennell* (2008) 249 ALR 300, 301, citing *Yorta Yorta* (2002) 214 CLR 422, 554.

14 Ibid. This was affirmed more recently in *Banjima People v Western Australia (No 2)* [2013] FCA 868 [376]–[377]. See also Nick Duff, "What's Needed to Prove Native Title? Finding Flexibility within the Law on Connection", Australian Institute of Aboriginal and Torres Strait Islander Studies Native Title Research Unit Research Discussion Paper No 35 (2014) at http://aiatsis.gov.au/sites/default/files/products/discussion_paper/whats-needed-to-prove-native-title.pdf (accessed 6 October 2015). At 27, Duff suggests that

> the concern is to ensure that the court does not recognise any parallel lawmaking entity subsequent to the Crown's initial assertion of sovereignty – that is, the insistence of substantial continuity is a consequence of the imperative to preserve the Australian legal system's monopoly on law-making.

15 Ibid., 318.

16 Ibid. (emphasis added)

17 *Sampi on behalf of the Bardi and Jawi People v Western Australia* (2010) 266 ALR 537, 553, 559. In this case, the internal view of claimants was considered in reference to the question of whether the Bardi Jawi were one society or two for the purpose of their claim.

18 *Bodney v Bennell* (2008) 249 ALR 300, 312, citing *Northern Territory v Alyawarr* (2005) 220 ALR 431; also citing *Western Australia v Ward* (2000) 170 ALR 159.

19 *Ward* (2002) 213 CLR 1, 246–7.

20 Current proposals for reform include an amendment to stipulate that "a connection with the land or waters . . . need not be a physical connection". Native Title Amendment (Reform) Bill 2014 (Cth), cl 13. See also discussion in the ALRC IP 45, above n 39 (Ch 9).

trial judge in *Bennell* considered whether the normative system revealed was consistent with continuity of a society since sovereignty, on appeal the court held that the question is, rather, whether "acknowledgment and observance of traditional laws and customs has continued *substantially uninterrupted* since sovereignty":

> [The question of continuity] is to be answered by ascertaining whether, *for each generation* of the relevant society since sovereignty, those laws and customs constituted a normative system giving rise to rights and interests in land, and in fact regulated and defined the rights and interests which those people had and could exercise in relation to the land and waters.[21]

This requirement for intergenerational continuity was established in *Risk v Northern Territory*,[22] in which Justice Mansfield held that native title claimants must prove, inter alia, that

> the acknowledgment and observance of the laws and customs has continued substantially uninterrupted by each generation since sovereignty, and the society has continued to exist throughout that period as a body united in and by its acknowledgment and observance of those laws and customs . . .

It has been suggested that this decision elevates "the *Yorta Yorta* decision's brief reference to generational transmission of laws and customs" to the status of an independent, prescriptive requirement and, more broadly, draws Australian native title doctrine toward "a more strict approach to proof", its methodology and terminology demonstrative of more restrictive notions of 'tradition'.[23]

The term "substantially uninterrupted" contemplates some non-Indigenous disruption to acknowledgment and observance of traditional law and custom, but only to the extent that such law and custom may still be considered '*traditional*', as a threshold of entitlement:

> European settlement is what justifies the expression "substantially uninterrupted" rather than "uninterrupted". It explains why it is that the common law will recognise traditional laws and customs that are not exactly the same

21 *Bodney v Bennell* (2008) 249 ALR 300, 317 (emphasis added).

22 [2006] FCA 404, [97](c). (2007) 240 ALR 74.

23 Young, above n 8, 110. In *Yorta Yorta*, the court acknowledged that some evolution and adaptation of law and custom may not necessarily be fatal to a native title claim: *Yorta Yorta* (2002) 214 CLR 422, 455 (Gleeson CJ, Gummow and Hayne JJ) and 463–4 (Gaudron and Kirby JJ). Nonetheless, it has been suggested that the current judicial approach to the notion of "traditional" is excessively onerous: see also Jumbunna Indigenous House of Learning Research Unit, *Submission for the Inquiry into the Native Title Amendment (Reform) Bill 2011, Prepared for the Senate Standing Committee on Legal and Constitutional Affairs* (July 2011).

> as they were at settlement. But if . . . there has been a substantial interruption, it is not to be mitigated by reference to white settlement. The continuity inquiry does not involve consideration of *why* acknowledgment and observance stopped. If this were not the case, a great many Aboriginal societies would be entitled to claim native title rights even though their current laws and customs are *in no meaningful way traditional*.[24]

In summary, to be considered 'traditional' within the meaning of the Act, law and custom must be shown to exist within an extant normative system, pertaining to rights and interests in land and waters to which the claimants possess a demonstrable connection. Observance of such normative law and custom must have continued 'substantially uninterrupted', transmitted across each generation *since sovereignty*. In the context of contemporary Indigenous communities, satisfaction of this (increasingly) exacting requirement is extraordinarily burdensome, if not impossible.[25]

Proposed statutory amendments[26] provide for the possibility of a more expansive description[27] of 'traditional', with "traditional laws acknowledged" and "traditional customs observed" to include laws and customs that "remain identifiable through time, regardless of whether there is a change in those laws [or customs] or in the manner in which they are acknowledged [or observed]".[28] The proposed

24 *Bodney v Bennell* (2008) 249 ALR 300, 325 (last emphasis added). See also *Yorta Yorta* (2002) 214 CLR 422, 457, in which it was held that if the requirement for continuity of acknowledgment and observance is not met, "examining why that is so is important *only* to the exent that the presence or absence of reasons might influence the fact-finder's decision about whether there was such an interruption".

25 Following the finding in *Risk v Northern Territory* (2007) 240 ALR 75, in which it was held that the laws and customs were not "traditional" in accordance with the requirement of s 223(1) of the *Native Title Act 1993* (Cth), at 96, and that the difference between the "body of laws" of the claimant at sovereignty and the "present-day laws and customs" were "significant and substantial", at 96–7, it has been suggested that "the construction of native title, specifically with respect to substantial interruption . . . [is] creating 'insurmountable barriers to cultural resurgence'": ALRC IP 45, above n 39 (Ch 9), [199], citing Commonwealth, *Parliamentary Debates*, Senate, 21 March 2011, 1303 (Rachel Siewert).

26 See proposals for legislative amendment in Chief Justice French, "Lifting the burden of native title: Some modest proposals for improvement" (2009) 93 *Reform* 10, 13 at www.austlii.edu.au/au/journals/FedJSchol/2008/18.html (accessed 6 October 2015). These proposals, among others, informed the Native Title Amendment (Reform) Bill 2011 (Cth), and its subsequent iterations, the Native Title Amendment (Reform) Bill (No. 1) 2012 (Cth) and Native Title Amendment (Reform) Bill 2014 (Cth).

27 The term "traditional" is not explicitly defined in the *Native Title Act 1993* (Cth), although the current Australian Law Reform Commission native title inquiry invites comment on whether a definition should be inserted into s 223 of the Act: ALRC IP 45, above n 39 (Ch 9), Question 11 [126].

28 Native Title Amendment (Reform) Bill 2014 (Cth), Schedule 1, 18 (to insert after s 223(1) of the *Native Title Act 1993* (Cth)).

amendments also include a rebuttable presumption[29] of continuous connection, in favour of Indigenous claimants. Accordingly, the onus of proof of connection, as a question of fact, would rest with the claimants. Unless proven otherwise, laws and customs observed by the native title claim group are presumed to be "traditional" and, therefore, to be those "observed at sovereignty", and the claim group is presumed to have "a connection with the land and waters by those traditional laws and traditional customs".[30] Additionally, the proposed amendments also provide that "if the native title rights and interests asserted are capable of recognition by the common law . . . the facts necessary for the recognition of those rights and interests by the common law are established."[31] Furthermore, the proposed amendment to section 61, in respect of continuing connection, provides that connection in accordance with section 223(1) may be satisfied despite a finding of "substantial interruption in the acknowledgment of traditional laws or the observance of traditional customs", or "a significant change to traditional laws acknowledged or traditional customs observed", provided the "primary reason for the substantial interruption or the significant change is the action of a State or a Territory or a person or other party who is not an Aboriginal person or a Torres Strait Islander".[32]

If passed, these amendments would appear to provide a more achievable standard of proof for Indigenous claimants. In practice, however, alleviation of the burden upon native title claimants is fundamentally limited.[33] Such limitation is apparent, for instance, where the presumption of connection may be set aside by evidence of "significant disruption".[34] It has also been suggested that a presumption may require "State and Territory Governments to place renewed emphasis on identifying the flaws in connection evidence".[35] Additional difficulties remain where the law continues in its commitment to a notion of "tradition" and,

29 This would be a persuasive, rather than evidentiary, presumption: see French, above n 26. See also discussion in the ALRC IP 45, above n 39 (Ch 9), [85], citing J.D. Heydon, *Cross on Evidence*, Vol 1 (at Service 164) [7295], [7300]; see also [82].

30 Native Title Amendment (Reform) Bill 2014 (Cth), Schedule 1, 14 (to insert after s 61 of the *Native Title Act 1993* (Cth) as s 61AA).

31 Ibid.

32 Ibid., Schedule 1, 14 (to insert after s 61 of the *Native Title Act 1993* (Cth) as s 61AB). See also judicial support for the proposition that " 'significant adaptations' may occur without depriving law and custom of their status as 'traditional' ": Duff, above n 14, 30. Judicial support is provided in *Yorta Yorta* (2002) 214 CLR 422, 443–4; *Neowarra v Western Australia* [2003] FCA 1402, [163]; *Rubibi Community v Western Australia (No. 5)* [2005] FCA 1025, [368].

33 See Aboriginal and Torres Strait Islander Social Justice Commissioner, Social Justice and Native Title Report (Australian Human Rights Commission, 2013) 77 at www.humanrights.gov.au/publications/social-justice-and-native-title-report-2013 (accessed 6 October 2015).

34 Explanatory Memorandum, Native Title Amendment (Reform) Bill 2014 (Cth) 2 (Outline).

35 Western Australian Government, Submission No 18 to Senate Committee on Legal and Constitutional Affairs, Parliament of Australia, *Inquiry into Native Title Amendment (Reform) Bill 2011*, August 2011. See discussion in the ALRC IP 45, above n 39 (Ch 9), [93].

therefore, to "traditional laws acknowledged and traditional customs observed at sovereignty", and to the threshold question of whether "the native title rights and interests asserted are capable of recognition by the common law".[36] Such requirements, despite the proposed amendments, fail to acknowledge the violence of common law *recognition* itself and, furthermore, while presenting a potential improvement upon existing legislative requirements for native title claimants, fail to fully relinquish the demand for intergenerational continuity despite the realities of intergenerational dispossession.[37]

Before delving further into the judicial interpretation of the current statutory requirements, I would like to momentarily dwell upon the significance of these in the context of my previous discussion of 'legitimate fictions'. The search for the 'traditional' as it is defined by the law, ascertained by reference to 'fact' in evidence pertaining to the practices of both historical and contemporary Indigenous communities, arguably represents a search for an impossibility.[38] The current requirement for evidence of a society governed by laws and customs predominantly *unchanged*[39] since the imposition of British sovereignty reveals a search for fantasy – that is, for the aforementioned fantasy of the " 'ancient tribe', who did acknowledge those laws and customs at the time of British acquisition of sovereignty in Australia", and the "judgment process can be understood as having a focus upon deciding if the last members of the tribe have yet come to pass".[40] The manifest differences between the historical vision of a fundamentally unaltered system of traditional law and custom, and the realities of contemporary societies, create an arguably insurmountable hurdle for claimants. Indeed, as Grbich suggests, the "judicial focus upon the finding of the 'traditional' in laws and customs" divides "the traditional and the modern or present", such that the latter

36 Explanatory Memorandum, Native Title Amendment (Reform) Bill 2014 (Cth) 2 (Outline) 6 (point 17). See also *Yorta Yorta* (2002) 214 CLR 422, 444 (Gleeson CJ, Gummow and Hayne JJ).

37 See discussion in ANTaR Submission to the Senate Legal and Constitutional Affairs Legislation Committee: Inquiry into a previous iteration of the bill, the Native Title Amendment (Reform) Bill 2011 (Cth). For a more detailed discussion of the 2011 bill, see Jumbunna Indigenous House of Learning Research Unit, above n 23.

38 See Boire, above n 63 (Ch 9), 234. Boire speaks of the nullification and elision of Indigenous legal and political systems as a necessary prerequisite to the imposition of "European juridical forms":

> [A]ny potential symbolic systems of the other are emptied of meaning, or filled with negative meaning in need of rectification, long before those symbolic systems are encountered, as a pre-condition of their impossibility.

39 The Full Court has acknowledged that some change to traditional laws and customs is not necessarily fatal to a claim: *Yorta Yorta* (2002) 214 CLR 422, 455. Note that the court has also held that some change to native title rights and interests themselves may be permissible, where "no greater burden" is imposed upon the Crown's radical title: *Bodney v Bennell* [2008] FCAFC 63, 329. See also discussion in Young, above n 8, especially 114–15. Note the acknowledgment of *some* change in the term "substantially uninterrupted", as detailed judicially and as contemplated in the Native Title Amendment (Reform) Bill (No. 1) 2012 (Cth).

40 Grbich, above n 43 (Ch 9), 128.

"must always be displaced or expelled by the jurisdiction of the court".[41] Moreover, she likens the contemporary judicial narrative of indigeneity to "the genre of the 'last of the tribe'" in the European literary archive, prominent during the 18th and 19th centuries:

> Each time the court finds the litigants are part of a modern or non-traditional indigenous society, that they have failed to prove an unbroken connection with the "ancient tribe", it constructs and preserves within the European archive a record of the dying of the ancient tribe, a written record is made of the "last of the tribe" in the form of the judgment.[42]

According to Povinelli, moreover, while the legitimacy of native title depends upon the existence of traditional laws and customs, the object of the judiciary is to decide whether these laws and customs have been "washed away by the tide of history" or, if they have survived this assault, whether "any of these real ancient customs violate contemporary common law values".[43] The adapted and hybrid realities of Indigenous peoples and societies, and their associated claims to country, may not be 'traditional' within current or proposed legislated meanings and, if so, are consequently rendered largely unrecognisable to the law. Native title law is therefore described as a narrative of "negative or absent communities", necessary to the perpetuation of "stories of enlightened Europeans and their regimes of sovereignty and jurisdiction in Australia".[44] Indeed, Povinelli describes the legal pursuit of a 'traditional' indigeneity, "untouched and untainted by the 'ravages' of colonial settlement", as akin to that of anthropologists and ethnographers,[45] and the demand for proof thereof as "inspiring in the indigenous subject a desire to identify with a lost indeterminable object . . . to be the melancholic subject of *traditions*".[46]

The pedantry of the current statutory requirements and common law interpretations is largely unique to Australian native title law, distinguishing it from other common law jurisdictions.[47] The *Bennell* trial decision was significant in its gesture toward a broader approach to proof of native title, moving away from that which has been described as an "overly particular (microscoping) methodology" and " 'tradition' focus",[48] largely derived from Justice Brennan's *Mabo* decision and subsequently intensified in *Yorta Yorta*.[49] The latter predominantly turned upon the definition of 'tradition' within the meaning of the Act, and the

41 Grbich, above n 43 (Ch 9), 128.
42 Ibid., 129.
43 Povinelli, above n 47 (Ch 11), 37.
44 Grbich, above n 43 (Ch 9), 129.
45 Povinelli, above n 47 (Ch 11), 37.
46 Ibid., 39 (emphasis added).
47 For a detailed comparative analysis, see Young, above n 46 (Ch 11).
48 Ibid., 97, 110.
49 See discussion in Young, above n 46 (Ch 11). At 234, Young suggests that the "strict 'tradition'-focused methodology" began with *Mabo* and subsequently "gathered momentum".

court clearly established the requirements for proof thereof, as being derived and largely unchanged from those laws and customs acknowledged and observed by the relevant (claimant) pre-sovereignty Indigenous society.[50] These two elements – laws and customs defined as 'traditional' and their acknowledgment and observance by an identifiable society, in addition to proof of connection with land and waters arising from those laws and customs – form the crux of current Australian native title law and, I argue, as questions of 'fact',[51] represent the aforementioned judicial search for fictions.[52]

As suggested, the trial decision in *Bennell* demonstrates a relatively expansive judicial treatment of the statutory elements and judicial interpretation of native title. Justice Wilcox explicitly acknowledged and accommodated some community change, difference, and dissent within the claim group and attenuation of the normative system of traditional laws and customs, though still maintaining the requirement for proof of continued law and custom in relation to surviving native title rights.[53] His Honour also noted the importance of recognition of these as a "normative system", irrespective of ontological and epistemological differences in respect of notions of property and "belonging".[54] The subsequent appeal decision, however, was a stern correction to Justice Wilson's broader emphases, re-establishing the exacting requirements of previous decisions – most particularly, the narrower interpretation of the statutory "recognition and protection" of "rights and interests in relation to land or waters . . . finding their origin in traditional law and custom".[55] An apparent broadening of this view was evidenced in *Sampi*, on appeal, in which the Full Court placed emphasis upon the internal view of the claimants, as it pertained to the question of whether they were a single society at the time of sovereignty, acknowledging one law.[56] More recently, however, in

50 *Yorta Yorta* (2002) 214 CLR 422, 433–4.

51 See explicit acknowledgment in *Western Australia v Sebastian* (2008) 248 ALR 61, 87.

52 As previously acknowledged, see illuminating discussion in Grbich, above n 43 (Ch 9), 128:

> The court's preference for written evidence of this unbroken connection, the oral traditions of indigenous people, and the largely absent settler record of indigenous possession has the effect of the court searching for fictions.

53 See detailed discussion in Young, above n 46 (Ch 11), 112.

54 *Bennell* (2006) 230 ALR 603, 605, citing *Yorta Yorta* (2002) 214 CLR 422 556, as followed by *Northern Territory of Australia v Alaywar, Kaytetye, Warumungu, Wakaya Native Title Claim Group* (2005) 145 FCR 442:

> The rights and interests under traditional laws and customs will often reflect a different conception of "property" or "belonging". But none of these considerations denies the normative quality of the laws and customs of the indigenous societies. It is only if the rich complexity of indigenous societies is denied that reference to traditional laws and customs as a normative system jars the ears of the listener.

55 *Yorta Yorta* (2002) 214 CLR 422, 452–3.

56 *Sampi on behalf of the Bardi and Jawi People v Western Australia* [2010] FCAFC 26 [77]. See also Marcelle Burns, "Challenging the Assumptions of Positivism: An Analysis of the Concept of Society in *Sampi on Behalf of the Bardi Jawi People v Western Australia* [2010] and *Bodney v Bennell* [2008]

Wyman on behalf of the Bidjara People v Queensland (No. 2),[57] while the court remained bound to interpret and apply the Act, it was suggested that it is a mere "construct", imposing "a set of requirements which bear no necessary relationship to contemporary Aboriginal Australia or . . . what might ordinarily be considered to be a society and its continuence".[58]

On the distinction between the common law and traditional law and custom, the court has vigorously defended the notion of judicial recognition of the autonomy of the latter. In *Yorta Yorta*, the court held that native title does not "[owe] its origins to the common law" as a creation thereof, but is, rather, derived from existing (yet, crucially, *traditional*) rights and interests.[59] This decision drew upon previous judicial affirmation of the integrity of the distinction between the common law and native title. In *Mabo*, Justice Brennan maintained that "[t]he general principle that the common law will recognise a customary title only if it be consistent with the common law is subject to an exception in favour of traditional native title";[60] in *Western Australia v Commonwealth*, Justice Dawson upheld this view, asserting that native title need not be consistent with the common law;[61] further, in *Yarmirr*, it was held that the existence of native title is not dependent upon the recognition of the court, or indeed by the legislature.[62] Nonetheless, the inescapable fact remains that the realisation of tangible rights and interests in land and waters is dependent upon such recognition and, in the case of native title, this recognition remains subject to the limitations of the "skeleton of principle which gives the body of our law its shape and internal consistency".[63] Indeed, in a footnote in *Ward*, Justice Callinan remarked upon such limitations:

> In *Mabo [No 2]* [1992] HCA 23; (1992) 175 CLR 1 at 42 per Brennan J, it was stated that a change in the law was necessary to make the common law non-discriminatory. But this Court and other legal bodies are founded on a post-dream time legal order. Although some may contend that we should, we do not in fact recognise Aboriginal criminal law, tort law or any aspects of indigenous laws, nor do we pretend to. The question then is why the

(May 2011) 4(7) *Land, Rights, Laws: Issues of Native Title* at http://aiatsis.gov.au/sites/default/files/products/issues_paper/burns-ntip-v4n7-challenging-assumptions-positivism-concept-of-society.pdf (accessed 6 October 2015).

57 [2013] FCA 1229.

58 Ibid., [472] (per Jagot J):

> Whether native title rights and interests can be established does not necessarily say anything about the existence of any contemporary Aboriginal society (in the sense of a body of persons united in and by its acknowledgment and observance of a body of laws and customs), the content or strength of any norms and values of that society, or the merits or otherwise of those norms and values.

59 *Yorta Yorta* (2002) 214 CLR 422, 453.

60 *Mabo* (1992) 175 CLR 1, 59.

61 (1995) 183 CLR 373, 492.

62 *Yarmirr* (2001) 208 CLR 1, 129; *Mabo* (1992) 175 CLR 1, 57; 82; 182–3.

63 *Mabo* (1992) 175 CLR 1, 29.

> common law of property, which had been regarded as settled for more than a century, should have been changed to recognise sui generis interests in land that had no counterpart in our legal system.[64]

The legal framework within which Indigenous relations to country receive recognition – as native *title* – is necessarily informed by the common law of property, "our land law",[65] which is inevitably constrained in its capacity to recognise such relations.[66] As Grbich contends, while the purported recognition of native title must be contained within the limits of the common law, specifically of 'our land law', actual recognition remains elusive:

> While the time of sovereignty purports to be a backward glance, the glance of recognition contains within itself the symbolic relations of "our land law" of the present, the feudalscapes of lord and serf – a symbolic relation in which there must be a use of a thing of such a kind that the owner is recognised as a lord.[67]

64 *Ward* (2002) 213 CLR 1, 399. On the point that "the discrimination argument is not obvious", his Honour further cites Ronald Sackville, "The Emerging Australian Law of Native Title: Some North American Comparisons" (2000) 74 *Australian Law Journal* 820, 830. See also discussion in Larissa Behrendt and Loretta Kelly, *Resolving Indigenous Disputes: Land Conflict and Beyond* (2008) 4. Cf recent judicial remarks in *McLennan on behalf of the Jangga People v Queensland* [2012] FCA 1082 [4], which suggest a broader interpretation of Indigenous law and its reception by Australian law:

> When the court makes an order for a determination of native title, it exercises the juridical power of the Commonwealth, on behalf of the whole Australian community, to validate the indigenous claimants' rights and interests as having the *force of law* in both social systems . . . (emphasis added).

65 *Mabo* (1992) 175 CLR 1, 45 (Brennan J):

> A basic doctrine of the land law is the doctrine of tenure, to which Stephen CJ referred in *Attorney-General v Brown*, and it is a doctrine which could not be overturned without fracturing the skeleton which gives our land law its shape and consistency. It is derived from feudal origins.

Compare also earlier reference to the "law of the land" that "cannot be questioned", in *Johnson v M'Intosh* 21 US 543, 591 (1823).

66 In a recent decision in respect of native title and commercial rights and interests, the court sought to distinguish traditional laws and customs from "the common lawyer's one-dimensional view of property as control over access": *Western Australian v Brown and Ors* [2014] HCA 8 (12 March 2014) [36]. While some elements of this decision were doctrinally significant, such that principles of common law extinguishment are arguably now more favourable to native title claimants than current legislative provisions, traditional laws and customs remain constrained by the limits of their recognition within the common law, where native title cannot be recognised in the event of inconsistency with certain common law or statutory rights: *Commonwealth v Yarmirr* (2001) 208 CLR 1, 68 (Gleeson CJ, Gaudron, Gummow and Hayne JJ). See also discussion in ALRC IP 45, above n 39 (Ch 9), [134].

67 Judith Grbich, "The Road to Jawi Country: Exilic Subjects and Legal Landscapes" in Anna Haebich and Baden Offord (eds), *Landscapes of Exile: Once Perilous, Now Safe* (2008) 43, 54.

Grbich describes such (mis)recognition as "the paradox at the heart of the legal interpretation of native title interests in Australia" as "one capable of recognising novelty or newness, but conditional upon that newness not being inconsistent in the form of 'our land law'".[68]

Ultimately, legal recognition of native title depends upon a performance of 'traditional' indigeneity, a determinate creation of the common law and, subsequently, of statute and its judicial interpretation. Indeed, it has been argued elsewhere, native title claimants must construct identities for the sole purpose of native title claims "in a singular and traditionalist modality", irrespective of their contemporary experiences and engagements.[69] Nonetheless, I recall Derrida once again, who describes the elements of law and justice, while distinct, as existing in a perpetual and necessary negotiation "between the calculable and the incalculable".[70] Similarly, I would suggest that while the legal conception of Indigenous 'tradition' violently constrains the Indigenous claimant, it remains in a state of perpetual negotiation with more expansive and indeterminate notions of indigeneity,[71] the latter encompassing 'traditions' that may not necessarily accord with those articulated by the law.

Law as literature

> We gotta be moving, remembering, singing our place little bit new, little bit special, all the time.[72]

Where indigeneity persistently moves between calculability and incalculability, in a perpetual and discomforting state of (il)legality, its determination or encapsulation within the limits of the common law also recall my earlier discussion of Nancy's notion of the 'proper' Indigenous subject. This subject is construed *as difference*, yet as difference that is *proper* to the law, and is thereby encapsulated within it.[73] While the law purports to identify the source and origin of native title in Indigenous law and custom, the legal recognition of these is necessarily constrained by the interpretative capacity of the court – a constraint that, the High Court has held,

68 Ibid., 52.

69 David Martin, "Alternative Constructions of Indigenous Identities in Australia's *Native Title Act*" in Toni Bauman and Lydia Glick (eds), *The Limits of Change: Mabo and Native Title 20 Years On* (AIATSIS, 2012) 356.

70 Derrida, above n 1 (Ch 9), 257. See also useful discussion in Peter Fitzpatrick, "Reading Slowly: The Law of Literature and the Literature of Law" in Ruth Buchanan, Stewart Motha and Sundhya Pahuja (eds), *Reading Modern Law: Critical Methodologies and Sovereign Formations* (2012) 193.

71 See generally Fitzpatrick and Joyce, above n 6, 171.

72 Kim Scott, *True Country* (1993) 225.

73 Nancy, above n 117 (Ch 9), 10. See also discussion in Motha, above n 6 (Ch 9). At 85, discussing the *Mabo* decision and the rejection of the doctrine of *terra nullius*, Motha notes: "The recognition of the 'existence' of the other should not be mistaken for the recognition of the 'difference' of the other".

"may require refusal of recognition to rights and interests which, in some way, are antithetical to fundamental tenets of the common law".[74] Recalling Benjamin, in order to sustain its own authority, for 'its own sake', the law cannot fully accommodate that which threatens these fundamental tenets; yet, it is these very interventions that *write* the law, as a literature, constituting it from within.[75]

The archive of precedent that comprises, compels, and constrains the common law, following and reiterating Derrida, may be understood as a literature; furthermore, once again, as "the impossible story of the impossible".[76] That is, as the impossible story of origin and foundation and, in the context of the Indigenous subject before the law of native title, as the impossible story of 'tradition'. From the moment of European arrival, the telescope directed toward the land and its contours marked and boundaries drawn, the straight lines on the maps of the colonisers were superimposed upon the "rivers and hills and the curves of the land", the songlines of Indigenous Law.[77] This cartographic imposition was and is, I continue to argue, reflected in the (non-Indigenous) 'law of the land', most particularly the law of native title. The law I have thus far described in this book, however, is possessed of two facets – mythic and divine, conditional and unconditional. I have described indigeneity as evoked in the movement between these poles, "the movement of deconstruction",[78] recalling once again Derrida's allusions to the fictitious core of legal thought.[79]

In anticipation of Part IV, I wish to introduce (an)other (legal) literature, which contemplates an immanent rather than a transcendent authority and is narrated via the curves or songlines of the earth, rather than via the constrained reasoning of the court. Indigenous author Alexis Wright, for instance, in her novel *Carpentaria*,[80] evokes a sentient landscape, forged by the ancestor creatures of the Dreaming, now manifest in the terrain, which provides both the source and force of Indigenous Law. In contrast, non-Indigenous literary depictions of the moment of encounter have echoed the classificatory urge exemplified in the law, such that indigeneity has been depicted as "the emblematic primitive against which the European order defined its modernity".[81] The Indigene coalesces with the

74 *Yorta Yorta* (2002) 214 CLR 422, 453, citing *Ward* (2002) 191 ALR 1, 17–18; 213 CLR 1, 66–7. At 454, the court then proceeded to define the bounds of such recognition:

> The native title rights and interests which are the subject of the Act are those which existed at sovereignty, survived that fundamental change in legal regime, and now, by resort to the processes of the new legal order, can be enforced and protected. It is those rights and interests which are "recognised" in the common law.

75 See useful discussion in Boire, above n 63 (Ch 9), 231, especially 243–4.

76 Derrida, above n 109 (Ch 9), 200.

77 Sally Morgan, "The Balance for the World", in Morgan, Mia and Kwaymullina, above n 26 (Ch 11), 262.

78 Derrida, above n 1 (Ch 9), 254.

79 Derrida, above n 109 (Ch 9), 190.

80 Alexis Wright, *Carpentaria* (2006).

81 Stephen Muecke, *Ancient and Modern: Time, Culture and Indigenous Philosophy* (2004) 138.

environment as, in Katherine Susannah Prichard's *Coonardoo*, the "blackened and broken sticks beside the fire"[82] or, in David Malouf's *Remembering Babylon*, as a threshold separating the known from "the abode of everything savage and fearsome . . . all that belonged to the Absolute Dark".[83] Furthermore, in the elegiac poetry of Judith Wright, Indigenous people are spectralised, as "night ghosts of a land . . . like a shadow cast".[84] Such depictions may be contrasted with the animated corporeality of connection to country in Indigenous literary renderings, such as *Carpentaria*, in which the author describes a young countryman who "carried the tide in his body",[85] and is triumphant witness to the reprisal of Indigenous Law in the awesome apparition of the Rainbow Serpent,[86] and of a tremendous cyclone that annihilates colonial civilisation with a bloodless and divine violence.[87]

The following and final part will embark upon a narrative of the "law of literature" which, according to Derrida, is "an instituted *fiction* but also a *fictive institution*".[88] As such, literature provides an escape from the prohibitions[89] and delusions[90] of the law via, I argue, evocations of the unconditional justice of a Derridean deconstruction,[91] and of a Benjaminian divine violence. Part IV will dwell upon the emergence of the unconditional, divine, and revolutionary within the literary, the importance of Indigenous narrative as a means of broader epistemological transfer,[92] and the more empirical ways in which such literature might function strategically, articulating the experiences, aspirations, and cultural imperatives of marginalised groups. Furthermore, I will consider the creation of indigeneities within textual imaginaries, both legal and literary, and the dissolution of such categories within a 'law and literature' paradigm, ultimately proposing a conception of law as literature, and of (Indigenous) literature *as law*.

82 Katherine Susannah Prichard, *Coonardoo* (1929) 232.
83 David Malouf, *Remembering Babylon* (1993) 3.
84 Judith Wright, "The Dark Ones" in *Collected Poems: 1942–1985* (1994).
85 Wright, above n 80, 401.
86 Ibid., 407.
87 Ibid., 494. My reference here is to Benjamin, above n 5 (Ch 9).
88 Derrida, above n 33 (Ch 10), 36.
89 Ibid. Derrida describes "the space of literature" as a "fictive institution", which allows one to "break out of [*franchir*] prohibitions". I will return to this particular argument more fully in Part IV (Literature).
90 See Martel, above n 21 (Ch 9), discussed more fully in Part IV (Literature).
91 Derrida, above n 1 (Ch 9).
92 See, for instance, Langton, above n 81 (Ch 10); Ginibi, above n 95 (Ch 11), 8.

Part IV

Literature

Chapter 13

Literary indigeneities

> The law of literature tends, in principle, to defy or lift the law.[1]

Law, as described by Derrida and throughout this book, is "lacking in pure essence, and structurally related to what [he] terms *différance* or, in its non-metaphysical sense, 'literature'".[2] That is, both law and literature are "always to come" and "[t]hus already past",[3] the substance of each contingent and indeterminate. While the law, in the pursuit of (a putative) justice, momentarily and methodically halts this indeterminate flow with the determinacy of decision, it is the literary that "deconstructs" and "renews law"[4] that enters into and acts *with-in* the law, that can "*play the law*, repeating it while diverting or circumventing it",[5] revealing both the literary qualities of the law, and the juridical qualities of literature. In this final Part, having dwelt upon questions of indigeneity and law, I now turn more fully to the question of literature. That is, literature as defined by its apparently *necessary* evasion of definition, rendered in the 'event' of its performance.[6] Returning to the concerns outlined in the introduction to this book, I will examine the literary work as a strategic response, generative of the historical or ideological subtext to which it responds[7] and, further, as an encounter or singular event[8] and, therefore, a subversive juridical source in its capacity to "create, and legislate meaning".[9] Furthermore, I will consider the experience of literature as an

1 Jacques Derrida, " 'This Strange Institution Called Literature': An Interview with Jacques Derrida" in Jacques Derrida (Derek Attridge, ed.), *Acts of Literature* (1992) 33, 36.
2 Derek Attridge, Preface to "Before the Law" in Jacques Derrida (Derek Attridge, ed.), *Acts of Literature* (1992), 181, 182.
3 Jacques Derrida, "Before the Law" in Jacques Derrida (Derek Attridge, ed.), *Acts of Literature* (1992) 181, 270.
4 See useful discussion in Peter Goodrich, *Law in the Courts of Love: Literature and Other Minor Jurisprudences* (1996) 6–7.
5 Derrida, above n 3, 216.
6 Derek Attridge, *The Singularity of Literature* (2004) 1.
7 Terry Eagleton, *The Event of Literature* (2012) 170.
8 Attridge, above n 6.
9 Maria Aristodemou, *Law and Literature: Journeys From Her to Eternity* (2000) 3.

expression of the possibility of an unconditional justice, understood in terms of Derrida's notion of deconstruction, evoked in both law and justice.[10] Ultimately, I will consider the Law invoked in the literary, specifically in Indigenous literature, as a force of recuperative and, indeed, revolutionary Benjaminian divine violence.[11]

As discussed in Part I, Derrida proposes a notion of the literary text as "radically *situated*" such that, in its writing, reading and re-reading, it possesses "a singularity (each time) which can never be reduced by criticism or theoretical contemplation".[12] His own emphasis, however, is upon the "puzzling yet productive relation between singularity and generality", such that these apparent opposites may be conceived as possessing a "structural interdependence".[13] To be meaningful, the text must be recognisable (as a genre, such as 'literature') and therefore capable of interpretation, thereby "imply[ing] a repetition, a law, an ideality".[14] Attridge summarises Derrida's argument:

> For Derrida the literary text is not, therefore, a rich verbal icon or a hermetically sealed space; it is not the site of a rich plenitude of meaning but rather a kind of emptying-out of meaning that remains potently meaningful; it does not possess a core of uniqueness that survives mutability, but rather a repeatable singularity that depends on an openness to new contexts and therefore on its difference each time it is repeated.[15]

It is the simultaneous "irreplaceability" and universality of the literary text that also define the law, where the latter is concerned with the (impossible) application of universalities to irreplaceable singularities.[16] That is, 'impossible' in the Derridean sense, as an 'event' of (in)decision, which "belongs to a *perhaps* which is in keeping not with the possible but with the impossible".[17] Discussing Derrida's

10 As discussed in Part II (Indigeneity), Derrida equates both law and justice with deconstruction. See Jacques Derrida, "Force of Law: The Mystical Foundation of Authority" in Jacques Derrida (Gil Anidjar, ed.), *Acts of Religion* (2002) 228. At 243, Derrida writes: "Justice in itself, if such a thing exist, outside or beyond law, is not deconstructible. No more than deconstruction itself, if such a thing exist. *Deconstruction is justice*". See also Jacques Derrida, James Adner, Kate Doyle and Glenn Hendler, "Women in the Beehive: A Seminar with Jacques Derrida" (2005) 16(3) *A Journal of Feminist Cultural Studies* 139, 149:

> Deconstruction *is* the Law. It's an affirmation, and affirmation is on the side of the Law . . . It's not something which limits the desire or forbids the transgression. As soon as you affirm a desire, you perform something which is the Law.

11 Walter Benjamin, "Critique of Violence" in Walter Benjamin, *Reflections: Essays, Aphorisms, Autobiographical Writings* (1978) 277.

12 Derek Attridge, "Introduction: Derrida and the Questioning of Literature" in Jacques Derrida (Derek Attridge, ed.), *Acts of Literature* (1992) 1, 15.

13 Ibid.

14 Ibid.

15 Ibid., 16.

16 Derrida, above n 10, 245.

17 Jacques Derrida, "The University Without Condition" in Jacques Derrida, *Without Alibi* (2002) 202, 235.

work on literature, Attridge describes this simultaneity as "iterability",[18] examined in Part III in the context of the origin, and in Part I in my discussion of the *singularity* of literature.[19] That is, the possibility and impossibility of repetition, where repetition is required for an item to be meaningful, yet it is impossible "since it has no essence that could remain unaffected by the potentially infinite contexts . . . into which it could be grafted".[20] Indeed, Fitzpatrick describes the potentially "endless variety of determinate existences of the [literary] work", realised in particular readings of it, such that the literary work, alongside the law, "remains a continually formative opening onto what lies beyond its realizations".[21] Yet, the work is not "simply evanescent", but asserts a "contained determinacy, transient as that will be in turn".[22] Accordingly, "[t]he literary text . . . is an act (both a doing and an imitation of doing, both a performance and a record, both an *event* and a law)"[23] that is disruptive of the oppositions it apparently straddles. Discussing Kafka's parable, "Before the Law", Derrida's analysis reveals the ways in which the apparently "stable categories or concepts" of the literary text *as such* are "put into question", thereby providing a unique commentary on the very relation between law and literature.[24]

In the context of discourses of indigeneity, the iterative performance of Indigenous identity within both literary and juridical texts may be understood in these terms and, further, in accordance with Derrida's notion of *différance* – that is, of identity, as it is expressed in text (and in speech), as both differing and deferred, a "movement" or "play of differences".[25] While literature, however, is "brought into being and governed by laws"[26] – that is, the laws of the "strange institution"[27] that is literature – for Derrida, the texts "under its aegis" are peculiarly subversive.[28] Indeed, the law of the legal institution (as opposed to the literary institution) is curiously dependent upon "some literary intervention" for its very presence and permanence: "only once it is 'put into writing' does the law remain 'on record',

18 Attridge, above n 12, 18.
19 Derrida, above n 1, 33; Attridge, above n 6.
20 Attridge, above n 12, 18.
21 Peter Fitzpatrick, " 'Reading Slowly': The Law of Literature and the Literature of Law" in Ruth Buchanan, Stewart Motha and Sundhya Pahuja (eds), *Reading Modern Law: Critical Methodologies and Sovereign Formations* (2012) 193, 198, citing Maurice Blanchot, *The Madness of the Day* (Lydia David trans., 1981 edn) 16 and Maurice Blanchot, "Literature and the Right to Death" in Maurice Blanchot, *The Station Hill Blanchot Reader: Fiction and Literary Essays* (Lydia David trans., 1999 edn) 365–6.
22 Fitzpatrick, above n 21, 198.
23 Attridge, above n 12, 1, 19 (emphasis added).
24 Attridge, above n 2, 181. I will return to this parable throughout the following chapters.
25 Jacques Derrida, "Différance" in Jacques Derrida, *Margins of Philosophy* (1982) 3, 11–12, 17. I will return to discuss both deferral and iterability, in the context of law and literature, in Chapter 15.
26 Attridge, above n 2, 181.
27 Derrida, above n 1, 33.
28 Attridge, above n 2, 181.

its permanence 'ensured [by the text] with the vigilance of a guardian'".[29] Accordingly, this law is "held 'in *suspense*'", having "no set content of its own",[30] whereas the institution of literature has been described as being in possession of a unique capacity to "stage and *suspend* all the presuppositions upon which any such institution rests – among them the operation of laws".[31]

For Goodrich, a "literary analysis" possesses the capacity to "destroy the idols of the legal form" with which law claims its authority, via the revelation of aberrant "minor jurisprudences".[32] Such jurisprudences may be conceived as "forms of legal knowledge that escape the phantom of a sovereign and unitary law", which thereby represent "the possibilities of interpretation as also of plural forms of knowledge".[33] This notion may be usefully brought to bear upon an examination of Indigenous literature. I would suggest, however, that the deconstructive and recuperative force of such literature exceeds Goodrich's conception of a 'minor jurisprudence',[34] deconstructing and, *literally*,[35] annihilating non-Indigenous law. Whereas the 'minor' jurisprudences of the literary might trouble the "law of genre", which defines the institutional classification of literature itself,[36] Indigenous literature, I argue, emerges as a "subversive juridicity"[37] – indeed, as a deconstructive law itself[38] – and, furthermore, as a textual rendering of an Indigenous oral tradition of storytelling, as a form of (Indigenous) legal pedagogy.

Via a Benjaminian political theology, the previous part was concerned with expressions of mythical violence within the historical foundations and

29 Susan Chaplin, "Textual Properties: The Limit of Law and Literature – Towards a Gothic Jurisprudence" (2008) 43 *Studies in Law, Politics and Society: Special Issue: Law and Literature Reconsidered* 113, 115, citing Jacques Derrida, "Plato's Pharmacy" in Jacques Derrida *Dissemination* (Barbara Johnson trans., 2000 edn) 113. At 115, Chaplin writes:

> Derrida compares textuality to a *pharmakon*, an ambivalent substance that has the capacity to act as both poison and cure. The "cure" that textuality offers to the law pertains to the law's inability to establish its own permanence, or presence, without some literary intervention.

30 Fitzpatrick, above n 21, 204, citing Derrida, above n 10, 269 (emphasis added).
31 Attridge, above n 2, 181 (emphasis added).
32 Goodrich, above n 4, 113.
33 Ibid., 2.
34 See further support for this argument in Laurent de Sutter and Kyle McGee, "Introduction" in Laurent de Sutter and Kyle McGee (eds), *Deleuze and Law* (2012) 1, 10. Discussing the contribution in the same volume by Penelope Pether, "On 'Cruelty': Law, Literature, and Difference", 69, de Sutter and McGee suggest:

> Minor literatures are not enough, we cannot expect idly that they will produce the changes that law-and-lit wants to effect – we must prolong the text, insert it into the extratextual flows passing through our very different worlds, to make it act.

35 *Literally*, in the sense that the annihilation to which I refer occurs in the literary text, yet also, where literature itself enters the law as a source of social and cultural meaning, it *literally* acts upon the text of the law itself.
36 Jacques Derrida, "The Law of Genre" in Jacques Derrida (Derek Attridge, ed.), *Acts of Literature* (1992) 221.
37 Derrida, above n 3, 216.
38 Derrida, Adner, Doyle and Hendler, above n 10, 149.

contemporary manifestations of Australian law, specifically native title. It provided a critique of the authority of this law, founded upon a denial of Indigenous occupation and, indeed, sovereignty, in the arrogation of British sovereignty and the preservation of its "skeleton of principle".[39] It also examined the requirement, in Australian native title law, of a "substantially uninterrupted"[40] traditional connection to land and waters, and the myriad difficulties for contemporary Indigenous individuals and communities in demonstrating such connection. This examination situated these requirements within a discussion of the legal, or 'legitimate', fiction,[41] where the origin and foundation of law rest upon that which is (necessarily) unknowable and, moreover, fictitious.[42] This included a discussion of the constructed (legal) Indigenous subject, and the relation between such fictions and opposing ideas of justice – "real justice" and the "idea of justice".[43] The former was conceived as Derrida's constrained notion of "justice *as law*",[44] and the latter as indeterminate and unconditional,[45] arising in moments of deconstruction.

The present part will dwell upon the indeterminate and unconditional, and upon the expiatory force of divine violence in Benjamin's critique.[46] While I have described the figuring of the Indigene within the law governing native title as the machination of a determinate, mythic violence, the momentary presentation of the unpresentable of indigeneity, as it is evoked in Indigenous literature, is imagined as that which both animates and annihilates this law, with a divine and bloodless violence. That is, a "sovereign violence"[47] that overflows, exceeds or surpasses, as, indeed, "*the law of the law*".[48] In contrast to the preserving violence of such lawmaking,[49] which preconceives the Indigenous legal subject, a Benjaminian "afformative"[50] violence is, I argue, evocative of an indeterminate indigeneity, as

39 *Mabo* (1992) 175 CLR 1, 30.

40 *Akiba and Another (on behalf of the Torres Strait Islanders of the Regional Seas Claim Group) v Queensland and Others* (No 2) (2010) 270 ALR 564, [544]–[552]. See more extensive citations in Part III (Law).

41 Derrida, above n 10, 240, citing and discussing Montaigne, *Essais* 3, Ch 13, "De l'expérience" (1962), 1203/*The Essayes of Montaigne* (John Florio trans., 1933 edn) 970.

42 See Jacques Derrida, ". . . That Dangerous Supplement . . ." in Jacques Derrida (Derek Attridge, ed.), *Acts of Literature* (1992) 76; Peter Fitzpatrick, *Modernism and the Grounds of Law* (2001), especially chapter 1.

43 Sherman Alexie, "The Trial of Thomas Builds-the-Fire", in Sherman Alexie, *The Lone Ranger and Tonto Fistfight in Heaven* (1993) 100. See also Derrida, above n 10, 254.

44 Derrida, above n 10, 240 (emphasis added).

45 See Derrida, above n 17, 234.

46 Benjamin, above n 11.

47 Ibid., 300. See earlier discussion of the definition of "sovereignty", in terms of Benjamin's critique, in Part III (Law), in which it is noted that whereas Benjamin describes divine violence as sovereign, the German word used is different to that used to describe state sovereignty, and should therefore be understood to refer to an alternative form of sovereignty. See further discussion in James R Martel, *Divine Violence: Walter Benjamin and the Eschatology of Sovereignty* (2012) 61.

48 Derrida, above n 3, 191.

49 Benjamin, above n 11, especially 284.

50 Werner Hamacher (Dana Hollander trans), "Afformative, Strike: Benjamin's 'Critique of Violence'" in Andrew Benjamin and Peter Osborne (eds), *Walter Benjamin's Philosophy: Destruction and Experience* (2000) 108, 125, footnote 12. See further detail in Ch 3, footnote 29..

"the movement of deconstruction within the law"[51] and as the condition for the enactment of such law.[52] Extending this discussion and following Martel, I will further consider this law as an antidote to the fetish of political sovereignty, a means of perceiving reality amidst " 'the phantasmagoria', a swirl of misreading and idolatry"[53] that constitutes political life and legal authority in sovereign states and, moreover, as productive of a "revolutionary chance",[54] in which those marginalised by existing political forms and representations might create an alternative politics.

In the course of this discussion, I will elaborate a subversive jurisprudence of Indigenous literature, in the sense of literature as a source of law and, therefore, as deconstructive,[55] but also of law as a literary genre.[56] To begin, I will further consider Derrida's analysis of Kafka's parable, "Before the Law",[57] as a means of identifying the constitutive relation between law and literature. This will be followed by a brief overview of the 'law and literature' theoretical paradigm and its centrality to my exploration of the question of indigeneity, and a more fulsome discussion of the situation of Indigenous literature within a postcolonial paradigm. This latter engagement will include a discussion of the resistance of some Indigenous authors to the term 'postcolonial', with respect to their writing,[58] and the counter that postcolonialism refers not to a temporal delineation but, rather more favourably, to disruptive and revelatory discourses.[59] I will then consider the situation of the coloniser and the colonised within a postcolonial context, the associated anxiety of cultural recognition,[60] and the notion of hybridity, as articulated by Bhabha. That is, hybridity conceived as "a difference within", defined by its relation to that which is 'beyond', to alterity.[61] In the context of a consideration of the "irresolute identity" of the postcolonial,[62] and of the interventions of postcolo-

51 Derrida, above n 10, 254.
52 Hamacher, above n 50.
53 Martel, above n 47, 11.
54 Ibid., 52.
55 Derrida, Adner, Doyle and Hendler, above n 10, 149.
56 Goodrich, above n 4, 112.
57 Franz Kafka, "Before the Law" in Franz Kafka (Nahum N Glatzer, ed.), *The Complete Short Stories of Franz Kafka* (Willa and Edwin Muir trans., 2005 edn) 3; Derrida, above n 3.
58 See, for instance, Linda Tuhiwai Smith, *Decolonizing Methodologies: Research and Indigenous Peoples* (1999) 24; Leela Gandhi, *Postcolonial Theory: A Critical Introduction* (1998) 171; Anne McClintock, "The Angel of Progress: Pitfalls of the Term 'Postcolonialism'" in Francis Barker, Peter Hulme and Margaret Iversen (eds), *Colonial Discourse/Postcolonial Theory* (1994) 253, 255.
59 See Peter Fitzpatrick and Eve Darian-Smith, "Laws of the Postcolonial: An Insistent Introduction" in Eve Darian-Smith and Peter Fitzpatrick, *Laws of the Postcolonial* (1999) 1.
60 Such anxiety is conceived in terms of Freud's notion of the "uncanny": Sigmund Freud, "The 'Uncanny'", in Albert Dickson (ed.), *The Pelican Freud Library: Art and Literature*, Vol. 14 (1990), discussed throughout this book.
61 Homi Bhabha, *The Location of Culture* (1994) (Routledge Classics Edition, 2004) xv, 19, 6.
62 Fitzpatrick and Darian-Smith, above n 59, 2.

nialism, this discussion will return to questions of cultural identity and 'authenticity', via an examination of controversial author, Mudrooroo (Colin Johnson), and his first novel, *Wild Cat Falling*.[63]

I will then turn to examine the notion that both law and literature – as texts – may be conceived as mimetic, and consider the narrative interventions that a subversion of the conventional hierarchy between representation and 'truth' might allow. That is, the ways in which textual representations might subvert putative 'truths' and, furthermore, might be themselves productive of 'other' truths. Postcolonial literatures, I argue, specifically Indigenous authored literatures, perform such interventions, subverting legal constructions of history and subjectivity with the presentation of aberrant narratives. Reading Deleuze, I will then follow the suggestion that the subversive capacity of the literary might provide a destabilising force, through "a movement of *subversion*".[64] The notion of a subversive literature has been described in the context of poetry, which, Lincoln argues, is in possession of a " 'particular power' . . . to destabilise 'established logical forms' (of power)":[65]

> Precisely *not* through a language of judgment (identification, recognition) that will either denounce or demystify (and in so doing run the risk of degenerating into the very established logic it sets out to denounce) or flight ("fleeing the world") but rather by a movement of *subversion*, an act of playful sabotage of the very rules that bind and define it . . . "to subvert from the bottom up through a cancellation of the established logical forms".[66]

As opposed to the notion of a 'minor' literature, discussed earlier, Lincoln argues that a Deleuzian "philosophy of law, in so far as it belongs to a philosophy of literature", may reveal "something deeper . . . an intimate connection between literature and the figures of law which is independent of the former's 'becoming minor' or not"; in short, she suggests, such an encounter "would be . . . far from minor".[67] I will engage with this notion of a subversive literature in the context of a Deleuzian reading of the simulacrum, and a textual analysis of *That Deadman Dance*,[68] by Kim Scott. In so doing, I will argue that such textual representations

63 Mudrooroo, *Wild Cat Falling* (1965). The *Wild Cat* trilogy is comprised of *Wild Cat Falling* (1965), *Doin' Wild Cat* (1988) and *Wild Cat Screaming* (1992). Mudrooroo is also author of the *Master* series, which comprises *Master of the Ghost Dreaming* (1991), *The Undying* (1998), *Underground* (1999) and *The Promised Land* (2000).

64 Lissa Lincoln, "Deleuze and Camus: Strange Encounters" in Laurent de Sutter and Kyle McGee (eds), *Deleuze and Law* (2012) 167, 181.

65 Ibid., 180.

66 Ibid., discussing, among others, Emmanuel Renault, *L'Experience de l'injustice: Reconnaissance et Clinique de l'injustice* (2004); see also 174.

67 Ibid., 182.

68 Kim Scott, *That Deadman Dance* (2010).

of indigeneities are productive of a radical newness or openness,[69] initiating a regenerative 'restaging' of Indigenous subjectivities.

Via a close reading of *Carpentaria*, by Alexis Wright,[70] I will then further consider the Derridean notion of a "subversive juridicity",[71] and of Indigenous literature as evocative of a recuperative and revolutionary law of alterity. In the context of these readings, this analysis will elaborate upon Derrida's (apparently) conflicting assertions in respect of the relations between law, justice, and deconstruction, ultimately revealing the juridical authority and, therefore, deconstructive force of these texts.[72] Moreover, I will demonstrate the ways in which these texts depict a regenerative force of law – of divine violence, I will suggest – that would disrupt, suspend, and, indeed, (re)constitute colonial law, via the recuperation and reassertion of Indigenous Law.

Through these readings, and drawing the elements of this book together in conclusion, I will situate the radical 'newness' of depictions of indigeneities within these texts alongside a Derridean unconditional justice and a Benjaminian divine violence, where such literary renderings penetrate and disrupt the hegemony of existing legal narratives, emerging *with-in* the law itself. Indeed, while it is stories that are formative of Indigenous jurisprudences, Indigenous Law being sourced in the songlines or ancestral stories traced geographically through lands, waters and sky, I argue that such narratives also triumphantly, yet nonviolently, penetrate non-Indigenous law via their expression in Indigenous literature.

A fictive institution

> In terms of a quest to reach the law, in order to stand before it . . . the story becomes the impossible story of the impossible. The story of prohibition is a prohibited story.[73]

"[T]he space of literature" is, for Derrida, "not only that of an instituted *fiction* but also a *fictive institution* which in principle allows one to say everything", by "gather[ing] . . . translating . . . totaliz[ing] by formalizing", yet also allowing one "to break out of prohibitions".[74] This "strange institution",[75] he further suggests, liberates the writer, to "say everything he wants to or everything he can", as a

69 Gilles Deleuze, *Difference and Repetition* (Paul Patton trans., 2004 edn).
70 Alexis Wright, *Carpentaria* (2006).
71 Derrida, above n 3, 216.
72 Derrida, above n 10; Derrida, Adner, Doyle and Hendler, above n 10, 149.
73 Derrida, above n 3, 199–200.
74 Derrida, above n 1, 36.
75 Ibid.

"powerful political weapon" that may be "neutralized as fiction".[76] Kafka's parable, "Before the Law", is exemplary of the critical analysis of law *in* literature and of law *as* literature and, furthermore, of literature as *law*. The parable functions simultaneously as a literary fiction, yet also as a meditation upon the origins of law and of the legal text, and of the literary text as juridical. Indeed, Derrida argues, Kafka writes a text "which in turn *becomes* the Law itself", since "[w]e are in front of it as in front of the law":[77]

> [Kafka] reproduces the situation, and the Franz Kafka signature or the signature of the text, makes the Law – in a deconstructing movement. So deconstruction affirms a new mode of Law. It becomes the Law.[78]

Derrida describes the prohibitive relation between the countryman and the law, and its rigorous doorkeepers, as that between the legal subject and the legal text. He describes the "original" text as the door, and "the 'I' of the doorkeeper [as] also that of the text or of the law",[79] which "lays down the law, and in the first place with respect to itself" such that, "[i]n its very act, the text produces and pronounces the law that protects it and renders it intangible".[80] This text is prohibited, yet not "in the sense of an imperative constraint; it is a *différance*".[81] The infinite doors and doorkeepers separating the countryman from the law are, for Derrida, akin to the infinite deferrals of *différance*, the origin of which "must not and cannot be approached . . . presented or represented and above all not penetrated":[82]

> The door is physically open, the doorkeeper does not bar the way by force. It is his discourse, rather, that operates at the limit, not to prohibit directly, but to interrupt and defer the passage, to withhold the pass.[83]

The legal text (and indeed, the literary text), however, is always "yet to come", instituted and constituted by the acts of the unwitting countryman, who appears before it. Derrida describes this "extraordinary paradox":

76 Derrida, above n 1, 37–8. Such neutralisation may also equate to impotence: Aristodemou, above n 9, 9. Aristodemou cites Theodor Adorno, *Aesthetic Theory* (Christian Lenhardt trans., 1984 edn), 325:

> Works are most critical when they first see the light of day; afterwards they become neutralized because, among other things, the social conditions have changed. Neutralization is the social price art pays for its autonomy.

77 Derrida, Adner, Doyle and Hendler, above n 10, 149 (emphasis added).
78 Ibid., 150.
79 Derrida, above n 3, 210–11.
80 Ibid., 212.
81 Ibid., 202–3.
82 Ibid., 205.
83 Ibid., 203.

> [T]he law [*loi*] is transcendent, violent and nonviolent, because it depends only on who is before it (and so prior to it), on who produces it, founds it, authorizes it in an absolute performative whose presence always escapes him.[84]

While the countryman patiently waits his entire life before the law, the parable ultimately reveals the futility of his endurance, where the law "has no essence", being "guarded by a doorkeeper who guards nothing, the door remaining open – and open onto nothing".[85] It is the countryman's own restraint that *makes* the law: "He must force himself, give himself an order, not to obey the law but rather to *not gain access* to the law . . .".[86] In the course of its very narration, therefore, Kafka's parable "allows one to think the essence of the law in the experience of this 'everything to say'",[87] thereby revealing the contingency and vacuity of the law, the textual production necessary to the foundation and maintenance of its authority and to deference before it[88] and, therefore, of the literary text as akin to the law, and as a source of law. The capacity to perceive such readings of the law, via literature, is a critical function of law and literature scholarship.

The law and literature movement, arguably begun with the writings of legal scholar, John Wigmore[89] (concerned with law *in* literature) and continued by Benjamin Cardozo[90] (concerned with law *as* literature) and, later, James Boyd White,[91] is now a common thread in critical legal studies.[92] This movement began with the notion that literature may impart some humanist morality to the common lawyer, and so favourably infuse the practice of law. Indeed, it has been suggested that literature might possess, and be defined by, "certain effects on readers: humanizing them, broadening their minds, alerting them to linguistic niceties,

84 Derrida, above n 10, 270.
85 Derrida, above n 3, 206.
86 Ibid., 203.
87 Derrida, above n 1, 36.
88 See also discussion in Aristodemou, above n 9, 25, who suggests that the parable is revealing of the paternalism of the doorkeeper, and consequently of law, and of the possibility of alternative entrances.
89 John L Wigmore, "A List of Legal Novels" (1908) 2 *Illinois Law Review* 574.
90 Benjamin Cardozo, "Law and Literature" (1925) 14 *Yale Law Review* 699.
91 James Boyd White, *The Legal Imagination* (1973); James Boyd White, *Heracles' Bow: Essays on the Rhetoric and Poetics of the Law* (1985); more recently, James Boyd White, "The Cultural Background of 'The Legal Imagination'" in Austin Sarat, Cathrine O Frank and Matthew Anderson (eds), *Teaching Law and Literature* (2011); James Boyd White, "An Old-Fashioned View of the Nature of Law" (2011) 12(1) *Theoretical Inquiries in Law* 381; James Boyd White, "The 'Legal Imagination' and the Beginning of Modern Law and Literature" in B Pozzo (ed.), *Teaching Law Through the Looking Glass of Literature* (2010) 9.
92 For a relatively recent and comprehensive overview of the relevant literature, see Austin Sarat, Matthew Anderson and Cathrine O Frank, "Introduction: On the Origins and Prospects of the Humanistic Study of Law" in Austin Sarat, Matthew Anderson and Cathrine O Frank (eds), *Law and the Humanities: An Introduction* (2010).

enlarging their sympathies, undermining their covert ideological assumptions, and so forth".[93] Furthermore, this notion emerged far earlier in the writings of the Romantics, which extolled the "moral force"[94] of the imagination, to the extent that Shelley declared poets "the unacknowledged legislators of the world".[95] Such aspirations, however, in the context of the relations between law and literature, have received criticism.[96] Moreover, the use of literature as a critique of law has also been subject to censure, where it is recalled that both law and literature are institutions, "created by social, legal, and political processes that themselves vary from one culture and historical period to the next".[97] Nonetheless, it has been suggested that literature itself, as distinct from the institution of literature ("literary *studies*"), may possess the capacity to "perform a liberatory role", removed from the limitations of epistemology.[98] Furthermore, as discussed in Part I, Eagleton has proposed a notion of literature as strategy, such that the experience of a literary work is itself generative of "the very historical and ideological subtext to which it is a strategic reply".[99]

According to Goodrich, as discussed at the outset, such literary interventions are revelatory of laws that are unrecognisable and, indeed, "imaginary", only insofar as "legal science and its history of power denie[s] reality to those jurisdictions, fictions or laws".[100] Where the literary is principally concerned with the imagination, its capacity to envisage and formulate alternative realities is productive of an extensive "register of imaginary laws".[101] It is with these imaginative tendencies that literary jurisprudences "[trouble] the boundaries of an institution, practice or tradition" and, in the case of law, "[question] its values and [transgress] its limits".[102] Literature, furthermore, troubles the "law of genre"[103] that would define literature *as literature* and, indeed, that would distinguish

93 Attridge, above n 6, 59–60. Attridge argues that literary works may indeed have these effects, "but it is not as a direct result of their being *literary*".

94 John L Mahoney, "The Idea of Mimesis in Shelley's A Defence of Poetry" (1984) 24(1) *The British Journal of Aesthetics* 59, 59. At 63, citing Percy Bysshe Shelley, "A Defence of Poetry" in Bruce R McElderry Jr (ed.), *Shelley's Critical Prose* (1967) 3, 12, Mahoney writes:

> Poetry for Shelley is not ethics, but pleasing contemplation . . . it is the ultimate moral vehicle; "it awakens and enlarges the mind itself by rendering it the receptacle of a thousand unapprehended combinations of thought".

95 Shelley, above n 94, 36.

96 See Aristodemou, above n 9, especially 5–6; Terry Eagleton, *Literary Theory: An Introduction* (1996), 15–46.

97 Aristodemou, above n 9, 7, citing Attridge, above n 12, 1 and Jacques Derrida, "The First Session" in Jacques Derrida (Derek Attridge, ed.), *Acts of Literature* (1992) 127.

98 Ibid., 10, citing Simon During, *Foucault and Literature: Towards a Genealogy of Writing* (1992) 113–18.

99 Eagleton, above n 7, 170.

100 Goodrich, above n 4, 3.

101 Ibid.

102 Ibid., 6.

103 Derrida, above n 36.

legal and literary texts, revealing the literary qualities of law itself. Such revelation "reinstate[s] the uncertainty and the undecidability of the writing of law" and, in so doing, draws "attention to the particular" – the aforementioned focus of both law and literature upon an application of universalities to the singular work – and to the "question of justice".[104] That is, returning to Derrida, "the operation of justice" within the law, conceived as "an impossible union of a singular occurrence and a general law"[105] and, therefore, as a movement between an indeterminate responsiveness and a determinate decisiveness. Returning briefly to Kafka's parable, Martel has suggested that the justice for which the countryman (everyman) waits has already arrived, evident in the "justice and democratic practices" already existing outside of the law.[106] The perpetual expectation of the waiting countryman renders such practices illegible, the ultimate realisation of the futility of his wait only revealed to him upon his death. For Derrida, however, this justice has not arrived, but perpetually haunts the law.[107] Nonetheless, the "law of literature" is conceived as possessing a tendency "to defy and lift the law",[108] thereby interrupting the institutionalised narratives of the law in a revolutionary – yet fleeting, ungraspable, perhaps impossible[109] – moment of justice.

The literary here stands in contrast to the law; yet, as Fitzpatrick remarks, "affinities loom".[110] Returning to his earlier conception of the non-closure of "the frame or border of the context", such that "[t]he outside penetrates and thus determines the inside",[111] Derrida similarly describes the law of genre, which "gathers together the corpus and, at the same time, in the same blinking of an eye, keeps it from closing, from identifying itself with itself".[112] In this way, the literary work and the law of genre are neither "immanent or identical to one another . . . neither one nor two".[113] As Fitzpatrick further suggests, while "literature rejects instrumental containment", there is "a generative contamination" between such containment and its release.[114] Derrida calls this simultaneous "inclusion and exclusion" the "genre-clause".[115] That is, a law of literature that

104 Goodrich, above n 4, 8.
105 Jacques Derrida, "Force of Law: The Mystical Foundation of Authority" (1990) 11 *Cardozo Law Review* 919, cited in Attridge, above n 12, 17–18.
106 Martel, above n 47, 70.
107 Jacques Derrida, "Force of Law": The "Mystical Foundation of Authority" in Drucilla Cornell, Michel Rosenfeld and David Gray Carlson (eds), *Deconstruction and the Possibility of Justice* (1992) 27, cited in Martel, above n 47, 74.
108 Derrida, above n 1, 36.
109 Derrida, above n 3, 201.
110 Fitzpatrick, above n 21, 199.
111 Simon Critchley, *The Ethics of Deconstruction: Derrida and Levinas* (1992), 32, citing Jacques Derrida, *Limited Inc* (1990) 281–2; *Limited Inc* (1988) 152–3. See further detail in Part II (Indigeneity).
112 Derrida, above n 36, 231.
113 Ibid.
114 Fitzpatrick, above n 21, 200.
115 Derrida, above n 36, 231.

would designate the genre of a literary work, yet would simultaneously maintain an openness to alterity, to the 'beyond'. Such simultaneity provides that literature might remain an 'institution', yet one that might also "overflow the institution"[116] or, at the very least, exceed its limits.[117]

Returning to my earlier discussion of the "literary event", following Attridge, the literary work as "an act, an event, of reading" may be conceived as "singular".[118] That is, as "*a set of active relations*, put in play in the reading, that never settle into a fixed configuration".[119] I might construe this argument to be a suggestion that the literary text may be fixed for the moment of its reading or performance, yet must *simultaneously* remain open to reconfiguration in the experience of another performance. Indeed, "literature . . . rejects any ultimate containment".[120] Similarly, following Derrida, Fitzpatrick argues that the law is necessarily a "calculable determinacy, yet this determinacy must be held in 'suspense' allowing law to empty itself of existing content, respond to alterity, and do so utterly" in a " 'moment of law', a moment instanced in the legal decision".[121] Nonetheless, this opening must not be a mere receptivity beyond all determinacy; rather, in the rendering of justice, the law must "extend beyond justice and bring it to bear".[122] Accordingly, both law and literature are created by simultaneous "constituent dimensions",[123] perpetually opening on to alterity yet momentarily resolving in singular events – readings, performances, decisions – of determinacy.

It is the "modest hope" of one, and perhaps other scholars engaged in critique within a law and literature paradigm, that "literary texts, and above all, our readings of them, will be less reductive of the world's varied meanings than legal texts".[124] Many scholars, however, are less concerned with the ameliorative effects of literature upon law than with the revelation of, as articulated above, the literary qualities of law and the juridical qualities of literature.[125] Nonetheless, this apparent philosophical mutuality has been described in less favourable terms for the law: "Literature is fundamentally the law's problem".[126] Derrida's analyses, alongside those of Fitzpatrick, reveal a responsive tension between a determinate law that would contain literature, and the indeterminacy of a literary 'event' that would resist any such containment[127] – that is, more broadly, between law and literature,

116 Derrida, above n 1, 36.
117 Attridge, above n 6, 60, suggests that the literary may exceed the limits of "the recognized institution of literature"; see also Fitzpatrick, above n 21, 200.
118 Ibid., 59.
119 Ibid., 68.
120 Fitzpatrick, above n 21, 200.
121 Ibid., 203, citing Derrida, above n 10, 269.
122 Ibid., 202–3.
123 Ibid., 202.
124 Aristodemou, above n 9, 9.
125 Ibid.
126 Chaplin, above n 29, 113.
127 Fitzpatrick, above n 21, 200.

as between law and justice.[128] It is the purpose of this part to consider the latter of each of these where Indigenous authored literature, in the 'event' of its reading, is uniquely expressive and, indeed, constitutive of disruptive and resistant indigeneities which, in turn, perpetually (re)constitute both juridical and literary laws in revolutionary "moment[s] of suspense".[129]

As mutually constitutive institutions and texts, law and literature have been described as "products of the same social, historical, and cultural forces", their effects upon society "not monolithic but contradictory and fragmentary".[130] Accordingly, these modes of cultural expression are further conceived as "sites of struggle", where law must relentlessly seek to establish its own authority in a mediation between its own textual categories and the realities appearing before it, while literature subverts this authority in the fictitious expression of imaginary worlds, "which may in turn become laws".[131] Indigenous literature, I argue, performs a unique role in this struggle, articulating the experiences and aspirations of marginalised groups and elaborating a vibrant Indigenous Law. Indeed, where such literature may be conceived as a subversive jurisprudence, expressive of "[t]he fragmentary and deterritorialised language of minority"[132] yet evocative of a revolutionary force beyond the limits of a 'minor' jurisprudence, it may be also conceived as critical to the broader postcolonial project.

The postcolonial project

> Our words are weapons too . . . We have only to wait and one day we will see change. This is the hope of writing. Believing the unbelievable.[133]

While law and literature scholars attribute to literature a capacity to "disrupt old meanings and create new ones",[134] postcolonial literature disrupts and creates via the marginalised language of the historically disempowered and dispossessed. Such literature has been described as "counter-discursive", insofar as it presents a challenge to dominant discourses, and "reinvests its own hybridised world with a provisionally normative perspective".[135] Indigenous literature, and its expression

128 See Derrida, above n 10; Derrida, above n 2.
129 Derrida, above n 10, 269.
130 Aristodemou, above n 9, 9–10.
131 Ibid., 11.
132 Goodrich, above n 4, 2.
133 Alexis Wright, "Politics of Writing" (Summer 2002) 62(2) *Southerly* 10, 20.
134 Aristodemou, above n 9, 24.
135 Helen Tiffin, "Post-Colonial Literatures and Counter-Discourse" from "Post-colonial Literatures and Counter-discourse" (1987) 9(3) *Kunapipi* 17, excerpted in Bill Ashcroft, Gareth Griffiths and Helen Tiffin (eds), *The Post-Colonial Studies Reader* (2006, 2nd edn) 99, 101. Tiffin notes that such perspectives are "deliberately constructed as provisional", since the postcolonial novel [she instances Jean Rhys's *Wide Sargasso Sea* (1966)] "is at pains to demonstrate the subjective nature of point of view and hence the cultural construction of meaning".

of Indigenous Law, operates in that which may be described as a postcolonial space, allowing the subaltern to 'speak back' to the imperial metropole.[136] Yet, it has been suggested that where Indigenous authors are concerned with expressing an experience of indigeneity that is extrinsic to imperialism, its mode of expression should not be dictated by occidental traditions.[137] Indigenous authors have resisted the situation of their writing within a postcolonial discourse, perceiving it to be an imperialist denial of continued colonisation. Tuhiwai Smith has described postcolonialism as, potentially, a "strategy for reinscribing or re-authorizing the privilege of non-Indigenous academics", for whom the 'post' remains a deceit.[138] Accordingly, it has been suggested that postcolonialism simply situates cultural and political expressions *in relation to* colonisation, rather than as extrinsic to it, whereby the prefix 'post' "semantically delivers the idea of a world historicised through the single category of colonialism"[139] and, further, "[o]ther cultures share only a chronological and prepositional relation to a Euro-centred epoch that is over (post) or not yet begun ('pre')".[140]

Postcolonialism as an intellectual field rather than a temporal delineation, however, has been described as indicative not of a linear sequentiality but rather, of "a disruption or fracturing of the West", which "is not to be contained by the West" and "cannot be 'part' of the West".[141] Within this reading, postcolonialism is conceived not as a marker of progress[142] but, according to Bhabha, as a revelation: "the image of post-Enlightenment man tethered to, *not* confronted by, his dark reflection", which "splits his presence", revealing not "Self and Other but the otherness of the Self".[143] Drawing upon the Freudian notion of the 'primal horde', which immediately precedes the instantiation of law, Fitzpatrick describes the "civilized man" of modernity, who "originates in stark opposition to savagery but savagery is also the connected and protean progenitor of this civilized man and persists within 'him'".[144] In the postcolonial context, both colonised and

136 Bill Ashcroft, Gareth Griffiths and Helen Tiffin, *The Empire Writes Back: Theory and Practice in Postcolonial Literatures* (2nd edn, 2002); see also Gayatri Chakravorty Spivak, "Can the Subaltern Speak?" in Cary Nelson and Lawrence Grossberg (eds), *Marxism and the Interpretation of Culture* (1988) 271. This imperative has also been applied to Indigenous researchers: Linda Tuhiwai Smith has spoken of her academic project as " 'researching back', in the same tradition of 'writing back' or 'talking back', that characterizes much of the post-colonial or anti-colonial literature": Tuhiwai Smith, above n 58, 7.

137 Ian Anderson, "Introduction: The Aboriginal Critique of Colonial Knowing" in Michele Grossman (ed.), *Blacklines: Contemporary Critical Writing by Indigenous Australians* (2003) 17, 23.

138 Tuhiwai Smith, above n 58, 24.

139 Gandhi, above n 58, 171.

140 McClintock, above n 58, 255; see also Simone Drichel, " 'How Newness (not) Comes into the World': Eva Rask Knudsen's *The Circle and the Spiral*" (October 2006) 22(4) *Australian Literary Studies* 507, 507.

141 Fitzpatrick and Darian-Smith, above n 59, 2.

142 See McClintock, above n 58, 254.

143 Bhabha, above n 61, 62–3.

144 Fitzpatrick, above n 42, 44; see also 63.

coloniser are immersed in a process productive of "an estrangement of familiar meanings and a mutual 'creolisation' of identities",[145] a process that should not be understood as generative of the new, but as a recognition of existing conditions, "the perverse palimpsest of colonial identity".[146] Perrin further elaborates upon the anxiety of this recognition:

> The proximity of indigenous peoples is anxious not because they threaten to upset some kind of already secure difference, but because they threaten to reveal the fact that this difference, which ought to have been excluded, never was.[147]

Hybridity, as articulated by Bhabha, is conceived not in terms of relationality, but as "a difference within".[148] In this way, traditional Indigenous "life-ways"[149] are "reinscribed" via "conditions of contingency and contradictoriness", and contemporary subjectivities emerge, which embrace incommensurabilities,[150] while rejecting imposed identities. Such incommensurabilities are not, Bhabha maintains, comparable to a "naïve and benevolent pluralism" [151] or "mere diversity" [152] but, rather, exhibit a gesturing toward the 'beyond', "embody[ing] its restless and revisionary energy" in the transformation of "the present into an expanded and ex-centric site of experience and empowerment".[153] The force of Indigenous literature, I argue, may be described as an " 'opening' to what is beyond, to alterity and possibility, to 'the void' ".[154] It is "here and there, on all sides,

145 Gandhi, above n 58, 131, citing Mary Louise Pratt, *Imperial Eyes: Travel Writing and Transculturation* (1992) 4–6.

146 Bhabha, above n 61, 63.

147 Colin Perrin, "Approaching Anxiety: The Insistence of the Postcolonial in the Declaration on the Rights of Indigenous Peoples" in Eve Darian-Smith and Peter Fitzpatrick, *Laws of the Postcolonial* (1999) 19, 30.

148 Bhabha, above n 61, xv, 19. See also Peter Hallward, *Absolutely Postcolonial: Writing between the Singular and the Specific* (2001), who remarks at 24, footnote 32: "Bhabha is only interested in a 'form of cultural value that does not depend on binary divisions'" (Homi Bhabha, "Unpacking my library. . . Again" in Iain Chambers and Lidia Curti (eds), *The Post-colonial Question: Common Skies, Divided Horizons* (1996) 199, 207).

149 Marcia Langton, "The 'Wild', the Market and the Native: Indigenous People face New Forms of Global Colonization" in William M Adams and Martin Mulligan (eds), *Decolonizing Nature: Strategies for Conservation in a Post-Colonial Era* (2003) 79, 80.

150 Bhabha, above n 61, 3.

151 Bhabha, above n 148, 203.

152 Bhabha, above n 61, 60, 124, 154–5.

153 Ibid., 6.

154 Maurice Blanchot, "Literature and the Right to Death" in Maurice Blanchot, *The Station Hill Blanchot Reader: Fiction and Literary Essays* (Lydia David trans., 1999 ed) 359, 388, cited and discussed in Peter Fitzpatrick, "Juris-fiction: Literature and the Law of the Law" (2004) 35(1–2) *ARIEL* 215, 222.

fort/da,[155] hither and thither, back and forth", offering an unconditional aesthetic, an "insurgent act of cultural translation . . . that innovates and interrupts the performance of the present".[156] As Wright asserts, "fiction penetrates more than the surface layers, and probes deep into the inner workings of reality".[157] It is these inner workings with which the law is "*not* confronted" but to which it is "tethered", as the coloniser is tethered to the colonised,[158] and to which it must continually respond.

The insurgent act of Indigenous literature – as postcolonial, hybrid, interstitial – vividly reveals the liminal experience of the marginalised. Speaking of the liminality of the migrant or minority experience, Bhabha writes:

> Living in the interstices of Lucretius and Ovid, caught in-between a "nativist", even nationalist, atavism and a postcolonial metropolitan assimilation, the subject of cultural difference becomes a problem that Walter Benjamin has described as the irresolution, or liminality, of "translation", the *element of resistance* in the process of transformation, "that element in a translation which does not lend itself to translation".[159]

This "irresolution", "liminality", and "element of resistance" is, I would suggest, that which interrupts or "punctures"[160] the narrative of the law with the " 'newness' of migrant or minority discourse",[161] and the articulation of subaltern identities. Yet, the newness to which Bhabha refers here is detached from the linearity of history, such that "the future becomes (once again) an *open question*, instead of being specified by the fixity of the past",[162] which avails marginalised or minority identities of "a mode of performative agency".[163] Indeed, for Bhabha, postcolonialism is "the space of intervention emerging in the cultural interstices that introduces creative invention into existence", and "demands an encounter

155 German: gone/there. This is a reference to Sigmund Freud, *Beyond the Pleasure Principle* (standard edn, Vol. 18, 1920) 14–15.
156 Bhabha, above n 61, 2, 10.
157 Wright, above n 133, 13.
158 Bhabha, above n 61, 62–3.
159 Ibid., 321, citing Walter Benjamin, *Illuminations* (Harry Zorn trans., 1968 edn) 75–6.
160 Derrida, above n 17, 234.
161 Bhabha, above n 61, 325.
162 John Forrester, "Dead on Time" in John Forrester, *The Seductions of Psychoanalysis: Freud, Lacan and Derrida* (1990) 206, cited in Bhabha, above n 61, 314.
163 Bhabha, above n 61, 314. Citing Judith Butler, "Decking Out: Performing Identities" in Diana Fuss (ed.), *Inside/Out, Lesbian Theories, Gay Theories* (1991) 17, Bhabha writes:

> The iterative "time" of the future as *a becoming "once again open"*, makes available to marginalized or minority identities a mode of performative agency that Judith Butler has elaborated for the representation of lesbian sexuality: "a specificity. . . to be established, not *outside* or *beyond* that reinscription or reiteration, but in the very modality and effects of that reinscription".

with 'newness' that is not part of the continuum of past and present".[164] That is, rather, an encounter with "[t]he borderline work of culture", which "renews the past, refiguring it as a performance of the present".[165] To dwell in the 'beyond', he suggests, is "to be a part of a revisionary time", such that intervention is in the "here and now".[166] Harnessing that which Fitzpatrick describes as "post-colonialism's revolutionary orientation towards history",[167] the interventions of postcolonial literature, and expressions of indigeneity in Indigenous literature, may be understood as evocations of Bhaba's 'newness', apparent in the aforementioned revolutionary moments of deconstruction,[168] and of justice.

Situated within the "fractured 'in-between'" of the postcolonial, however, such writing must conform to that which Fitzpatrick and Darian-Smith describe as "the double demand of occidental modernity: the demand for an assured position integrated with a responsiveness to all that is beyond a position".[169] This 'double demand' recalls, once again, Derrida's notion of the "genre-clause", which entails a simultaneous "inclusion and exclusion", or non-closure.[170] In terms of the law, Fitzpatrick has elsewhere described the postcolonial as "an aporetic combination of law as capable of determinate self-realization and law as 'abstract' or vacuous and thence infinitely responsive".[171] Accordingly, the interventions of the postcolonial – challenging and, indeed, re-writing hegemonic narratives – require both the determinacy of a speaking position that would tend to ossify postcolonial identities, as was discussed in the introduction to this book, and a responsivity to "the constituent conditions of society or community itself",[172] which extends to the indeterminacy of the literary.[173] The tendency toward such ossification, juxtaposed with the liberatory capacities of the literary, assume a particular poignancy in considering Mudrooroo (Colin Johnson), an enormously influential author of fiction, poetry and Indigenous literary and cultural criticism.

164 Bhabha, above n 61, 12, 10.

165 Ibid., 10.

166 Ibid.

167 Peter Fitzpatrick, "The Revolutionary Past: Decolonizing Law and Human Rights" (2014) 2(1) *Metodo: International Studies in Phenomenology and Philosophy* 117, 123.

168 See Derrida, above n 17, 234.

169 Fitzpatrick and Darian-Smith, above n 59, 3.

170 Derrida, above n 36, 231. See also Derrida, above n 97, 153.

171 Fitzpatrick, above n 167, 125. See also Eve Darian-Smith and Peter Fitzpatrick (eds), *Laws of the Postcolonial* (1999).

172 Ibid., 125, citing Jacques Derrida, *Politics of Friendship* (George Collins trans., 1997 edn) 231.

173 See broader discussion of the aforementioned "double demand of occidental modernity", of which the determinacy of a speaking position and indeterminacy of postcolonial literatures are an example, in Fitzpatrick and Darian-Smith, above n 59, especially 3.

First published to great acclaim in 1965,[174] Mudrooroo's variously contested assertions of cultural identity are, in themselves, demonstrative of the unsettled positioning of postcolonial identities and, most particularly, of indigeneities. His (Australian) Aboriginality has now been widely denounced on the basis of descent, despite an uncertain genealogy and a previous personal conviction of his own Aboriginality. As the recipient of a national literary award for Indigenous authors and having held various positions as expert in Aboriginal Studies, the revelation of Mudrooroo as, arguably, non-Indigenous, was and remains of great significance to questions of Indigenous 'authenticity' and entitlement, most particularly in literary and academic spheres. While some have leapt to his defence,[175] others remain circumspect, and yet others have denounced his entire *oeuvre*, as no longer relevant to 'Indigenous Studies'.[176] The latter response has been described as reflective of a particular "deployment of authenticity as a concept which is meant to validate the categorization, reception and reading of literature", a non-Indigenous fascination with the "aura of exoticism"[177] of the " 'authentic' native".[178] Indeed, his denunciation has been placed alongside other Australian literary 'hoaxes', particularly those concerning authorial claims to indigeneity.[179] Whereas other non-Indigenous renderings of indigeneity frequently depend upon a pristine 'authenticity', the uncertain and unknowable hybridity of Mudrooroo's fictional characters, and indeed of his own identity, is unsettling. The evocations of indigeneity expressed within his literary and critical texts are evocative of this hybridity, and are of particular interest in the context of broader contestation concerning Indigenous identity.

Mudrooroo's first novel, *Wild Cat Falling*, depicts a nameless protagonist in prose that is both reflective of the beat writers and an "existentialist ennui",[180] and of the traditions of oral storytelling and the Dreaming. Attempting to escape after shooting a police officer, the character encounters a local Aboriginal man who

174 Mudrooroo (1965), above n 63. Despite an initially positive public reception to the book, Heiss describes Mary Durack's Foreword to *Wild Cat Falling* as "essentially racist": "There we have it: Johnson's [Mudrooroo's] introduction to the literary world as a noble savage": Anita M Heiss, *Dhuuluu-Yala: To Talk Straight* (2003) 4.

175 Ruby Langford Ginibi, "The Right to be a Koori Writer", Letter to the Editor, *The Australian* (7 August 1996) 12, cited in Adam Shoemaker, "Mudrooroo and the Curse of Authencity" in Annalisa Oboe (ed.), *Mongrel Signatures: Reflections on the Work of Mudrooroo* (2003) 1, 4.

176 See Shoemaker, above n 175, 4–5.

177 Ibid., 8, 9.

178 Rey Chow, "Where Have All the Natives Gone?" in Angelika Bammer (ed.), *Displacements: Cultural Identities in Question* (1994) 136, cited in Shoemaker, above n 175, 9.

179 Shoemaker, above n 175, 12–13.

180 Suzanne Ruta, "Collapsing Into Himself", Review of Mudrooroo, *Wild Cat Falling* (January 9, 1994) *New York Times*, at http://query.nytimes.com/gst/fullpage.html?res=9B0DE5DC173EF93AA35752C0A962958260&scp=1&sq=mudrooroo+wildcat+falling&st=nyt# (accessed 6 October 2015).

relates the story of a wild cat and a crow, in which the cat is deceived by the crow to believe he is able to fly to the moon.[181] The protagonist, a so-called 'half-caste', relates to both the cat and the crow, "in tormented double identification":[182]

> Wild cat plunging downwards through the night with terror in its glazed cat eyes. I am watching and the terror is my own. I am the crow laughing to see such fun. It is I falling, falling, plunging to my certain doom.[183]

This dual recognition has been described as "a capsule psychoanalysis",[184] depicting the pain and terror of the half-caste. Ultimately, the novel articulates both a desire for knowledge and acceptance in non-Indigenous society, and a deep yearning for an autochthonous, Indigenous self. The angst of the protagonist is echoed in the self-description of its author, following his unveiling, as "some kind of weird mongrel" or "some sort of a blackfella masquerading as a blackfella".[185]

While Mudrooroo's ancestral, cultural and intellectual 'authenticity' remain contested, and his fictional and critical works should not be considered alongside those of Scott and Wright, his texts nonetheless present a challenge to static figurings of indigeneity. His written renderings of Indigenous oral stories are expressive of that which he describes as "maban reality"[186] – a mode of 'magic realism' that recreates moments of colonial encounter from multiple and alternate perspectives. Moreover, Mudrooroo has asserted that his writing attempts to recuperate the "great oral discourses and spiritual narratives of preliterate Aboriginal Australia",[187] which "allow for the opening of the doors of perception through language and imagination", and a reimagining of truth and reality.[188] In a postcolonial mode, it has been suggested, such writing "stor[ies] a new sense of place" within a polyphonic indigeneity, which "refutes boundaries and evokes recuperative change through the endless definitions of place and the real".[189] That is, Archer-Lean suggests, "the idea of created and creative worlds",[190] which are simultaneously expressive of the "specifics of land and treaty rights" and the imaginary.[191]

181 Mudrooroo, above n 63, 127.
182 Ruta, above n 180.
183 Mudrooroo, above n 63, 127–8.
184 Ruta, above n 180.
185 Mudrooroo, *Personal Interview with Adam Shoemaker* (17 April, 2001), cited in Shoemaker, above n 175, 19.
186 Mudrooroo, *The Indigenous Literature of Australia: Milli Milli Wangka* (1997) 97–8.
187 Ibid., 95–6.
188 Ibid., 97–8.
189 Clare Archer-Lean, "Place, Space and Tradition in the Writings of Mudrooroo" in Oboe, above n 175, 203, 222.
190 Ibid., 203.
191 Ibid., 222.

Chapter 14

Mimetic indigeneities

Becoming indigeneity

The imaginative interventions of Indigenous literature, constitutive of law and evocative of justice, present a challenge to the putative 'truths' of hegemonic juridical narratives, and most particularly to their claim to originary 'truth'.[1] This challenge reveals the literary nature of the law, in accordance with Derrida's conception of both law and literature as *différance*.[2] As discussed, both law and literature are conceived as relational, in terms of a constant "play of differences".[3] Both literary and juridical narratives or 'texts' are understood in terms of a perpetual openness or "non-closure", such that the outside productively penetrates the inside.[4] Furthering this discussion, Derrida elsewhere evokes the notion of deferral, or *différance*, and the productive interventions entailed within a process of iteration or repetition, in an examination of mimesis. Speaking of the contested relation that is said to exist between textuality and 'truth', and a "certain play" between literature and truth, Derrida describes the history of this relationship as "organized by . . . a certain interpretation of *mimēsis*".[5] That is, an interpretation of a text as 'mere' (re)presentation, rather than 'truth' and, therefore, as mimetic of reality. Derrida suggests that "writing *in general* is interpreted as an imitation, a duplicate of the living voice or present *logos*"[6] and, furthermore:

1 Derrida, above n 10 (Ch 13), 277–8, cited and discussed in Fitzpatrick, above n 42 (Ch 13), 78. See further discussion in Part III (Law).

2 Attridge, above n 2 (Ch 13), 182.

3 Derrida, above n 25 (Ch 13), 11–12, 17.

4 Critchley, citing Derrida, above n 111 (Ch 13), 32.

5 Derrida, above n 97 (Ch 13), 129–31. Derrida traces this history and discusses this relation in the context of a segment from Plato's *Philebus* and Mallarmé's "Mimique". See also Aristodemou, above n 9 (Ch 13), 20–1, who writes:

> Literature may reveal the repressed rhetoricity, production, and contingency of societal constructs that deny their own artificiality and reopen the gap between representation and reality to a time *before* existing practices, begun as myths and plays, became law and started to take themselves (extremely) seriously.

6 Ibid., 133.

> [M]imēsis is lined up alongside truth: either it hinders the unveiling of the thing itself by substituting a copy or double for what is; or else it works in the service of truth through the double's resemblance (homoiōsis). Logos, which is itself imitated by writing, only has value as truth . . .[7]

Accordingly, mimesis poses a threat to 'truth', where the former "*supervenes* upon reality, the representation upon the present in presentation, the imitation upon the thing, the imitator [*l'imitant*] upon the imitated".[8] Indeed, as Chaplin argues, "[m]imesis is the abject ordering principle of literature and law", since the 'truth' of each depends upon its textual rendering, which is necessarily mimetic of the acts such texts reproduce.[9]

Whereas the 'double' produced by mimesis is, in Platonic terms, considered inferior to the original, however, the relation is fraught. Returning to Kafka's parables, Martel has suggested that these texts do not even attempt truth; rather, "in Kafka's texts, representation can unmake the very pseudo truths that it posits".[10] Derrida's reading of Mallarmé's "Mimique", in "The Double Session",[11] reveals the ways in which Mallarmé's text subverts the inferior positioning of mimesis within a Platonic hierarchy and is, furthermore, described by Derrida as a "handbook of literature".[12] According to Derrida, " 'Mimique' describes a scene of writing within a scene of writing and so on without end, through a structural necessity that is marked in the text".[13] That is, the text describes the mime of a future crime, the story of which may be itself regarded as a mimetic copying of another story.[14]

"The Mime", Derrida suggests, does not attempt verisimilitude; rather, "[t]he act always plays out a difference without reference, or rather without a referent, without any absolute exteriority, and hence, without any inside",[15] recalling Derrida's description of the "non-closure" of the context.[16] In his preface to "The First Session", Attridge usefully interprets Derrida's revelations:

> "Mimique" puts into play notions of mimesis, imitation, truth, representation, reference, and temporality, unsettling any absolute distinctions between that

7 Derrida, above n 97 (Ch 13), 135.
8 Ibid., 140.
9 Chaplin, above n 29 (Ch 13), 116.
10 Martel, above n 47 (Ch 13), 53.
11 Derrida, above n 97 (Ch 13); see also discussion in Chaplin, above n 29 (Ch 13), 114; 117–18.
12 Ibid., 176–7. For further discussion of Platonic *mimēsis*, at 139, footnote 9, the editor refers the reader to Derrida, above n 29 (Ch 13), 136–7.
13 Ibid., 177.
14 The "referent" for Mallarmé's text is a story by Fernand Beissier, in which a man tickles his wife to death: Ibid., 149. Derrida further remarks upon the extended origins of this pantomime: see especially 154–155, footnotes 15 and 16.
15 Derrida, above n 97 (Ch 13), 172.
16 Jacques Derrida, *Of Grammatology* (Gayatri Spivak trans., 1976 edn) 163, cited in Critchley, above n 111 (Ch 13), 25.

> which is imitated and that which imitates, between truth and the representation of truth, between referent and reference, between present and past . . . Instead of abiding within the opposed domains of metaphysical concepts, clearly separated by a border that marks an inside and an outside, literature operates in a realm that undermines alternatives and the logic of identity.

For Derrida, the " 'allusion,' not 'illusion' " of Mallarmé's text may be described as "undecidable", such that "one can never know what the allusion alludes to, unless it is to itself in the process of alluding".[17] Derrida here further recalls his conception of the *hymen* or the *entre* (between), which, like the "*pharmakon, supplément, différence*", possess "a double, contradictory, undecidable value that always derives from their syntax".[18] The mime, therefore, cannot be reduced to the Platonic conception of a mere *copy*, since its very performance entails the production of difference. Moreover, Derrida describes the simulacrum, "a copy of a copy, a simulacrum that simulates the Platonic simulacrum", that has "lost here the lure of the present referent", and is therefore "lost for absolute knowledge".[19] That is, the origin or original 'truth' of a mimetic text is not only lost but, moreover, illusory, where such truth is, itself, "mimed".[20] Ultimately, Derrida reveals the ways in which Mallarmé's text is demonstrative of the constitutively iterative nature of literature:

> If this handbook of literature meant to *say* something . . . it would proclaim first of all that there is no – or hardly any, ever so little – literature; that in any event there is no essence of literature, no truth of literature, no literary-being or being-literary of literature.[21]

Reading Derrida, Chaplin argues that it is via this "aberrant, yet *exemplary* literary work" – Mallarmé's "Mimique", Derrida's "handbook of literature"[22] – that the hierarchical positioning of truth and text is subverted, and the subversive elements of the literary are revealed.[23] Postcolonial literatures, I argue – specifically, Indigenous literatures – assume this subversive role, as aberrant narrativities, challenging, disrupting and, indeed, transforming claims to historical, juridical and literary 'truths'. In the texts with which this part is principally engaged, mimesis

17 Derrida, above n 97 (Ch 13), 172.
18 Ibid., 174.
19 Ibid., 172.
20 Ibid., 172.
21 Ibid., 177.
22 Ibid., 176–7.
23 Chaplin, above n 29 (Ch 13), 114. At 114, Chaplin instances the literary Gothic, which "enters into legal and literary discourse . . . as an aberrant, yet exemplary narrativity that simultaneously guarantees and repudiates the possibility of authentic juridical and literary 'truth' ".

– both literal mimicry, as 'mime', and mimetic text – function to reveal and subvert dominant narratives with the appearance of revisionary and, indeed, revolutionary perspectives.

This notion of subversive mimesis, as it appears in Indigenous literature, may be more generatively conceived in the context of the Deleuzian simulacrum,[24] which, rather than functioning reductively in accordance with a Platonic hierarchy, remains open to perpetual renewal. Drichel suggests an account of "indigenous creativity", expressed in Indigenous literature, as just such a simulacrum – not "an enslaved shadow of a luminous prior presence", but "a paradoxical 'being of becoming'" that "is therefore coextensive with a radical openness, or newness: the newness of 'becoming unlimited, [. . .] a becoming always other'".[25] Distinguishing the Platonic notion of the simulacrum as "an image without resemblance" (as opposed to a copy), positioned lowest in "the great Platonic trinity: user, producer, imitator", Deleuze instead identifies a limitless potentiality within the simulacrum.[26] Rather than being a "degraded copy", he suggests that the simulacrum "contains a positive power which negates *both original and copy, both model and reproduction*".[27] He writes:

> The simulacrum includes within itself the differential point of view, and the spectator is made part of the simulacrum, which is transformed and deformed according to his point of view. In short, folded within the simulacrum there is a process of going mad, a process of limitlessness . . . a constant development, a gradual process of subversion of the depths, an adept avoidance of the equivalent, the limit, the Same, or the Like: always simultaneously more and less, but never equal.[28]

Such limitlessness and its 'madness' recall my earlier discussion of "the irreducible madness" of the judicial decision, which is necessarily transgressive.[29] For Deleuze, the simulacrum creates a newness that is extrinsic to the original, which, "in rising to the surface, causes the Same and the Like, the model and the

24 Gilles Deleuze and Rosalind Krauss, "Plato and the Simulacrum" (Winter 1983) 27 *October* 45; Deleuze, above n 69 (Ch 13).

25 Drichel, above n 140 (Ch 13), 511, citing Gilles Deleuze, *Logic of Sense* (1969) 258; see also Deleuze, above n 69 (Ch 13); Deleuze and Krauss, above n 24; Daniel W Smith, "The Concept of the Simulacrum: Deleuze and the Overturning of Platonism" (2006) 38 *Continental Philosophy Review* 89; Scott Durham, *Phantom Communities: The Simulacrum and the Limits of Postmodernism* (1998); Kir Kuiken, "Deleuze/Derrida: Towards an Almost Imperceptible Difference" (2005) 35 *Research in Phenomenology* 290.

26 Deleuze and Krauss, above n 24, 49.

27 Ibid., 53.

28 Ibid., 49.

29 See Peter Fitzpatrick, "Why the Law Is Also Nonviolent" in Austin Sarat (ed.), *Law, Violence and the Possibility of Justice* (2001) 142, 156; Derrida, above n 10 (Ch 13), 255, citing Kierkegaard; Fitzpatrick, above n 42 (Ch 13), 78.

copy, to fall under the power of the false (phantasm)" and, further, "[f]ar from being a new foundation, it swallows up all foundations, it assures a universal collapse, but as a positive and joyous event, as de-founding (*effondement*)".[30] Moreover, he suggests, where the simulacrum "is constructed around disparity, a difference . . . [and] interiorizes a dissimilitude", it is distinguishable from the copy. Indeed, its model may be the Other, "from which it follows an interiorized dissimilarity".[31]

Drawing upon this reading of the simulacrum, "based on a concept of pure *difference* (rather than identity)",[32] indigeneity, as expressed in Indigenous authored literature, may be conceived as this notion of dissimilitude – not a copy of indigeneity created by controlling discourses, but an opening into the space of alterity, of creation, of *becoming*. Deleuze describes the simulacrum as a symbol of repetition itself, which includes difference "by way of disguise and by the order of the symbol".[33] Indeed, for Deleuze, the simulacrum is difference itself: "It is not an implosion, but a differentiation; it is an index not of absolute proximity, but of galactic distances".[34] Where repetition "is by nature transgression or exception", it reveals "a singularity opposed to the particulars subsumed under laws, a universal opposed to the generalities which give rise to laws".[35] Moreover, for Deleuze, repetition "puts laws into question":

> If repetition is possible, it is due to miracle rather than to law. It is against the law: against the similar form and the equivalent content of law. If repetition can be found, even in nature, it is in the name of a power which affirms itself against the law, which works underneath laws, perhaps *superior to laws*.[36]

Where the law, for Deleuze, governs and is governed by "good sense" and "common sense" – "the *doxa*" – it is only able to recognise the same: "form will never inspire anything but conformities".[37] In contrast, the simulacrum, as the

30 Deleuze and Krauss, above n 24, 53.
31 Ibid., 49. At 49, footnote 3, Deleuze and Krauss suggest: "The Other is, indeed, not only a defect that affects images; it, itself, appears as a possible model against the good model of the Same."
32 Smith, above n 215, 106.
33 Deleuze, above n 69 (Ch 13), 20.
34 Brian Massumi, "The Simulacrum According to Deleuze and Guattari" (1987) 1 *Copyright* 90.
35 Deleuze, above n 69 (Ch 13), 6. On the pursuit of a "Universal Jurisprudence" (to which Deleuze apparently aspired), in which the creation of legal principle and concepts such as "law" are privileged over their application as "Law", see de Sutter and McGee, above n 34 (Ch 13), 9:

> To free law from Law, then, requires that law become devoted to the "free and savage" creation on non-decomposable, non-transposable principles extracted from singular cases, remaining always within the strict limits of the case or singularity.

36 Ibid., 3 (emphasis added). This delineation between "law" and "Law" should be distinguished from my description of non-Indigenous *law* and Indigenous *Law*.
37 Deleuze, above n 69 (Ch 13), 169–70.

symbol of difference and repetition, produces an uncanniness, which bears only a "deceptive resemblance" to its model, concealing an "inner dynamism".[38] Its creation entails a rebellion against the model, opening a new space – a process described as "going mad"[39] or "mad proliferation".[40]

Drichel has proposed indigeneity as a simulacrum appearing in Indigenous literature – a simulacrum that is liberated from "a metaphysics of presence which privileges an original 'presence' of culture and tradition, and devalues all later articulations as derivations and copies", and is revealed to be an "original presence", in and of itself.[41] Drawing upon Bhabha's reading of the 'new', Drichel asserts:

> [T]he new that comes into the world is . . . never truly new. The simulacrum, on the other hand, brings "a newness that is not part of the 'progressivist' division between past and present, or the archaic and the modern; nor is it a newness that can be contained in the mimesis of the 'original and copy'" . . . The simulacrum, in other words, registers the "double-time" of (indigenous) narration, whose hallmark is "a split between the continuist, accumulative temporality of the pedagogical, and the repetitious, recursive strategy of the performative".[42]

Such remarks evoke Deleuze's distinction between the "established", which "was always established from the outset, even if a certain amount of time was necessary for this to be recognised", and "the new", which he equates to difference, "with its power of beginning and beginning again", which "remains forever new".[43] Indeed, difference resists the "derisory struggles for recognition", founded upon "established values".[44] Further, Deleuze argues, difference "calls forth forces in thought which are not the forces of recognition, today or tomorrow, but the powers of a completely other model, from an unrecognised and unrecognisable *terra incognita*".[45]

For Drichel, the simulacrum offers "radical potential", as a means of articulating a much needed critique of "postcolonial theory *from within*" on questions of indigeneity.[46] Countering aspirations to 'authenticity' in previous readings of Indigenous expression,[47] Indigenous literature may be read as a repetition or

38 Massumi, above n 34, 91.
39 Deleuze and Krauss, above n 24, 49.
40 Massumi, above n 34.
41 Drichel, above n 140 (Ch 13), 510–11.
42 Ibid., 510, citing Bhabha, above n 61 (Ch 13), 325; 208–9.
43 Deleuze, above n 69 (Ch 13), 172.
44 Ibid. See useful discussion in Lincoln, above n 64 (Ch 13), 179.
45 Ibid.
46 Drichel, above n 140 (Ch 13), 511, 512.
47 Such as Eva Rask Knudsen, *The Circle and the Spiral: A Study of Australian Aboriginal and New Zealand Maori Literature* (2004), which Drichel is here reviewing.

'restaging' of Indigenous subjectivity which, rather than being a degraded thing, is "*a good thing*".[48] Where Wright has articulated a desire, as an Indigenous author, to "create a truer replica of reality"[49] on questions of indigeneity and Indigenous experience, Drichel's proposition accords with my broader discussions of the liberatory capacities of literature, "provok[ing] people to *think*, rather than merely recognise, represent or consume".[50] Further, for Deleuze, "[t]hought is primarily trespass and violence"; that which "forces us to think" is "an object not of recognition but of a fundamental *encounter*", that which must be "sensed", rather than "recognised":[51]

> The conditions of a true critique and a true creation are the same: the destruction of an image of thought which presupposes itself and the genesis of the act of thinking in thought itself.[52]

Conceived as a simulacrum, Indigenous literature reveals the difference and newness of indigeneity as that which "denounces" the "nominal or general character" of the law, "in favour of a more profound and more artistic reality".[53]

The notion of a regenerative 'restaging', or iterative performance, of subjectivities within Indigenous literature presents a radical challenge to static notions of cultural 'authenticity' in Indigenous political and cultural expression, within the literary and the juridical. This critical repetition – indeed, a (re)imagining – of Indigenous subjectivities is expressed in the novels with which this part will engage, most explicitly in scenes of literal mimicry, and their recuperative and transformative intent. Such scenes evoke a Deleuzian escape from the struggle for recognition via the simulacrum – that is, the production of unsettling uncanniness and creative potential via the performance of difference and repetition.[54] In the fictional text to which I will now turn, *That Deadman Dance*, literary form, as well as national and cultural identities, are all subject to disruptive, mimetic subversions. Animated by overlapping historical and contemporary imperatives, this novel, alongside those yet to be discussed, expresses Indigenous perspectives that subvert the familiar narratives of colonisation by restaging both Indigenous and non-Indigenous subjectivities, thereby presenting an aberrant mimesis or simulacrum of the 'truth' of colonial history. Furthermore, I argue, these texts reveal a subversive jurisprudence within the laws of literature,

48 Drichel, above n 140 (Ch 13), 511.
49 Wright, above n 133 (Ch 13), 13.
50 Hallward, above n 148 (Ch 13), xx.
51 Deleuze, above n 69 (Ch 13), 175–6.
52 Ibid., 176.
53 Ibid., 3.
54 Deleuze and Krauss, above n 24; Deleuze, above n 69 (Ch 13); see also discussion in Massumi, above n 34.

as within the laws of the state, troubling arrogations of authority and completeness. This subversion is apparent in the literary (re)imagination of historical Indigenous subjectivities, and the revelation of a transformative Indigenous Law.

(Re)imagining indigeneity

> It was not easy talking back then; you shook hands and grinned, danced and mimed and laughed, but you never knew what the other fellow was thinking, not really (do we ever, dear friends?).[55]

Kim Scott's acclaimed novel, *That Deadman Dance*,[56] presents just such a (re)imagination of historical encounters and ensuing relationships between Indigenous and non-Indigenous people, as a means of "re-representing Aboriginality".[57] Differing narrative perspectives are interwoven throughout, depicting the shifting allegiances and aspirations of early settlers and Noongar people occasioned by the imposition of non-Indigenous juridical, cultural, and linguistic norms. By (re)imagining the possibilities of interracial relationships begun at this historical moment, Scott's lyrical prose radically rearticulates literary and historic renderings of Indigenous subjectivities and agency, and of Indigenous Law.

Set in and around Albany, Western Australia – described by historians as the "friendly frontier"[58] – the story of the settlement, and its inevitable trauma and dispossession, are largely expressed through song and dance, as performed by the pivotal Noongar character, Bobby Wabalanginy. His Noongar name, translated at poignant moments in the novel as "all of us playing together",[59] is itself a lament for the lost opportunities of this historical period. The title of the novel and the impetus for its narrative are inspired by a particular historical moment, in 1801, when an English expedition under Captain Matthew Flinders stayed briefly in King George Sound, Western Australia. Before departing, Flinders "ordered the

55 Scott, above n 68 (Ch 13), 80.

56 Scott, above n 68 (Ch 13). This novel has received several awards, including the prestigious Miles Franklin Literary Award (2011) and the Commonwealth Writers' Prize for Fiction (Regional Winner, Southeast Asia and the Pacific, 2011).

57 Kim Scott, quoting Mick Dodson (citation unknown), in Radio National Best of Festivals broadcast (18 January 2012), "Native Titles: Can fiction reveal the truth of the earliest encounters between Indigenous and settler Australians more honestly than conventional history?" (2011 Melbourne Writers' Festival), featuring panellists Kate Grenville, Kim Scott and Rohan Wilson, hosted by Stephen Romei, literary editor of *The Australian* newspaper, at www.abc.net.au/radionational/programs/bestoffestivals/native-titles/3785914 (accessed 6 October 2015).

58 See Kim John Scott, *An Anomalous History and a Noongar Voice: A Literary Investigation of the "Friendly Frontier"* (PhD Thesis, Creative Writing, University of Western Australia, 2009), abstract available at https://repository.uwa.edu.au/R/-?func=dbin-jump-full&object_id=29349&local_base=GEN01-INS01 (accessed 6 October 2015).

59 Scott, above n 68 (Ch 13), 39, 350.

party of marines on shore ... to be exercised", for the benefit of the Noongar people present:

> The red coats and white crossed belts were greatly admired, having some resemblance to [the Noongar] manner of ornamenting themselves; and the drum, but particularly the fife, excited their astonishment; but when they saw these beautiful red-and-white men, with their bright muskets, drawn up in a line, they absolutely screamed with delight; nor were their wild gestures and vociferation to be silenced, but by commencing the exercise, to which they paid the most earnest and silent attention.[60]

The ensuing performance elicited a mimetic response by several among the audience and, subsequently, the attribution of Noongar meaning to the drill, "the exchange of new dances" apparently being "an appropriate contact ritual" among neighbouring Noongar tribes:[61]

> Several of them moved their hands, involuntarily, according to the motions; and [an] old man placed himself at the end of the rank, with a short staff in his hand, which he shouldered, presented, grounded, as did the marines their muskets, without, I believe, knowing what he did.[62]

These acts of mimesis subtly attribute meaning to the military drill in accordance with Indigenous Law such that, it has been suggested, "Flinders's splendid spectacle was 'a suitable gift bequeathed in exchange for [Noongar] hospitality – they were being taught a new ceremony'".[63] This historical "moment of cultural exchange", alongside other similarly theatrical moments of mimicry and mockery, reveal "a certain pathos, suggesting the possibility that the future might have turned out differently".[64] Indeed, this textual encounter itself may be conceived as mimetic of the 'truth' of the imperial spectacle occasioned by the military drill – that is, of its 'truth' as an assertion of British sovereignty. In Scott's literary text, this moment is subversively reimagined as a moment of cultural exchange and humour.

Anthropologist Daisy Bates subsequently recorded an interview with a man in Albany, in 1908, who claimed that "the Aborigines of King George's Sound believed that Flinders and his men were the ghosts of their own dead ancestors,

60 Paul Carter, *Living in a New Country: History, Travelling and Language* (1992) 161.

61 Ibid., 162.

62 Ibid., 161, citing an account by Captain Matthew Flinders. See also description in Tiffany Shellam, *Shaking Hands on the Fringe: Negotiating the Aboriginal World at King George's Sound* (2009) 17–18.

63 Carter, above n 60, 162, citing Sylvia Hallam, "The Other Side of the Western Frontier" (1983) 7(2) *Aboriginal History* 146–7.

64 Ibid., 163–4. See also Inga Clendinnen's discussion of British sailors and Indigenous peoples dancing together, described as "a phase of the imperial process": Inga Clendinnen, *Dancing with Strangers* (2003) 8. See also Scott, above n 68 (Ch 13), 12, 263.

come back from Kooranup, the home of the dead across the sea", and their performance a Kooranup ceremony.[65] This man further revealed that the military drill was later incorporated into an Aboriginal dance ceremony,[66] a demonstration of the subversive capacity of mimesis, as expressed in Noongar ritual and, most recently, in the literary text authored by Scott, himself a Noongar man. In contrast to the arguably infantalising descriptions of Indigenous people contained within the aforementioned historical accounts, Scott's descriptions are richly evocative of Indigenous interpretative authority and, indeed, subversive mimesis. Through the narrative perspective of Bobby, Scott describes the particulars of the 'dance' itself, as the original military drill was (re)imagined:

> The dance? You paint yourself in red ochre, neck to waist and wrist, and leave your hands all bare. White ochre on your thighs, but keep your calves and feet bare, like boots, see? A big cross of white clay painted on every chest.
>
> Each man takes a stick about the size of an emu's leg, and sometimes you wave it about, sometimes carry it on your shoulder as you walk up and down very stiffly, sometimes hold it away from yourself with your arms outstretched. . . .
>
> Over and over again, the many copy the one. And people clap – oh, that is a wild and stirring rhythm – and they whistle. All point their stick into the air – like a rifle, of course – and bang bang bang like the boom boom boom of thunder or ocean swell meeting rock. But sharper, and the echoes roll on and on in the silence after.[67]

The text richly evokes the drama and rhythm of the mimetic performance. As a literary work, however, it simultaneously recalls the aforementioned historical accounts while subverting them, 'restaging' the encounter. The performance is no longer involuntary or unknowing, but redefined as a Noongar tradition, the "Dead Man Dance"; further, its details are defined within that frame of reference – the rifle becomes "a stick about the size of an emu's leg", its explosive sound akin to the "boom boom boom of thunder or ocean swell meeting rock".[68] As a simulacrum of colonial history, Scott's literary work expresses Indigenous subjectivities in this reimagined moment of encounter.

This "appropriation", and the suggestion of an alternative historical trajectory elicited by such amicable encounters, animate Scott's novel.[69] Via a literary

65 Isobel White, "Birth and Death of a Ceremony" (1980) 4(1) *Aboriginal History* 35, cited in Carter, above n 60, 162.

66 Ibid., cited in Shellam, above n 62, 18.

67 Scott, above n 68 (Ch 13), 68.

68 Ibid., 67–8.

69 Kim Scott, Interview discussing *That Deadman Dance*, at www.youtube.com/watch?v=xqY8v1I9Pls (accessed 6 October 2015).

rendering of this cultural exchange of dance, among other such exchanges, the text presents the possibility that these early relationships may have continued as peaceably as they began. Through Bobby, Scott further describes the significance of the dance, as a familiar mode of cross-cultural exchange, "from way past the ocean's horizon".[70] Again, the text reimagines frontier encounters within a subversive frame of reference, as a "dance of life, a lively dance for people to do together", rather than a military drill designed to intimidate.[71] Furthermore, Scott's protagonist describes "these visitors", arriving and departing on "[t]he wind, blowing to the horizon and back", who "danced like dead men, cruel brutal men", but "were never dead".[72] The performance is no longer a military drill but is reimagined as a dance, the soldiers reimagined as spectral figures, forebears who would pass their traditions to "our old people".[73]

Situating this moment, and its subsequent manifestations, at the centre of his novel, Scott's narrative provides a commentary on tentative frontier relationships and their ultimate tragedy.[74] Most poignantly, he depicts the initial hope and ultimate despair of such relations in the tender intimacy between the settlement doctor and Bobby's Noongar relative:

> Content after a shared meal, Wunyeran and Cross sat within the glow of fire and candle, heads close and nodding to one another, gesticulating with wrists and fingers, speaking slowly and softly . . . We are two men of such different backgrounds, thought Cross and, attempting to fuse them, we are preparing for the birth of a new world.[75]

Succumbing to the illnesses prevalent in the settlement, the two men are buried together. This unity is lost, however, when the remains of Cross are disinterred and moved to the town cemetery, his memory honoured, and in this very act the remains of Wunyeran are desecrated, as are the aspirations of their friendship – the latter a cipher for the initial aspirations of the settlement. Wunyeran's body, which in a spiritual return to the ancestors of country had "begun to dissolve into the earth along with ochre and leaves and ash", is unceremoniously "exposed and disordered" by the gravedigger's spade.[76] The abrasive action of the spade is, itself, representative of the unrelenting desecration of colonial settlement:

> It was not like the passion of flood, or a persistent wind lifting the soil to expose bones at the core of country . . . Small bones were left to grey in the

70 Scott, above n 68 (Ch 13), 67.
71 Ibid.
72 Ibid., 72.
73 Ibid., 67.
74 See, for instance, ibid., 68–9.
75 Ibid., 128–9.
76 Ibid., 353–4.

> sun, be trodden in horseshit and piss and vomit as the town grew and bright moons waxed and waned.[77]

A subversive assertion of Indigenous Law, however, is imaginatively rehearsed throughout the text, as envisaged and evoked by Noongar Elder, Menak.[78] As in Wright's novel, to which I will shortly turn, Scott depicts the animation of the landscape in accordance with Indigenous Law, the ancestors hindering their British assailants while aiding the Noongar. Pursuing the latter through inhospitable tracts of bushland for alleged acts of theft, among other things, the British are thwarted:

> It was as if a great many limbs restrained them, disinterestedly; as if thousands of fingers plucked at their hair and clothing. Tree roots tripped them.[79]

Escaping their pursuit, the Noongar are apparently borne aloft by and concealed beneath this very same landscape:

> Wind rocked the trees and shrubs, and the Noongar disappeared and rose again, so light on their feet they seemed to glide . . . The same branches that alternately supported or concealed them clutched at [the British Sergeant's] jacket, and tree roots tripped him.[80]

Most dramatically, as the novel draws to a close and the destruction of Indigenous peoples and 'life-ways'[81] appears inevitable, Menak and his wife, Manit, alongside Bobby, elicit a destructive and, perhaps, recuperative storm through their song, drawing the bones of their deceased relative, Wunyeran, to their final resting place: "Bones from riverbanks washed down toward the sea, and only a kindred spirit and tongue can find them, maybe bring them alive again, even if in some other shape".[82] Scott imagines an uncanny intermingling of bodily remains and settlement debris, closing the passage with a vision of bones collected on the ocean floor. These bones, he suggests, might eventually "reach the sea and join a path of whalebones across the ocean floor" or, alternatively, might become "part of the foundations of the town hall", on top of which, "right at the very steeple top", is perched "that very great weight: a nation's fluttering flag".[83] The resting place for Wunyeran's bones, beneath these markers of British sovereignty, suggests

77 Scott, above n 68 (Ch 13), 353–4.

78 See, for instance, ibid., 338, at which point Noongar Elder, Menak, imagines the reprisal of the whales and, indeed, of the ocean, to the whales' annihilation: "Menak spoke of whales rising from the water; of whale tails beating the water, striking men and splintering whaleboats; of whales charging, and energy from beneath the sea's skin bursting forth. . ."

79 Ibid., 49.

80 Ibid., 121.

81 Langton, above n 149 (Ch 13), 80.

82 Scott, above n 68 (Ch 13), 357.

83 Ibid.

a subversive and, indeed, subterranean ancestral presence, despite colonial imposition. Concealed beneath the 'idols'[84] of non-Indigenous law, this presence may be interpreted as a spiritual manifestation of a potentially recuperative force, of Indigenous Law, to be summoned at will.[85]

At the climactic conclusion to the novel, Bobby dances a diplomatic plea for peaceful relations before the dignitaries and law enforcers of the British settlement, expressing a desire to share his ancestral land: "We will share it with you, and share what you bring".[86] He also provides his own rationale for such cooperation: "Because you need to be inside the sound and the spirit of it, to live here properly. And how can that be, without we people who have been here for all time?"[87] While his Noongar elders are dismissive, Bobby is convinced of his powers of persuasion, evinced in his performance of song and dance: "It is like the dance to dodge the spears; they cannot match us".[88] Through this performance, Bobby attempts to unify the settlement, to "sing and dance the spirit of any gathering, show them what we gathered together here really are . . . show them how people must live here, together".[89] Alluding perhaps to the erroneous notion that racial tensions might be resolved by the universal application of the rule of (British) law and, indeed, of British cultural mores,[90] Scott's character petitions, rather, for the accommodation of cultural difference: "My friends . . . *blackfellas* and *whitefellas* . . . we are not just our colour".[91]

Dressed in formal British attire, Bobby begins his performance with the theatrical removal of each item of clothing in the course of describing the scope of this

84 See Martel, above n 47 (Ch 13).

85 For a similar literary depiction of Indigenous resistance to imperialism, see José Mariá Arguedas, *Deep Rivers* (1958), in which the ancient stones of Cusco, once the capital of the Inca Empire, initiate a revolutionary flood (chapters 7 and 11). See also discussion in Fitzpatrick, above n 167 (Ch 13), 118:

> The stones are both foundational of, yet subordinated to, imperial structures. But the same stones are radiant. They seethe, they move, talk, frolic. Their streets flow like rivers, deep rivers, rivers akin to primordial serpents. This foundational fusion with movement and change is later aligned in the novel with Indigenous rebellions, with a primal or abyssal capacity to sweep away the existent, to sweep it away in a flood, a flood of rivers.

86 Scott, above n 68 (Ch 13), 394.

87 Ibid.

88 Ibid., 390.

89 Ibid.

90 While Scott's novel is set on a specific frontier, in Western Australia, this notion was more overtly promoted elsewhere: see, for instance, the apparently aspirational image commonly known as "Governor Davey's Proclamation to the Aborigines, 1816": Manuscripts, Oral History & Pictures (State Library of New South Wales, 2008) at http://acms.sl.nsw.gov.au/item/itemDetailPaged.aspx?itemID=442502 (accessed 6 October 2015). This pictorial proclamation, actually issued in Van Diemen's Land by Lieutenant-Governor Arthur, circa 1828–1830, depicts the principles of the rule of law, alongside British cultural mores, and their apparently impartial application to both British settlers and Indigenous peoples.

91 Scott, above n 68 (Ch 13), 391.

cultural difference. Juxtaposing English and Noongar languages, and eloquently expressing the spiritual precepts of an Indigenous Law made manifest in an enduring relationship to land, waters and sky, Bobby confounds his audience:

> He stepped lightly out of the shoes, and left them balanced on their toes, propped against the base of the naked hatstand in the corner of the room. *Booja djena baranginy.* Sand can hold my feet instead. . . .
>
> *Naatjil kaatbwok.* Why wear this hat? *Ngayn yirra yak koombar maar-ang kaat koombar.* Clouds around my head just like a mountain top; *Ngaitj nol-ok darrp koorl, dabakan, dabakan, dat nyin.* I want shade? Slip beneath the big trees, slow down, stop. . . .
>
> *Nitjak bwoka.* My shirt. . . . *Bwokabt, ngaank ngayn maarak ngabiny.* No shirt means the wind and sun caress you better.[92]

Liberating himself from the constraints of this attire, Bobby hangs each item on a hatstand, "[t]he hat up high, the shoes balanced on their toes", and the coat "buttoned and secure as if there were still a body within".[93] The final description of Bobby's near-naked appearance, and the spectralised appearance of the discarded clothing of the coloniser, evoke a subversive alterity, which is productive of the anxiety and resultant trauma of colonial recognition to which I alluded earlier in this part. That is, a recognition of difference in the colonial subject, "which ought to have been excluded [yet] never was"[94] and, furthermore, of an uncanny hybridity:

> In moments, Bobby wore little more than a thin belt made of human hair, with blonde strands woven through it. A mysterious, well-dressed human form hovered on its toes in the corner of the room like a ghost, a silent witness, a hanging man; like all those things at once . . .[95]

In this scene, Scott deftly evokes the terrible anxieties elicited by such cultural juxtaposition. Through the perspective of his Indigenous protagonist, it is the accoutrements of British civilisation that are spectralised, subverted by a visceral and, indeed, uncanny experience of indigeneity through the performance of difference and repetition:[96] "Bobby knew his audience felt animal fur and feathers

92 Scott, above n 68 (Ch 13), 392–3.
93 Ibid.
94 Perrin, above n 147 (Ch 13), 30.
95 Scott, above n 68 (Ch 13), 393.
96 Deleuze and Krauss, above n 24; Deleuze, above n 69 (Ch 13); see also discussion in Massumi, above n 34.

brush their skin, so softly, knew they breathed the scent of sandalwood smoke wisping across them . . ."[97]

At the close of his performance, the spectacular failure of Bobby's plea is apparent: "Faces . . . had turned away from him. Bobby felt as if he had surfaced in some other world. Chairs creaked as people stirred, coughing".[98] Whereas the "terrible beauty of Bobby's spell", elicited in previous performances, had once transfixed his audiences, this 'terrible beauty' is apparently transformed into a "terrible anxiety",[99] in both Bobby and his non-Indigenous audience, and its inevitable violence. That is, I would suggest, an anxiety evoked by the appearance of the uncanny, or *unheimlich*,[100] in Bobby's performance – in his subversion of English language and custom and his expression of Noongar language and Law – unfathomable and, indeed, absurd to those he would entreat.[101]

As a dramatisation of indigeneity before the law, this moment is of great significance to the imaginative and, indeed, juridical force of the novel. Bobby's uncanny appearance – the speech of a British subject issuing from his mouth, above which "[a] fine bright bone pierced [his] nose, brightly coloured feathers bobbed in his hair"[102] – create a retrospective moment of rupture in the 'mythical' force[103] of the British legal narrative. Such rupture recalls Derrida's description of the *unheimlich* or uncanny, and therefore "terrifying" moment – indeed, the moment of revolution – in which one law is suspended in order to found another.[104] Indeed, this revolutionary moment reveals a terrifying rupture in law where, according to de Ville (reading Derrida, following Benjamin), "[t]he violence that founds law is not alien to law, but that in law which suspends law; an instance of non-law in law".[105] This founding, furthermore, "is terrifying", since such moments "are in themselves and in their violence uninterpretable or indecipherable – that is, an ungraspable revolutionary instant".[106] It is the very evocation of indigeneity and of Indigenous Law in this scene, as a radical newness, which provides the subversive and, therefore, revolutionary momentum of the novel, revealing the constituently iterative capacity of Indigenous literature, and its articulation of identity as *différance*.[107]

97 Scott, above n 68 (Ch 13), 393.
98 Ibid., 395.
99 Ibid., 377, 395.
100 Freud, above n 60 (Ch 13).
101 See also other similar moments of subversion, in Scott, above n 68 (Ch 13), 44, 59, 68, 318–19, 376, 385, 390.
102 Scott, above n 68 (Ch 13), 394.
103 See Benjamin, above n 11 (Ch 13); Derrida, above n 10 (Ch 13).
104 Derrida, above n 10 (Ch 13), 269.
105 Jacques de Ville, *Jacques Derrida: Law as Absolute Hospitality* (2011) 156, citing Derrida, above n 10 (Ch 13), 268–70.
106 Ibid., citing Derrida, above n 10 (Ch 13), 269, 274.
107 Derrida, above n 25 (Ch 13), 11–12, 17.

Chapter 15

A law of alterity

A subversive juridicity

> The Law is the Law and the Law will be looking after all of us.[1]

The imaginative evocation of Indigenous Law, as a "subversive juridicity"[2] and, furthermore, as a recuperative force, is amply provided in Alexis Wright's *Carpentaria*, to which I will shortly turn. In the context of a nation concerned with contested historical stories, the stories within novels such as this, Davison suggests, "present as something other than myth", being "real stories that tie people to their past and give voice to the laws and protocols of the land".[3] These literary reassertions of Indigenous Law are a reminder of the importance of laws that, for Aristodemou, reside "in the worlds of dream":

> The fact that these laws reside in the worlds of dreams or possibility rather than in the so-called real world makes them more, rather than less, important for enabling us to map and envision new selves and new conditions.[4]

In this way, the dream world of the literary may be conceived as generative of and strategically responsive to political and ideological imperatives[5] and, further, as a subversive jurisprudence, emergent in the undecidable, pervading every legal decision.

Appearing in novelistic and poetic form, as well as in storytelling, song, and film, it has been suggested that the variety of Indigenous narrative expression is

1 Wright, above n 70 (Ch 13), 446.
2 Derrida, above n 3 (Ch 13), 216.
3 Liam Davison, *Sydney Morning Herald Review* of Alexis Wright, *Carpentaria* (18 September 2006) at www.smh.com.au/news/book-reviews/carpentaria/2006/09/18/1158431619821.html (accessed 6 October 2015).
4 Aristodemou, above n 9 (Ch 13), 11.
5 Eagleton, above n 7 (Ch 13), 170.

consistent with "Indigenous jurisprudential tradition, with its blending of legality and narrative".[6] Black describes Indigenous jurisprudence not in terms of the linear trajectory of common law precedent, but as "a circular movement in which the information/story goes around the camp".[7] Moreover, she describes "what goes around the camp" as "a *feeling* of knowledge",[8] which informs her understanding of Indigenous jurisprudence. This understanding is portrayed most vividly in the writing of Senior Law Man Neidjie, in his richly expressive book, *Story about Feeling*, in which he describes a visceral connection between oneself and one's land:

> This story e can listen careful
> And how you want to feel on your feeling.
> This story e coming through your body
> E go right down foot and head
> Fingernail and blood . . . through the heart
> And e can feel it because e'll come right through.[9]

Accordingly, the narratives of Indigenous literatures may be conceived as expressive of Indigenous Law such that, in the context of the Jabiru of the Northern Territory of Australia, for example, Neidjie writes: "If you listen to this story . . . [y]ou will feel the spirit [of the Jabiru, Badbanarrarr] beside you".[10] Discussing Wright's early novel, *Plains of Promise*, Black describes "a narrative that reveals the 'bottom story', the story of the underbelly of the Law of the Land".[11] Wright also expresses this Law elsewhere, particularly emphasising its ultimate authority:

> I am country. Listen to me!
> I am your government – I am the land.
> This country speaks proper way.
> Law right up top.
> It has to be above other laws.[12]

Similarly, in the novels addressed in this book, a recuperative, transformative, and authoritative Indigenous Law is revealed, which is governed, as previously

6 CF Black, *The Land is the Source of the Law: A Dialogic Encounter with Indigenous Jurisprudence* (2011) 11.
7 Ibid., 13.
8 Ibid.
9 Bill Neidjie, *Story About Feeling* (1989) 1. See discussion in Black, above n 6, 27.
10 Ibid., 33. See also discussion in Black, above n 6, 33.
11 Black, above n 6, 100.
12 Alexis Wright, words written in recognition of the recorded voices of elders in Alexis Wright (ed., for the Central Land Council), *Take Power Like This Old Man Here: An Anthology of Writings Celebrating Twenty Years of Land Rights in Central Australia, 1977–1997* (1998) and Neidjie, above n 9, in *Dirtsong*, performed by The Black Arm Band, Melbourne International Arts Festival, October 2009.

discussed, by relationships to country. Frequently expressed (in part) in Indigenous languages, and alluding to a complex and intricate jurisprudence, the very alterity of such writing presents a disruptive juridical force.

The works of Wright and Scott have received wide acclaim, having been awarded or shortlisted for the prestigious Australian Miles Franklin Literary Award, among other prizes.[13] Awarded annually since 1957, the prize is intended to foster Australian literature: "Without an indigenous literature, people can remain alien in their own soil".[14] While Franklin's remark may not have been intended as a specific reference to Indigenous authored literature, the award of this prize to Wright and Scott is particularly apt, given these authors might be described as writers of both 'indigenous' and 'Indigenous' literature.[15] Their literary works depict an "Indigenous world that is both ancient and modern, both colonial experience and contemporary reality",[16] (re)imagining historical renderings of Indigenous subjectivities and agency and presenting uniquely Indigenous perspectives. Wright's novel, *Carpentaria,* is an interweaving web of narratives that defies the limits of conventional literary forms, depicting the multiplicity of Australian indigeneities. Simultaneously evocative of the ancient and modern,[17] spiritual and political, this novel is overtly politically engaged, providing a unique contribution to Australian literature. More specifically, it contributes to the ever-expanding body of Indigenous Australian literature, and to the broader written expression of Indigenous knowledge and lived experience – as a mode of, as discussed previously, "Indigenous intellectual activism".[18]

I have thus far described Indigenous literature as a means of intervention, disruptive of dominant discourses and expressive of the myriad inflections of Indigenous subjectivities and associated cultural and political imperatives. The writing and reading of such literature may, in fact, constitute a "strategic reply"[19]

13 Kim Scott, *Benang* (1999), Miles Franklin Literary Award winner, 2000; Kim Scott, *That Deadman Dance* (2010), Miles Franklin Literary Award winner, 2011; Alexis Wright, *Carpentaria* (2006), Miles Franklin Literary Award winner, 2007; Alexis Wright, *The Swan Book* (2013), shortlisted for the Miles Franklin Literary Award, 2014. Both *Carpentaria* and *That Deadman Dance* also received several other literary awards.

14 Miles Franklin, *Laughter, Not for a Cage* (1956) 3.

15 Jen Webb, "Living Wound: The Swan Book", *Australian Book Review* at www.australianbookreview.com.au/component/k2/105-abr-previews/1597-living-wound-the-swan-book (accessed 6 October 2015). Webb describes the works of Wright in these terms.

16 Alexis Wright, "On Writing *Carpentaria*." (2007) 13 *HEAT Magazine* 79–95, reprinted at http://logincms.uws.edu.au/__data/assets/pdf_file/0011/385949/Wright-HEATessay.pdf (accessed 6 October 2015), 11.

17 See interesting discussion of this juxtaposition, beyond the context of the literary, in Stephen Muecke, *Ancient and Modern: Time, Culture and Indigenous Philosophy* (2004).

18 Michele Grossman, "After Aboriginalism: Power, Knowledge and Indigenous Australian Critical Writing" in Michele Grossman (ed.), *Blacklines: Contemporary Critical Writing by Indigenous Australians* (2003) 1, 9. See my discussion in Part I (Narratives).

19 Eagleton, above n 7 (Ch 13), 170.

– that is, a response to and intervention upon its historical and ideological subtext, facilitating the iterative production of new thought and meaning.[20] The imaginative force of this reply presents an extraordinary alternative to historical narratives, particularly those that feature Indigenous peoples as passive, unable to resist, and, indeed, perhaps unaware of their dispossession. The literary works of Wright and Scott, among others, depict an enlivened Indigenous reality, suppressed but unconquered, reawakening at the instigation of ancestral land and waters and their Indigenous custodians, who are liberated from the corporeal and spiritual violence of their oppressors through the force of a recuperative Indigenous Law. This Law, which must be "above other laws",[21] is articulated not in a court of law but in storytelling, its juridical force made manifest not in judicial decision, but in the ancestral governance of country. Following Attridge once again, the singular experience of reading or hearing such literature is itself productive of reality, introducing "an element of foreignness, something unanticipated, not immediately graspable . . .".[22] Departing from conventional literary form and language – Wright has expressed a desire to "write in the way we tell stories and in the voice of our own people and our own way of speaking" – *Carpentaria* presents a story of "law and country",[23] as well as a critique of contemporary community attitudes, political rhetoric, and unsustainable commercial imperatives. Furthermore, it expresses a lament for a dispossessed people in the context of an unresponsive nation,[24] and the persistence of a people seeking hope in stories, "the big stories and the little ones in between".[25]

Discussing the imaginative impetus for the writing of *Carpentaria*, Wright has suggested it was her intention that the novel should be derived from the perspective of the "everyday contemporary Indigenous story world", which "follows the original pattern of the great ancient sagas that defined the laws, customs and values of our culture".[26] Written as a "long song, following ancient tradition, reaching back as much as it reach[es] forward", the novel is uniquely expressive of Indigenous identity, and of the vibrancy of country.[27] Lamenting the environmental degradation of the Gregory River and its surrounds in the Gulf of Carpentaria – "[t]angling invasive vines grew here and there, smothering the slender young trees that are Indigenous to this savannah-zoned country" – Wright

20 Attridge, above n 6 (Ch 13), 136.
21 Wright, above n 12.
22 Derek Attridge, "The Singular Events of Literature" (2010) 50(1) *British Journal of Aesthetics* 81, 83.
23 Maryam Azam, "Alexis Wright: 'It was like writing a story to the ancestors'", *The Guardian* (25 May 2014) at www.theguardian.com/books/australia-culture-blog/2014/may/25/alexis-wright-it-was-like-writing-a-story-to-the-ancestors (accessed 6 October 2015).
24 Wright, above n 70 (Ch 13), 1.
25 Ibid., 12.
26 Wright, above n 12, 2.
27 Ibid., 7.

nonetheless describes the river as a recuperative ancestral force, "like an animal, very much alive, not destroyed, that [is] stronger than all of us":[28]

> [W]hat I saw was the mighty flow of an ancestral river rushing through the weeds, which were only weeds fruitlessly reaching down into the purity of this flowing water. The water rushed past the natural vegetation of ancient paperbarks, palms and fig trees that lined the river bank, and through the ancient serpentine track it had once formed while it continued racing forever forward, coursing its way to the sea.[29]

This imagery is evocative of the ancestral Rainbow Serpent, a recuperative presence throughout the novel, while also suggesting an opposition between notions of the "quantifiable measure of impact" of the "eco-footprint", and the Indigenous "ancestral footprint . . . a signature of ecological coherence, human care, and mutual life-giving".[30] Wright's rich evocation of a serpentine ancestral 'footprint' or 'track' is suggestive of this recuperative force, and of the imagination as a force of law. She writes: "*Carpentaria* is the land of the untouched: an Indigenous sovereignty of the imagination".[31] Indeed, where the novel "imagines the cultural mind as sovereign", the transformative possibilities of "other worlds" and jurisprudences are revealed.[32]

Recuperative jurisprudences

As a work of literary, political, and cultural significance, *Carpentaria* presents a radical depiction and evocation of the recuperative and transformative force of Indigenous Law. This Law stands in contrast to a determinate non-Indigenous law, empowered not by judicial authority enforced by the state, but by an ancestral authority manifest in and (literally) enforced by land, waters and sky. The novel contains several climactic sequences, in which Indigenous Law is evoked as an annihilating force, destructive of non-Indigenous law. These sequences resonate with a Benjaminian notion of divine violence, located beyond the law as revolutionary potential.[33] The transformation effected by such force is envisaged at several moments, including the dramatic explosion of a commercial mine in an act of guerrilla warfare, and an apocalyptic scene in which a cyclone initiates a flooding of the land, literally washing away the fabric of colonial settlement, and an imaginative rebirth and creation of a new Eden is enacted, re-establishing

28 Wright, above n 12, 1.
29 Ibid.
30 Deborah Bird Rose, *Reports from a Wild Country: Ethics for Decolonisation* (2004) 4; 177.
31 Wright, above n 12, 16.
32 Ibid., 6.
33 Benjamin, above n 11 (Ch 13), 297.

an ancient order.[34] This order may be understood to be an intrinsic Indigenous Law that had not lain dormant, but "rest[ing], while Aboriginal man was supposed to care for the land",[35] and now, in response to the violence imposed upon it, acts in reprisal. Indeed, in this transformative moment, ancient realities rumble to the surface and, rather than Indigenous Law and custom being washed away by "the tide of history", it is non-Indigenous law that succumbs to the tide.[36] In this novel, and in Scott's, this washing away and other recuperative acts of the ancestors are imagined as restorative of country – as, perhaps, "*the law of the law*".[37]

As a politically and semantically transgressive narrative, *Carpentaria* reframes non-Indigenous renderings of indigeneity and challenges conventional common law modes of Indigenous recognition, in accordance with which the subaltern is simply reinserted into non-Indigenous law and public discourse.[38] Inherent within this endeavour is a unique challenge to non-Indigenous law, not only in terms of political protest but also in the presentation of Indigenous Law, as a transformative aesthetic to which non-Indigenous law is called to respond. Expansive and sprawling, the novel is enlivened by the poetic evocation of the ancestral Rainbow Serpent and its creative path across the land of the ancestors, forging the river systems of the Gulf of Carpentaria, "scoring deep into – scouring down through – the slippery underground of the mudflats, leaving in its wake the thunder of tunnels collapsing to form deep sunken valleys".[39] These ancestral tracks of traditional country are, for Wright, illustrative of the continuity of time, uniting "all stories, all realities from the ancient to the new"; furthermore, they provide the motif for the entirety of her writing, illuminating the "what ifs" of alternative visions, "fly[ing] above the bitterness of pure logic and rational thought".[40] The Indigenous characters exhibit a postcolonial hybridity, existing simultaneously within the (non-Indigenous) law of Uptown yet beyond its net, mocking the pursuit of presumptive authenticity: "You got to be more than traditional",[41] and of a certain intellectual capital: "Aborigine people were different now, they knew the scientify as well".[42]

34 Wright, above n 70 (Ch 13), 494.

35 Ibid., 492.

36 By the expression, "the tide of history", I refer to *Mabo and Others v Queensland (No. 2) ("Mabo")* (1992) 175 CLR 1, 60 (Brennan J), discussed in Part III (Law). To reiterate, his Honour concluded:

> The common law can, by reference to the traditional laws and customs of an indigenous people, identify and protect the native rights and interests to which they give rise. However, when the tide of history has washed away any real acknowledgment of traditional law and any real observance of traditional customs, the foundation of native title has disappeared.

37 Derrida, above n 3 (Ch 13), 191.

38 Elizabeth Povinelli, *The Cunning of Recognition: Indigenous Alterities and the Making of Australian Multiculturalism* (2002).

39 Wright, above n 70 (Ch 13), 1–2.

40 Wright, above n 133 (Ch 13), 14.

41 Wright, above n 70 (Ch 13), 486.

42 Ibid., 123.

As a member of the Waanyi nation of the southern highlands of the Gulf of Carpentaria, Wright displays a nuanced comprehension of the cultural politics of that region, including such petty intricacies as are indicative of small-town mentalities. Her political engagements extend further, however, to address Aboriginal deaths in custody and race-based brutality, forms of social exclusion that deny the suffering of extreme material poverty and childhood addictions, and environmental degradation and cultural decimation resulting from large-scale commercial mining, scraping ore from "the growth rings of a powerful, ancient being".[43] Wright articulates the impositions of "WHITE MAN",[44] a mobilisation of 21st-century environmental discourses to translate and articulate an Indigenous, ancient responsibility to country.[45] Mozzie Fishman, leader of a separatist travelling mob, journeying "along the spiritual travelling road of the great ancestor" and possessed of the self-appointed responsibility for "keeping the Law strong",[46] speaks this language: "We mobs got to start acting locally. Show whose got the Dreaming. The Laaaw".[47] Wright's characterisation of "the Fishman" depicts a particular spiritual and juridical commitment, his convoy assuming the very reptilian proportions of the ancestor along whose creative path it travels:

> The men in this moving mirage of battered vehicles felt they had well and truly followed the Dreaming. Travel had become *same, same* and mandatory, as the convoy moved in reptile silence over the tracks of the travelling mighty ancestor whom they worshipped through singing the story that had continued for years. The crossing of the continent to bring the ceremony north-east to the Gulf, to finish it up, was a rigorous Law, laid down piece by piece in a book of another kind covering thousands of kilometres . . . The pilgrims drove the roads knowing they had one aim in life. They were totally responsible for keeping the one Law strong by performing this one ceremony from thousands of creation stories for the guardians of Gondwanaland.[48]

43 Wright, above n 70 (Ch 13), 10.

44 Ibid., 408.

45 As discussed previously, particularly in Part I of this book, the term "country" refers to the relationship between Indigenous Australians and the land, waters and sky of their ancestors. See, for instance, Bob Morgan, "Country – A Journey to Cultural and Spiritual Healing", in Sally Morgan, Tjalaminu Mia and Blake Kwaymullina (eds), *Heartsick for Country: Stories of Love, Spirit and Creation* (2008) 201, 204; Ambelin Kwaymullina, "Introduction: A Land of Many Countries" in Morgan, Mia and Kwaymullina 6, 6; Deborah Bird Rose, *Nourishing Terrains: Australian Aboriginal Views of Landscape and Wilderness* (Australian Heritage Commission 1996) 7, available at www.environment.gov.au/heritage/ahc/publications/commission/books/nourishing-terrains.html (accessed 6 October 2015).

46 Wright, above n 70 (Ch 13), 124.

47 Ibid., 409.

48 Ibid., 124.

The story is set largely in Desperance, a fictitious town in the "red never-never land"[49] on the Gulf of Carpentaria, "marked on no map" as a result of resistance to State bureaucracy intent upon changing the name of the town.[50] Situated "in the middle of a warzone",[51] the town is both racially and culturally divided, isolated and insular: "*they were changing the guards at Buckingham Palace* but nobody in the world cared what happened to Desperance".[52] The Indigenous inhabitants, the "[f]ringe mob, the edge people",[53] while separated by the "distance of tolerance"[54] and all but invisible to the averted eyes of Uptown, are subsequently splintered into smaller fringe camps – the Eastside, the Westside, and the Pricklebush elders, who "saw huge, powerful, ancestral creation spirits occupying the land and sea moving through the town, even inside other folk's houses, right across any piece of the country".[55] These communities describe the non-Indigenous residents as without origin or tradition, greeting one another with "Hey stranger",[56] as "deluded will-o-the-wisps from nowhere [who] reigned in a glorious separateness".[57] In contrast, through her Indigenous characters, Wright expresses a sense of autochthony, described elsewhere as a connectivity to "all things on Earth . . . [themselves] as part human".[58] This includes Will Phantom, depicted as both political activist and ephemeral chameleon, who literally *becomes* country – "mud",[59] the trunk of a dead tree,[60] a puff of smoke,[61] able to hide behind thin air, every dust storm.[62] He is the son of Normal Phantom, a man able to "grab hold of the river in his mind and live with it as his father's fathers did before him":

> His ancestors were the river people, who were living with the river before time began. Normal was like ebbing water; he came and went on the flowing waters of the river right out to the sea.[63]

Likewise, Will is "[a]t home on the sea, at home on the land".[64] Escaping the "technical men [of the Gurfurrit mine] in navy raincoats and yellow helmets", he

49 Wright, above n 70 (Ch 13), 60.
50 Ibid., 59.
51 Ibid., 203.
52 Ibid., 73.
53 Ibid., 58; see also 86.
54 Ibid., 100.
55 Ibid., 59.
56 Ibid., 56–7; see also 49, 321.
57 Ibid., 62.
58 Silas Roberts, first Chairman of the Northern Land Council, cited in Rose, above n 30, 26.
59 Wright, above n 70 (Ch 13), 182.
60 Ibid., 469.
61 Ibid., 444.
62 Ibid., 378.
63 Ibid., 6.
64 Ibid., 182.

is protected by "the wax-green foliage of the stick trees", which "became a procession of spirits moving across the soft earth of darkness, protecting the country of the water people".[65] He repeatedly encounters his ancestors throughout the novel, including in a rock cave, the walls of which are animated by "ancestral paintings telling stories of human history, made and remade by ochre paints, as the forefathers whispered the charter of their land".[66]

Such literary depictions evoke a landscape enlivened by the ancestors, governed by a recuperative Indigenous Law. Indeed, Wright has suggested that the act of writing is, for her, "like writing a story to the ancestors, to the spirits of the country".[67] In *Carpentaria*, the ancestors again appear, animating the landscape, as Will escapes the destruction of the mine. Following the initiative of Will and his guerrilla comrades, the ancestors create an explosion in the mine:

> The finale was majestical. Dearo, dearie, the explosion was holy in its glory. All of it was gone. The whole mine, pride of the banana state, ended up looking like a big panorama of burnt chop suey. On a grand scale of course because our country is a very big story.[68]

Awed, the men watch as the Rainbow Serpent assumes fiery form, "full of fascination at the fire's life, roaring like a fiery serpent, looking over to [them] with wild eyes".[69] They listen:

> Wonderment was the ear on the ground listening to the great murmuring ancestor, and the earth shook the bodies of those ones lying flat on the ground in the hills. Then, it was dark with smoke and dust and everything turned silent for a long time.[70]

Escaping the explosion, Will's murderous pursuer is tripped and killed by the ancestors manifest in a rock, "that had, up to that moment, lain on the ground, embedded in soil that was thousands of seasons old, untouched by humankind since the ancestor had placed it in this spot, as if it had planned to do this incredible thing".[71] These ancestors simultaneously rescue Will and his comrades, who are "thrown down for shelter behind the boulders, in the fold of the ancestral spirit who governed the land".[72]

65 Wright, above n 70 (Ch 13), 180–1.
66 Ibid., 181.
67 Azam, above n 23.
68 Wright, above n 70 (Ch 13), 411.
69 Ibid., 407.
70 Ibid., 408.
71 Ibid., 405.
72 Ibid., 407.

Throughout the novel, the laws of the land, both imposed and ancestral, are juxtaposed, revealing a seismic retaliation to colonial intrusion. Wright describes the intrusion of colonial law in phallic terms, as a rape of her homeland, revealed by the act of writing. "Writing is", she suggests, "like taking the snake out of the hole. The snake that has killed, maimed and stolen . . . It is about dragging our memories, realities and losses back up to the surface and letting the whole world see them in the full, glaring light of day".[73] This intrusion is most tangibly depicted in her description of oceans of hands, at one point "a whole industry of invisible [white] hands", relentlessly "killing Aboriginal people . . . [and] still sitting themselves on top of traditional Law"[74] and at another, a sea of black hands rescuing Will and others.[75] Following the explosion, the "Fishman's men", who "agreed that only the greatness of the mighty ancestor had saved them",[76] literally coalesce with this ancestral earth:

> The fine dust fell slowly, and when it settled on those men who were trying to regain a sense of the enormity of what had happened, they took on the appearance of the earth itself. One by one, camouflaged by dust, they began spiriting themselves away, quickly, carefully, as dust covered their tracks, back to the lagoon of the dancing spirits.[77]

This event is then eclipsed by the scene of a cyclone, a force that washes away the settlement. The laws of Uptown, which cast an "invisible safety net"[78] across the non-Indigenous inhabitants of Desperance, are torn apart by the literal and figurative cyclone of the ancestral spirits of the land. The net itself is porous and pathetic, ultimately swept away by the tremendous cyclone of "the creation spirits, who come down out of the skies like a tempest when they start looking for Law breakers".[79]

This restorative annihilation, "a madness [that] went on and on",[80] is a dramatic illustration of the principal philosophical arguments I have advanced in this book. Wright's novel depicts and enacts the destruction of the mythic, determinate laws of Uptown by, I would suggest, a force akin to the force of a Benjaminian bloodless and divine violence,[81] elsewhere described as a "purifying hurricane" and

73 Wright, above n 70 (Ch 13), 14.
74 Ibid., 127–8.
75 Ibid., 407.
76 Ibid., 416.
77 Ibid., 416.
78 Ibid., 33.
79 Ibid., 479.
80 Ibid., 493.
81 Benjamin, above n 11 (Ch 13), 297.

subsequent "storm of forgiveness".[82] Such climatic events,[83] literally enacted in this novel,[84] dramatically liberate land, waters, and sky, and their Indigenous custodians, from the impositions of non-Indigenous settlement through the reassertion of Indigenous Law. Accordingly, this literary moment of subversion and (re)constitution may be further understood in terms of the Deleuzian simulacrum, folded within which is "a process of going mad, a process of limitlessness", which "swallows up all foundations" in the expression of difference and dissimilitude.[85] Furthermore, this reassertion and (re)constitution recall Derrida's notion of the "madness" of judicial (in)decision,[86] a moment in which the determinacy of law is suspended in unrestrained responsiveness to an indeterminacy beyond it. The singular event[87] of this literary work – in its reading or hearing – is an experience of juridical revolution in which, following Derrida once again, one law is suspended in order to found another.[88] In this way, each reader's experience of this moment may be iteratively productive of new meaning[89] and, therefore, retrospectively productive of historical and political context.

In the wake of the cyclone, afloat in the oceans of the creative spirits on a "serpentine flotation" comprised of the detritus of the town, Will Phantom is a witness to the "watery [re-]birth"[90] of the country upon which the settlement is imposed:

> It was at this point he realised how history could be obliterated when the Gods move the country. He saw history rolled, reshaped, undone and mauled as the great creators of the natural world engineered the bounty of everything man had ever done in this part of the world into something more of their

82 Walter Benjamin, "The Meaning of Time in the Moral Universe" in Marcus Bullock and Michael W Jennings (eds), *Walter Benjamin: Selected Writings, Vol. I 1913–1926* (1996) 286–7, cited in Martel, above n 47 (Ch 13), 102.

83 See Derrida's discussion of the "event" in Derrida, above n 17 (Ch 13), especially 234; see also Martel, above n 47 (Ch 13), 133, who makes reference to singular acts of political recuperation, enacted in "the anarchism of every day life". He describes such acts, in Benjaminian terms, as Messianic – moments of subversion and revelation, "singularities" (94, citing Alain Badiou, *The Communist Hypothesis* (2010) 221, in which existing relations are liberated from the determinacy of fetishism.

84 This comparison is mine alone; neither Alexis Wright, nor the authors of the novels to which I otherwise refer, make explicit reference to Benjaminian political theology.

85 Deleuze and Krauss, above n 24 (Ch 14), 49.

86 Derrida, above n 10 (Ch 13), 255, citing Kierkegaard; Fitzpatrick, above n 29 (Ch 14), 156; Fitzpatrick, above n 42 (Ch 13), 78.

87 Attridge, above n 6 (Ch 13).

88 Derrida, above n 10 (Ch 13), 269.

89 Attridge, above n 6 (Ch 13), 136. Attridge argues that the literary work emerges in

> a performance in which the authored signature, alterity, and inventiveness of the work as an exploitation of the multiple powers of language are experienced and affirmed in the present, in a creative, responsible reading.

90 Wright, above n 70 (Ch 13), 493–4.

> own making . . . The bulwark of the spirits rose from the waters, and he saw nothing monstrous or hideous in this new creation taking shape, moving, rolling, changing appearance, and beauty in its strident crashing back into the water.[91]

The laws of Uptown are swept away in a literary space, in which the reader is transformed by an alternative vision of reality. Will's father, Normal Phantom, and his grandson Bala walk home through the streets of a town "that no longer existed", as the country reverberates with the song of "a mass choir of frogs . . . wafting off the watery land, singing the country afresh",[92] thereby inaugurating the decolonisation of country. Indeed, it is the challenge of these evocations that interrupts the flow of colonial narratives, opening a new space for dialogue between law and literature and, of greater import, between non-Indigenous law and Indigenous Law.

91 Wright, above n 70 (Ch 13), 491–2.
92 Ibid., 519.

Chapter 16

Decolonising country

Beyond the law

Throughout this book, I have counterposed Indigenous and non-Indigenous laws, and their expression and evocation in legal and literary texts. Furthermore, according to Benjamin's "Critique of Violence", which opposes mythical violence as lawmaking and divine violence as law-destroying,[1] and Derrida's analysis thereof,[2] I have described an antinomy within the law. This law is able to contain and secure fixity and remains apparently intangible, creative of impossible fictions, yet also remains receptive to an alterity beyond it. Such alterity, I have argued, is evoked in the literary – specifically, Indigenous literature, which frequently depicts a creative Indigenous Law to which non-Indigenous law must respond and by which its narratives are radically re-contextualised and, indeed, (re)constituted. Wright's novel, *Carpentaria*, is exemplary in this regard, depicting a literal and figurative cleansing of the landscape by ancestral spirits in moments of Indigenous resistance to the impositions of colonial settlement, and a reassertion of Indigenous Law.

This resistance and reassertion, I have argued, may be elicited by a force I have described in terms of Benjamin's 'divine' violence, a moment of "pure violence" that is "pre-positional . . . pretemporal and thus not representable" and that, itself, "brings on the demise of what is represented", since "every violence must decay in its positing".[3] That is, divine violence is destructive of a positive, mythic law, representing the sovereign authority or state power.[4] Reading Benjamin on this point, Martel describes sovereignty, in its determinate and ubiquitous form, as

1 Benjamin, above n 11 (Ch 13), 297.

2 Derrida, above n 10 (Ch 13).

3 Hamacher, above n 50 (Ch 13), 110.

4 Benjamin, above n 10 (Ch 13), 300; see also discussion of Benjaminian political theology in Martel, above n 47 (Ch 13), most succinctly at 7:

> In his concept of divine violence and in his larger understanding of the way that time, order, progress and history are to be understood as discontinuous and "in ruins", Benjamin shows how to scramble and dissipate the sovereign order, without seeking to annihilate it altogether.

inherently "idolatrous", and the idolater as a fetishist, bound to signs that are "false, misleading and misread".[5] In contrast, the anti-fetishist is in possession of an awareness of this misreading, of its inevitability and false promise, thus overcoming the "mythologies" with which fetishists are engaged.[6] The means of liberation from such misreading, Martel argues, is the "slight adjustment"[7] resulting from the expiatory force of divine intervention, or violence. Divine violence annihilates and expiates the sin of idolatry, in an "ellipsis"[8] or suspension of law, potentially resulting in "alternative sovereign practices, alternative forms of representation and politics".[9]

In summary, whereas mythical violence "creates laws . . . establishes boundaries . . . [and] is tied up with the business of [human] sovereignty" and is therefore idolatrous, divine violence "cleanses away the sin of idolatry", and we are thus "purified of law" and its "mythical projections".[10] These periodic acts of annihilation, however, do not resolve our perpetual misreading. Rather, they each create "a revolutionary chance", or "the possibility of our own response", where human agency is wrested from "the fictions of sovereign authority".[11] This possibility of a politics other than that currently subject to the rule of (sovereign) law, realised by recognition and action in such moments, is a provocative proposition, particularly for Indigenous peoples. Indeed, the revolutionary force of divine intervention – "divine violence" – may be conceived as a force that would enliven a repressed body politic and enable the revelation and recuperation of an extant "anarchism".[12] That is, an "anarchism marked by justice, order, forgiveness and judgment".[13] In the context of this book, I would identify such anarchism in the disruptive evocation of alterity in such moments of 'revolution',[14] apparent in the dynamic and constitutive relation between law and literature and resulting in the emergence of an unconditional justice.[15]

Briefly recalling my earlier recourse to Deleuze, such justice may be also described as the "inner dynamism" of the simulacrum,[16] and the "forever new"[17] of indigeneity. The simulacrum, understood in accordance with Deleuze as the

5 Martel, above n 47 (Ch 13), 12.
6 Ibid., 11.
7 Ibid., 93, citing Walter Benjamin, "Franz Kafka: On the Tenth Anniversary of his Death" in Walter Benjamin, *Illuminations, Essays and Reflections* (1968) 134.
8 Hamacher, above n 50 (Ch 13), 125, footnote 12.
9 Martel, above n 47 (Ch 13), 8. See also remarks on the translation of "sovereign violence" in Part III (Law).
10 Ibid., 52.
11 Ibid., 52, 59.
12 Ibid., 146–7.
13 Ibid., 147.
14 See ibid., 52, 59.
15 Derrida, above n 10 (Ch 13), 257; see also Derrida, above n 17 (Ch 13).
16 Massumi, above n 34 (Ch 14).
17 Deleuze, above n 69 (Ch 13), 172.

symbol of difference and repetition, is productive of uncanniness, a rebellion against "the *doxa*" of the same.[18]

While the Indigene before the law is subject to its violent impositions, Indigenous narrative, expressed more fully and disseminated more widely in literary form, evokes a disruptive dynamism that is justice. Where such justice cannot be contained within the bounds of non-Indigenous law and, indeed, overturns such law, the Indigene becomes, as previously argued, following Deleuze, "an object not of recognition but of a fundamental *encounter*".[19] That is, a notion of encounter as productive of creative thought, rather than recognition, where "thought . . . must be impacted by an external encounter, one that it can neither engender nor anticipate".[20] The notion of *encounter* is of significance to a consideration of the appearance of the subject before the law, who is construed as a legal subject within the text – the 'word' – of the law,[21] and to the rupture of such law,[22] as it is evoked in Indigenous literature. This encounter, I would suggest, momentarily liberates both law and literature from the laws of their respective institutions,[23] allowing each to partake of an alterity that exists beyond it, in a "responsive reaching to 'non-law'".[24]

The justice described by Derrida that "is not law . . . [but] the very movement of deconstruction at work in law"[25] may be also understood in accordance with Benjamin's "principle of all divine end making", which is in contrast to "power[,] the principle of all mythical law making".[26] Indeed, Benjamin writes, "mythical violence is confronted by the divine", such that the latter may arrest the former.[27] Martel describes this divine violence as a "storm of forgiveness . . . [which is] a kind of tumult that constantly roils the phantasmagoria, creates a context for us to be able to act . . . without the crushing, preordained certainties of idolatry".[28] That is, the "misreading and idolatry" of the fetishist, who is consumed by the myths of sovereign authority, liberated only by human resistance and action

18 Deleuze, above n 69 (Ch 13), 169–70.
19 Ibid., 175–6.
20 Lincoln, above n 64 (Ch 13), 179, citing Alexandre Lefebvre, *The Image of Law: Deleuze, Bergson, Spinoza* (2008) 59.
21 See discussion, in Part III (Law), of Robert M Cover, "Violence and the Word" in Bruce B Lawrence and Aisha Karim, *On Violence: A Reader* (2007) 293.
22 See discussion in Fitzpatrick, above n 29 (Ch 14). At 145, Fitzpatrick describes the "word" that is law as that which "can only endure in a continuing relation to what is necessarily and constantly rejected, suppressed, or adapted to *make* it complete . . . the word cannot exist and endure in a solitary stasis".
23 See Derrida, above n 36 (Ch 13).
24 See discussion in Fitzpatrick, above n 21 (Ch 13), 204, citing Derrida, above n 10 (Ch 13), 269. See also Derrida, above n 3 (Ch 13), 216.
25 Derrida, above n 10 (Ch 13), 254.
26 Benjamin, above n 11 (Ch 13), 295.
27 Ibid., 297.
28 Martel, above n 47 (Ch 13), 103.

enabled by moments of divine violence.[29] Martel cites Benjamin's evocative description:

> As the purifying hurricane speeds ahead of the thunder and lightening, God's fury roars through history in a storm of forgiveness, in order to sweep away everything that would be consumed forever in the lightening bolts of divine wrath.[30]

The force of Indigenous Law, as it is depicted in the literary works previously discussed, may be understood as akin to this Benjaminian 'storm of forgiveness' – though in accordance with an Indigenous ancestral and therefore immanent, rather than transcendent, authority. The resultant 'anarchism' is creative of a revolutionary space in which a new political order might be enacted, in accordance with this law of alterity.

For the Indigenous peoples of Australia, and elsewhere, the "slight adjustment" to legal (and historical) narratives effected by such counterperspectives and, more specifically, the revelation of Indigenous Law within Indigenous literature is, perhaps, all that is required "to avoid being utterly determined".[31] That is, to provide alternative historical trajectories and legal subjectivities via the revelation of indigeneities within the subversive jurisprudences of the literary. While legal narratives appear to be complete and authoritatively so, this book has suggested that this apparent order is mere contrivance, revealed by the appearance of alterity. That is, a law of alterity that troubles, deconstructs, and annihilates the law of the coloniser with the emergence of the indeterminate, divine, and revolutionary. Following Fitzpatrick's suggestion that the law must remain responsive to social and historical change, drawing upon and deriving its content from external sources,[32] I argue that the Law evoked in Indigenous literature enters the fabric of social and cultural understanding, recontextualising and thereby legislating acceptable norms.[33] From the singular Indigenous claimant before the law to the global movement that is 'indigeneity', this disruptive capacity may be productive of new cultural and political forms and representations and, indeed, juridical narratives, in which indigeneities may be more expansively conceived.

29 Martel, above n 47 (Ch 13), 11.

30 Benjamin, above n 82 (Ch 15), cited in Martel, above n 47 (Ch 13), 102.

31 Martel, above n 47 (Ch 13), 93, citing Benjamin's reference to the "slight adjustment" effected by divine violence, in Benjamin, above n 7, 134.

32 Peter Fitzpatrick, "Bare Sovereignty: *Homo Sacer* and the Insistence of Law", in Andrew Norris (ed.), *Politics, Metaphysics and Death: Essays on Giorgio Agamben's Homo Sacer* (2005) 49, 62. See further discussion in Part I (Narratives).

33 See similar and extended discussion in Aristodemou, above n 9 (Ch 13), 10. More broadly, see Ben Golder and Peter Fitzpatrick, *Foucault's Law* (2009), especially Chapter 3.

To conclude

> Sore, sore the tears you shed
> When hope seemed folly and justice dead.
> Was the long night weary? Look up, dark band,
> The dawn is at hand.[34]

This book has dwelled upon the appearance of indigeneity, both *before* and *beyond* the law. That is, indigeneity as the determinate construction of a Benjaminian mythic law, and as the indeterminate evocation of the divine. I have identified the mythic in non-Indigenous (Australian) law, specifically in the law concerning native title, and the divine in expressions of indigeneity, appearing in Indigenous authored literature. Throughout, I have argued that the revolutionary, recuperative, and redemptive potentiality of this literature reveals an alterity that is always already evident *with-in* the law – subject to its determinacy, yet simultaneously constitutive of it. Indigeneities, while violently misrecognised and marginalised by the force of a determinate law, nonetheless emerge within it in the excesses and contradictions of the indeterminate, such that the law is ultimately constituted by alterity.[35] While the law persists in a positivist calculation of the Indigene and of her legal rights and interests, the alterity of an indeterminate indigeneity emerges in the fleeting moment of indecision and, indeed, of "non-law" – the moment, according to Derrida, of justice.[36] As a persistent spectre yet constitutive force, indigeneity is "caught, as a ghost at least, but an essential ghost, in every decision, in every event of decision",[37] expressed in the redemptive and transformative potentiality of intervening narratives and, ultimately, within the wider legal archive.[38]

My discussion of Australian native title law has entailed a consideration of the performance and (mis)recognition of indigeneity in the violent narrative of *terra*

34 Oodgeroo Noonuccal, "The Dawn is at Hand" in Anita Heiss and Peter Minter (eds), *Macquarie PEN Anthology of Aboriginal Literature* (2008) 45.

35 See interesting discussion in de Ville, above n 105 (Ch 14), 162–4. At 164, de Ville discusses the "application" of a Derridean notion of justice, recalling Derrida's own remark that "[d]econstruction cannot be applied and cannot *not* be applied" (citing Jacques Derrida, "As if I were Dead: An Interview with Jacques Derrida" in John Brannigan, Ruth Robbins and Julian Wolfreys (eds), *Applying: To Derrida* (1996) 218). At 164, de Ville further suggests:

> While justice does not therefore simply demand a concern for suffering or marginalised others, this structure of law and justice should, depending on whether the decision-maker indeed "gives" herself over to the impossible decision, in most instances lead to an invention of law which favours those who are marginalised.

36 Ibid., 269. See also Fitzpatrick, above n 21 (Ch 13); Fitzpatrick, above n 42 (Ch 13).

37 Derrida, above n 10 (Ch 13), 253.

38 Ann Curthoys, Ann Genovese and Alexander Reilly, *Rights and Redemption: History, Law and Indigenous People* (2008) 166.

nullius, and recent manifestations of this violence in the appearance of the Indigene *before* the law, in native title case law and legislation. As an ambivalent and unsettling notion, an anxiety surrounds the uncanny notion of indigeneity, the misrecognition of which is productive of the (legal) fictions exemplified in the law of native title. Such fictions are entailed within the Australian native title requirement, in the face of manifest dispossession and imposed cultural change, for acknowledgment and observance of 'traditional' laws and customs that constitute the 'origin and content' of native title,[39] and the requirement for continuous or 'substantially uninterrupted' connection to land and waters claimed.[40] In contrast, where native title pertains to questions of ontological significance, Indigenous relations to 'country' are understood in terms of spiritual relation and obligation,[41] rather than hierarchical right and entitlement.

Indigenous literature, I have asserted, might be understood as a critical and interventionist force, and as part of a broader postcolonial discourse. For Indigenous peoples, however, storytelling is also considered a cultural imperative. While Indigenous Law is sourced in the land,[42] it is predominantly expressed in narrative – in both oral and, more recently, textual narrratives. Indeed, Indigenous identities, and their expression in Law, are located "not in human sociality but in relationship to the land"[43], and in the telling of stories of the land – in the words of Wright: "[O]ur country is a very big story".[44] Within this tradition of storytelling, "knowledge of the natural world is gathered through personal experience and passed on through tradition and culture",[45] and land is regarded "not just as a physical resource, but as a social resource".[46] Accordingly, the landscape is radically reconceptualised within such literature, as an integral source of Law, and non-Indigenous perspectives are challenged.

39 *Mabo* (1992) 175 CLR 1, 58.

40 *Akiba and Another (on behalf of the Torres Strait Islanders of the Regional Seas Claim Group) v Queensland and Others (No 2)* (2010) 270 ALR 564, [544]–[552], citing s 223(1)(b) of the *Native Title Act* 1993 (Cth).

41 See, for instance, Marcia Langton, "The Estate as Duration: 'Being in Place' and Aboriginal Property Relations in Areas of Cape York Peninsula in North Australia" in Lee Godden and Maureen Tehan (eds), *Comparative Perspectives on Communal Lands and Individual Ownership: Sustainable Futures* (2010) 75; Bradley Bryan, "Property as Ontology: On Aboriginal and English Understandings of Ownership" (2000) 13 *Canadian Journal of Law and Jurisprudence* 3; Langton, above n 149 (Ch 13), 93.

42 Black, above n 6 (Ch 15).

43 Nellie Green, "Chasing an Identity, An Aboriginal Perspective on Aboriginality" in Kerry Reed-Gilbert (ed.), *The Strength of Us as Women: Black Women Speak* (2000) 47, cited in Heiss, above n 174 (Ch 13), 19.

44 Wright, above n 70 (Ch 13), 411.

45 Bruce Rose, Land Management Issues: Attitudes and Perceptions Amongst Aboriginal People of Central Australia (1995) xvii, cited in Langton, above n 149 (Ch 13), 94.

46 Langton, above n 149 (Ch 13), 94.

Reading such literature, particularly as a non-Indigenous scholar, I have drawn upon broader notions of literature as that which "unsettles the law",[47] of the literary work as a strategic response, generative of the historical or ideological subtext to which it responds,[48] and as a singular event or encounter,[49] such that Indigenous authored literature might be conceived as a subversive jurisprudence.[50] Moreover, I have described the imaginative interventions of such literature as comprehensible in terms of the disruptive capacity of mimesis which, rather than producing an inferior copy of Indigenous subjectivity, is revolutionary in its very subversiveness. Drawing upon Deleuze's notion of "limitless potentiality" and "positive power" within the simulacrum,[51] I have identified the evocation of a radical newness in literary expressions of indigeneity. Where such literature expresses a Law that is perceived to be distinct from, and perhaps even superior to, non-Indigenous law, this antinomy may be understood in terms of Benjamin's opposition between mythic and divine violence. While the former is evident in the determinate narratives of non-Indigenous law, such as the Australian common law creation and recognition of native title, the latter is expressed in Indigenous literature. This latter force is described as the force of a Benjaminian "storm of forgiveness"[52] and, in Derridean terms, as a deconstructive force.[53] This force figuratively and literally suspends and annihilates the law[54] and, in its reformation, is productive of the "slight adjustment"[55] that might, reiterating Wright's words, "[sing] the country afresh".[56] In recognition of the difficulties inherent in (non-Indigenous) postcolonial critique, I initially expressed a desire to speak not *for* Indigenous Australians, but to be ever more attentive to Indigenous voices. In my reading of Indigenous literature, and my examination of the intersections between such literature and the law, I have indeed attended to such voices and, moreover, to their revolutionary and juridical force.

I will close with the opening lines of a chapter in Wright's novel, *Carpentaria*, which express hope in the transformative potential of the stories of a dispossessed people:

> One evening in the driest grass in the world, a child who was no stranger to her people, asked if anyone could find hope.

47 Patrick Hanafin, Adam Gearey and Joseph Brooker, "Introduction: On Writing: Law and Literature" in Patrick Hanafin, Adam Gearey and Joseph Brooker (eds) *Law and Literature* (2004) 31(1) Special Issue of the *Journal of Law and Society* 1, 2.

48 Eagleton, above n 7 (Ch 13), 170.

49 Attridge, above n 6 (Ch 13).

50 Goodrich, above n 4 (Ch 13), 113.

51 Deleuze and Krauss, above n 24 (Ch 14), 53; Deleuze, above n 69 (Ch 13).

52 Martel, above n 47 (Ch 13), 103.

53 Derrida, above n 10 (Ch 13), 254.

54 Ibid., 269; Benjamin, above n 11 (Ch 13), especially 300.

55 Martel, above n 47 (Ch 13), 93, citing Benjamin, above n 7, 134.

56 Wright, above n 70 (Ch 13), 519.

> The people of parable and prophecy pondered what was hopeless and finally declared they no longer knew what hope was.
>
> The clocks, tick-a-ty tock, looked as though they might run out of time. Luckily, the ghosts in the memories of the old folk were listening. And said anyone can find hope in the stories: the big stories and the little ones in between. So . . .[57]

And the stories begin.

57 Wright, above n 70 (Ch 13), 12.

Bibliography

Articles/books

Adams, William M, "Nature and the Colonial Mind" in William M Adams and Martin Mulligan (eds), *Decolonizing Nature: Strategies for Conservation in a Post-Colonial Era* (2003) 16. London and Sterling, VA: Earthscan Publications.

Adorno, Theodor, *Aesthetic Theory* (Christian Lenhardt trans., 1984 edn). London and Boston, MA: Routledge & Kegan Paul.

Agamben, Giorgio, *Homo Sacer: Sovereign Power and Bare Life* (1998). Stanford, CA: Stanford University Press.

Althusser, Louis, "Ideology and Ideological State Apparatuses (Notes towards an Investigation), in Slavoj Žižek (ed.), *Mapping Ideology* (1994) 100, 128. London and New York: Verso.

Álvarez Molinero, Natalia, "From the Theory of Discovery to the Theory of Recognition of Indigenous Rights: Conventional International Law in Search of Homeopathy" in Saladin Meckled-García and Başak Çali, *The Legalization of Human Rights: Multidisciplinary Perspectives on Human Rights and Human Rights Law* (2006) 165. London and New York: Routledge.

Anaya, S. James, *Indigenous Peoples in International Law* (2004, 2nd edn). Oxford and New York: Oxford University Press.

Anderson, Ian, "Introduction: The Aboriginal Critique of Colonial Knowing" in Michele Grossman (ed.), *Blacklines: Contemporary Critical Writing by Indigenous Australians* (2003) 17. Carlton, Australia: Melbourne University Press.

Ang, Ien, *On Not Speaking Chinese: Living Between Asia and the West* (2001). London: Routledge.

Appaduri, Arjun, *Modernity at Large: Cultural Dimensions of Globalization* (1996). Minneapolis, MN: University of Minnesota Press.

Archer-Lean, Clare "Place, Space and Tradition in the Writings of Mudrooroo" in Annalisa Oboe (ed.), *Mongrel Signatures: Reflections on the Work of Mudrooroo* (2003) 203. Amsterdam and New York: Rodopi.

Archuleta, Elizabeth, "'An Extreme Need to Tell the Truth': Silence and Language in Sherman Alexie's 'The Trial of Thomas Builds-the-Fire'" in Jeff Berglund and Jan Roush (eds), *Sherman Alexie: A Collection of Critical Essays* (2010) 44. Salt Lake City, UT: University of Utah Press.

Aristodemou, Maria, *Law and Literature: Journeys From Her to Eternity* (2000). Oxford: Oxford University Press.

Asch, Michael, *Home and Native Land: Aboriginal Rights and the Canadian Constitution* (1984). Toronto and New York: Methuen.

Asch, Michael and Colin Samson, Discussion of Adam Kuper, "The Return of the Native" (April 2004) 45(2) *Current Anthropology* 261.

Ashcroft, Bill, Gareth Griffiths and Helen Tiffin, "Issues and Debates", in Bill Ashcroft, Gareth Griffiths and Helen Tiffin (eds), *The Post-Colonial Studies Reader* (1995, 2nd edn) 9. London and New York: Routledge.

Ashcroft, Bill, Gareth Griffiths and Helen Tiffin, *The Empire Writes Back: Theory and Practice in Post-Colonial Literatures* (2002, 2nd edn). London and New York: Routledge.

Attridge, Derek, "Introduction: Derrida and the Questioning of Literature" in Jacques Derrida (Derek Attridge, ed.), *Acts of Literature* (1992) 1. New York: Routledge.

Attridge, Derek, Preface to "Before the Law" in Jacques Derrida (Derek Attridge, ed.), *Acts of Literature* (1992) 181. New York: Routledge.

Attridge, Derek, *The Singularity of Literature* (2004). London; New York: Routledge.

Attridge, Derek, "The Singular Events of Literature" (2010) 50(1) *British Journal of Aesthetics* 81.

Azam, Maryam, "Alexis Wright: 'It was like writing a story to the ancestors'", *The Guardian* (25 May 2014) at www.theguardian.com/books/australia-culture-blog/2014/may/25/alexis-wright-it-was-like-writing-a-story-to-the-ancestors (accessed 6 October 2015).

Badiou, Alain, *The Communist Hypothesis* (2010). London and New York: Verso.

Barnard, Alan, "Indigenous Peoples: A Response to Justin Kenrick and Jerome Lewis" (2004) 20, *Anthropology Today* 19.

Barnard, Alan, "Kalahari Revisionism, Vienna and the 'indigenous peoples' Debate" (2006) 14(1) *Social Anthropology* 1.

Bartlett, Richard H, *Native Title in Australia* (2000). Sydney, Australia: Butterworths.

Bayet-Charlton, Fabienne, "Overturning the doctrine: Indigenous Peoples and Wilderness – Being Aboriginal in the Environmental Movement", in Michele Grossman (ed.), *Blacklines: Contemporary Critical Writing by Indigenous Australians* (2003) 171. Carlton, Australia: Melbourne University Press.

Behrendt, Larissa, "The Relevance of the Rights Agenda of Practical Reconciliation" in Rosemary Hunter and Mary Keyes (eds), *Changing Law: Rights, Regulation and Reconciliation* (2005) 137. Aldershot, UK and Burlington, VT: Ashgate.

Behrendt, Larissa and Loretta Kelly, *Resolving Indigenous Disputes: Land Conflict and Beyond* (2008). Leichhardt, Australia: The Federation Press.

Benjamin, Walter, *Illuminations* (Harry Zohn trans., 1968 edn). New York: Harcourt Brace Jovanovich.

Benjamin, Walter, "Critique of Violence" in Walter Benjamin, *Reflections: Essays, Aphorisms, Autobiographical Writings* (1978) 277. New York: Harcourt Brace Jovanovich.

Benjamin, Walter, "The Meaning of Time in the Moral Universe" in Marcus Bullock and Michael W Jennings (eds), *Walter Benjamin: Selected Writings, Vol. I 1913–1926* (1996) 286. Cambridge, MA: Belknap Press.

Benjamin, Walter, *The Origin of German Tragic Drama* (1998). London: Verso.

Benjamin, Walter, "Central Park" in Howard Eiland and Michael W Jennings (eds), *Walter Benjamin: Selected Writings* (Vol 4) (2006) 164. Cambridge, MA: Belknap Press.

Bhabha, Homi, "Of Mimicry and Man: The Ambivalence of Colonial Discourse" (1984) 28 *Discipleship: A Special Issue on Psychoanalysis* 125.

Bhabha, Homi, "The Other Question: The Stereotype and Colonial Discourse" in Mandy Merck *The Sexual Subject: A Screen Reader in Sexuality* (1992) 312. London and New York: Routledge.

Bhabha, Homi, "Unpacking my library . . . Again" in Iain Chambers and Lidia Curti (eds), *The Post-colonial Question: Common Skies, Divided Horizons* (1996) 199. London and New York: Routledge.

Bhabha, Homi, *The Location of Culture* (1994) (Routledge Classics Edition, 2004). London and New York: Routledge.

Bhandar, Brenna, "Re-covering the Limits of Recognition: The Politics of Difference and Decolonisation in John Borrows" *Recovering Canada: The Resurgence of Indigenous Law* (2007) 27, *Australian Feminist Law Journal* 125.

Bhandar, Brenna, "'Spatialising History' and Opening Time: Resisting the Reproduction of the Proper Subject" in Scott Veitch (ed.), *Law and the Politics of Reconciliation* (2007) 93. Aldershot, UK and Burlington, VT: Ashgate.

Bhandar, Brenna, "Plasticity and Post-Colonial Recognition: 'Owning, Knowing and Being'" (2011) 22(3) *Law and Critique* 227, 228.

Biber, Katherine, "Being/Nothing: Native Title and Fantasy Fulfilment" (2004) 3, *Indigenous Law Journal* 1.

Birch, Tony, "'Real Aborigines': Colonial Attempts to Re-Imagine and Re-Create the Identities of Aboriginal People" (1993) 4, *Ulitarra* 13.

Birch, Tony, "'Black Armbands and White Veils': John Howard's Moral Amnesia" (1997) 25, *Melbourne Historical Journal* 8–16.

Birrell, Kathleen, Lee Godden and Maureen Tehan, "Climate Change and REDD+: Property as a Prism for Conceiving Indigenous Peoples' Engagement" (2012) 3(2) *Journal of Human Rights and the Environment* 196.

Black, CF, *The Land is the Source of the Law: A Dialogic Encounter with Indigenous Jurisprudence* (2011). New York: Routledge.

Blackstone, William, *Commentaries on the Laws of England* (1830, 17th edn), Book II, Chapter I. New York: Collins and Hannay.

Blanchot, Maurice, *The Unavowable Community* (Pierre Joris trans., 1988 edn). Barrytown, NY: Station Hill Press.

Blanchot, Maurice, "Literature and the Right to Death" in Maurice Blanchot, *The Station Hill Blanchot Reader: Fiction and Literary Essays* (Lydia David trans., 1999 edn) 359. Barrytown, NY: Station Hill Press.

Boire, Gary, "'Ratione Officii': Representing Law in Postcolonial Literatures" (1994) 27(4) *Mosaic: Journal for the Interdisciplinary Study of Literature* 199.

Boire, Gary, "Symbolic Violence: Law, Literature, Interpretation: An Afterword" (2004) *ARIEL* 35 (1–2) 231.

Borrows, John, "Practical Reconciliation, Practical Re-Colonisation?" (May 2004) 2(27) *Land, Rights, Laws: Issues of Native Title* (Native Title Research Unit, AIATSIS).

Bourdieu, Pierre, "The Force of Law: Towards a Sociology of the Juridical Field" *The Hastings Law Journal* 38 (Richard Terdiman trans., 1987 edn) 814.

Brady, James B and Newton Garver (eds), *Justice, Law, and Violence* (1991). Philadelphia, PA: Temple University Press.

Bright, April, "Burn Grass" in *Country in Flames: Proceedings of the 1994 Symposium on Biodiversity and Fire in North Australia*, Biodiversity Series, Paper No 3 at http://www.environment.gov.au/archive/biodiversity/publications/series/paper3/ (accessed 9 February 2016).

Brown, Wendy, "Suffering the Paradoxes of Rights" in Wendy Brown and Janet Halley (eds) *Left Legalism/Left Critique* (2002) 420. Durham, NC: Duke University Press.

Brown, Wendy, *Regulating Aversion: Tolerance in the Age of Identity and Empire* (2006). Princeton, NJ: Princeton University Press.

Bryan, Bradley, "Property as Ontology: On Aboriginal and English Understandings of Ownership" (2000) 13 *Canadian Journal of Law and Jurisprudence* 3.

Burns, Marcelle, "Challenging the Assumptions of Positivism: An Analysis of the Concept of Society in *Sampi on Behalf of the Bardi Jawi People v Western Australia* [2010] and *Bodney v Bennell* [2008] (May 2011) 4(7) *Land, Rights, Laws: Issues of Native Title* at http://aiatsis.gov.au/sites/default/files/products/issues_paper/burns-ntip-v4n7-challenging-assumptions-positivism-concept-of-society.pdf (accessed 6 October 2015).

Butler, Judith, *Gender Trouble: Feminism and the Subversion of Identity* (1990). New York: Routledge.

Butler, Judith, "Decking Out: Performing Identities" in Diana Fuss (ed.), *Inside/Out, Lesbian Theories, Gay Theories* (1991) 17. New York: Routledge.

Butler, Judith, *Excitable Speech: A Politics of the Performative* (1997). New York: Routledge.

Butler, Judith, *Precarious Life: The Powers of Mourning and Violence* (2004). London and New York: Verso.

Campbell, David, "Voice of the New Tribes" *The Guardian* (4 January 2003) at www.theguardian.com/books/2003/jan/04/artsfeatures.fiction (accessed 6 October 2015).

Cardozo, Benjamin, "Law and Literature" (1925) 14 *Yale Law Review* 699.

Carter, Paul, *The Road to Botany Bay: An Essay in Spatial History* (1987). London and Boston, MA: Faber and Faber.

Carter, Paul, *Living in a New Country: History, Travelling and Language* (1992). London: Faber and Faber.

Chaplin, Susan, "Textual Properties: The Limit of Law and Literature – Towards a Gothic Jurisprudence" (2008) 43 *Studies in Law, Politics and Society: Special Issue: Law and Literature Reconsidered* 113.

Charters, Claire, Les Malezer and Victoria Tauli-Corpuz (eds), *Indigenous Voices: The UN Declaration on the Rights of Indigenous Peoples* (forthcoming). Oxford: Hart Publishing.

Chow, Rey, "Where Have All the Natives Gone?" in Angelika Bammer (ed.), *Displacements: Cultural Identities in Question* (1994) 136. Bloomington, IN: Indiana University Press.

Clendinnen, Inga, *Dancing with Strangers* (2003). Melbourne, Australia: Text Publishing.

Clifford, James, "Indigenous Articulations" (Fall, 2001) 13(2) *The Contemporary Pacific* 468.

Cohen, Felix, "Original Indian Title" (1947) 32 *Minnesota Law Review* 28.

Collard, Len, "Kura, Yeye, boorda 'from the past, today and the future'", in Sally Morgan, Tjalaminu Mia and Blake Kwaymullina (eds), *Heartsick for Country: Stories of Love, Spirit and Creation* (2008) 59. North Fremantle, Australia: Fremantle Press.

Constable, Marianne, "The Silence of the Law: Justice in Cover's 'Field of Pain and Death'" in Austin Sarat (ed.), *Law, Violence, and the Possibility of Justice* (2001) 85. Princeton, NJ and Oxford: Princeton University Press.

Coombe, Rosemary J, "The Properties of Culture and the Politics of Possessing Identity", in Jonathan Hart and Richard W Bauman (eds), *Explorations in Difference: Law, Culture and Politics* (1996) 252. Toronto: Published in association with the Centre for Constitutional Studies, University of Alberta, by University of Toronto Press.

Cornell, Drucilla, "Post-Structuralism, the Ethical Relation, and the Law" (1988) 9 *Cardozo Law Review* 1587.

Cornell, Drucilla, *The Philosophy of the Limit* (1992). New York: Routledge.

Coulthard, Glen S, "Subjects of Empire: Indigenous Peoples in the 'Politics of Recognition' in Canada" (2007) 6 *Contemporary Political Theory* 437.

Cover, Robert, "Violence and the Word" (1986) 95 *Yale Law Journal* 1601.

Cover, Robert M, "Nomos and Narrative" in Martha Minnow, Michael Ryan and Austin Sarat (eds), *Narrative, Violence, and the Law* (1992) 95. Ann Arbor, MI: University of Michigan Press.

Cover, Robert M, "Violence and the Word" in Bruce B Lawrence and Aisha Karim, *On Violence: A Reader* (2007) 293. Durham, NC: Duke University Press.

Critchley, Simon, *The Ethics of Deconstruction: Derrida and Levinas* (1992). Oxford and Cambridge, MA : Blackwell.

Critchley, Simon, *Ethics-Politics-Subjectivity: Essays on Derrida, Levinas and Contemporary French Thought* (1999). London: Verso.

Culler, Jonathan, "Derrida and the Singularity of Literature" (2005) 27(2) *Cardozo Law Review* 869, 874.

Curthoys, Ann, Ann Genovese and Alexander Reilly, *Rights and Redemption: History, Law and Indigenous People* (2008). Sydney, Australia: University of New South Wales Press.

Daes, Erica-Irene, "An Overview of the History of Indigenous Peoples: Self-Determination and the United Nations" (2008) 21 *Cambridge Review of International Affairs* 7.

Davis, Colin, *Levinas: An Introduction* (1996). Cambridge: Polity Press.

Davis, Megan, "Indigenous Struggles in Standard-Setting: The United Nations Declaration on the Rights of Indigenous Peoples" (2008) 9(2) *Melbourne Journal of International Law* 43.

De Montaigne, Michel, *The Essayes of Montaigne* (John Florio trans., 1933 edn). London: Gibbings & Company.

De Sutter, Laurent and Kyle McGee, "Introduction" in Laurent de Sutter and Kyle McGee (eds), *Deleuze and Law* (2012) 1. Edinburgh, UK: Edinburgh University Press.

De Ville, Jacques, "On Law's Origin: Derrida Reading Freud, Kafka and Lévi-Strauss" (2011) 7(2) *Utrecht Law Review* 77.

De Ville, Jacques, *Jacques Derrida: Law as Absolute Hospitality* (2011). Oxford and New York: Routledge.

De Vitoria, Francisco, "On the American Indians" in Francisco de Vitoria (Anthony Pagden and Jeremy Lawrence, eds), *Political Writings* (1991) 231. Cambridge: Cambridge University Press.

Deleuze, Gilles, *Logic of Sense* (1969). New York: Columbia University Press.

Deleuze, Gilles, *Difference and Repetition* (Paul Patton trans., 2004 edn). New York: Columbia University Press.

Deleuze, Gilles and Rosalind Krauss, "Plato and the Simulacrum" (Winter 1983) 27 *October* 45.

Derrida, Jacques, *Of Grammatology* (Gayatri Spivak trans., 1976 edn). Baltimore, MD: Johns Hopkins University Press.

Derrida, Jacques, "Violence and Metaphysics: An Essay on the Thought of Emmanuel Levinas" in Jacques Derrida, *Writing and Difference* (1978) 97. Oxford and New York: Routledge.

Derrida, Jacques, "Outwork, Prefacing", in Jacques Derrida, *Dissemination* (Barbara Johnson trans., 1981 edn) 1. Chicago, IL: University of Chicago Press.

Derrida, Jacques, "Différance" in Jacques Derrida, *Margins of Philosophy* (A Bass trans., 1982 edn) 3. Chicago, IL: University of Chicago Press.

Derrida, Jacques, "Différance" in Jacques Derrida, *Margins of Philosophy* (1982) 11. Chicago, IL: University of Chicago Press.

Derrida, Jacques, "The Parergon", in Jacques Derrida, *The Truth in Painting* (Geoff Bennington and Ian McLeod trans., 1987 edn) 37. Chicago, IL: University of Chicago Press.

Derrida, Jacques, *Limited Inc* (1988). Evanston, IL: Northwestern University Press.

Derrida, Jacques, "Psyche: Inventions of the Other" in Lindsay Waters and Wlad Godzich (eds), *Reading de Man Reading* (Catherine Porter trans., 1989 edn) 55. Minneapolis, MN: University of Minnesota Press.

Derrida, Jacques, "Force of Law: The Mystical Foundation of Authority" (1990) 11 *Cardozo Law Review* 919.

Derrida, Jacques, " Force of Law: The 'Mystical Foundation of Authority'" in Drucilla Cornell, Michel Rosenfeld and David Gray Carlson (eds), *Deconstruction and the Possibility of Justice* (1992) 27. New York: Routledge.

Derrida, Jacques, "This Strange Institution Called Literature: An Interview with Jacques Derrida" in Jacques Derrida (Derek Attridge, ed.), *Acts of Literature* (1992) 33. New York: Routledge.

Derrida, Jacques, ". . . That Dangerous Supplement . . ." in Jacques Derrida (Derek Attridge, ed.), *Acts of Literature* (1992) 76. New York: Routledge.

Derrida, Jacques, "The First Session" in Jacques Derrida (Derek Attridge, ed.), *Acts of Literature* (1992) 127. New York: Routledge.

Derrida, Jacques, "Before the Law" in Jacques Derrida (Derek Attridge, ed.), *Acts of Literature* (1992) 181. New York: Routledge.

Derrida, Jacques, "The Law of Genre" in Jacques Derrida (Derek Attridge, ed.), *Acts of Literature* (1992) 221. New York: Routledge.

Derrida, Jacques, *Archive Fever: A Freudian Impression* (Eric Prenowitz trans., 1995 edn). Chicago, IL: University of Chicago Press.

Derrida, Jacques, "Passions: An Oblique Offering" in Jacques Derrida (Thomas Dutoit, ed.), *On the Name* (David Wood, John P Leavey, Jr and Ian McLeod, trans., 1995 edn) 3. Stanford, CA: Stanford University Press.

Derrida, Jacques, "As if I were Dead: An Interview with Jacques Derrida" in John Brannigan, Ruth Robbins and Julian Wolfreys (eds), *Applying: To Derrida* (1996) 218. New York: St. Martin's Press.

Derrida, Jacques, "On Forgiveness" in Jacques Derrida, *On Cosmopolitanism and Forgiveness* (Mark Dooley and Michael Hughes trans., 1997 edn) 27. London and New York: Routledge.

Derrida, Jacques, *Politics of Friendship* (George Collins trans., 1997 edn). London and New York: Verso.

Derrida, Jacques, *Monolingualism of the Other, or The Prosthesis of Origin* (Patrick Mensah trans., 1998 edn). Stanford, CA: Stanford University Press.

Derrida, Jacques, *Adieu to Emmanuel Levinas* (Pascale-Anne Brault and Michael Naas, trans., 1999 edn). Stanford, CA: Stanford University Press.

Derrida, Jacques, *Of Hospitality* (Rachel Bowlby trans., 2000 edn). Stanford, CA: Stanford University Press.

Derrida, Jacques, "Plato's Pharmacy" in Jacques Derrida *Dissemination* ((Barbara Johnson trans., 2000 edn) 113. Chicago, IL: University of Chicago Press.

Derrida, Jacques, (Gil Anidjar, ed.), *Acts of Religion* (2002). New York and London: Routledge.

Derrida, Jacques, "Archive Fever in South Africa" in Carolyn Hamilton, Verne Harris, Michèle Pickover, Graeme Reid, Razia Saleh and Jane Taylor (eds), *Refiguring the Archive* (2002) 38. Dordrecht, The Netherlands and London : Kluwer Academic.

Derrida, Jacques, "Force of Law: The Mystical Foundation of Authority" in Jacques Derrida (Gil Anidjar, ed.), *Acts of Religion* (2002) 228. New York and London: Routledge.

Derrida, Jacques, "From Restricted to General Economy: A Hegelianism without Reserve" in Jacques Derrida, *Writing and Difference* (2002) 317. Oxford and New York: Routledge.

Derrida, Jacques, "The University without Condition" in Jacques Derrida, *Without Alibi* (2002) 202. Stanford, CA: Stanford University Press.

Derrida, Jacques, *Who's Afraid of Philosophy? Right to Philosophy 1* (2002). Stanford, CA: Stanford University Press.

Derrida, Jacques, "Autoimmunity: Real and Symbolic Suicides – A Dialogue with Jacques Derrida" in Giovanna Borradori, *Philosophy in a Time of Terror: Dialogues with Jürgen Habermas and Jacques Derrida* (2003) 85. Chicago, IL: University of Chicago Press.

Derrida, Jacques, James Adner, Kate Doyle, and Glenn Hendler, "Women in the Beehive: A Seminar with Jacques Derrida" (2005) 16(3) *A Journal of Feminist Cultural Studies* 139.

Dix, Andrew, "Escape Stories: Narratives and Native Americans in Sherman Alexie's *The Lone Ranger and Tonto Fistfight in Heaven*" (2001) 31 *The Yearbook of English Studies* 155.

Docherty, Thomas, *Aesthetic Democracy* (2006). Stanford, CA: Stanford University Press.

Dodson, Michael, "From Lore to Law: Indigenous Rights and Australian Legal Systems" (1995) 72(2) *Aboriginal Law Bulletin* 2.

Dodson, Mick, "Linking International Standards with Contemporary Concerns of Aboriginal and Torres Strait Islander Peoples" in Sarah Pritchard (ed.), *Indigenous Peoples, the United Nations, and Human Rights* (1998) 18. Leichhardt, Australia: Federation Press.

Douzinas, Costas, *The End of Human Rights: Critical Legal Thought at the Turn of the Century* (2000). Oxford: Hart Publishing.

Douzinas, Costas, "Identity, Recognition, Rights or What Can Hegel Teach Us About Human Rights?" (Sept. 2002) 29(3) *Journal of Law and Society* 379.

Douzinas, Costas, *Human Rights and Empire: The Political Philosophy of Cosmopolitanism* (2007). London: Routledge-Cavendish.

Douzinas, Costas and Adam Gearey, *Critical Jurisprudence: The Political Philosophy of Justice* (2005). Oxford and Portland, OR: Hart Publishing.

Douzinas, Costas and Ronnie Warrington, "The Face of Justice: A Jurisprudence of Alterity" (1994) 3 *Social and Legal Studies: An International Journal* 23.

Dove, Michael R, "Indigenous People and Environmental Politics" (2006) 35 *Annual Review of Anthropology* 191.

Drichel, Simone, "'How Newness (not) Comes into the World'": Eva Rask Knudsen's *The Circle and the Spiral* (October 2006) 22(4) *Australian Literary Studies* 507.

Duff, Nick, "What's Needed to Prove Native Title? Finding Flexibility within the Law on Connection", Australian Institute of Aboriginal and Torres Strait Islander Studies Native Title Research Unit Research Discussion Paper No 35 (2014) at http://aiatsis.gov.au/sites/default/files/products/discussion_paper/whats-needed-to-prove-native-title.pdf (accessed 6 October 2015).

Durham, Scott, *Phantom Communities: The Simulacrum and the Limits of Postmodernism* (1998). Stanford, CA: Stanford University Press.

During, Simon, *Foucault and Literature: Towards a Genealogy of Writing* (1992). London and New York: Routledge.

Eagleton, Terry, *Literary Theory: An Introduction* (1996). Cambridge, MA: Blackwell

Eagleton, Terry, *The Event of Literature* (2012). New Haven, CT: Yale University Press.

Engle, Karen, "From Skepticism to Embrace: Human Rights and the American Anthropological Assocation from 1947 to 1999" (2001) 23 *Human Rights Quarterly* 536.

Evans, Julie, "Beyond the Frontier: Possibilities and Precariousness along Australia's Southern Coast" in Lynette Russell (ed.), *Colonial Frontiers: Indigenous-European Encounters in Settler Societies* (2001) 151. Manchester, UK and New York: Manchester University Press; Distributed exclusively in the USA by Palgrave.

Everett, Jim, "Aboriginality in Tasmania" (2000) 12 *Siglo* 2.

Fanon, Frantz, *The Wretched of the Earth* (Richard Philcox trans., with commentary by Jean-Paul Sartre and Homi K Bhabha, 1963 edn). New York: Grove Press.

Fanon, Frantz, *Black Skin, White Masks* (Charles Lam Markmann trans., 1967 edn). New York: Grove Press.

Fee, Margery, "Who can Write as Other?" from "Why C.K. Stead Didn't Like Kerry Hulme's *The Bone People* or Who Can Write as the Other" (1989) 1 *Australian and New Zealand Studies in Canada*, in Bill Ashcroft, Gareth Griffiths and Helen Tiffin (eds), *The Post-Colonial Studies Reader* (1995, 2nd edn) 169. London and New York: Routledge.

Fish, Stanley, *Doing What Comes Naturally: Change, Rhetoric, and the Practice of Theory in Literary and Legal Studies* (1989). Durham, NC: Duke University Press.

Fitzpatrick, Peter, "Law and Societies", (1984) 22 *Osgood Hall Law Journal* 115.

Fitzpatrick, Peter, *The Mythology of Modern Law* (1992). London; New York: Routledge.

Fitzpatrick, Peter, "'Enacted in the Destiny of Sedentary Peoples': Racism, Discovery and the Grounds of Law" (2000) 1(1) *Balayi* 11.

Fitzpatrick, Peter, *Modernism and the Grounds of Law* (2001). Cambridge and Melbourne, Australia: Cambridge University Press.

Fitzpatrick, Peter, "Why the Law Is Also Nonviolent" in Austin Sarat (ed.), *Law, Violence and the Possibility of Justice* (2001) 142.

Fitzpatrick, Peter, "No Higher Duty: Mabo and the Failure of Legal Foundation" (2002) 13 *Law and Critique* 233.

Fitzpatrick, Peter, "Juris-fiction: Literature and the Law of the Law" (2004) 35 (1–2) *ARIEL* 215

Fitzpatrick, Peter, "Bare Sovereignty: *Homo Sacer* and the Insistence of Law", in Andrew Norris (ed.), *Politics, Metaphysics and Death: Essays on Giorgio Agamben's Homo Sacer* (2005) 49. Durham, NC: Duke University Press.

Fitzpatrick, Peter, "Making Difference: Modernity and the Political Formations of Death" in Charles J Ogletree Jr and Austin Sarat (eds), *The Road to Abolition: The Future of Capital Punishment in the United States* (2009) 319. New York: New York University Press.

Fitzpatrick, Peter, "Necessary Fictions: Indigenous Claims and the Humanity of Rights" (20 February 2010) *Human Rights and Human Welfare Working Paper No 57*, 17, at www.du.edu/korbel/hrhw/workingpapers/archive/index.html (accessed 6 October 2015).

Fitzpatrick, Peter, "Reading Slowly: The Law of Literature and the Literature of Law" in Ruth Buchanan, Stewart Motha and Sundhya Pahuja (eds), *Reading Modern Law: Critical Methodologies and Sovereign Formations* (2012) 193. New York: Routledge.

Fitzpatrick, Peter, "The Revolutionary Past: Decolonizing Law and Human Rights" (2014) 2(1) *Metodo: International Studies in Phenomenology and Philosophy* 117.

Fitzpatrick, Peter and Eve Darian-Smith, "Laws of the Postcolonial: An Insistent Introduction" in Eve Darian-Smith and Peter Fitzpatrick, *Laws of the Postcolonial* (1999) 1. Ann Arbor, MI: University of Michigan Press.

Fitzpatrick, Peter and Richard Joyce, "Copying Right: Cultural Property and the Limits of (Occidental) Law" in Fiona Macmillan (ed.), *New Directions in Copyright* (Vol. 4) (2007) 171. Cheltenham, UK and Northampton, MA: Edward Elgar.

Forrester, John, "Dead on Time" in John Forrester, *The Seductions of Psychoanalysis: Freud, Lacan and Derrida* (1990) 206. Cambridge and New York: Cambridge University Press.

Foucault, Michel, *Power/Knowledge: Selected Interviews and Other Writings 1972–77* (Colin Gordon *et al.* trans., 1980 edn). Brighton, UK: Harvester Press.

Foucault, Michel, "Nietzsche, Genealogy, History" in Michel Foucault (Paul Rabinow, ed.) *The Foucault Reader* (1984) 76. New York: Pantheon Books.

Foucault, Michel, "Maurice Blanchot: The Thought from Outside" in Michel Foucault and Maurice Blanchot, *Foucault/Blanchot* (Brian Massumi trans., 1987 ed) 7. New York: Zone Books and Cambridge, MA: MIT Press, distributor.

Franklin, Miles, *Laughter, Not for a Cage* (1956). Sydney: Angus and Robertson.

French, Justice Robert and Patricia Lane, "The Common Law of Native Title in Australia" (2002) 2 *Oxford University Commonwealth Law Journal* 15.

French, Chief Justice Robert "Lifting the burden of native title: Some modest proposals for improvement" (2009) 93 *Reform* 10 at www.austlii.edu.au/au/journals/FedJSchol/2008/18.html (accessed 6 October 2015).

Freud, Sigmund, *Beyond the Pleasure Principle* (Standard edn, Vol. 18, 1920). London: Hogarth Press.

Freud, Sigmund, "Delusions and Dreams in Jensen's 'Gradiva' (1906–07)" in Sigmund Freud, *The Standard Edition of the Complete Psychological Works of Sigmund Freud* (James Strachey trans., 1953–1974 edn) 80. London: Hogarth Press.

Freud, Sigmund, "The 'Uncanny'", in Albert Dickson (ed.), *The Art and Literature*, Vol. 14 (1990). London: Penguin Books.

Gadamer, Hans-Georg, *Wahreit und Methode* [Truth and Method] (1975). New York: Seabury Press.

Gandhi, Leela, *Postcolonial Theory: A Critical Introduction* (1998). New York: Columbia University Press.

Geertz, Clifford, "From the Native's Point of View: On the Nature of Anthropological Understanding" in Paul Rabinow and WM Sullivan (eds), *Interpretive Social Science* (1979) 225. Berkeley, CA: University of California Press.

Geertz, Clifford, *Local Knowledge: Further Essays on Interpretative Anthropology* (1983). Berkeley, CA: University of California Press.

Giddens, Anthony, *The Constitution of Society: Outline of the Theory of Structuration* (1984). Cambridge, MA: Polity.

Gilroy, Paul, *Small Acts: Thoughts on the Politics of Black Cultures* (1993). London and New York: Serpent's Tail.

Ginibi, Ruby Langford, "Aboriginal Traditional and Customary Laws" (1994) (1) *Law, Text, Culture* 8.

Ginibi, Ruby Langford, "My Mob, My Self" in Kerry Reed-Gilbert (ed.), *The Strength of Us as Women: Black Women Speak* (2000) 19. Charnwood, Australia: Ginninderra Press.

Godden, Lee, "Indigenous Heritage and the Environment: 'Legal categories are only one way of imagining the real'" (August 2002) 19(4) *Environmental and Planning Law Journal* 258.

Godden, Lee and Maureen Tehan, "Introduction: A Sustainable Future for Communal Lands, Resources and Communities" in Lee Godden and Maureen Tehan (eds), *Comparative Perspectives on Communal Lands and Individual Ownership: Sustainable Futures* (2010) 10. Abingdon, UK: Routledge.

Golder, Ben and Peter Fitzpatrick, *Foucault's Law* (2009). Oxford: Routledge-Cavendish.

Goodrich, Peter, *Law in the Courts of Love: Literature and Other Minor Jurisprudences* (1996). London and New York: Routledge.

Graham, Mary, "Some Thoughts about the Philosophical Underpinnings of Aboriginal Worldviews" (2008) 45 *Australian Humanities Review* 181.

Gray, Geoffrey and Christine Winter (eds), *The Resurgence of Racism: Howard, Hanson and the Race Debate* (1997). Clayton, Australia: Department of History, Monash University.

Grbich, Judith, "The Scent of Colonialism: Mabo, Eucalyptus and Excursions within Legal Racism" (2001) 15 *Australian Feminist Law Journal* 119.

Grbich, Judith, "Tracing the Figure of the Native in Postcolonial Theory and Native Title Law: Enlightenment, Aesthetics and Charles Harpur" (2005) 22 *Australian Feminist Law Journal* 127.

Grbich, Judith, "The Road to Jawi Country: Exilic Subjects and Legal Landscapes" in Anna Haebich and Baden Offord (eds), *Landscapes of exile: Once perilous, Now safe* (2008) 43. Oxford: Peter Lang.

Green, Nellie, "Chasing an Identity, An Aboriginal Perspective on Aboriginality" in Kerry Reed-Gilbert (ed.), *The Strength of Us as Women: Black Women Speak* (2000) 47. Charnwood, Australia: Ginninderra Press.

Grossman, Michele, "After Aboriginalism: Power, Knowledge and Indigenous Australian Critical Writing" in Michele Grossman (ed.), *Blacklines: Contemporary Critical Writing by Indigenous Australians* (2003) 1. Carlton, Australia. Melbourne University Press.

Hachamovitch, Yifat, "The Ideal Object of Transmission: An Essay on the Faith which Attaches to Instruments (*de fide instrumentorum*)" (1991) 2(1) *Law and Critique* 85.

Hallam, Sylvia, "The Other Side of the Western Frontier" (1983) 7(2) *Aboriginal History* 146.

Hallward, Peter, *Absolutely Postcolonial: Writing between the Singular and the Specific* (2001). Manchester, UK: Manchester University Press.

Hamacher, Werner (Dana Hollander trans.), "Afformative, Strike: Benjamin's 'Critique of Violence'" in Andrew Benjamin and Peter Osborne (eds), *Walter Benjamin's Philosophy: Destruction and Experience* (2000) 108. London and New York: Routledge.

Hamacher, Werner, "Guilt History: Benjamin's Sketch 'Capitalism as Religion'" (2002) Fall–Winter *Diacritics* 81.

Hamilton, Jennifer Anne, *Indigeneity in the Courtroom: Law, Culture and the Production of Difference in the North American Courts* (2009). New York and London: Routledge.

Hanafin, Patrick, Adam Gearey and Joseph Brooker, "Introduction: On Writing: Law and Literature" in Patrick Hanafin, Adam Gearey and Joseph Brooker (eds) *Law and Literature* (2004) 31(1) Special Issue of the *Journal of Law and Society* 1.

Handler, Richard, "Authenticity" (1986) 2 *Anthropology Today* 2.

Harris, Mark, "Mapping Australian Postcolonial Landscapes: From Resistance to Reconciliation?" (2003) 7 *Law/Text/Culture* 71.

Harris, Mark, "Mythologising 'Recollections of Squatting in Victoria': Law's Intersection with Colonial Memory" (2003) 1 *Law, Social Justice & Global Development Journal* at www2.warwick.ac.uk/fac/soc/law/elj/lgd/2003_1/harris (accessed 3 June 2015).

Harris, Verne, "A Shaft of Darkness: Derrida in the Archive" in Carolyn Hamilton, Verne Harris, Michèle Pickover, Graeme Reid, Razia Saleh and Jane Taylor (eds), *Refiguring the Archive* (2002) 75. Dordrecht, The Netherlands and London: Kluwer Academic.

Healy, Chris, *Forgetting Aborigines* (2008). Sydney: University of New South Wales Press.

Hegel, Georg Wilhelm Friedrich, "Self-Consciousness: The Truth and Self-Certainty: Independence and Dependence of Self-Consciousness: Lordship and Bondage", in *Phenomenology of Spirit* (AV Miller trans., with analysis and forward by JN Findlay, 1977 edn) 111. Oxford: Oxford University Press.

Heidegger, Martin, *Being and Time* (John Macquarie and Edward Robinson trans., 1962, 7th edn). New York: Harper & Row.

Heidegger, Martin, "What is Metaphysics?" in Martin Heidegger (David Farrell-Krell, ed.), *Basic Writings* (1993) 101. Abingdon, UK: Routledge Classics.
Heiss, Anita M, *Dhuuluu-Yala: To Talk Straight* (2003). Canberra, Australia: Aboriginal Studies Press.
Heiss, Anita and Peter Minter, "Aboriginal Literature" in Anita Heiss and Peter Minter (eds), *Macquarie PEN Anthology of Aboriginal Literature* (2008) 1. Crows Nest, Australia: Allen & Unwin.
Hirtz, Frank, "It takes Modern Means to be Traditional: On Recognizing Indigenous Cultural Communities in the Philippines" (2003) 34(5) *Development and Change* 887.
Hirvonen, Ari, "The Politics of Revolt: On Benjamin and Critique of Law" (2011) 22(2) *Law and Critique* 101.
Hornborg, Alf, "Ecology as Semiotics: Outlines of a Contextualist Paradigm for Human Ecology" in Philippe Descola and Gísli Pálsson, *Nature and Society: Anthropological Perspectives* (1996) 45. London: Routledge.
Huddart, David, "Making an Example of Spivak" (April 2001) 6 *Angelaki: Journal of Theoretical Humanities* 35.
Huggan, Graham, *The Postcolonial Exotic: Marketing the Margins* (2001). New York: Routledge.
Husserl, Edmund, *The Crisis of European Sciences and Transcendental Phenomenology* (David Carr trans., 1970 edn). Evanston, IL: Northwestern University Press.
Jackson, Jean E, "Culture, Genuine and Spurious: The Politics of Indianness in the Vaupés" (1995) 22(1) *American Ethnologist* 3.
Jackson, Jean E, "The Politics of Ethnographic Practice in the Columbian Vaupés" (1999) 6(2–3) *Identities* 281.
Jenks, Edward, *A History of the Australasian Colonies: From their Foundation to the Year 1893* (1896). Cambridge: Cambridge University Press.
Kafka, Franz, *The Penguin Complete Novels of Franz Kafka* (Willa and Edwin Muir trans., 1983 edn). Harmondsworth, UK: Penguin.
Kafka, Franz, "Before the Law" in Franz Kafka (Nahum N Glatzer, ed.), *The Complete Short Stories of Franz Kafka* (Willa and Edwin Muir trans., 2005 edn) 3. London: Vintage.
Kafka, Franz, "The Problem of Our Laws" in Franz Kafka (Nathum Norbert Glazer, ed.), *The Complete Short Stories of Franz Kafka* (Willa Muir and Edwin Muir trans., 2005 edn) 437. London: Vintage.
Kaintz, Howard P, *Hegel's Phenomenology of Spirit* (1994). University Park, PA: Pennsylvania State University Press.
Kant, Immanuel, *Critique of Pure Reason* (John Miller Dow Meiklejohn trans., 1855 edn). London: Bohn.
Kant, Immanuel, *Critique of Practical Reason* (Lewis White Beck trans., 1956 edn) published in *Kant's Critique of Practical Reason and Other Writings in Moral Philosophy* (1949). Chicago, IL: University of Chicago Press.
Kant, Immanuel, *Critique of Judgment* (James Creed Meredith trans., 1964 edn). Oxford: Clarendon.
Katz, Cindi and Andrew Kirby, "In the Nature of Things: The Environment and Everyday Life" (1991) 16 (2) *Transactions of the Institute of British Geographers* 259.
Keal, Paul, *European Conquest and the Rights of Indigenous Peoples: The Moral Backwardness of International Society* (2003). New York: Cambridge University Press.
Keating, Paul, "The Redfern Park Speech" in Michelle Grattan (ed.), *Reconciliation: Essays on Australian Reconciliation* (2000) 60. Melbourne, Australia: Bookman Press.

Keenan, Thomas, "Deconstruction and the Impossibility of Justice" (1990) 11 *Cardozo Law Review* 1680.

Kenrick, Justin, Discussion: The Concept of Indigeneity (2006) 14(1) *Social Anthropology* 17, 19.

Kenrick, Justin and Jerome Lewis, Discussion of Adam Kuper, "The Return of the Native" (April 2004) 45(2) *Current Anthropology* 263.

Kenrick, Justin and Jerome Lewis, "Indigenous Peoples' Rights and the Politics of the Term 'Indigenous'" (2004) 20 *Anthropology Today* 4.

Kerruish, Valerie, "Imperatives of Extinguishment: *Kartinyeri v The Commonwealth of Australia*" (2008) 3 Jahrgang *DILEMMATA: Jahrbuch der Altonaer Stiftung für philosophische Grundlagenforschung* 1.

Knudsen, Eva Rask, "Fringe Finds Focus: Developments and Strategies in Aboriginal Writing in English" (1991) 15(2) *Australian Literary Studies* 32.

Knudsen, Eva Rask, *The Circle and the Spiral: A Study of Australian Aboriginal and New Zealand Maori Literature* (2004). Amsterdam and New York: Rodopi.

Kuiken, Kir, "Deleuze/Derrida: Towards an Almost Imperceptible Difference" (2005) 35 *Research in Phenomenology* 290.

Kuper, Adam, "The Return of the Native" (Current Anthropology Forum on Anthropology in Public, June 2003) 44(3) *Current Anthropology* 389.

Kuper, Adam, Reply to Discussion of Adam Kuper, "The Return of the Native" (April 2004) 45(2) *Current Anthropology* 265.

Kwaymullina, Ambelin, "Seeing the Light: Aboriginal Law, Learning and Sustainable Living in Country" (2005) 6(11) *Indigenous Law Bulletin* 12.

Kwaymullina, Ambelin, "Introduction: A Land of Many Countries" in Sally Morgan, Tjalaminu Mia and Blake Kwaymullina (eds), *Heartsick for Country: Stories of Love, Spirit and Creation* (2008) 6. North Fremantle, Australia: Fremantle Press.

Kwaymullina, Ambelin, "Living together in country: Creation, *terra nullius* and 'the trouble with tradition'" in Simon Young, *The Trouble with Tradition: Native Title and Cultural Change* (2008) xvi. Sydney: Federation Press.

Lacan, Jacques (Jacques Alain-Miller, ed.), *The Seminar of Jacques Lacan: Book I, Freud's Papers on Technique, 1953–1954* (John Forrester trans., 1988 edn). London: W. W. Norton & Co.

Langton, Marcia, *Well I Heard it on the Radio and I saw it on the Television: An Essay for the Australian Film Commission on the Politics and Aesthetics of Filmmaking by and about Aboriginal people and Things* (1993) Australian Film Commission.

Langton, Marcia, "The 'Wild', the Market and the Native: Indigenous People face New Forms of Global Colonization" in William M Adams and Martin Mulligan (eds), *Decolonizing Nature: Strategies for Conservation in a Post-Colonial Era* (2003) 79. London and Sterling, Australia: Earthscan Publications.

Langton, Marcia, "The Estate as Duration: 'Being in Place' and Aboriginal Property Relations in Areas of Cape York Peninsula in North Australia" in Lee Godden and Maureen Tehan (eds), *Comparative Perspectives on Communal Lands and Individual Ownership: Sustainable Futures* (2010) 75. Abingdon, UK: Routledge

Lefebvre, Alexandre, *The Image of Law: Deleuze, Bergson, Spinoza* (2008). Stanford, CA: Stanford University Press.

Lehman, Greg, "Being Black" in Goran Burenhult (ed.), *Traditional Peoples Today: Continuity and Change in the Modern World* (1994) 89. St Lucia, Australia: University of Queensland Press.

Lehman, Greg, "The Palawa of Tasmania" in Göran Burenhult (ed.), *Traditional Peoples Today: Continuity and Change in the Modern World* (1994) 85. St Lucia, Australia: University of Queensland Press.

Lehman, Greg, "A Snake and a Seal", in Sally Morgan, Tjalaminu Mia and Blake Kwaymullina (eds), *Heartsick for Country: Stories of Love, Spirit and Creation* (2008) 132. North Fremantle, Australia: Fremantle Press.

Leitch, Vincent, *Deconstructive Criticism* (1983). New York: Columbia University Press.

Leung, Gilbert and Matthew Stone, "Otherwise than Hospitality: A Disputation on the Relation of Ethics to Law and Politics" (2009) 20 *Law and Critique* 193.

Levinas, Emmanuel, *Totality and Infinity: An Essay on Exteriority* (Alphonso Lingis trans., 1969 edn). Pittsburgh, PA: Duquesne University Press.

Levinas, Emmanuel, "Ethics as First Philosophy" in Sean Hand (ed.), *The Levinas Reader* (1989) 75. Oxford; Cambridge, MA: B. Blackwell.

Levinas, Emmanuel, *Entre Nous* (1998, Michael B Smith and Barbara Harshav trans., 2006 edn). London and New York: Continuum.

Levinas, Emmanuel, "Philosophy and the Idea of Infinity" in Emmanuel Levinas, *Collected Philosophical Papers* (1957) (Alphonso Lingis trans., 1998 edn) 47. Pittsburgh, PA: Duquesne University Press.

Li, Tania, "Articulating Indigenous Identity in Indonesia: Resource Politics and the Tribal Slot" (2000) 42(1) *Comparative Studies in Society and History* 149.

Li, Tania, "Ethnic Cleansing, Recursive Knowledge, and the Dilemma of Sedentarism" (2002) 173 *International Journal of Social Sciences* 361.

Lincoln, Lissa, "Deleuze and Camus: Strange Encounters" in Laurent de Sutter and Kyle McGee (eds), *Deleuze and Law* (2012) 167. Edinburgh, UK: Edinburgh University Press.

Macneil, Rod, "Time after Time: Temporal Frontiers and Boundaries in Colonial Images of the Australian Landscape" in Lynette Russell (ed.), *Colonial Frontiers: Indigenous-European Encounters in Settler Societies* (2001) 47. Manchester and New York: Manchester University Press; Distributed exclusively in the USA by Palgrave.

MacNeil, William P, "'It's the vibe!': The Common Law Imaginary Down Under" in Leslie J Moran, Emma Sandon, Elena Loizidou and Ian Christie (eds), *Law's Moving Image* (2004) 31. London: Cavendish Publishing, GlassHouse Press.

Maggio, Jay, "Can the Subaltern Be Heard? Political Theory, Translation, Representation, and Gayatri Chakravorty Spivak" (2007) 32(4) *Alternatives* 419.

Mahoney, John L, "The Idea of Mimesis in Shelley's A Defence of Poetry" (1984) 24(1) *The British Journal of Aesthetics* 59.

Martel, James R, *Divine Violence: Walter Benjamin and the Eschatology of Sovereignty* (2012). London and New York: Routledge.

Martin, David, "Alternative Constructions of Indigenous Identities in Australia's *Native Title Act*" in Toni Bauman and Lydia Glick (eds), *The Limits of Change: Mabo and Native Title 20 Years On* (Australian Institute of Aboriginal and Torres Strait Islander Studies, 2012) 356. Canberra, Australia: AIATSIS Research Publications.

Massumi, Brian, "The Simulacrum According to Deleuze and Guattari" (1987) 1 *Copyright* 90.

McClintock, Anne, "The Angel of Progress: Pitfalls of the Term 'Postcolonialism'" in Francis Barker, Peter Hulme and Margaret Iversen (eds), *Colonial Discourse/Postcolonial Theory* (1994) 253. Manchester, UK and New York: Manchester University Press; New York: Distributed exclusively in the USA and Canada by St. Martin's Press.

McNeil, Kent, "A Question of Title: Has the Common Law Been Misapplied to Dispossess the Aboriginals?" (1990) 16 *Monash University Law Review* 91.

Menga, Ferdinando, "Interculturality and the Limits of a Globalized Order. Some Paradigmatic Insights on the Unavoidable Intervention of Contingency Within Human Institutions" (2012) 3–2 *Rivista Internazionale di Filosofia e Psicologia* 254.

Mertes, Tom, *A Movement of Movements: Is Another World Really Possible?* (2004). London and New York: Verso.

Messer, Ellen, "Anthropology and Human Rights" (1993) 22 *Annual Review of Anthropology* 221.

Milroy, Gladys and Jill Milroy, "Different Ways of Knowing: Trees are our Families Too" in Sally Morgan, Tjalaminu Mia and Blake Kwaymullina (eds), *Heartsick for Country: Stories of Love, Spirit and Creation* (2008) 22. North Fremantle, Australia: Fremantle Press.

Milsom, SFC, *The Legal Framework of English Feudalism: The Maitland Lectures Given in 1972* (1976). London, New York and Melbourne, Australia: Cambridge University Press.

Minnow, Martha, Michael Ryan and Austin Sarat (eds), *Narrative, Violence, and the Law: The Essays of Robert Cover* (1992). Ann Arbor, MI: University of Michigan Press.

Moore-Gilbert, Bart, *Postcolonial Theory: Contexts, Practices, Politics* (1997). London and New York: Verso.

Moran, Joe, *Reading the Everyday* (2005). Oxford and New York: Routledge.

Moreton-Robinson, Aileen, "I Still Call Australia Home: Indigenous Belonging and Place in a White Post Colonizing Society" in Sara Ahmed, Claudia Castañeda, Anne-Marie Fortier and Mimi Sheller (eds), *Uprootings/Regroundings: Questions of Home and Migration* (2004) 23. New York: Berg Publishers.

Morgan, Bob, "Country – A Journey to Cultural and Spiritual Healing", in Sally Morgan, Tjalaminu Mia and Blake Kwaymullina (eds), *Heartsick for Country: Stories of Love, Spirit and Creation* (2008) 201. North Fremantle, Australia: Fremantle Press.

Morgan, Sally, "The Balance for the World" in Sally Morgan, Tjalaminu Mia and Blake Kwaymullina (eds), *Heartsick for Country: Stories of Love, Spirit and Creation* (2008) 254. North Fremantle, Australia: Fremantle Press.

Motha, Stewart, "Mabo: Encountering the Epistemic Limit of the Recognition of 'Difference'" (1998) 7 *Griffith Law Review* 79.

Mowaljarlaiand, David and Jutta Malnic, *Yorro Yorro, Everything Standing Up Alive: Spirit of the Kimberley* (2001). Broome, Australia: Magabala Books.

Mudrooroo (Narogin), *Writing from the Fringe: A Study of Modern Aboriginal Literature* (1990). South Yarra, Australia: Hyland House.

Mudrooroo, *The Indigenous Literature of Australia: Milli Milli Wangka* (1997). Melbourne, Australia: Hyland House.

Muecke, Stephen, *Ancient and Modern: Time, Culture and Indigenous Philosophy* (2004). Sydney: University of New South Wales Press.

Naas, Michael, *Derrida From Now On* (2008). New York: Fordham University Press.

Nancy, Jean-Luc, "Abandoned Being" in Jean-Luc Nancy, *The Birth to Presence* (Brian Holmes trans., 1993 edn) 36. Stanford, CA: Stanford University Press.

Nancy, Jean-Luc, "Identity and Trembling" in Jean-Luc Nancy, *The Birth to Presence* (Brian Holmes trans., 1993 edn) 9. Stanford, CA: Stanford University Press.

Nancy, Jean-Luc, *The Sense of the World* (1997). Minneapolis, MN: University of Minnesota Press.

Nancy, Jean-Luc, *Corpus* (2000). Paris: Éditions Métailié.

Nancy, Jean-Luc (Simon Sparks, ed.), *Finite Thinking* (2003). Stanford, CA: Stanford University Press.

Narveson, Jan, "Force, Violence, and Law" in James B Brady and Newton Garver, *Justice, Law, and Violence* (1991) 149. Philadelphia, PA: Temple University Press.

Neidjie, Bill, *Story About Feeling* (1989). Broome, Australia: Magabala Books.

Neumann, Franz, *The Democratic and the Authoritarian State: Essays in Political and Legal Theory* (1957). Glencoe, IL: Free Press.

Neumann, Iver B, "Self and Other in International Relations" (1996) 2(2) *European Journal of International Relations* 139.

Niezen, Ronald, *The Origins of Indigenism: Human Rights and the Politics of Identity* (2003). Berkeley, CA: University of California Press.

Norrie, Alan, *Crime, Reason and History* (1993) 23. Cambridge: Cambridge University Press.

Omura, Keiichi, Comment on Adam Kuper, "The Return of the Native" (Current Anthropology Forum on Anthropology in Public, June 2003) 44(3) *Current Anthropology* 389.

Oxenham, Darlene, Kim Collard, Pat Dudgeon, Darren Garvey, Marion Kickett, Tracey Kickett, Jeannie Roberts and Jules Whiteway, *A Dialogue in Indigenous Identity: Warts 'n' All* (1999). Perth, Australia: Gunada Press.

Pahuja, Sundhya, "Decolonization and the Eventness of International Law" in Fleur Johns, Richard Joyce and Sundhya Pahuja (eds), *Events: The Force of International Law* (2011) 91. London and New York: Routledge.

Palmer, Kingsley, "Anthropologist as Expert in Native Title Cases in Australia" (2011) Australian Institute of Aboriginal and Torres Strait Islander Studies Native Title Research Unit at http://aiatsis.gov.au/sites/default/files/products/research_outputs/palmer-2011-anthropologist-expert-native-title-cases.pdf (accessed 6 October 2015).

Paradies, Yin C, "Beyond Black and White: Essentialism, Hybridity and Indigeneity" (2006) 42 *Journal of Sociology* 355.

Parfitt, Rose, "Theorizing Recognition and International Personality" in Florian Hoffman and Anne Orford (eds), *The Oxford Handbook of International Legal Theory* (forthcoming). Oxford: Oxford University Press.

Pearson, Noel, "Concept of Native Title at Common Law" in Galarrwuy Yanupingu (ed.) *Our Land is our Life: Land Rights Past Present and Future* (1997) 150. St. Lucia, Australia: University of Queensland Press and Portland, OR: Distributed in the USA and Canada by International Specialized Book Services.

Pereira, Pedro Schacht, Review of Derek Attridge, *The Singularity of Literature* (2004) in (2007) 104(4) *Modern Philology* 560.

Perrin, Colin, "Approaching Anxiety: The Insistence of the Postcolonial in the Declaration on the Rights of Indigenous Peoples" in Eve Darian-Smith and Peter Fitzpatrick, *Laws of the Postcolonial* (1999) 19. Ann Arbor, MI: University of Michigan Press.

Pether, Penelope, "On 'Cruelty': Law, Literature, and Difference" in Laurent de Sutter and Kyle McGee (eds), *Deleuze and Law* (2012) 69. Edinburgh, UK: Edinburgh University Press.

Pinkoski, Marc and Michael Asch, "Anthropology and Indigenous Rights in Canada and the United States: Implications in Steward's Theoretical Project" in Alan Barnard (ed.), *Hunter-Gatherers in History, Archaeology and Anthropology* (2004) 187. Oxford and New York: Berg.

Plaice, Evie, Comment on Adam Kuper, "The Return of the Native" (Current Anthropology Forum on Anthropology in Public, June 2003) 44(3) *Current Anthropology* 396.

Plaice, Evie, "Discussion: The Concept of Indigeneity" (2006) *Social Anthropology* 14(1) 17, 22.

Povinelli, Elizabeth, "The State of Shame: Australian Multiculturalism and the Crisis of Indigenous Citizenship" (Winter 1998) *Critical Inquiry* 575.

Povinelli, Elizabeth, *The Cunning of Recognition: Indigenous Alterities and the Making of Australian Multiculturalism* (2002). Durham, NC: Duke University Press.

Pratt, Mary Louise, *Imperial Eyes: Travel Writing and Transculturation* (1992). London and New York: Routledge.

Pryor, Benjamin S, "Law in Abandon: Jean-Luc Nancy and the Critical Study of Law" (2004) 15 *Law and Critique* 259.

Pulido, Laura, "Ecological Legitimacy and Cultural Essentialism" in Daniel Richard Faber (ed.), *The Struggle for Ecological Democracy: Environmental Justice in the United States* (1998) 293. New York: Guilford Press.

Rajaram, Prem, "Dystopic Geographies of Empire" (October–December 2006) 31(4) *Alternatives* 475.

Ramos, Alcida Rita, Comment on Adam Kuper, "The Return of the Native" (Current Anthropology Forum on Anthropology in Public, June 2003) 44(3) *Current Anthropology* 397.

Reichman, Ravit, "Undignified Details: The Colonial Subject of Law" (2004) 35(1–2) *ARIEL* 81.

Renault, Emmanuel, *L'Experience de l'injustice: Reconnaissance et Clinique de l'injustice* (2004). Paris: La Découverte, Armillaire.

Reynolds, Henry, *The Law of the Land* (1987) (revised edns in 1992 and 2003). Ringwood, Australia: Penguin.

Reynolds, Henry, *Aboriginal Sovereignty: Reflections on Race, State and Nation* (1996). St. Leonards, Australia: Allen & Unwin.

Riles, Annelise, "Anthropology, Human Rights and Legal Knowledge: Culture in the Iron Cage" (2006) 108(1) *American Anthropologist* 52.

Ritter, David, "Tilting at Doctrine in a Changing World: The Three Editions of Henry Reynolds' *The Law of the Land*" (2008) 32(3) *Journal of Australian Studies* 393.

Roberts-Cady, Sarah E, "Rethinking Justice with Levinas" in Desmond Manderson (ed.), *Essays on Levinas and Law: A Mosaic* (2009) 241. Basingstoke, UK: Palgrave Macmillan.

Roberts-Wray, Kenneth, "The Adaptation of Imported Law into Africa" (1960) 4(2) *Journal of African Law* 66.

Robins, Steven, "Whose 'Culture'? Whose Survival?" in Alan Barnard and Justin Kenrich (eds), *Africa's Indigenous Peoples: 'First Peoples' or 'Marginalized Minorities'?* (2001). Edinburgh, UK: Centre of African Studies, University of Edinburgh.

Robins, Steven, Comment on Adam Kuper, "The Return of the Native" (Current Anthropology Forum on Anthropology in Public, June 2003) 44(3) *Current Anthropology* 398.

Rose, Bruce, *Land Management Issues: Attitudes and Perceptions amongst Aboriginal People of Central Australia* (1995). Central Land Council Australia.

Rose, Deborah Bird, "Land Rights and Deep Colonising: The Erasure of Women" (1996) 28 *Aboriginal Law Bulletin* 6.

Rose, Deborah Bird, *Nourishing Terrains: Australian Aboriginal Views of Landscape and Wilderness* (Australian Heritage Commission 1996) 7, available at www.environment.gov.au/heritage/ahc/publications/commission/books/nourishing-terrains.html (accessed 6 October 2015).

Rose, Deborah Bird, "Indigenous Ecologies and an Ethic of Connection" in Nicholas Low (ed.), *Global Ethics and Environment* (1999) 175. London: Routledge.

Rose, Deborah Bird, *Reports from a Wild Country: Ethics for Decolonisation* (2004). Sydney: University of New South Wales Press.

Rushdie, Salman, "In Good Faith" in *Imaginary Homelands: Essays and Criticism 1981–1991* (1991) 393. London: Granta Books and New York: In association with Penguin Books.

Sackville, Ronald, "The Emerging Australian Law of Native Title: Some North American Comparisons" (2000) 74 *Australian Law Journal* 820.

Said, Edward, *Orientalism* (1978). New York: Pantheon Books.

Sandall, Roger, *The Culture Cult: Designer Tribalism and Other Essays* (2001). Boulder, CO: Westview Press.

Sandhu, Jaimal, "Caliban Rediscovered? On the Rise of the Global Indigenous Movement" (2012) 1 *Burgmann Journal* 27.

Sarat, Austin (ed.), *Law, Violence, and the Possibility of Justice* (2001). Princeton, NJ and Oxford: Princeton University Press.

Sarat, Austin, "Situating Law between the Realities of Violence and the Claims of Justice: An Introduction" in Austin Sarat (ed.), *Law, Violence and the Possibility of Justice* (2001) 3. Princeton, NJ and Oxford: Princeton University Press.

Sarat, Austin, Matthew Anderson and Cathrine O. Frank, "Introduction: On the Origins and Prospects of the Humanistic Study of Law" in Austin Sarat, Matthew Anderson and Cathrine O. Frank (eds), *Law and the Humanities: An Introduction* (2010). Cambridge, (UK); New York: Cambridge University Press.

Sartre, Jean-Paul, *Being and Nothingness* (Hazel E Barnes trans., 1969 edn). London: Methuen.

Saugestad, Sidsel, *The Inconvenient Indigenous: Remote Area Development in Botswana, Donor Assistance and the First People of the Kalahari* (2001). Sweden: The Nordic Africa Institute.

Saugestad, Sidsel, Discussion of Adam Kuper, "The Return of the Native" (April 2004) 45(2) *Current Anthropology* 263.

Schaap, Andrew, "Political Reconciliation Through a Struggle for Recognition" (2004) 13 *Social Legal Studies* 523.

Schmitt, Carl, *The Nomos of the Earth in the International Law of Jus Publicum Europaeum* (GL Ulman trans. and annotation, 1950 edn). New York: Telos Press.

Schulte-Tenckhoff, Isabelle, "Reassessing the Paradigm of Domestication: The Problematic of Indigenous Treaties" (1998) 4(2) *Review of Constitutional Studies* 239.

Scott, Joan Wallach, "Multiculturalism and the Politics of Identity" (1992) 61 *October* 18.

Shellam, Tiffany, *Shaking Hands on the Fringe: Negotiating the Aboriginal World at King George's Sound* (2009). Crawley, Australia: University of Western Australia Press.

Shelley, Percy Bysshe, "A Defence of Poetry" in Bruce R McElderry Jr (ed.), *Shelley's Critical Prose* (1967) 3. Lincoln, NE: University of Nebraska Press.

Shetty, Sandhya and Elizabeth Jane Bellamy, "Postcolonialism's Archive Fever" (Spring 2000) 30(1) *Diacritics* 25.

Shoemaker, Adam, "Mudrooroo and the Curse of Authencity" in Annalisa Oboe (ed.), *Mongrel Signatures: Reflections on the Work of Mudrooroo* (2003) 1. Amsterdam and New York: Rodopi.

Sieder, Rachel and Jessica Witchell, "Advancing Indigenous Claims through the Law: Reflections on the Guatemalan Peace Process" in Jane K Cowen, Marie-Bénédicte Dembour and Richard A Wilson (eds), *Culture and Rights: Anthropological Perspectives* (2001) 201. Cambridge and New York: Cambridge University Press.

Smith, Daniel W, "The Concept of the Simulacrum: Deleuze and the Overturning of Platonism" (2006) 38 *Continental Philosophy Review* 89.

Smith, Linda Tuhiwai, *Decolonizing Methodologies: Research and Indigenous Peoples* (1999). London and New York: Zed Books; Dunedin, NZ: University of Otago Press; New York: Distributed in the USA exclusively by St. Martin's Press.

Smith, Nick, "Questions for a Reluctant Jurisprudence of Alterity" in Desmond Manderson (ed.), *Essays on Levinas and Law: A Mosaic* (2009) 55. Basingstoke, UK: Palgrave Macmillan.

Soguk, Nevzat, "Indigenous Peoples and Radical Futures in Global Politics" (March 2007) 29(1) *New Political Science* 1.

Spivak, Gayatri Chakravorty, "Can the Subaltern Speak?" in Cary Nelson and Lawrence Grossberg (eds), *Marxism and the Interpretation of Culture* (1988) 271. Urbana, IL: University of Illinois Press.

Spivak, Gayatri Chakravorty, *A Critique of Postcolonial Reason: Toward a History of the Vanishing Present* (1999). Cambridge, MA: Harvard University Press.

Spivak, Gayatri Chakravorty, "Translating into English" in Sandra Bermann and Michael Wood, *Nation, Language, and the Ethics of Translation* (2005) 93. Princeton, NJ: Princeton University Press.

Stanner, William Edward Hanley, *After the Dreaming: The Boyer Lectures 1968* (1972). Sydney: Australian Broadcasting Commission.

Strelein, Lisa, "'Beliefs, Feelings and Justice' – Delgamuukw v British Columbia: A Judicial Consideration of Indigenous Peoples' Rights in Canada" (1998) *Land, Rights, Laws: Issues of Native Title* (Issues Paper No 22).

Strelein, Lisa, "The Vagaries of Native Title: Partial Recognition of Aboriginal Law in the Alice Springs Native Title Case" (1999) 4(26) *Indigenous Law Bulletin* 13.

Strelein, Lisa, "From *Mabo* to *Yorta Yorta*: Native Title Law in Australia" (2005) 19 *Washington University Journal of Law and Policy* 225.

Sutton, Peter, "The Politics of Suffering: Indigenous Policy in Australia since the Seventies" (10 April typescript) revised version of the Inaugural Berndt Foundation Biennial Lecture, University of Western Australia (23 September 2000).

Sutton, Peter, *The Politics of Suffering: Indigenous Australia and the End of the Liberal Consensus* (2009). Carlton, Australia: Melbourne University Press.

Suzman, James, Comment on Adam Kuper, "The Return of the Native" (Current Anthropology Forum on Anthropology in Public, June 2003) 44(3) *Current Anthropology* 389.

Taylor, Charles, *Reconciling the Solitudes: Essays on Canadian Federalism and Nationalism* (1993). Montreal & Kingston; London and Ithaca, NY: McGill-Queens University Press.

Taylor, Charles, "The Politics of Recognition" in Amy Guttman (ed.), *Multiculturalism: Examining the Politics of Recognition* (1994) 25. Princeton, NJ: Princeton University Press.

Taylor, Mark C, "Desire of Law Law of Desire" (1990) 11 *Cardozo Law Review* 1269.

Thomas, Nicholas, *Possessions: Indigenous Art/Colonial Culture* (1999). New York: Thames and Hudson.

Thuen, Trond, "Anthropological Knowledge in the Courtroom: Conflicting Paradigms" (2004) 12 *Social Anthropology* 265.

Thuen, Trond, "Discussion: The Concept of Indigeneity" (2006) *Social Anthropology* 14(1) 17, 24.

Tiffin, Helen, "Post-Colonial Literatures and Counter-Discourse" from "Post-colonial Literatures and Counter-discourse" (1987) 9(3) *Kunapipi* 17, excerpted in Bill Ashcroft, Gareth Griffiths and Helen Tiffin (eds), *The Post-Colonial Studies Reader* (2006, 2nd edn) 99.

Tinamin, George, "One Land, One Law, One People", in Lorraine Mafi-Williams (ed.), *Spirit Song: A Collection of Aboriginal Poetry* (1993) 4. Norwood, Australia: Omnibus Books.

Tourme-Jouannet, Emmanuelle, *What is a Fair International Society? International Law between Development and Recognition* (2013). Oxford: Hart Publishing.

Tourme-Jouannet, Emmanuelle, "The International Law of Recognition" (2013) 24(2) *European Journal of International Law* 691.

Tuitt, Patricia, *Race, Law, Resistance* (2004). London: Glasshouse.

Turner, Terry, Discussion of Adam Kuper, "The Return of the Native" (April 2004) 45(2) *Current Anthropology* 264.

Van Marle, Karin, "Constitution as Archive" in Scott Veitch (ed.), *Law and the Politics of Reconciliation* (2007) 215. Aldershot, UK and Burlington, VT: Ashgate.

Venn, Couze, *The Postcolonial Challenge: Towards Alternative Worlds* (2006). London and Thousand Oaks, CA: Sage Publishing.

Venne, Sharon Helen, *Our Elders Understand Our Rights: Evolving International Law Regarding Indigenous Peoples* (1998). Penticton, Canada: Theytus Books.

Vizenor, Gerald, "A Postmodern Introduction", in Gerald Vizenor (ed.), *Narrative Chance: Postmodern Discourse on Native American Indian Literatures* (1993) 3. Norman, OK: University of Oklahoma Press.

Wall, Illan Rua, *Human Rights and Constituent Power: Without Model or Warranty* (2012). Abingdon, UK; New York: Routledge.

Watson, Irene, "De-colonising the Space: Dreaming back to Country", in Sally Morgan, Tjalaminu Mia and Blake Kwaymullina (eds), *Heartsick for Country: Stories of Love, Spirit and Creation* (2008) 82. North Fremantle, Australia: Fremantle Press.

Watson, Irene, *Aboriginal Peoples, Colonialism and International Law: Raw Law* (2014). Abingdon, UK: Routledge.

Webber, Jeremy, "Beyond Regret: Mabo's Implications for Australian Constitutionalism" in Duncan Ivison, Paul Patton and Will Sanders (eds), *Political Theory and the Rights of Indigenous Peoples* (2000) 60. Cambridge; Melbourne: Cambridge University Press.

Weber, Samuel, "A Touch of Translation: On Walter Benjamin's 'Task of the Translator'" in Sandra Bermann and Michael Wood (eds), *Nation, Language and the Ethics of Translation* (2005) 65. Princeton, NJ: Princeton University Press.

White, Isobel, "Birth and Death of a Ceremony" (1980) 4(1) *Aboriginal History* 35.

White, James Boyd, *The Legal Imagination* (1973). Chicago, IL: University of Chicago Press.

White, James Boyd, *Heracles' Bow: Essays on the Rhetoric and Poetics of the Law* (1985). Madison, WI: University of Wisconsin Press.

White, James Boyd, "The 'Legal Imagination' and the Beginning of Modern Law and Literature" in Barbara Pozzo (ed.), *Teaching Law Through the Looking Glass of Literature* (2010) 9. Bern, Switzerland: Staempfli Publishers.

White, James Boyd, "An Old-Fashioned View of the Nature of Law" (2011) 12(1) *Theoretical Inquiries in Law* 381.

White, James Boyd, "The Cultural Background of 'The Legal Imagination'" in Austin Sarat, Cathrine O. Frank and Matthew Anderson (eds), *Teaching Law and Literature* (2011). New York: Modern Language Association of America.

Wigmore, John L, "A List of Legal Novels" (1908) 2 *Illinois Law Review* 574.

Williams, Robert A, *The American Indian in Western Legal Thought: The Discourses of Conquest* (1990). New York: Oxford University Press.

Williams, Robert R, *Hegel's Ethics of Recognition* (2000). Berkeley, CA: University of California Press.

Wolfe, Patrick, *Settler Colonialism and the Transformation of Anthropology* (1999). London and New York: Cassell.

Wolfe, Patrick, "Discussion: The Concept of Indigeneity" (2006) *Social Anthropology* 14(1) 17, 27.

Wright, Alexis, "On Writing *Carpentaria*." (2007) 13 *HEAT Magazine* 79–95, reprinted at http://logincms.uws.edu.au/__data/assets/pdf_file/0011/385949/Wright-HEATessay.pdf (accessed 6 October 2015).

Wright, Alexis, "Politics of Writing" (Summer 2002) 62(2) *Southerly* 10.

Yar, Majid, "Recognition and the Politics of Human(e) Desire" (2001) 18(2–3) *Theory, Culture & Society* 57.

Yinirrakun, April Bright, "Burn Grass" in Deborah Bird Rose (ed.), *Country in Flames: Proceedings of the 1994 Symposium on Biodiversity and Fire in North Australia*, Biodiversity Series, Paper No 3, Department of the Environment, Sport and Territories and the North Australia Research Unit (ANU), Canberra (1995).

Young, Simon, *The Trouble with Tradition: Native Title and Cultural Change* (2008). Sydney: Federation Press.

Young, Simon, "Tides of History and Jurisprudential Gulfs: Native Title Proof and the Noongar Western Australia Claim" (2010) 8(1) *Indigenous Law Journal* 95.

Zips, Werner, "Discussion: The Concept of Indigeneity" (2006) *Social Anthropology* 14(1) 17, 27–28.

Case law

Australia

Akiba and Another (on behalf of the Torres Strait Islanders of the Regional Seas Claim Group) v Queensland and Others (No 2) (2010) 270 ALR 564.

Akiba v Queensland (No 3) (2010) 204 FCR 1.

Banjima People v Western Australia (No 2) [2013] FCA 868.

Bennell v Western Australia (2006) 230 ALR 603.

Bodney v Bennell [2008] FCAFC 63.

Bodney v Bennell (2008) 249 ALR 300.

Bodney v Bennell and Others (2008) 249 ALR 300.

Commonwealth v Akiba (2012) 204 FCR 260.

Commonwealth v Yarmirr (2001) 208 CLR 1.

De Rose v South Australia (2003) 133 FCR 325.

Fejo v Northern Territory (1998) 195 CLR 96.

Kartinyeri v Commonwealth (1998] 195 CLR 337.

Mabo and Others v Queensland (No. 2) (1992) 175 CLR 1.

Members of the Yorta Yorta Aboriginal Community v Victoria and Ors [1998] FCA 1606.

McLennan on behalf of the Jangga People v Queensland [2012] FCA 1082.

Members of the Yorta Yorta Aboriginal Community v Victoria (2002) 214 CLR 422.

Milirrpum v Nabalco Pty Ltd (1971) 17 FLR 141.

Neowarra v Western Australia [2003] FCA 1402.

Northern Territory v Alaywar, Kaytetye, Warumungu, Wakaya Native Title Claim Group (2005) 145 FCR 442.

Northern Territory v Alyawar (2005) 220 ALR 431.

Rubibi Community v Western Australia (No. 5) [2005] FCA 1025.
Sampi v Western Australia [2005] FCA 777.
Sampi on behalf of the Bardi and Jawi People v Western Australia [2010] FCAFC 26.
Shaw v Wolf (1999) 163 ALR 205.
Western Australian v Brown and Ors [2014] HCA 8.
Western Australia v Commonwealth (1995) 183 CLR 373.
Western Australia v Sebastian (2008) 248 ALR 61.
Western Australia v Ward (2000) 170 ALR 159.
Western Australia v Ward (2002) 213 CLR 1.
Wik Peoples v Queensland & Ors; The Thayorre People v Queensland & Ors (1996) 187 CLR 1.
Wyman on behalf of the Bidjara People v Queensland (No. 2) [2013] FCA 1229.

Other

Adeyinka Oyekan v Musendiku Adele [1957] 1 WLR 876.
Amodu Tijani v Secretary, Southern Nigeria [1921] 2 AC 399.
Calder et al. v Attorney General (British Columbia) (1973) 34 DLR (3d) 145.
Campbell v Hall (1774) 94 ER 1045.
Cooper v Stuart [1889] 14 AC 286, 291.
Delgamuukw v British Columbia (1997) 153 DLR (4th) 193.
Fletcher v Peck, 10 US (6 Cranch) 87 (1810).
Guerin v R (1984) [1984] 2 SCR 335.
R v Sparrow [1990] 1 SCR 1075.
R v Van der Peet (1996) 137 DLR (4d) 289.
Re Southern Rhodesia (1919) AC 211.
Sobhuza II. v Miller [1926] AC, 525.
Thomas Johnson and Graham's Lessee v William M'Intosh 21 US 543 (1823).

Legislation

Aboriginal and Torres Strait Islander Act 2005 (Cth).
Evidence Amendment Act 2008 (Cth).
Hindmarsh Island Bridge Act 1997 (Cth).
Native Title Act 1993 (Cth).
Native Title Amendment (Reform) Bill 2011 (Cth) (lapsed).
Native Title Amendment (Reform) Bill (No. 1) 2012 (Cth) (lapsed).
Explanatory Memorandum, Native Title Amendment (Reform) Bill (No. 1) 2012 (Cth).
Native Title Amendment (Reform) Bill 2014 (Cth).
Explanatory Memorandum, Native Title Amendment (Reform) Bill 2014 (Cth).

Treaties/resolutions/UN materials

Cobo, JR Martinéz, *Study of the Problem of Discrimination against Indigenous Populations* (UN Doc. E/CN.4/Sub.2/1983/21/Add.8 1983) 67. See www.iwgia.org/culture-and-identity/identification-of-indigenous-peoples (accessed 6 October 2015).
Communication from the United Nations Permanent Forum on Indigenous Issues Chairperson on a Third International Decade of the World's Indigenous Peoples at

http://undesadspd.org/IndigenousPeoples/tabid/70/articleType/ArticleView/articleId/201/Communication-from-the-UNPFII-Chairperson-on-a-Third-International-Decade-of-the-Worlds-Indigenous-Peoples.aspx (accessed 6 October 2015).

International Labour Organization (ILO) Convention (No. 107) *Concerning the Protection and Integration of Indigenous and Other Tribal and Semi-Tribal Populations in Independent Countries* (1957), accompanied by the ILO Recommendation (No. 104) (1957).

International Labour Organisation Convention (No. 169) *Indigenous and Tribal Peoples Convention* (1989).

Resolution on the Second International Decade of the World's Indigenous People, (A/RES/59/174), 74th Plenary Meeting, 20 December 2004, to commence on 1 January 2005. See http://social.un.org/index/IndigenousPeoples/SecondDecade.aspx (accessed 6 October 2015).

Statement on the United Nations Declaration on the Rights of Indigenous Peoples, The Hon Jenny Macklin, Minister for Families, Housing, Community Services and Indigenous Affairs, 3 April 2009, Parliament House Canberra: www.un.org/esa/socdev/unpfii/documents/Australia_official_statement_endorsement_UNDRIP.pdf (accessed 6 October 2015).

United Nations Declaration on the Rights of Indigenous Peoples (A/RES/61/295), 107th plenary meeting, 13 September 2007. See http://social.un.org/index/IndigenousPeoples/DeclarationontheRightsofIndigenousPeoples.aspx (accessed 6 October 2015).

United Nations Draft *Declaration on the Rights of Indigenous Peoples* (1993) UN Doc E/CN.4/Sub.2/1993/29/Annex I.

United Nations Final Report of the Second International Decade of the World's Indigenous People GA, 69th Session, August 2014, UN Doc A/69/271 at http://undesadspd.org/indigenouspeoples/seconddecade.aspx (accessed 6 October 2015).

United Nations Universal Declaration of Human Rights, adopted by the United Nations General Assembly on 10 December 1948, at www.un.org/en/documents/udhr/ (accessed 6 October 2015).

United Nations Reducing Emissions from Deforestation and Degradation Programme (REDD+): www.un-redd.org/Home/tabid/565/language/en-US/Default.aspx (accessed 6 October 2015).

World Bank Operational Directive 4.10 (July 2005, revised April 2013): see http://web.worldbank.org/WBSITE/EXTERNAL/PROJECTS/EXTPOLICIES/EXTOPMANUAL/0,,contentMDK:20553653~menuPK:4564185~pagePK:64709096~piPK:64709108~theSitePK:502184,00.html#F6 (accessed 6 October 2015).

World Bank Operational Manual: Operational Directive 4.20 (September 1991): Indigenous Peoples.

Fictional works

Achebe, Chinua, *Things Fall Apart* (1958). London: Penguin Books.

Alexie, Sherman, "A Drug Called Tradition" in Sherman Alexie, *The Lone Ranger and Tonto Fistfight in Heaven*" (1993) 12. London: Vintage, Random House.

Alexie, Sherman, "Imagining the Reservation" in Sherman Alexie, *The Lone Ranger and Tonto Fistfight in Heaven* (1993) 149. London: Vintage, Random House.

Alexie, Sherman, "The Trial of Thomas Builds-the-Fire", in Sherman Alexie, *The Loneranger and Tonto Fistfight in Heaven* (1993) 100. London: Vintage, Random House.

Arguedas, José Mariá, *Deep Rivers* (1958). USA: Frances Horning Barraclough.
Malouf, David, *Remembering Babylon* (1993). Milsons Point, Australia: Random House Australia.
Mudrooroo, *Wild Cat Falling* (1965). Sydney: Angus and Robertson.
Mudrooroo, *Doin' Wild Cat* (1988). Melbourne, Australia: Hyland House.
Mudrooroo, *Master of the Ghost Dreaming* (1991). North Ryde, Australia: Angus and Robertson.
Mudrooroo, *Wild Cat Screaming* (1992). Pymble, Australia: Angus and Robertson.
Mudrooroo, *The Undying* (1998). Pymble, Australia: Angus and Robertson.
Mudrooroo, *Underground* (1999). Pymble, Australia: Angus and Robertson.
Mudrooroo, *The Promised Land* (2000). Pymble, Australia: Harper Collins.
Noonuccal, Oodgeroo, "The Dawn is at Hand" in Anita Heiss and Peter Minter (eds), *Macquarie PEN Anthology of Aboriginal Literature* (2008) 45. Crows Nest, Australia: Allen & Unwin.
Prichard, Katherine Susannah, *Coonardoo* (1929). Sydney: Angus and Robertson.
Rhys, Jean, *Wide Sargasso Sea* (1966). London: Deutsch.
Scott, Kim, *True Country* (1993). South Fremantle, Australia: Fremantle Arts Centre Press.
Scott, Kim, *That Deadman Dance* (2011). Sydney: Pan Macmillan.
Wright, Alexis, *Plains of Promise* (1997). Queensland, Australia: University of Queensland Press.
Wright, Alexis, *Carpentaria* (2006). Artamon, Australia: Giramondo Publishing Company.
Wright, Alexis, *The Swan Book* (2013). Artamon, Australia: Giramondo Publishing Company.
Wright, Judith, "The Dark Ones" in *Collected Poems: 1942–1985* (1994). Sydney: Angus and Robertson.

Other sources

Aboriginal and Torres Strait Islander Social Justice Commissioner, Social Justice and Native Title Report (Australian Human Rights Commission, 2013) at www.humanrights.gov.au/publications/social-justice-and-native-title-report-2013 (accessed 6 October 2015).
ANTaR Submission to the Senate Legal and Constitutional Affairs Legislation Committee: Inquiry into the previous iteration of the bill, the Native Title Amendment (Reform) Bill 2011 (Cth).
Apology to Australia's Indigenous Peoples, House of Representatives, Parliament House, Canberra (13 February 2008). See full text and video at http://australia.gov.au/about-australia/our-country/our-people/apology-to-australias-indigenous-peoples (accessed 6 October 2015).
Australian Law Reform Commission Review of the Native Title Act (IP 45) at www.alrc.gov.au/publications/native-title-ip-45 (accessed 6 October 2015).
Brown, Lesley (ed.), *The New Shorter Oxford English Dictionary on Historical Principles* (1993). Oxford: Oxford University Press.
Calma, Tom, Aboriginal and Torres Strait Islander Social Justice Commissioner, Australian Human Rights Commission Native Title Report 2008, at www.hreoc.gov.au/social_justice/nt_report/index.html (accessed 6 October 2015).
Davison, Liam, Sydney Morning Herald Review of Alexis Wright, *Carpentaria* (18 September 2006) at www.smh.com.au/news/book-reviews/carpentaria/2006/09/18/1158431619821.html (accessed 6 October 2015).

Ginibi, Ruby Langford, "The Right to be a Koori Writer", Letter to the Editor, *The Australian* (7 August 1996) 12.

"Governor Davey's Proclamation to the Aborigines, 1816": Manuscripts, Oral History & Pictures (State Library of New South Wales, 2008) at http://acms.sl.nsw.gov.au/item/itemDetailPaged.aspx?itemID=442502 (accessed 6 October 2015).

Journal of the H.M.S. Endeavour, 1768–1771 [manuscript] National Library of Australia, MS 1. See also discussion at http://pandora.nla.gov.au/pan/44385/20040920–0000/www.nla.gov.au/collect/treasures/mar_treasure.html (accessed 6 October 2015).

Jumbunna Indigenous House of Learning Research Unit, *Submission for the Inquiry into the Native Title Amendment (Reform) Bill 2011, Prepared for the Senate Standing Committee on Legal and Constitutional Affairs* (July 2011).

Keynes, RD (ed.), *Charles Darwin's Beagle Diary* (2001) at http://darwin-online.org.uk/content/frameset?itemID=F1925&viewtype=text&pageseq=1 (accessed 6 October 2015).

Ruta, Suzanne, "Collapsing Into Himself", Review of Mudrooroo, *Wild Cat Falling* (January 9, 1994) *New York Times*, at http://query.nytimes.com/gst/fullpage.html?res=9B0DE5DC173EF93AA35752C0A962958260&scp=1&sq=mudrooroo+wildcat+falling&st=nyt# (accessed 6 October 2015).

Scott, Kim John, *An Anomalous History and a Noongar Voice: A Literary Investigation of the "Friendly Frontier"* (PhD Thesis, Creative Writing, University of Western Australia, 2009), abstract available at https://repository.uwa.edu.au/R/-?func=dbin-jump-full&object_id=29349&local_base=GEN01-INS01 (accessed 6 October 2015).

Scott, Kim, quoting Mick Dodson (citation unknown), in Radio National Best of Festivals broadcast (18 January 2012), "Native Titles: Can fiction reveal the truth of the earliest encounters between Indigenous and settler Australians more honestly than conventional history?" (2011 Melbourne Writers' Festival), featuring panellists Kate Grenville, Kim Scott and Rohan Wilson, hosted by Stephen Romei, literary editor of *The Australian* newspaper, at www.abc.net.au/radionational/programs/bestoffestivals/native-titles/3785914 (accessed 6 October 2015).

Scott, Kim, Interview discussing *That Deadman Dance*, at www.youtube.com/watch?v=xqY8v1l9Pls (accessed 6 October 2015).

The Oxford English Dictionary (1991, 2nd edn).

Western Australian Government, Submission No 18 to Senate Committee on Legal and Constitutional Affairs, Parliament of Australia, *Inquiry into Native Title Amendment (Reform) Bill 2011*, August 2011.

Wright, Alexis, words written in recognition of the recorded voices of elders in Alexis Wright (ed. for the Central Land Council), *Take Power Like This Old Man Here: An Anthology of Writings Celebrating Twenty Years of Land Rights in Central Australia, 1977–1997* (1998) and Bill Neidjie, *Story About Feeling* (1989) in *Dirtsong*, performed by The Black Arm Band, Melbourne International Arts Festival, October 2009.

Index